Human Cannon, The Bundle, Jackets, in the Company of Men

Human Cannon charts the struggle against Fascism in Spain through the stories of the village community of Estarobon and one of its members, Agustina and her family. She begins by learning to fire her enemies' cannon, and ends by herself becoming – through the strength of human will – the most effective weapon in the armoury of resistance and revolution.

The Bundle 'opens with the poet/judge Basho spurning an unwanted baby left by the river-bank as he strides off searching for enlightenment . . . Capturing both the panoramic sweep of history and the rich density of everyday life, Bond shows – and not by polemics but through the actions, motivations and dreams of his multitudinous characters – that "goodness" is not a quality of individuals, that "government makes not only laws but morality" . . . an optimistic, invigorating masterpiece.' *Time Out*

'It has the force and the onward movement of a tidal wave. It communicates narrative joy; a complicated tale is to be told, spanning many years, and the playwright's craft in keeping us aware of our bearings is immaculate . . . Bond returns us to the weight and rhythm of epic theatre.' *Observer*

'*Jackets* is a double-bill, exploring the machinations behind political martyrdom in eighteenth-century Japan and twentieth-century Europe . . . it's a rich, complex, resonant piece, exhaustive in its probings . . . an astonishingly powerful piece of political, polemical poetry.' *Guardian*

In the Company of Men, described by the RSC as 'a vast meditation on the twenty-first century', makes a vivid and coruscating attack on the values encapuslated by boardroom power games, where the battle between successful tycoons Oldfield and his ambitious young son moves from skirmishing to violence.

The volume also contains Notes on Post-Modernism, originally published with *Jackets* and *In the Company of Men*, and the Bundle Poems.

Edward Bond was born and educated in London. His plays include *The Pope's Wedding* (Royal Court Theatre, 1962), *Saved* (Royal Court, 1965), *Early Morning* (Royal Court, 1968), *Narrow Road to the Deep North* (Belgrade Theatre, Coventry, 1968; Royal Court, 1969), *Black Mass* (Sharpeville Commemoration Evening, Lyceum Theatre, 1970), *Passion* (CND Rally, Alexandra Palace, 1971), *Lear* (Royal Court, 1971), *The Sea* (Royal Court, 1973), *Bingo* (Northcott, Exeter, 1973; Royal Court, 1974), *The Fool* (Royal Court, 1975), *The Bundle* (RSC Warehouse, 1978), *The Woman* (National Theatre, 1978), *The Worlds* (New Half Moon Theatre, London, 1981), *Restoration* (Royal Court, 1981), *Summer* (National Theatre, 1982), *Derek* (RSC Youth Festival, The Other Place, Stratford-upon-Avon, 1982), *The Cat* (produced in Germany as *The English Cat* by the Stuttgart Opera, 1983), *Human Cannon* (Quantum Theatre, Manchester, 1986), *The War Plays* (*Red Black and Ignorant*, *The Tin Can People* and *Great Peace*), which were staged as a trilogy by the RSC at the Barbican Pit in 1985, *Jackets* (Leicester, Haymarket, 1989), *September* (Canterbury Cathedral, 1989), *In the Company of Men* (Paris, 1992; RSC at the Barbican Pit, 1996), *At the Inland Sea* (toured by Big Brum Theatre-in-Education, 1995); *Olly's Prison* (BBC 2 Television, 1993), *Tuesday* (BBC Schools TV, 1993). His *Theatre Poems and Songs* were published in 1978, *Poems 1978–1985* in 1987, and his latest play *Coffee* in 1995.

EDWARD BOND

Plays: 5

Human Cannon
The Bundle
Jackets
In the Company of Men

Methuen Drama

METHUEN CONTEMPORARY DRAMATISTS

This collection first published in Great Britain in 1996
by Methuen Drama
an imprint of Reed International Books Ltd
Michelin House, 81 Fulham Road, London SW3 6RB
and Auckland, Melbourne, Singapore and Toronto
and distributed in the United States of America
by Heinemann, a division of Reed Elsevier Inc.
361 Hanover Street, Portsmouth, New Hampshire NH 03801 3959

Reprinted 1997

Human Cannon first published in Great Britain in 1985 as a Methuen
New Theatrescript by Methuen London Ltd; copyright © 1985, 1996 by
Edward Bond
The Bundle, 'A Note on Dramatic Method' and 'The Bundle Poems' first
published in Great Britain in 1978 by Eyre Methuen Ltd in the Methuen
Modern Plays series; copyright © 1978, 1996 by Edward Bond
Jackets, In the Company of Men and 'Notes on Post-Modernism' first
published in Great Britain in 1990 by Methuen Drama in a volume
entitled *Two Post-Modern Plays* in the Methuen Modern Plays series
Jackets copyright © 1990, 1996 by Edward Bond
In the Company of Men copyright © 1990, 1996 by Edward Bond
'Notes on Post-Modernism' copyright © 1990, 1996 by Edward Bond

Copyright in this collection © 1996 by Edward Bond
The author has asserted his moral rights

ISBN 0-413-70390-8

A CIP catalogue record for this book
is available from the British Library

Typeset by Wilmaset Ltd, Birkenhead, Wirral
Printed and bound in Great Britain by
Cox & Wyman Ltd, Reading, Berkshire

Caution

Contents

Edward Bond
A Chronology

PLAY	*First performance*
The Pope's Wedding	9.12.1962
Saved	3.11.1965
A Chaste Maid in Cheapside (*adaptation*)	13.1.1966
The Three Sisters (*translation*)	18.4.1967
Early Morning	31.3.1968
Narrow Road to the Deep North	24.6.1968
Black Mass (*part of* Sharpeville Sequence)	22.3.1970
Passion	11.4.1971
Lear	29.9.1971
The Sea	22.5.1973
Bingo: Scenes of money and death	14.11.1973
Spring Awakening (*translation*)	28.5.1974
The Fool: Scenes of bread and love	18.11.1975
Stone	8.6.1976
We Come to the River	12.7.1976
The White Devil (*adaptation*)	12.7.1976
Grandma Faust (*part one of* A-A-America!)	25.10.1976
The Swing (*part two of* A-A-America!)	22.11.1976
The Bundle: New Narrow Road to the Deep North	13.1.1978
The Woman	10.8.1978
The Worlds	8.3.1979
Restoration	21.7.1981
Summer	27.1.1982
Derek	18.10.1982
After the Assassinations	1.3.1983
The Cat (*performed as* The English Cat)	2.6.1983
Human Cannon	2.2.1986
The War Plays	
Part I: Red Black and Ignorant	29.5.1985
Part II: The Tin Can People	29.5.1985
Part III: Great Peace	17.7.1985
Jackets	24.1.1989
September	16.9.1989
In the Company of Men	1.2.1992
Lulu (*translation*)	2.3.1992
Olly's Prison (*TV*)	1.5.1993
Tuesday (*TV*)	1.6.1993
Coffee	(published 1995)
At the Inland Sea	16.10.1995

Notes on Post-Modernism

1.   These notes concern the history and present state (known as post-modernity) of the relationship between people, technology and authority; and the way in which theatre and other arts are part of that relationship.

2.   People organise themselves into societies in order to fulfill their needs more efficiently. They experience the social as the private. Because of this the relationship between them and society does not develop mechanically. The development is reciprocal – as a plant helps to biologize the soil and climate in which it grows.

3.   The human mind's capacity is greater than that which people would use if they only fulfilled their needs individually. This over-capacity makes possible the ramifications of society and culture. The total capacity is invocable in immediate experience and so the mind is radically interrogative. No answer stops it because the capacity to interrogate engulfs the answer. For this same reason of over-capacity societies interpret their needs not in relation to their locality but to the world. People cannot live in society without interpreting the world.

4.   Meaning cannot be derived from the world but must be given to it. The world is the boundary – the cosmic world. The boundary is unknowable and is a fact without meaning. In the way in which societies use it it does not exist.

5.   Because of their mind's over-capacity people must interrogate the nature of the boundary. Even children do this. They ask the questions of philosophy. Why? What? Whence? Whither? The answers to these questions must unite the lowest human functions and behaviour with the highest culture.

6.   Authority claims to speak to and for the boundary. The boundary is seen as the source of meaning and value.

7.   When people organize themselves into societies some of them exercize authority in the organisation. The organizers may be stronger, wiser, more devious and so forth. I shall call them the 'authority'. Authority organizes society to use technology in the seemingly most efficient way to meet the common needs. In the course of doing this the relationships between people and authority, people and the boundary, and authority and the boundary, must be interrogated. Belief and consent are forms of

interrogation in which the same questions are constantly repeated. That they are forms of doubt is concealed by the prohibition (by self or state) of other questions. Belief is a form of boredom.

8.   The threefold model of people, authority and boundary can be used to understand the history and present state referred to in note 1. The three elements are not as mutually exclusive as the model suggests but it is able to throw light on their relationship.

9.   The boundary is unknowable. Its mystery is analogous to the mystery people know as their 'self'. Light plays on exterior things but not on the self and its thoughts, passions and dreams. The things of the world have analogues in the structure sensed in the self. It is as if the exterior boundary had knowledge of the interior boundary, but not the other way around. The interior is contained in the exterior but encompasses it in ceaseless interrogation. Society depends on the natural world to meet its needs. But accidents, the hazards of the seasons, natural disasters, all threaten society; so it propitiates, induces and thanks the boundary. Authority stipulates and regulates these practices and rites.

10.   Authority relates people, technology and the boundary to each other. In speaking for the boundary and interpreting the relationship authority increases the humanness of the human mind. This is the reason for optimism. Authority does not derive humanness from the human mind. Humanness is socially, culturally created within the mind's excess capacity. (So its characteristics cannot be acquired genetically.) The mind's consent to authority's story is part of the process by which humans create their humanness. Authority partly represses people but at the same time it must increase their collective humanness. In time repression of people greater than that needed for technological efficiency forces them into interrogating authority. The mind creates its humanness by living in the threefold relationship. In this way even barbarism is a source of humanness, though barbarism is not necessary; it is a disharmony between the social and the individual's perception of the social. Authority's story – its account of the threefold relationship – is false: the boundary has no story. So it is as if the rabbit believed in the conjuror's tricks.

11.   Authority may use force as well as or instead of its story. As the human mind must interrogate, authority itself eventually becomes a barrier. This happens in slave and prison cultures and under all forms of social exploitation. Authority secures power,

privilege and prestige more easily if it tells a story which wins willing consent.

12.   Authority is not free. It declares the meaning of the boundary and so of people but is coerced by the necessity of meeting people's needs. Technology disturbs social relations and this stimulates interrogation of the boundary. As the technology by which needs are met changes, so authority changes its story or gives way to the next storyteller. Authority cannot return to the beginning. It inherits a story which legitimizes human needs; needs are then seen not as coming from the individual but as being given to them by the boundary. Raw need is culturally legitimized. It is the legitimizing of needs and not the fulfilling of them which gives authority its greatest power: people will sacrifice their needs to preserve their legitimacy and will sacrifice their lives to preserve their icon of the self. Authority inherits a story which legitimizes the existing humanness of the human mind and it must develop the story. The new story can only be understood as a further episode in the story from the past – as if the new story were an episode in a serial novel. The new story must enable people to recognise themselves in terms of the humanness they have come to believe of themselves; the belief has become an essential part of their economic and cultural life. These beliefs and practices are – together with the interrogation of them – their humanness. If this were not so it would be as if we had to tell a story before we had learned a language.

13.   It is important that in its relation to the boundary authority uses the boundary to legitimize people's needs. Ultimately the legitimization depends on the need of the mind's over-capacity to interrogate. Authority's story tells why people are entitled to their needs, how having them is evidence of their humanness. People relate to their needs in accordance with the boundary's approval or condemnation of their needs. Authority legitimizes both needs and interrogation; and interrogation even subverts needs, turning fulfillment into need and need into what is desired; in this way interrogation justifies the answers to its questions, giving them the authority of questions. Legitimizing authority cannot act arbitrarily; its story is defined by people's needs and the possibilities of technology and organisation. Even tyranny cannot be arbitrary for long. Corruption of people is not arbitrary but is defined by the virtue it excludes; and to this extent it serves virtue's ends in the dialectical changes in the threefold relationship.

14. Throughout history much human behaviour remains the same. People must meet the needs of their physiology and these change little. They must eat, sleep and multiply. But humanness changes radically. This is because technology and social organisation change. To eat, for example, is a constant need, but the generalization of the behaviour by which needs are met creates each society's culture and so each individual's culture.

15. Instincts are commonly misunderstood. We learn our instincts when we learn our social roles; but they are not rational and easily corrigible. They are learned in the context of social stories, especially in the versions told to children – told not only verbally, but shown in uniforms, agendas, punishments, architecture and so forth. Children are dramatized by their induction into society. Instincts do not determine culture. On the contrary, culture gives instincts a social character. Instincts are not biologically determined but culturally manipulable. This removes them from the private to the public. This is true even of antisocial instinctive behaviour. That behaviour is the objectification of the tensions in unjust society. The tensions need not be consistently abrasive and may be emollient in the way they manipulate sentiment and even in the norms of behaviour they encourage (as in the chaos of a shipwreck there may be order). These distortions – which give us the wrong reasons for our instincts – are unavoidable because of the vulnerability in which children grow. It means, however, that in contesting their own antisocialism people should not think they should repress their animal nature and feel guilt for their self-assertion: that may be provocation or at best expedience. Instead they should criticise society – the mind's need to interrogate is their natural ability to do this.

16. Individuals have the instincts of their social roles, just as they do their language; and their own *use* of language – in Saussureian terms their *parole* as distinct from their *langue* – is also derived from their social role. Individuality has the same origin as class generalisation. The former is the shape of the fragment chipped from the block of the latter. Individuality is authentic but it cannot be expressed or understood outside its class context. Individual diversity comes from class uniformity and class experience is derived from individual diversity. Individuality is the product of generality. The private is how the public expresses itself – the statue embraces its sculptor. Hence the instability of class roles. They are not instinctive, or even politically determined except in shifting generalities; so that if self autonomy is to be achieved there

is need not only for political understanding but also for self understanding. Both forms of understanding are the subject of drama. If individuality is discounted in politics, then need is stripped of legitimization; authority cannot then increase the humanness of mind; it attempts to take the boundary's place and any authority which does that becomes a barrier; it has stifled or, worse, diverted into regimentation, the need to interrogate.

17. The individual is dramatized because the over-capacity of mind makes him or her a spectator of his or her self, which is (by analysis) a spectator of himself or herself in society: an actor on stage. The combination of reason and the capacity for instinct dramatizes the child as it becomes a social agent.

18. Understood in this way instincts explain much of the drama of knowing yourself to be human. We are not tools of instinct. Our reasoning, interrogating mind severs instinct from the natural world and our instincts are not our birthright but are donated to us in the drama of childhood and our later need to redramatize that drama. Instincts and cognition make up a whole, like weft and warp; neither exists nor changes without the other. Instincts are humanizing since they help to make the mind interrogative; if they are corrupt that is because they are wrongly thought. But thought does not control instinct, it creates it – sometimes as Frankenstein created. All pleasure is the satisfactory – that is, precise – asking of a question: because the flesh is made literature. But we cannot remember the question, only its interrogative form. The question is lost in its first dramatization in the child; redramatizing the drama means understanding the new situation and letting the old answer – which we cannot remember – serve as part of the question; then our ignorance teaches us and our knowledge of the new may be precise – we have no need of lies and find no security or comfort in corruption. Plato is wrong in saying we learn only what we know. What we know is the truth – but the facts are against it. The facts are the new. They must change the truth – and that is the redramatization of childhood necessary to maturity; the new must constantly be integrated into the old so that the truth may become fiction. We would die without our trauma.

19. We can only think of society in our role as spectators of the boundary. The corruption of instinct is ultimately derived from society. But as drama precedes rational understanding, culture is in two respects founded on falsehoods: the child's and authority's.

In the rationality of drama instincts can elucidate their humanness – or in the corruption of drama they turn interrogation of authority into belief and obedience. Belief is the constant reiteration of the same questions in order to avoid answers.

20.   This account of instincts is compatible with theories of mind as diverse as Locke's and Chomsky's. A modular understanding of the brain must allow for information and performance ultimately to be generalized in the cortex and so in experience. Otherwise we would in effect be working on other people's memories. We do not have *other people's* memories even of the times two multiplication table but *our own* memory of it, and this would be true even if the table were innate knowledge. I am not making the simple point that knowledge is what we think of it or need it for, but what the things we know keep secret from us.

21.   Authority does not discern an existing story but creates one. God does not speak till he is spoken to by authority. Authority does not pray. Just as people create – in submission or resistance – their humanity in their relationship to authority, so does authority in relationship to the boundary. It believes it knows its story just as it knows the language in which it tells it. People do not necessarily lose their humanness under tyranny. They lose it only when authority with their consent replaces the boundary with itself as barrier; usually this happens only when authority delegates authority to subordinates in a way which (through fear or prestige) prohibits interrogation – it creates a chain of vavasours. Then the child's philosophical birthright is lost and the functionality of the good citizen is produced.

22.   Madness unlike officiousness is not corruption. Madness, when its cause is not chemical, bodily etc., occurs when the questioner turns on himself or herself in fear – not in self-questioning but in the process of questioning the boundary; then the individual haunts the boundary as if it were no man's land. The exterior is internalized and questions become answers; yet the madman or madwoman does not have the sanctuary of belief (which depends on outside authority) but must constantly fantasize reality.

23.   Some changes in the threefold relationship are culturally more important than others. Their importance is that later developments have to take account of them – they cannot rescind the earlier humanness but must incorporate it into their own.

24. Early cultures related people to the jungle, veldt or desert in which their society lived. For them the world was not mapped beyond the community's tracks. It was the demesne of spirits and animal-spirits. The natural was seen as the supernatural. Authority's story described the spirits and controlled the rituals that ensured good relations between them and society, so that needs were met. The totem animal might be eaten and actors might be sacrificed. (The first actors were killed at the end of the performance but this is no longer done in modern theatre.) The iconography was of animals and humans and their symbiosis. Ritual and theatre can only be combined in such primitive societies. Politics hardly existed because it was synonymous with culture and wisdom. Opposition came from without, from the boundary which was alien and malevolent.

25. The tendency of greek society was discursive not ritualistic. The boundary was partly literalised by asia on the greek frontier – not a jungle inhabited by animal spirits but a place of barbarous political darkness. And technology had changed. Slash and burn and hunting were replaced by husbandry and herding. Plato's ideal world had a perfection absent in this world. Yet people were victims of the ideal world. In Plato's myth of the cave people are bound like slaves. The world was imagined as controlled by gods. The gods were frivolous. Judged by human standards they were mad. The boundary was fate – and perhaps fate was even the graveyard of the gods. In greek drama human suffering was enormous and served no natural, totemic purpose. It was – amazingly – endured for the purposes of the inner boundary, so that it might interrogate the outer boundary. The drama of people and animals was replaced by the drama of people and gods. But people achieved their humanity in defying the gods. Their ability to choose to submit to fate was a moral condemnation of its arbitrariness. A judgement on it. The radicalness of the greeks in doing this has not been surpassed. In the greek world authority was not free to create culture by its interpretation of the boundary, founding its power on fear of the world. The gods were judged, the world was explored and new maps were made. Culture was divided into the poetic, the philosophical and the administrative. The division meant that ritual was once and for ever excluded from theatre. In the past ritual had increased the humanness of mind. In future ritual would function as a politics that excluded understanding; ritual is without interrogation. Philosophy interrogated authority's institutions.

This openness produced self knowledge that later cultures would have to take into account. In greek society answers were not dictated but came through discussion. Even oracles were ambiguous, not out of sacerdotal cunning but out of respect of the questioner: ambiguity was not a trap but a dialogue. Of course the institutions were imperfect, and when the oracle was acted on, the hand came off with the glove. But it meant the gods did not know – or did not respect – the truth. The greeks were not the chosen people but the people who chose themselves. Their statues showed the gods as superhuman, heroic and harmonious even in discord; but drama showed them as arbitrary, entangled, inhuman. The first is the human utopia, the second is the reality. The function of any religion is, in order to explain the boundary, to create gods who in their dealings with this world are able to behave worse than human beings could in that situation. If human beings behaved as badly they would lose their self-respect and destroy their icon of humanity. Religion does not idealise our goodness but licenses – in the acts of the gods – the worst in us. Gods are not sacrificial scapegoats, either, but the actors of *Realpolitik* in the world of ethics and emotions. Their miracles are only a moral figleaf. We misunderstand god because we have not understood ourselves.

26. There were flaws. The greeks could not have achieved their openness and still have organized society if they had been truly democratic. Democracy could not have been created without the support of slavery; greek technocracy was too primitive to allow humanness to be generalised. The economy needed slaves – two-footed cattle. In this matter the greeks were forced to be as frivolous as their gods. Plato's story of the cave is political not metaphysical.

27. Slaves cannot accept their master's evaluation of slaves. They cannot be corrupted in this way; but free people are corrupted by accepting their masters' description of freedom. Authority cannot have the institutions and forms in which slaves can question it and so it cannot give slaves answers that increase their humanity. Slavery cannot be legitimized for slaves, at best it is endured in resentful fear. Slaves must question the boundary directly and that is the advantage they often have over the free. They create their own culture, which is the way they answer their questions. But if the masters seem technologically competent the slaves might adapt their masters' culture to their own ends. This means that in order to escape from slavery slaves will lose some of their freedom. That is part of the drama of being human, the way the psyche is enmeshed in politics; and why we can only live by

human law when our humanity does not depend on the legitimizing of our need to be criminal.

28.   Slavery was the classical world's weakness. ('If all slaves were dressed alike they would see how great was their number and murder us.') To accept that all people were equal before the boundary would have weakened authority and made the administration of technology too hard. Greek society's discursiveness was not a viable model for the organisation of ancient technology. Christianity resolved the resulting crisis between psychic tension and political efficiency. Christian authority spoke dogmatically for the boundary. Dogma was the price of making god human. The new freedom was based on a rigidity which must in time become a prison – when god will turn into the devil in order to escape again from human beings and make machines his chosen people.

29.   Societies migrating to new lands or developing new economies often seek dictatorial leaders. Judeo-christianity created the single god as a moral counterpart to political need. When humans became political ethics had to replace ritual. As christianity made everyone equal before god it was not in the common interest to see gods as frivolous: that would have devalued the equality of humanness. The frivolity of the greeks' gods had seeped through into the relation between masters and slaves; what a culture cannot use as a strength becomes a weakness, a corruption of the state. In fact the christian god's acts were as frivolous (or were as bound by fate) as those of the greek gods. But they were monotheistic, tyrannical, ineffable signs of love: god became moral and jealous. He was not to be defied and judged. Perhaps in criticising the gods Euripides abdicated human responsibility for them. We must accept, with all their faults, the gods we create; we create their faults because we need them; the gods have a graveyard but they must not go to it too soon. Greek drama had to accept the criminality of the gods so that the utopian heroic greek statues could dance in the orchestra of dionysus.

Christianity could not accept responsibility for its god and he was not to be interrogated though he redeem the world with murder. Christianity closed theatres because they cannot exist without questioning. It closed the arenas because they were the scenes of its martyrdom. But they were also the scenes of the martyrdom of heathens. The church closed the arenas less to prevent victims' sufferings (it inflicted suffering on its own kind) than to prevent the spectators' delight. This was wise, because to the state pleasure is more dangerous than suffering; when people suffer a tyranny already begins to control the authority that will replace it. To be human drama must be fiction, not real. Otherwise people behave like gods and that is not how to become human. To put it crudely, our gods do our dirty work for us and allow us to keep our human icon. Its often thought that gods are a projection of the best in human beings, the utopian. But gods are created to do what human beings would find it inhuman to do, but which (at the time it is done) must be done if authority is to administer technology and the economy and still legitimize the human mind – which means to increase its humanness. The moral accountability which people are supposed to have to god they really have to authority: god keeps the hands of the police clean. Gods are our moral slaves and combine ethics and *Realpolitik*. When we created tools we had to create god to take responsibility for the effects of their use. If we look at it analytically we see that we create gods to drive our machines.

30.   Christianity's drama is in the past in the days of conception, golgotha and resurrection; but it is also timeless and always at its moment of crisis. The church-state administered culture as an open wound. Theatre must question the boundary, and so authority replaced theatre with ritual, the constant making and healing of the wound. But christian ritual is different from the early ritual of people-and-animals. *That* combined ritual and theatre; god had not yet chosen martyrdom for his son and so taken ritual and theatre out of history – and so in primitive ritual real martyrdom (real even when symbolic) was still repeatedly acted *as theatre*. There was no functional difference between the stage in the mind and the stage in society. At each ritual performance the god was re-won; there is no prayer in ritual, only invocation and presence and the question is erased by blood or chant. But the christian martyrdom of god occurs only once. This enables authority to control dogma, within limits extending it as necessary to meet the remapping of the world and to enable society to change technology efficiently to meet new ends. In fact technology did not greatly develop, but many different technologies and ways of living in different climates and terrains were brought into economic contact and administration was extended. The administration of souls meant the overseeing of these new technologies and the start of turning the map of the world from a rune into a market diagram. Doctrine involved politics but was outside history. The church could adapt its foundations without destroying its edifice; till in time it would be shown a map it could not survive.

31. Fiction must be built into the threefold relationship and the purposes of fiction respected. Otherwise stages in the mind and stages in society become confused. Finally you cannot stage in society what must be staged in the mind, without corrupting the humanising process. It is not that the stage is a way of avoiding reality. We cannot have the facts of reality – survive them – unless we teach the facts our fictions; a knife has no morality, a machine has no appetite – yet they are martinets that instruct us. The child is both murderer and murderers' victim – many times – and because of its vulnerability it must be so; the emulsifying of instinct and reasoning is tragic and dramatic. When the process is understood the stage in the mind and the stage in society can be used to increase our humanness. Drama uses a dead language which, although it cannot be known, corrupts unless the facts of the new are clearly articulated in the memory of the old. This is true also of politics. That is why politics must not be confined to administering and ordering. We speak of the dictatorship of the proletariat: but we need the *diction* of the proletariat, the anarchy of the party and the dictatorship of (I mean from) the self. Like golgotha, the nazi parade ground and the lager appellplatz were real stages where the fictive ought to have been; and perhaps golgotha was a fiction? – as fictive as the resurrection. But golgotha was dogmatized as real. At least, unlike the nazi sites, it was creative because it freed slaves. The nazi sites were prisons. The problem set christian authority was how to make golgotha a prison, and it did this by declaring it to be a place of love.

32. Where there is no theatre society is the dramatic stage. What the theatre cannot stage must be staged in reality. Christianity's story is a drama of family and state. It legitimizes criticism at many levels but turns it into a means of repression. The son-god was born into a poor family. He dealt with earthly authority patronizingly and destructively. He dealt with the god of the boundary submissively. His mother is made pregnant not by god but by the son-like Gabriel; as if the unborn son made his mother pregnant. Oedipus fathers himself on his mother and treats his father as his son. The son is punished with crucifixion. Death becomes birth. Punishment becomes love. And forbidden love becomes love of the world: how else could it be concealed? By these contortions an elemental drama is suspended over people and state. Authority rewrites the story in which the child was originally dramatized and the psyche produced as the scene of drama. As children grow up the first story must be rewritten so that children can make the new practical; so that the victims can use technology

and become citizens and perhaps victimizers. But as the private can only think the public, children rewrite the story collectively as classes; the child's memory of events which did not occur are transmuted into mystical 'facts' of his or her culture. Unfortunately the old may be fictionalised as the new – the frequent cost of being human. Whenever organization must change, authority can enter the gap between the child's story of childhood, the story of events which did not take place (but which are remembered) and the new facts of the present world – which then become facts about the old story. Culturally it is the job of the individual to return as detective to the scene of the old crime with a bagful of facts from the new (the present) and litter them about the place – where they become clues of a crime that did not happen. Thus the present makes the past real so that the individual (murderer and victim) may take responsibility for the present: in this way childhood becomes maturity, with the moral mandate of that word or with the obedience of a good citizen whose soul is the taking of orders. The psyche is a plot; the stories of epochs are at the same time domestic dramas.

33.   Catharsis is not the evacuation of emotion but the means by which inhuman acts of *Realpolitik* are legitimized, in the face of needs, as part of the human icon. Culture is graffiti written on the wall at the boundary; graffiti, because doctrine is inventive and made 'on the run' as authority responds to crises. The wall does not exist but is actualized by the graffiti. Later, doctrine slowly changes into dogma and the boundary becomes a barrier and is actualized in bureaucracy, financial devices, schools, police cells and so on.

34.   In christianity all are equal. The authority of church and state speaks for the boundary. People may shut themselves off from the love of god and lose their place in society: a great garbage bin is set at the edge of the world, hell. Authority punishes heresy in the name of the boundary. In this way authority achieves administrative competence but legitimizes (as part of the human icon) its right to coerce when its other means fail. It legitimizes its violence in the same process by which it adds humanness to the human mind. Christian authority increased the humanness of the human mind by the story it told of god and his people. The individual's need to interrogate was co-ordinated into authority's power. Conflict stems from the injustice of the real world, but so long as authority can administer technology (which often means, so long as there are no leaps in technological development) conflict

may be acted out in terms of the story, not in terms of ownership. Authority donates humanness both to believers and heretics; heretics turn authority into a barrier; and this means turning authority's story of the boundary into a barrier. Heresy speaks directly to the boundary and so creates a new boundary which may humanize the mind. Provided it is not reactionary (reaction is nostalgia for the dramatization of childhood; it treats the events which did not happen as if they had, and brings the dead past into the present as clues: nostalgia is the utopia of the sexton; in submitting to his condemnation Socrates died of nostalgia for his childhood) interrogation itself is humanizing.

35.   Christianity removes drama from the stage to reality. Drama is turned into ritual. Ritual is not cathartic. Saints and sinners are constantly coerced with their unworthiness, impurity and sin. Because it abrogates interrogation the church's iconography is static; the soul must be an invalid. A god in movement forbids images because they immobilize; a static god allows images of martyrdom, disease, weakness, torture, captivity. At first christianity created other memorial martyrdoms, not merely because of the conflicts involved in the conversion of a continent – it used the inevitable and turned what would have been repressive into creation. Later as more of the world was mapped and marketed there were more martyrdoms, for the same reasons. The martyrdom of golgotha was replicated till its shadow fell everywhere and the memory of it sank into the stones of cathedrals and the proceedings of chancelleries and the angelus became the victim's wail in the fields. Only the market place was untouched. When there were enough sites of martyrdom the martyrdom of the orthodox ceased; since authority had now changed places with the past, the holy act became a crime. Now martyrs went to hell not heaven.

36.   Christianity combined rigidity with flexibility. It severed doctrine from administration and legitimized state violence; but it restrained violence so that it did not become so tyrannous that it could not represent the boundary and still legitimize need and add to the humanness of the human mind. Christianity's flaw was that it freed the soul and legitimized slavery. That is a common paradox in the dealings between state and people.

37.   Christian ritual allows people direct contact with the boundary but only through the mediation of authority. In its ritual (which is without theatre) communion with others is achieved through isolation from them. People experienced social unity only

by accepting their isolation. Ritual which creates community, as it once did in earlier times, is no longer possible because ritual cannot co-exist with theatre and the interrogative. Kierkegaard showed that christian fellowship is isolation before the holy. Ritual is possible only in a static society which does not have to treat the new as clues because there is no new and the present is eternal; for christian ritual to *tell* the new it would be necessary, say, to change the number of nails used in the crucifixion. Only theatre (and other fiction) has a hold on reality strong enough to do that. That is why christianity is foolishness to Oedipus and all greeks.

38.   In times of radical change the mind anticipates and (so to say) experiences the future. When it does this the mind still works materialistically: it experiences changes that *will* occur by its experience of past and present change; in the same mental event the mind is public and private. It is because the mind is materialistic – that is, a unity with the body's needs – that fiction and imagination are possible for us; their reality is created by the gap between the public and private, and the old and the new, which is opened and bridged in every act of thought. Because the mind anticipates the future, to understand what happened in the threefold relationship we can consider the renaissance and reformation together.

39.   Authority's story changed in the Reformation. There was a new map of the world and the rate of change of technology increased. To use the new technology in ways which seemingly best met human needs social organisation had to change and so had the humanness of the mind. Individuals had to accept more self-authority, which meant to become more complicated to themselves (and thus to know themselves less). The existing authority of church and state could not adapt because its own humanity (and its privileges) were invested in a particular arrangement of the threefold relationship. The state freed itself from this arrangement and claimed to speak directly to the boundary. Authority's change (though part of the forces of change could not yet be institutionalised in authority: that could wait for the eighteenth century bourgeoisie) increased the humanness of people's minds. It brought people and machines closer together. The relationship of people and state can be seen as that of a statue that carves itself with a mallet and chisel – but to understand the human drama we must see that the mallet and chisel are made of dust from the stone – and also see, in the end, that just as god was imagined as making men from clay we make our machines from the statue's dust. What

is iron, is the will. In the new world technology intruded more and more into natural cycles and more utopian dreams were disciplined on paper and in statutes, maps and literature and so ceased to be utopian and began to be the autopsy of births. Authority could not completely rewrite events; many of the changes of mind must be resolved in the mind; the watchdog barks at itself and does tricks to entertain itself in the mistaken belief that it is already the master, and soldiers are seen eating their uniforms.

40. The puritan conscience broke away from the state. It questioned authority's interpretation of the boundary and spoke directly to the boundary itself. So the state could not exercise authority and administer technology and the economy so as best to meet needs. This led to civil war. War is a ritual and therefore an aberration in civilization; it takes over the proper role of god (to act out and take responsibility for our humanity) and so is always pagan. For this to happen the necessity must be dire; war is the clumsy attempt of human beings to make a miracle. It follows that god must always be on the wrong side in war. There are no good wars, but, like accidents, they cannot always be avoided. War cannot close the gap between ritual and doctrine and so war and utopia become each other's illusion.

41. The Reformation disturbed the feudal settlement. Afterwards christianity could never be a doctrine (which imprisons in order to free) but must be dogma. Instead of imprisoning society it imprisons itself; mentally it passes to torturing the psyche. Modern christianity turns its back on society except in its fantasies.

42. Because the Reformation questioned authority's story theatre again became necessary. Theatre interrogates and so cannot be confined to ritual knowledge of another world. Theatre deals with mental and social changes which the existing mind and society cannot deal with. The mind could not go on experiencing society in the old way. Administration and the economy were disturbed by new energy from coal, water, minerals, maps (scripture accepts new maps only by fantasizing itself). The new energy was both mysterious and astonishingly practical: a machine has all the chief characteristics of the human soul *and* of the utopian image of heaven. It was as if the mechanical clockwork of animated idols were turned inside out and the gears and pulleys worshipped for themselves – as if the simulacrum of the human form which masked god was ripped off and behold there were the gears and pulleys which were the real workings of nature and

history. Truly the puritan god moved among his people, not in rural grottos but in workshops and market places. Even now faced with a new machine we become a little hysterical; and machines are still the true sublime. The new theatre had to create an iconography to serve as social plan, psychological diagram and invocation and legitimization of the new forces (perhaps the legitimization was not legality but danger, not order but offence) to build the plan. Once there had been a theatre of people and animals, then there was a theatre of people and gods. Now there was to be a theatre of people and the devil.

43. Jacobean theatre's one chief study is the devil. The first operas dealt with Orpheus's descent into hell; but, after the classical model of loss and defiance, Orpheus loses utopia. The new theatre reversed the story. The devil was brought out of hell. Oedipus unknowingly offends but gains self-knowledge; Iago is the unconscious agent of evil but never knows himself (the name is like a squashed fly). Iago is the true soldier, the doer. Othello is a toy soldier. He murders Eurydice not after looking back – as all men desire Utopia – but after spying on her. Othello is black and should (in the iconography of that time) be the devil (and in Shakespeare's first play the devil *is* black). Iago had to be the white devil (though conventionally with dark hair and eyebrows, as if to authenticate him his own shadow flitted for a moment across his face) because the new machines are owned and worked by whites. People had looked upon the iron guts of god and seen the devil – and it was good: the devil is a white mechanic. Shakespeare's history plays try to establish a Reformation without industrialism. They offer a patriotic political theology for modern feudalism, as if people could build great factories in which to carry on cottage industries. In the end of the history cycle, when the new feudal sovereign appears, he is accompanied by the new reality: Richard the Third is the devil. Theology fails in the presence of the new god. Richard's death cry for a horse is the complete strategy for the new world: I throw away the old kingdom if I may have the energy of the new – the symbolic horsepower, in which machines are still measured. All Shakespeare's next plays examine the new individuals: the creatures of machines and the devil. Evil is in all these plays and they are all studies of Faust. Shakespeare would certainly have written *Faust* if Marlowe had not already written it so well that there was no excuse to rewrite it.

44. The Reformation needed the devil for the reason the primitive world needed animals, the classical world needed gods and the

christian world needed one god: to increase the humanness of the human mind. God could no longer do it because the new technology took creation out of his (too human) hands. Machines do not need to be handled with piety and the experimental way of finding knowledge is not an approach to god: no one carries out experiments on god and who will wait for a miracle when they might have a machine? The new industrial satanic energy was not only humanizing in destroying an old authority and an old mind and creating new ones – it was a danger to the new. Theatre interrogated and created a new consciousness to bear new human responsibility. At the end of Othello authority calls for guards and torture not god.

45.   The Reformation disturbed the mind so radically that the mental energy involved in the change could not be contained in the change; it destroyed the old structures and ignited the anticipation of the new; the impulse became the goad, the need became the danger, and the future was presented in fate's hands – to pass through that sanely the mind had to treat the real as the mental: fantasize it – the world must go mad. And so the real drama of witch hunting and witch burning was created – an extraordinary craze of torturing, burning and hanging took place in the future lands of industrialism. The classical gods had behaved with human frivolity, the more draconian christian god showed human goodness (dangerous in such powerful hands because it sanctified *Realpolitik*) – the Reformation needed the creative anarchism of the devil. But its culture could legitimize itself only in terms of the humanness that went before it – the dignity of the greeks and the severity of the romans, among other things. One way of being the devil – allowing his energy to work in the mind – was to become the devil's persecutor: to come face to face with the devil is evidently an embrace in which you see yourself in the light of the devil's flames.

But puritanism punished the devil only in ways convenient for manufacture and trade; in harmless women too old to exploit for manual work and sometimes in children – and in a few token men. In this way puritanism harboured the devil as its living god; punished the devil where he had no political, military or commercial value; and exercised the devil in its own mind by violence and cruelty and so practised the mental energy it needed to wreck the old economy and build the new. The mental energy that created the industrial revolution could not be accommodated in its creators' minds and had to lead to either madness or theology.

The witch hunter knows – and so does not have to confess to himself
– that as manufacturer he is the devil's agent, so it is vital that he
always choose victims who are innocent: hence the old women and
children. He must destroy the innocent because it is diabolic to do
so. The confessions of the torture chamber, the bestial, remorseless
torture to obtain confessions from the innocent, is really the witch
hunter's way of keeping his own silence. He tortures others to
perfect his silence. That is why he is merciless – he must be blinded
by the torture's eerie brilliant light, as if satan were blinded by his
own fire. The witch-hunter uses satan to sanctify the good works
of his hands. There was no way other than torture to increase the
humanness of his mind. We have our machines because he
tortured. Is this so surprising? – later, when the need for religious
adventure was past, the devil became institutionalised in the
factory, survival wages, slums and the lottery of stocks and shares;
the poor were degraded so that profit could produce the glories of
enlightenment culture; and when whole communities can be
barbarized in the name of the good, it will be good, enlightened,
the voice of humanity, to legislate against the barbarity of burning
witches.

46.   It is not that there is no difference between good and evil.
There is all the difference. Our icons do our dirty work for us, or
permit us to do it; they legitimize our inhumanity; sometimes we
call them good and other times evil – in the end they do the same
work. It need not be so. There should be a time when people will
accept responsibility for being human, for what they do, and then
they will know what they do. Good and evil have only one suit of
clothes and they take it in turns to go out in it. Sometimes to be
human we have needed the devil. Perhaps the worst we do is to use
the devil to remove tragedy from politics.

47.   Jacobean theatre ended as abruptly as it began. It existed
during the disturbance of the exercise of authority and the way the
mind told itself it was human, when the existing relationship to the
boundary broke down. A new authority which spoke to the
boundary had to be established, otherwise technology could not be
owned and administered in ways seemingly best to meet common
needs. Puritans closed the theatres because they interrogate. The
puritans also broke images. Drama was removed from the stage
and went back to reality. But there were as yet no new rituals
because they must be administered by authority, and authority
represents the community in its relations to the boundary; but the
protestant church could not revoke the puritan conscience

(humanness must be built on existing humanness) which itself claimed to speak to the boundary. In fact the self-autonomy created by this could be useful in a society of machines: authority could form an alliance with it and corrupted conscience into conformity and the taking of orders. The blood of the mass became symbolic and the orderly ritual became the Walpurgis day of the shakers and then the silence of the quakers. The new society's ritual would be factory labour – good in the sight of the lord. In the factory the relationship with the boundary will be forged and people will say what they are. That was the nearest society came to ritual, because it came from the economy as part of the threefold relationship and not from the story – *that* would have made it mere aestheticism. Industrialism replaced the witch hunt as a social discipline.

48.   What causes the fanatical animus of all puritans against theatre? For them theatre is a torture chamber demanding that they confess. The restoration re-opened theatres to plays which did not tragically question the boundary. The king was resurrected and the constitutional monarchy became the Garden of Eden from which the serpent had been driven out. Restoration plays honour cynicism and give thanks for the stupidity of the poor. The boundary was the counting house. The factory existed outside Restoration theatre in the way slavery had existed outside the theatre of Dionysus. Cynicism protected the individual; when the new institutions are more extensive they will need more support; cynicism will give way to sentiment and licentiousness to respectability in order that things may stay the same.

49.   Some authorities survive upheavals. The Counter-Reformation used the old story to achieve ends which the reformation could only achieve by new stories. Old stories may be used in new ways but this does not give them a lasting truth. Generals may be buried in their uniforms but they cannot give orders. In history, eternity seems to come to an end every one or two hundred years or so.

50.   Before the Reformation iconoclasm was always followed by iconography. The puritans broke old images but they did not make new ones. They would have had to create images of their living god, the devil, and no matter how assiduously authority worships and works with the devil it does not create images of him. Witch burning broke the devil's telltale image even as the witch-hunters placed it in its niche in the new mind. And as the puritans could not create a new image of their god they changed their clothes and gave christ to the devil as a doll.

51.   God does not paint pictures or compose music because they are static images. God talks, always as a poet or dramatist. That is because he comes from the child's first dramatisation. God is created by children and worshipped by adults. Talking is the foundation of theatre because theatre is interrogative. So when god talks there can be no theatre – no one is allowed to question god. Job questioned him for a time and might even have become a greek but he ended by loving god as he loved his neighbour.

52.   The industrial revolution settled much of the turmoil it had created in the human mind. Labour became ritual and the nonconformist conscience sober and diligent. Energetic struggle with the devil, necessary to make him a familiar and install him in the mind as reason and not fear, gave way to the administration of both conformity and nonconformity; authority which is establishing itself can at first use the antagonism it incites as a means of support – when a hoop moves over a surface parts of the hoop recede as other parts advance; only later can antagonism harden into political opposition (this is the story of Stalinism).

53.   Authority built the geomorphic body of the devil in the factory town. It needed to protect the physical body of satan, not the idea; the idea had become property. So heresey lost its use and instead morality, obedience, became politically important. Crime was invented to replace witch burning and the gallows was erected as satan's altar. Authority set about teaching god good manners. Satan, securely buried in the foundations of factory towns, was banished – a typical confusion of morality. Satan did not attack the mind but property (his claim to property was merely moral not legal). Crime became a public institution. (Really this was a return to the primitive: satan was constantly being hanged and then like the ancient corn god resurrected; capitalism cannot exist without crime, not merely because it provokes crime, or because crime makes it respectable, but because crime serves a religious function for it. If there were no crime capitalism would be forced to take on the responsibilities of tyranny.) The statutory list of capital offences was grotesquely extended and children were publicly hanged for petty offences. Theatre became melodrama, the ritual of the dying; and later the modern musical, the ritual of the dead. (I do not deny that the dying and the dead need consolations or even that they find their humanness in them.)

54.   Literary novels were (and most of them still are) written to be read by robots: members of society with established incomes

who need to cultivate their subjectivity to prevent them from doing anything about the state of things. 'Novel' really means 'conservative'. Unlike christian rituals novels do not create isolation in the individual; they create an elite confident that wherever it casts its pearls there will be swine. Novels are written by the devil after he has been reformed; that is why there is no poetry in them. God is a poet but the devil is a statistician.

55.   Crime made it possible to remove interrogating drama from the stage. Reality was dramatized in prisons and hulks and on scaffolds. The scaffold does not exhibit the victim as possessed but as devil incarnate. Satanism became instrumental in rationalism – the dead rose from the graves and threw stones at the devil so that the state might administer the economy. Surely only the dead are interested in watching people being killed?

56.   Fielding, one of the first novelists, was a magistrate; and crime was an obsessive subject for Dostoevsky, Dickens, Balzac, Flaubert, Tolstoy and others. The novel is a sort of bible of crime. Later, class relations became atrophied and antagonism could not be creatively shared between classes – and a vast social division was created, a fact that could never be destroyed or rationalised away or bought off; it will remain under every gloss and will have to be settled with. Authority lost its responsibility for the human image; this created the frigidity of modern capitalism, the rigor mortis of the living. A literary sign of this was the detective novel. One of Sherlock Holmes' first recorded remarks is his claim that if he had been listened to many more people would have been hanged. The detective novel offers no hope; its rigidity comes from moral sclerosis not sureness of judgement; it does not use *Realpolitik* to achieve (tragically or farcically) ethical action, instead it takes *Realpolitik* for the ethical; all we may do is administer fate; it reifies the child's first story and makes it into a suicide note; the blood which is always in it is sacrificial in the most primitive way; it is the pornography of the death warrant; it is nothing more than the diary of a corpse.

57.   Crime serves a social purpose. Authority's aim in the threefold relationship is to establish and legitimize itself and contingently add to the humanness of the human mind. Authority uses the boundary to discipline the social discord its own injustice creates. This injustice derives from its economic and cultural privileges, which (it says) must be accepted by people as part of the all-important relationship with the boundary. Industrial

society's injustice promotes resistance. Crime develops from the puritan conscience's mode of opposition. But the criminal is more religious, closer to godliness, than the institutionalised puritan because the criminal speaks directly to the boundary but the puritan establishes authority as a false boundary: god is his constable and clerk. Crime, with its cynicism, desperation, viciousness and brutality is the purer religion because it is less corrupt – and its arsenals are smaller. Authority turns punishment into theatre; law and order isolates people from the boundary; and crime takes on the role first performed by christian martyrs and then by heresy.

58.   The state's increasing brutality undermined its authority. It transgressed against the humanness established in the mind by earlier stages of the three-fold relationship. Science was part of industrial technology; now it was used to codify resistance and the antisocial and it created the category of deviance. Authority sought to be more liberal and tolerant so that it could economically exploit its intricate technology more easily. Deviance could be dealt with quasi-medically (though more in apologetics than practice). Church-and-state gave way to science-and-state. People were not seen as the cultural creations of interrogation but as the products of scientifically studiable and corrigible determination. This led to conflicts with the historical development of humanness and cultural memory. Art was split off from science, theology and politics and pursued as an end in itself; this split culture from authority; and this removed responsibility for culture from authority and handed culture to it as something it could use. The politics and aesthetics of fascism became inevitable.

59.   Picasso's *Demoiselles d'Avignon* exemplifies the art that smashed the image. Modern art was iconoclastic in the way puritans were iconoclastic. The academic icon of human beings was destroyed because it no longer added to humanness: unlike the great art of the renaissance it was not a portrait of the scientist but a diagram of the object of instrumental science, a laboratory exhibition. It was potentially the icon of fascism. In this respect modern art was an attack on authority; but unlike puritan iconoclasm, modern iconoclasm was also iconographic; in the end in desperation it sought the new icon in the rubble of the old. The puritans swept away the fragments of the idols they broke, modern iconoclasm venerated the fragments. This process took place over and over again in many forms and to various degrees; it provoked counter formulations (the pretty and decorative) which served to

legitimize the original iconoclasm. Even authority was prepared to patronize iconoclasm; two icons were acceptable to it – the public academic art of monuments, portraits etc, and the private-public art of modernism: authority could seek to legitimize itself by patronizing both. The iconoclastic-icon disturbed the threefold relationship by creating an elite which claimed to have its own contact with the boundary. Often a new-icon god must speak in a half-gabble: as authority does not understand even its own role it cannot interpret the new scripture – and the artist wont or cant, because in the past he was part of the scripture and because in the present he poses on the boundary of the avant-garde. This made modern art a dictatorship without power; so that in time the ad-man could loot it. Children born in the ad-age are born with their parents' memories and so the new becomes part of the old and change is accelerated and made static.

60.   The arbitrariness of dada, surrealism, the novel cut up and pasted randomly together, or the mathematical precision of some abstract art – all are icons of chaos. The cut-and-pasted novel functions in the same way as the bureaucratic form; both administer emptiness and find value in the act of administration: the street leads only to the office which reminds you which side of the street to drive on. The cut-and-pasted novel wants value without administration; administration wants meaning without value. Public and private are not related but the public is seen as the private; this over-values the individual by cutting him off from himself. The threefold relationship itself becomes the boundary; science an ineffable mystery; authority the administration of the mystery and not of knowledge; and the individual a thing to be studied scientifically. That is the foundation of modern pseudo-democracy.

61.   In pseudo-democracy there is enjoyment as duty – or, for the bohemian or drop out, meaningless pleasure. The philosophical questions are corrupted; political movements seem to ask questions but see people as things and the boundary as history; and reaction sees the boundary as a wall that is a static dance of death. This reduces change to the contortions of administration and people are not free to question the boundary.

62.   Reaction uses the social aggression caused by its own or past injustice to justify itself and its use of repression. Often progressive politics denies the subjective and so cannot add to people's humanness. People must be free to question the boundary and

accept the best answers they can give – even if they are mistaken; it is better if people pay for their own errors than for their government's errors. Humanity cannot be created in any other way. But because this is so humanity may even be created in suffering (though suffering should not be made a fetish) and happiness may not always create humanness. Good and evil, devils and gods, have changed roles many times. Puritans needed the devil to become more human. The greeks – being promethean – needed to defy their gods to become more human. In our time – for the first time – we have no need to murder to become human. That is the problem of post-modernism. What can murderers do with their idleness?

63.　Authority claims itself and the economy as the boundary. To administer science is more deterministic than to administer ethics. In the old language, its as if you set out to teach god morality.

64.　Science extends human purpose into the macroscopic and the microscopic and takes over god's territory. The sacred has become the commercial. In the past the threefold relationship was disciplined by the meeting of needs. Authority legitimized needs in the name of the boundary and this legitimized its own role. Need was the foundation of technology, organisation and morality. It led to the increase in the humanness of the human mind. But in post-modernity needs are met; or if they are not met it is a matter of mere interruptions or shortfalls in organisation and not because meeting needs is sometimes impossible because the boundary (seemingly) does not will it. Post-modern society is a society of wants. Wants cannot function in the threefold relationship as needs or be broken down into needs. The extraordinary consequence of this is that we can no longer have a utopian vision and so any mystery of any boundary cannot have any ethical content. It is as if instead of cultural development there had been a mutation in culture.

65.　In terms of the threefold relationship post-modern people live on the boundary. So we are in heaven. The point is not rhetorical. If there is no boundary beyond authority and people there can be no utopia. In heaven we lose all need and so the meaning of suffering, discontent and lack changes forever Their biological foundation is recast. The idea of imperfection in heaven is not new. Before he was cast out satan was in heaven. We cannot cast out satan because we are in heaven and the imperfections are part of it; changing it would be like trying to change our skin as we change our clothes. Imperfections are to be dealt with by science and technology, but science and technology are the *origins* of the imperfections. Science and technology cause terror. Terrors arise from the proper working of technology: the waste of environment; industrial pollution; the disorientation of fact by the new media which disperse culture; the danger of nuclear weapons; political terrorism when the injustices inherited from the old world of needs are made more destructive and vehement by new technology; sabotage; hostages; city violence; glass in supermarket food; debt. We are in heaven but cannot get out of hell. We live by an iconography of perfection which is self-iconoclastic. Once we destroyed the images, now the images destroy us. The icon of goodness has become the lord of evil. We may, if we can survive it, stoically endure our situation; or we may create an ideology not of fictions but of the real. And that is the resurrection of satan.

66.   We are in heaven and so we do not need god. We live on the boundary and so there is nothing for him to do: if he existed he would become one of us. In the past people needed religion in order to have god and so add to the humanness of their minds. The devil was the contingency that explained the imperfections of god's world. In the post-modern world people have god because they need the devil; and in future god will remain absent from religion, like the image broken by the puritans. (Art can aestheticize rubble, but religion cannot make capitalism moral.) In post-modernity love of god is the pretext for worship of the devil. The substance of all post-modern religion is the devil; god is merely the spell that conjures him up. Why do the religious need the devil? To account for the terror created by technology. The devil has no practical work, as he had in the industrial revolution; he is the explanation created by frightened minds when they contemplate the stirrings of their insanity. The devil can no longer add to our humanness or improve society. He is needed only to account for the terrors in the post-modern world. He is its salvation. But if you found reason on fantasy, then reason itself works in a mad way – but without the saving weaknesses of madness. One consequence has been the spate of books – such as *The Clockwork Orange* and *The Lord of the Flies* – diabolizing children and young people. Such fictions are quite barbarous. The Royal Shakespeare Company has turned two of them into musicals.

67.   Wants cannot become needs and so cannot be a foundation for the threefold relationship which has been our means to humanness. We are in a world culture in which those who still seem

to have needs have only wants. A child starves to death in the third world not because it has needs, and because no one comes with bread and water, but because it wants luxuries. The paradox is that the child dies of wanting luxuries because it is in a world of wants and so is part of that world culture. In post-modernity the boundary moves for everyone. It cannot move for some and not others. And because for the affluent wants cannot serve as needs, the fulfillment of their wants cannot add to the humanness of their minds; their wants are fulfilled but not met and they are left 'starving' of fulfillment – and so the third world's starving and dying are, for the affluent, icons of their own psyche. The ultimate terror of unjust technology is that it pollutes the inner boundary and creates, there, desolation: it asks us to live with our own death – we are dead haunted by ghosts. In the post-modern world of wants human life cannot be sustained by either the have nots or the haves; and if the starving child were saved it would still be in the world of wants. Charity is no longer a gesture of humaneness. Acts of charity by the dead-in-want are fascistic just as post-modern love of god is really need of the devil. These harsh paradoxes make our post-modern world clear; in the end we are creators of a threefold relationship which substantiates our humanity. We are guardians of history and creators of the threefold relationship or we are not human.

68.   The child starves not because it lacks needs but because it has wants – does not *need* sustenance but *wants* affluence. Why do I say this? I say it not just because there is no place on earth not surveyed by satellites; not explored for minerals or cheap labour; not considered as a site for nuclear weapons or markets for big business; not even just because any starving child may be filmed for TV (the viewer is as helpless as the camera); or because its governments buy weapons so that it can die in freedom among friends; or because in our nuclear wars of freedom even the sky would be taken away from it – I say it simply because of the way the child's mind relates to the boundary and so to how its humanness is sustained. The affluence of the world is not a secret to the poor; we have created their boundary just as, often, our agrochemical industry and our politics have created their starvation. The starving no longer sacrifice or dance to their gods for food, and even if they wished to they have no strength to dance and nothing to sacrifice. The boundary has changed for all of us. The child wants a just world because a post-modern world of wants which is politically and economically unjust kills it. The dying

child knows that this is so – that it dies not because the gods are displeased but because people are unjust. Death has become more bitter. Perhaps the starving child knows the legend of the future, and perhaps only the starving have Utopia? If that is so, we are the starving child's Utopia. That is why I say our charity is fascistic. We buy the right to be unjust and our good conscience and our self-esteem: and we would buy the Utopia from the dying if we could and hang it on the wall as a tourist souvenir. Those who need the devil make a pact with him.

69. In the world of needs the boundary was always the site of Utopia. Utopia was presented either as desire or a fierce command. It parodied needs but also transcended them. In reality needs could be met but not escaped from and so their fulfillment was both total and partial. The mere fulfilling of needs could not have humanized the threefold relationship. Legitimizing needs – making them human – required a Utopia. Needs were met but Utopia was unobtainable. That was its function and it related needs to the radical interrogation produced by the mind's over-capacity. Utopia transcended need but was not a dream and had in it the grit of hunger, cold and mortality. Wants can have no Utopia – if you are in heaven you cannot have Utopia. What is wanted is more of the same or a new variety or fashion of the same. That is a radical mutation in our species; the brain has lost its main cultural activity. Needs (because they invoked Utopia in practical, daily, economic life, and in political and religious dealings, and because they made interrogation ethical) were the means by which we created our humanity – in the teeth of our inhumanity, which, certainly, needs also created. We could not have the first without the last. Wants cannot be such a means and so they alter the *nature* of the threefold relationship. If we invented god now he would not be a poet; I refrain from saying what he would be. We have lost the icon of our humanness. *We* are the image that has been smashed and we cannot find a new image in the debris of commercialism. Our society is a frenzy of media and ad-imaging, of cutting up and refashioning – but we only catch glimpses of ourselves in the blades of the scissors and knives. Post-modern iconoclasm destroys the icon maker.

70. The threefold relationship has developed so that now neither gods nor devils can add to the humanness of our mind. If we destroy ourselves it will not be because we do not fear ourselves enough or lack good will but because we did not learn to be human in the new world of technology and space. We cannot keep the

humanness we inherit from history without adding to it. It is really a technical question, where decision must replace the luxury of time in evolution. Goodness and evil have served many ends; and our emotions cannot induce behaviour which our emotions can adequately judge. That is why I described an understanding of instincts in notes 15 and 16. We are creations of our understanding of our situation. The space between the individual and society is the invisible lever by which each creates the other. Because our emotions are defined (and learn their story) in childhood they cannot be solely rational – such would be the emotions of god. If there were a god he would be the last to judge us on whether we had been good or bad because he would know the irrelevance of such considerations to human welfare.

71. People in uniforms and civilian clothes will go on murdering each other. They will do it for justice, which in the end is the legitimation of their needs. But in the post-modern world no one has needs. That is the paradox of our time of dearth, wastelands, dereliction, destitution, debt, drugs and crime. We have only wants because technology has placed the boundary under our feet. And so we cannot continue to be human without political justice. Religion serves only reaction and if our situation deteriorates religion will become openly fascistic, and in the United States it has already started to be that: it will treat crime as heresy and punish it as such.

72. Post-modernity is the result of the exponentially increasing productivity of technology in goods and in the passing of information. This has given new spasms of vitality to capitalism. Socialism has not failed but many of the things which socialism was intended to struggle for (and in the struggle the threefold relations would have changed so that products could become humanizing) have been produced as it were out of the hat by technology, as if science had played a trick on history. But technology confounded with capitalism will produce terror, partly simply as the result of the performance of machines but more profoundly because it has destroyed the boundary.

73. Why can't wants function as needs and so humanize the threefold relationship? Money can be a need only for those who do not wish to spend it; otherwise it is a want. When there are no needs the economy cannot integrate money into a humanizing threefold relationship. Money serves as a want, as a means to other wants. Perhaps the economy – which in capitalism depends on an invisible hand – could do the work once done by the mysteries of

good and evil, and perhaps even be less demanding of sacrifice? The economy cannot serve as the boundary. We are integrated into the economy by behaviour which the economy changes and for this reason no economy of wants can be well run and no safe predictions can be made about it. In capitalism everyone sees the economy as the enemy to be subverted – this is called competition. The consumer is the fifth column in the economy. The invisible hand becomes a strangler's hand. The consumer manipulates the economy to his or her advantage and so it is no more mysterious than roulette or the stock exchange – an inwardly-facing mystery with a starting line instead of a boundary and rules of procedure instead of morals. Imperialism tried to give the laws (not rules) of cricket ethical value, but that was trying to impose the objectivity of a game onto the *Realpolitik* of trade; the stock exchange is not a game but deadly earnest; you might as well ask criminals to make laws. The economy assumes a predetermined human nature, but economic loss and gain, expectations, solidarity etc change that nature.

The economist is like someone who tries to build bricks out of seawater because he's heard that the sea's currents are strong. Eventually government must intervene, with force or fraud, in the economy. But institutional defences against the economy's inherent self-enmity merely ramify manipulations. Just as the need to raise capital creates new ways of extending and managing debt, so institutions become the enemy of markets they are meant to defend. That is why we have an economy in the first place – it is the prison to be free in. If it were not so we could abolish the economy and our natural grace would see us through. The present surgence between technology and capitalism is a mirage with real consequences. It destroyed utopian vision and put consumption in its place. Almost anything is better than a Utopia, but our humanness has depended on two things: the structural discipline brought into politics and administration by our needs, and being able to use the boundary as the site of Utopia. What we have now are wants and markets. Utopia would be more wants. They cannot humanize the mind because they are outside it. We seem to have stepped out of history back into evolution but without the limitless time of evolution: instead we need to make decisions.

74.   If we survive we will have a technology without an economy. We can have that only when we have lived through our lack of need and Utopia. The devil and charity are the only Utopias available to capitalism; and charity is the devil's only virtue. The

devil will not work for capitalism as he did for puritanism. Capitalism must end in fascism because that is the end of its mechanisms; we cannot ethically bank on the past.

75.   A just society would not need democracy because democracy would be implicit in the working of its technology. We did not need democracy to tell us we had needs but to legitimize them in the face of the technology with which we met them – and to use our needs as a way of being human. And we will not need democracy to tell us we need justice. These paradoxes belong to the world that post-modernism will create.

76.   Each radical change in the threefold relationship records how people got rid of the existing form of humanness and created a new form, a new meaning in the infinity of mind which runs like a river between the bank of civil corruption and the bank of private madness to an open sea. We cannot sustain our humanness without justice and we can no longer create justice by murder, either the calculated murder of politics or the blind murder of crime. Communities threatened by fascist regimes or fascist banditti must defend their young by arms. But all murder is now either the last dance before morning or the first slouchings of a beast. A just world would not arm fascists or take them into the commercial community.

77.   In the nineteenth century the old royal and republican arsenals were replaced by the armaments industries. In the twentieth century we produced weapons that will remain a scandal in any human memory; our ambition was not to torture individuals but whole nations at a time. Nuclear weapons provoked surrogate wars around the world; but even if it were true that they kept the peace it does not follow that peace could not have been kept without them; and they leave for others a legacy of enormity, a politics based on violence that could have destroyed the world. We would not have much regard for a man mounting the scaffold who boasted that he had survived the walk there. By any judgement the half century of peace will be regarded as a time of unprecedented barbarity. As each child was born we held a pistol to its head – what else is nuclear deterrence? Technology will be able to make weapons more destructive than H bombs. If we go on making weapons they will be taken into the threefold relation as a fourth factor; the devil will not be a medieval apparition invoked at need, but an autonomous robot-satan with a permanent seat in our councils. Weapons will become the emblem

of fascism – it is what we must choose to make them. And in a just world a sawn-off shotgun would be as scandalous as a nuclear rocket.

78.   The administration of things seems a utopian wish but becomes possible to people who live on the boundary. It is difficult to believe this because our culture has not yet built its own foundations. Its said that post-modern politics are aestheticised and ordinary life has become theatre. In many ways our situation is comparable to that of the christians and puritans when they closed theatres and created a church-god and a factory-devil. But capitalism theatricalizes life *and* uses theatres. Its aesthetics are iconoclastic, the ad-man's detritus. It manufactures (sometimes unintentionally) problems and solves them by medication and entertainment. This makes the problems static. The greeks used problems to humanize the mind; capitalism uses problems to belittle us. Spectacle becomes vicious excitement that appeals to biological resonances which capitalism wrongly supposes to be free of cognition; with the best intentions it trivializes spectators.

79.   Theatre need not formalise questions and consume audiences by empty entertainment. It could be iconoclastic but not static; not the dream world of performance art, the autistic world of minimalism or a return to the young Brecht. It has to be both iconoclastic and iconographic because that is the function imposed on it by the mind's need to humanize itself. It could create a new method of graphism. Texts would still have sub-texts (because they cannot be written wholly objectively) but they would now have a meta-text. A meta-text is designed to be broken down into smaller 'theatre events', either incidents in scenes or whole scenes. The production is a structured series of 'theatre events' (TEs). The actor does not leave his character to play the meta-text but creates his character in playing it. In this way the individual is generalised. Text, sub-text and meta-text form a unity. Unlike happenings, TEs are a means of analytical understanding. They make clear the cause and consequence of events, collecting the diffuseness of real life into illustration and demonstration – not dogmatically or symbolically but still in units of conflict: in this way the future would be chosen, not determined by the past. The deconstructivist problem of closure would disappear: *that* after all is how people live – they rewrite the story of their childhood in the precision of the new, so that the past becomes clues of what will happen. Theatre creates in the same way, but it can take things apart so that they subvert the past we know. This sort of theatre would free

us from the illusions of Ibsen's determinism, the nihilism of absurdity, and the enervating sensitivity of Beckett; it would use the theatre pioneered by Brecht but not reify his techniques – TEs make alienation narrative. The theatre would have the objectivity appropriate to post-modernism.

80.   The difference between fiction and reality would disappear, as it did for the greeks, because it would have no use. Hyper-technology makes convention and tradition obsolete and much of their ways destructive; that means that living humanely means living a meta-text. But hasn't interrogation always made it that? The difference is that now it is a meta-text without a boundary. The mind's need to interrogate lost its earlier function when want swamped need (not as a psychological trait but as a technological, social imperative). The interrogator is now a prisoner in rags shuffling on a stage between the site of the old boundary and a barrier. That is the inner-icon of our affluence. For such a prisoner everything becomes a tool and an image. His theatre does not disinter the cause or meaning of things but creates them by his own actions. One day people will be amazed that their forebears thought ghosts had power over the living. Theatre will not be scripture, but there will be discipline in it, just as there was in the stages of the threefold relationship: but truths will harden not into dogma but into ambiguity – and then the clues will be oracles. We will not need Utopia because we will have real political responsibility. The difference between fiction and reality will disappear because for the first time we will know which is which.

81.   First there was the theatre of people and animals, then of people and gods, then of people and the devil. Now we need the theatre of people and people. It is made possible by the use of interrogation in post-modernity. If we don't realise it, it is because we are as greedy as the man who wanted two graves.

82.   All revolutions are written on the back of the calendar.

Edward Bond
from Notebooks
written in November 1989

Notes on Post-Modernism was originally published with Jackets *and* In the Company of Men *in a volume entitled* Two Post-Modern Plays.

Human Cannon

For Yvonne Bryceland

Characters who appear in the first part of the play

PRIEST	JUDGE 2
AGUSTINA	JUDGE 3 (MIGUEL)
TINA	SENTRY 1 (TOMASO)
NANDO	SENTRY 2
IGNACIO	SENTRY 3 (MARCO)
PACO	GRANDMOTHER
CATALINA	ANTONIA
TOMASO	RICO
MARCO	BLIND MAN
MIGUEL	CRIPPLED MAN
GLORIA VERGARA	WOMAN WITH SMALL
MARGARITA ARRANCE	GIRL
VILLAGER 1	JUAN
VILLAGER 2	GENERAL
VILLAGER 3	BISHOP
VILLAGER 4	CHAPLAIN
VILLAGER 5	FACTORY MANAGER
JUDGE 1 (IRENE)	ASSISTANT

Characters who appear for the first time in the second half of the play

JOSE ALBANA	GUADALUPE
MARIA	PIO
MANI	INVESTIGATOR
CORPORAL	CLERK
PORTLY MAN	CIVIL GUARD 1
WIFE	CIVIL GUARD 2
SON (AURELIO)	CIVIL GUARD 3
HARRISON-LEIGH	CIVIL GUARD 4
FAWCETT	BERTA TORBADO
VENDOR	RENATA ORTIZ
SOLDIER 1	NINA MIRAN
SOLDIER 2	TERESA MARTIN
SOLDIER 3	MARIA BARRIOS
PRISONER 1	RENATA RAMONES
PRISONER 2	MARIA CORVES
ROSITA	JUNITA MURCIANO

Part One

Part Two

An interval after Part One

Spain
The first scene in the late twenties
The other scenes from 1936 to 1940

PART ONE

One: The Nameless Child

A house with a field sloping behind it.

AGUSTINA *is in the house with her dead child.* NANDO *works in the field with their young daughter* TINA.

The PRIEST *comes to the door. He is about thirty.*

PRIEST. Good morning. My housekeeper told me your child had died. I'm sorry.

    AGUSTINA *pours water from a bucket into a bowl.*

PRIEST. She'll make you up a box of vegetables. Your husband can collect it at the funeral.

AGUSTINA. Send it. He's busy. (*She undresses the child and washes it.*)

PRIEST. Will he be long? You know Im often asked to send men up to do odd jobs on the estate. I cant recommend your husband over the heads of my flock. Tell him to come to church. What he does there's between him and his maker. It wouldnt be a compromise: he'd be paid for an honest day's work. You're too isolated up here. You see everything in black and white. If you werent so poor the child would have had a better chance of living.

The PRIEST *goes to the door.*

    (*Calls.*) Nando!

TINA. The priest called.

NANDO (*making a wooden box*). Once there were two men. One day one of them went to the forest. There was a stone on the ground. Suddenly he saw that he could use it to cut down a tree. The stone was the first tool. Till then people had only collected fallen branches. Now he cut down four trees. Naturally his neighbour said 'I'll have one'. When the man said they were his, his neighbour said no they came from *their* wood and he took one. The man sat and pondered and his eye fell on the stone. Next time his neighbour came for a tree he killed him with the stone. The first tool became the first weapon. Give me the nails. (TINA *gives him the nail box and he counts out eight nails.*) Eight. (TINA *takes back the nail box.*) Next the dead man's family said we'll kill him. So the man cut down ten trees and brought home a pile of sharp stones and said to some of his other neighbours, take these stones and protect me. In return I'll give you some of my wood. They were the first policemen. Next the man used them to guard the trees he *hadnt* cut down. Now if you wanted wood you had to work for him. Soon the world became complicated but the story didnt change. At different times its a tragedy or farce or mystery but the plot is always the same.

The Argument of the Story (NANDO)

When someone else owns the machines you use to earn
   your living then you are owned
Those who own the machines own the state, which is the
   system of ownership – and so they own everything
The result is terrible: When everything is owned everything becomes a weapon
Its as if even the tools you hold in your hand as you work
   turn into weapons you use against yourself

How can such a world be at peace?
   People are angry and cruel not by nature – but because
   society requires anger and cruelty from its citizens
This is the argument of the story: When the machines are

owned by those who dont use them everything becomes
a weapon and the world's filled with enmity

NANDO *gives the box to* TINA.

TINA. Is it a true story?

NANDO. Yes – but all governments ban it. Your mother cant
have any more children. Line it with hay.

NANDO *and* TINA *go down to the house.*

PRIEST. Im sorry the child's dead. What was its name?

NANDO (*gestures* TINA *to give the box to* AGUSTINA). Everyone takes an interest in it when its dead. It hasn't got a
name.

PRIEST. We'll need one for the Register.

NANDO. Its not being buried in the churchyard.

PRIEST. You mean to bury it in your field?

NANDO. I cant, I'd ruin my pick – you get to the rock after
two inches. Anyway I cant spare the land.

PRIEST. Its your duty to protect your wife, not add to her
sufferings. We cant know what a mother suffers when she
loses a baby. Now when her body heals her mind will
suffer even more if the child's buried in common ground.
What's the sense in that? I'll send the doctor to her.

NANDO. We need a harrow if you could send that.

PRIEST. Your conduct is an offence to the parish! The
behaviour of animals! You cant even bury your dead
properly yet you complain you're not allowed to run your
own lives! God save us from the day! I'll be in the vicarage
till midday tomorrow. I'll tell the sexton to dig the grave.
There wont be a fee.

The PRIEST *goes out right.*

AGUSTINA. I've taken the clothes to sell at the weekend.

NANDO (*as* AGUSTINA *puts the child in the box*). I'll be away
overnight. If I bury it here they'd dig it up. I know a gulley

where we camped when we were boys. Dropped stones in it.

AGUSTINA (*to* TINA). Put something to eat in your father's tin. (*Flatly as* NANDO *nails the lid on the box and* TINA *puts food in the tin.*) The pain doesnt stop after you give birth, it turns into the grief when you bury it.

NANDO (*kisses* AGUSTINA *and* TINA). Goodbye.

TINA. Shall I come?

AGUSTINA. No stay with me.

NANDO *takes his jacket, puts the tin in his pocket and the box under his arm and goes up the slope.*

AGUSTINA. Clear up for me.

TINA. Wont it have a name?

AGUSTINA (*half-hearing the question*). No it wasnt born in a human world, it was born in this world.

IGNACIO.

On the fifteenth of February nineteen thirty-six the Spanish Popular Front defeated reaction at the poles

The reactionaries began to plot

Franco had the appetite of the wolf

The caution of the snail

The eye of the hawk

And the arrogance of a man

After four months he revolted in Morocco with an army of thirty-six thousand

He had to move his army to Spain before the Popular Front could create an army to fight him

The Republican fleet blockaded Morocco

Franco sent messengers to Hitler and Mussolini

Within days Fascist planes were carrying his army to Spain

The people's militia – poorly armed and untrained – stopped Franco forty miles from Madrid

The snail spoke to the wolf and Franco opened a new front
  in the north

In the first days of the Fascist rebellion the villagers of
  Estarobon stood ready to defend the Republic
The landowner fled

Two: The Trial

*A school room and a hut in Estarobon. Desks, chairs and benches
in the school room.*

A group of villagers, among them AGUSTINA, NANDO, TINA,
IGNACIO, PACO, CATALINA, TOMASO, MARCO, MIGUEL,
GLORIA VERGARA, MARGARITA ARRANCE.

IGNACIO. We need places for the judges, witnesses,
  accused, prosecutor, defender –
VILLAGER 1. These little chairs will give under our weight.
VILLAGER 2. They make them as tough as bar stools so the
  children cant break them.

*The furniture is rearranged for a court. When it is done the
adults sit in the children's chairs.*

VILLAGER 3. Who has the teacher's desk?
TINA. The prosecutor!
NANDO. Judges!
IGNACIO. A revolutionary court doesnt use oaths. The
  enemy says that's because we're a rabble. No, in our court
  no one needs to lie! The facts arent in dispute, we have to
  decide the meaning of the facts! A revolutionary court's
  the only one that can give justice, the rest just tuck the rich
  up in bed. All our witnesses do is tell us how they live! Let
  them have the teacher's place!
VILLAGER 2. We're all judges.

AGUSTINA. We all have the right to speak but we need judges to run our court.

IGNACIO. A bag of stones picked up from our streets. Black or white. The first three to pick white are judges.

The VILLAGERS *pick stones. Those who pick white stones hold them up in the air. All those who pick stones put them in their pockets. Quietly three judges are chosen.*

IGNACIO. These are the three.

JUDGE 1 (*a woman*). We didnt ask for the job but if you want us we'll do it.

VILLAGER 1 (*points at* JUDGE 1). Irene is stubborn.

JUDGE 2. She stands up for the right.

VILLAGER 4 (*points to* JUDGE 3). Miguel loses his temper.

JUDGE 1. Only when there's an injustice.

VILLAGERS. They'll do.

The JUDGES *take their place.* IGNACIO *beckons* PACO *and* CATALINA *forward.*

JUDGE 1. Catalina, Paco: answer the questions and dont be afraid.

CATALINA. Why am I here?

JUDGE 1. This is a trial.

CATALINA. I havent done anything wrong.

JUDGE 3. You're a witness.

CATALINA. What will they do to the church? They're piling the pews in the street and throwing the statues and hymn books on top.

JUDGE 1. Let's begin.

SENTRY 1 *fetches the* PRIEST *from the hut.*

IGNACIO. Neighbours no court can be more just than the society in which it sits. Are there rich and poor, owners and workers? Then in that society there will be two of everything: schools, hospitals, houses and law – one for the rich and one for the poor. So if you want to know the

court, look at the society. Today let's have a wise decision
– and then we'll begin to respect ourselves after the years
when we lived like their animals. (*To the* PRIEST.) These
are your judges. D'you object to them? (*No response.*) I
prosecute. Name someone to defend you.

PRIEST. Pablo, Luise, Im ashamed that you older members
of the parish allow this to happen! The Marquis and the
civil guard have run away – so you pick on me because Im
the only one left.

JUDGE 1. You mustn't interrupt.

JUDGE 3. Please name someone. We want to be fair.

IGNACIO. You're charged with murder.

PRIEST. Ridiculous! Who have I murdered?

IGNACIO. Manuel Barrios.

PRIEST. Its disgraceful to use the poor man's death in this
way.

IGNACIO. Paco, go to the teacher's desk. (PACO *cant be seen
behind the desk.*) Stand on the chair. (PACO *stands on the
chair.*) Tell us about the time in the orchard.

PACO. I was going to my aunty's. I have dinner at her house.
Mr Barrios was in the orchard.

IGNACIO. What did he do?

PACO. His stream was dry. He was walking up and down it as
if he was looking for something.

CATALINA. There never was such a time.

IGNACIO. Did he speak?

PACO. No.

IGNACIO. What happened later?

PACO. After dinner I came home. It was very hot. At first I
thought the saddle was hanging on the tree. Mr Barrios
was in his black suit and straight and the white ground
hurt my eyes. Then I saw the rope round his neck. He was
hanging from a branch and the saddle was on his
shoulders. He'd put his cap on the ground. I ran to the
bottom of the orchard and called him but he didnt answer.
I went home. The civil guard put him in a cell in the police

station. I dont use the orchard now when I go to my aunty's.

JUDGE 1 (*to the* PRIEST). D'you want to ask the boy anything? (*No response.*) Paco you can go.

PACO. Good.

PACO *runs out right.*

IGNACIO. Catalina go to the teacher's desk.

CATALINA. I dont know what you want.

SENTRY 3 (*takes* CATALINA *to the teacher's desk*). Sit down.

CATALINA (*cries briefly*). Its about Manuel. What can I tell you? (*She sits.*) Our land was hard to work. We were tired even when we got up. But we made a living. Then when we were old it was all taken away from us. As if a wind came one night and blew everything away. In the morning we were beggars. You youngsters do what you have to do. Im too old to understand. (*She gets up and walks away from the teacher's desk.*) Its too complicated to explain – yet its so simple I can see I cant do anything about it. Take me home.

IGNACIO. We're here to give you justice.

CATALINA. Too late.

JUDGE 1. D'you want others to suffer like Manuel?

CATALINA. No no god forbid.

IGNACIO. Then help us. You had a stream.

CATALINA (*nods, staying where she is*). It ran through the orchard. We dug gullies down to our field and blocked them off with stones. In the evening we lifted the stones and the water flowed down to us. It was a great joy. Better than ten sons. Sons work but –

IGNACIO. Tell us about the mortage.

CATALINA. – they eat. With a stream you only have to pray for rain. When the work was too much for us Don Roberto gave us a loan. The steward came every week for the interest. Then every day. Manuel gave up making excuses. The steward said 'It'll have to be the water'. That

Saturday they built the wall that stopped the stream running through the orchard. Concrete. The steward said we could fetch water but we're too old to fetch it. Now Don Roberto's tomatoes are full of our water. Our seedlings shrivelled up. Lay on the ground like dead insects. There never was such a time. (*She cries briefly.*) Why am I here?

IGNACIO. What did Manuel do?

CATALINA. He shrivelled up like our crop. His body frightened me. He was like a little monkey. Then he shaved and put on his good suit and hanged himself. There wasnt enough weight on him to do it quickly so he put the ass's saddle on his neck. What does god say to such things, father?

IGNACIO. You can go now Catalina.

CATALINA. And what good did it do Don Roberto? (*She laughs.*) He's run off like our water! Everything's upside down. Soon they'll have a square sun. (*She goes to a chair and dozes.*)

PRIEST. Agustina speak for me. They'll listen to you.

AGUSTINA. Me? Ask a churchgoer. Get someone who understands you.

PRIEST. They want to kill me. You know I didnt harm Manuel. I loved him.

JUDGE 2. If he wants your help you should give it Agustina.

AGUSTINA. Well – I'll do what I can. (*To the* JUDGES.) For a start he didnt take Manuel's water so why does he have to defend himself?

IGNACIO. A crime was committed. He was paid to look after the village's morals. What did he do about it?

PRIEST. What could I do?

AGUSTINA. You knew Serosan wanted the stream?

PRIEST. The whole parish knew. He wanted to farm on the hill so he needed water. He could have let his steward burn Manuel's house or set up an accident to break his ass's legs – I've seen such things since I came here – but Manuel was

old and it would have caused comment. So he gave him a
mortgage, knowing he couldnt pay it back. That way he
got the water legally and the village didnt complain.

AGUSTINA. What did you do?

PRIEST. When my housekeeper told me the steward was
worrying Manuel every day I went to the Marquis as his
spiritual adviser and told him he was endangering his soul.
It could have been a nasty interview. I spoke without
hope.

AGUSTINA. Didnt he listen?

PRIEST. He always listened to a priest. But he said the
economy was depressed. Capital wasnt investing because
they didnt like the liberal government. Strikes in the
cities. Terrorism. The law had to be enforced. He had
other mortgages and the people who owed them would
take any leniency he showed Manuel as an excuse for not
paying. As I told you, I spoke without hope. The Marquis
acts on what he was taught are the principles of a christian
gentleman. The law must be enforced with rigour because
it must be feared: the church is the fountain of mercy –
and so he endows it with money. He said the mortgage had
given Manuel a year on his farm and now the church
should put him in one of the almshouses he paid for.

AGUSTINA. What did you do?

PRIEST. You will laugh. I prayed for the village.

AGUSTINA. Did you go to anyone else?

PRIEST. There was no one else.

AGUSTINA (to the VILLAGERS). Yet the whole village knew
what was happening. (To the JUDGES.) Why didnt you do
something? Suppose the village had decided to stop
Serosan stealing the water. You could have burned his
crops. Poisoned the stream. The government wouldnt
have sent troops. If you have to go to that extreme to
uphold the law you do more harm than if you neglect it.
They'd have stopped Serosan stealing the water. Or you
could have clubbed together and paid Manuel's debts.

VILLAGERS. No no!

AGUSTINA. No because some of you would have said what about my mortgage?

VILLAGER 1. We're worse off than Manuel! We've got children to feed.

VILLAGER 4. We need new tools. A new roof.

AGUSTINA. And then you'd have sat hunched over your fists which are worn down like spent flints yet still empty – and finally realised how much you had to do! But you did nothing. A priest's power depends on persuasion but your power is your strength when you act. Suppose he'd spoken from the pulpit? The bishop would have shut him up. He couldnt have done anything, he takes on obedience with the cassock. But you could have spoken on the streets in the clothes you're wearing now – and you can make far more noise on the street than you can in the pulpit! But you did nothing. You're worse than the priest, you're as bad as the Marquis.

JUDGE 1. Well Ignacio, what's your answer to that?

IGNACIO. Manuel was illiterate and so he couldnt leave a suicide note. I'll try to speak for him. The theft of this water was as blatant as if one of you had coshed him on the street and taken his wallet. You'd have been charged with murder. Yet the Marquis was allowed to profit from his crime! Agustina if we'd burned the crops Manuel would still be alive but we'd be in prison. Our land would be neglected and Serosan could buy it up dirt cheap. Who gives him his money? The papers – in which he owns shares – say he works for it. As hard as two men? Three? Ten? No one could work that hard without dying of exhaustion – and anyone who says he could has never done a day's work! Yet Serosan has the money of a thousand men! You get that by theft. There is no other way. Men like him steal all they have. How? The law keeps them rich and us poor. We work to make them rich enough to employ us! When we obey their law we commit a crime:

we allow their thieving to go on, and with it all the waste and ignorance that make this world sordid – and hanged Manuel. To maintain so much injustice almost every truth has to be corrupted. Those who do it get paid, but worse – they do it in good faith. Priests, officers, teachers, men who call themselves philosophers and scientists, editors, judges, public oracles – they look at this terrible world and say men are beasts and without us their state would be even worse. And we – we are the people who allow this to happen! Why? Because we have founded our lives, our acts, our characters on believing their falsehoods. We have become their cattle. Forgive me, I have waited years for this day. (*Slight pause.*) Then neighbours, is our situation hopeless? The dyer's hands are stained by his dye. If one day there is no more dye the water is clear. But his hands are still foul. How will he make himself clean? By washing his hands in the water that dyed them! How else? We change ourselves by struggling to change our society. That's how we become human. There is no other way. I accuse the priest – not because he said we'd get justice in another world but because he makes the injustice of this world possible! He doesnt fire the gun. He's the silencer on the gun.

VILLAGER 2. My mother couldn't get treatment! Serosan went to a sanatorium to get rid of his fat!

VILLAGER 3. We protested when he raised our rent! After that our son couldn't get work!

NANDO. They keep a blacklist!

VILLAGER 4. My husband joined a strike in the city. They put him in prison. It took a civil war to get him out!

JUDGE 2. Wait – wait –

JUDGE 3. If you all tell your story we'll never finish.

VILLAGER 4. We've heard enough.

VILLAGER 3. Shoot him!

JUDGE 1. Agustina.

AGUSTINA. There are a lot worse priests. He sees both sides.

He's at home with rich and poor. But what sort of man can go from a house where a family is crowded together, eats badly, has no privacy and no time to think but has to live as if the world ended at their doorstep – to a house where everyone eats well, has their own room and enough clothes for ten families, and there are gardens to rest in, and time to read and think and learn how to fool or force the people in the poor house to provide all this for you? He might be wandering from one continent to another, one century to another, but all this takes place in one parish. He even wanders between worlds! When he's bewildered he runs to god like a child running to mother with a grazed knee. He's learned nothing from the twentieth century, yet tells us how we should live in it! He believes bread turns into meat, the dead come to life, virgins can fly. He also believes little children are born guilty of the sins they havent yet had time to commit. That if long ago an old man hadn't murdered his son we'd all spend eternity burning in hell – and some of us will. What sort of man is he? He's mad. No sane man could believe such things. Well the insane arent responsible for their crimes. Let him go. Good riddance. Soon he wont have any power over us.

VILLAGER 2. There wouldn't be this talk if we were Serosan's prisoners!

VILLAGER 4. That's how they get their power!

VILLAGER 2. They always use violence when they cant get what they want without it!

VILLAGER 3. What's the verdict?

VILLAGER 1. Sentence!

VILLAGER 5. Stand him against the wall!

The VILLAGERS *are silent.*

JUDGE 2. We cant shuffle our feet.

JUDGE 3. He's as guilty as hell.

JUDGE 1.
    We sat in court and searched for justice
    It was as if we polished a silver plate that had lain in the
        soil for years
    Where it had been buried when our village had been
        pillaged and put to the sword
    Now we see ourselves in the silver
    And we say he is guilty and sentence him to be shot
JUDGE 3.
    But we do not ask the people to knock down the wall that
        makes Manuel's small field as dry as a dead lizard
    The water still sparkles in the light as it hurries over the
        stones
    And it has covered the barren hillside with maize and red
        and green peppers and brazen corn
    Let the river stay and the new fields go to the villagers
JUDGE 2.
    The tree on which Manuel hanged still bears fruit
    Let us pick it and give it away in the market
    His tomb shall not be a place of shame
    But a monument to this just decision

PRIEST (*to* AGUSTINA). Ask them to let me pray.
JUDGE 1. He can pray.

The three SENTRIES *put the* PRIEST *in the hut and fasten the door. They stand guard.* CATALINA *sleeps.* PACO *runs in from the right.*

PACO. They're burning the church. They took the paraffin from the stores and threw it up the walls. They let me throw a candle on the fire!
JUDGE 2. Dont set fire to yourself!

PACO *runs out right and the other villagers follow him.* GLORIA VERGARA *comes on from the left.*

GLORIA VERGARA (*with pan*). Look. Copper. Weighs a ton. Half the village are at Serosan's house.

SENTRY 1. We said no looting.

SENTRY 2. The Marquis looted it from us.

SENTRY 3. There should be a proper share-out.

PRIEST (*in the hut*). My sons dont murder your priest. The secret fraternities will take revenge. Follow you night and day. They swear an oath that –

SENTRY 2 (*kicks the hut*). Pray!

GLORIA VERGARA. They're stripping it bare. Walls. Floors. Ceilings. Piling everything on the carts from the stables.

SENTRY 2 *goes out left.*

SENTRY 1. What about the farm machinery?

SENTRY 3. Those who suffered most should get first pick.

MARGARITA ARRANCE *comes in from the left.*

MARGARITA ARRANCE (*with cushions*). Look. Embroidered gentry hunting in a forest. I'll get home from work and put that under my bum.

GLORIA VERGARA. Copper.

MARGARITA ARRANCE. We'll all have pans how. I'll never get another chance to have something like this. Girls went blind making those stiches.

SENTRY 3. Our women'll be up there. They'll get our share.

SENTRY 1. He had farm tools from America. Tools like that save labour – you live longer! We sit here two hours and that's costing us our life!

SENTRY 1 *and* 3 *go out left.*

PRIEST (*in the hut*). Boys, unfasten the door. I must stop them burning the church!

GLORIA VERGARA (*to* MARGARITA ARRANCE, *finger to lip*). Sh. (*She wakes* CATALINA.) Talk to father. (*She points to the hut.*)

GLORIA VERGARA *and* MARGARITA ARRANCE *go out right.*

PRIEST (*in the hut*). Who's there?

CATALINA. They're all gone, father. What are you doing in the hut?

PRIEST (*in the hut*). Catalina god's sent you to save the village. They'll all suffer if they harm me. Open the door.

CATALINA. They seemed sorry for Manuel, I didn't mean to harm you father. If they –

PRIEST (*in the hut*). God has forgiven you. Now thank him by opening the door.

CATALINA. They ought to take me home.

PRIEST (*in the hut*). How is the door locked?

CATALINA. A spike's wedged against the hasp.

PRIEST (*in the hut*.) Catalina you're old. You'll need a priest when you die. Take the spike out.

CATALINA. Gloria Vergara's stolen one of Don Roberto's saucepans. She'll cop it when he gets back.

PRIEST (*in the hut, crying*). O god, Catalina please. Please.

CATALINA. In the morning you go round the traps. The creatures inside stare at you through the bars. You take them out and knock them on the head or lower the cage in the stream. (*She tries the spike.*) Wedged.

PRIEST (*in the hut*). Use your strength woman! (*He rattles the door.*) Quickly! Quickly!

CATALINA. I cant open it if you kick the door. (*The door stops shaking. She struggles with the spike.*) The barber's radio says the roads arent safe. You run away. I dont want to make them angry for nothing.

CATALINA *opens the door and the* PRIEST *comes out.*

PRIEST. God will bless you. Say your prayers.

The PRIEST *starts to go, comes back, shuts the door, puts the spike in the staple and goes out.* CATALINA *wanders back to her chair.*

CATALINA. I shant hang. I said to Manuel 'You're too proud. What's the use of that? Beg!' I dont care what they think of me. (*She dozes off.*)

SENTRIES 1 *and* 2 *come on from the left.*

SENTRY 1 (*with a gaming table, bangs the lid*). A gaming table full of dice. His chauffeur had a set of stainless steel wrenches. I bet kids are playing with them!

SENTRY 2 (*with cutlery*). Silver cutlery with saints' heads. We'll flog this junk in Barcelona. Get a good price in the docks.

VILLAGERS *come on right.*

SENTRY 2. Comrades he's had time to pray.

IGNACIO. Do we go through with it?

NANDO (*to* SENTRIES 1 *and* 2). Someone else can take your place.

SENTRY 1. We'll do it.

SENTRY 2 (*goes into the hut and comes out*). He's gone.

Others look in the hut.

AGUSTINA. Who opened the door? When?

SENTRY 2. I went to the big house to stop the –

SENTRY 1. Shut up!

NANDO. You left him alone?

SENTRY 2. No the other two were there. Otherwise I wouldnt have –

SENTRY 1. We went to rescue the farm machinery. The village needs –

NANDO. Where's Marco?

IGNACIO. Looting!

SENTRY 1. No, guarding the house! We went to –

IGNACIO. Saboteurs!

VILLAGERS. Saboteurs!

NANDO. Take their guns!

SENTRY 1. No!

IGNACIO. They cant be trusted with guns!

VILLAGERS *disarm* SENTRIES 1 *and* 2.

SENTRY 1. Comrades we shouldnt have left our – but we're not traitors!

SENTRY 2 (*to* SENTRY 1). Why did you leave him on his own?

SENTRY 1. There was a crowd about. We thought it was safe. The door was bolted.

SENTRY 2. Who opened it? The wind didnt do it!

CATALINA. I did. I was sorry for him. I told you to take me home. You know I lost my wits when Manuel hanged. (*Holds out her hand like a beggar.*) Help an old woman.

IGNACIO. Put them on trial!

NANDO. What's the use of trials if prisoners get away?

NANDO, IGNACIO *and* VILLAGERS. In the hut!

IGNACIO. Comrades!

VILLAGERS. In the hut!

SENTRIES 1 and 2 are put in the hut. The door is shut.

SENTRY 1 (*in the hut, banging on its door and sides*). The good life's beginning.

SENTRY 2 (*in the hut, banging on its door and sides*). Let us share it!

Pause. It is quiet in the hut; the men inside are listening. Outside the men silently load their rifles.

SENTRY 2 (*in the hut*). We'll catch the priest, comrades . . .

SENTRY 1 (*in the hut*). . . . He cant be far . . .

Silently the VILLAGERS *aim at the hut.*

NANDO. Fire! (*Volley. Shouts from in the hut.*) Learn how to live! (*Volley. Shouts from in the hut.*) Learn how to live! (*Volley.*) Learn how to live!

VILLAGER 3. Fire lower!

IGNACIO. No they'll cling to the roof.

Two stray shots.

NANDO. Wait. (*He strikes the side of the hut. Silence. He kicks open the door and goes in. He comes out carrying* SENTRY 2.) Take him to the Murciano's house. She's saved people before.

VILLAGERS 2 *and* 4 *start to carry* SENTRY 2 *out.* (*Cf. Goya's 'Wounded Workman'.*)

VILLAGER 2. Gently.

VILLAGER 4 (*to* TINA). Hold this in the wound.

VILLAGER 4 *gives* TINA *a cloth and she walks beside* SENTRY 2 *plugging his wound as* VILLAGERS 2 *and* 4 *carry him out right.*

NANDO. Tomaso's dead. Shoot me if you want.

IGNACIO (*looking off left*). Marco. Shall I shoot him with the grin on his face?

MARCO (SENTRY 3) *comes in left. He is grinning.*

MARCO. Comrades, have you been in the big house? Enormous! Our hospital – or factory! There's a swimming pool with huge glass walls to close in the winter! (*Shows guitar.*) Look mother-of-pearl in the handle and a silk strap. I never thought I'd play a guitar. I shall take lessons! (*He plays chords.*)

NANDO. Look in the hut.

MARCO (*looks in the hut*). Was there an attack?

NANDO. You left your post.

MARCO. There were people about – we thought it was all right to –

NANDO. It's useless to say that! You just went!

MARCO. I see: the good times have come! The comrades shoot each other. (*Lifts rifle.*) Not me!

NANDO. Put it down.

MARCO. You shot my mate!

NANDO. The anger's gone, it was used up. Bury him. (MARCO *goes into the hut.*) The Marquis left in his fast car. Then a private plane. He banked abroad, he'll live well. And the priest slid behind him like his shadow. There are priest holes everywhere. We'll try to find him. We're pushing down a prison wall with our bare shoulders. When it falls we have to straighten up quickly or we'll fall with it. This is the first day of the war. I hope its the worst.

MARCO *has come from the hut carrying* SENTRY 1. *No one helps him. He goes out right, with the other* VILLAGERS *clustered round him.* CATALINA *is last. She holds out her hand to beg from the dead man as he is carried past her.*

TINA.

For three years the people's militia slowly retreated before Hitler Mussolini and Franco

In December nineteen thirty-eight Barcelona fell

Soon Madrid would fall

And on the first of April nineteen thirty-nine the Republic would fall

Three: The Surrender

A city factory workshop.

Large, bare, light. Noises of machines and goods being moved in metal trolleys.

A GRANDMOTHER *sleeps in a deck-chair. Beside her is a bag with a few personal things.*

ANTONIA *comes in left.*

ANTONIA. Mother come to the canteen.

GRANDMOTHER. Not hungry.

AGUSTINA *and* TINA *come in right.*

ANTONIA. You don't know when you'll get your next meal.

GRANDMOTHER. 'S too noisy.

ANTONIA *goes out left.*

AGUSTINA. Your father asked me to wait for him here. He says its the only quiet place in the factory: the glass roof would be dangerous in an air raid so its not used. We've been walking through the city this morning. We haven't walked together for so long. Even before the war. You marry and settle down. A child comes. You meet at meals and talk about the day's problems.

TINA. You two have always been like one pair of eyes.

AGUSTINA (*laughs*). Have we? This morning we stood and held hands on the bridge. I let my hair down. I'd forgotten how it suits me. There were gulls squabbling and starlings strutting up the quay. I haven't seen the world like that since I was a girl. Everyone looks happy. The enemy's coming but they're not here yet. No one works to make someone else rich. No one's confused by the lies they used to call the news. People even dress more casually. No ties, only a few buttons. Before they went about the streets as if they were visiting the sick. Now they walk as if they owned the earth – no, the sky. Freedom makes you happy. We said it would. Not many people will have it. But everyone who was in this city will always think of those who werent as strangers.

ANTONIA *comes in left with a tray on which there are three bowls and three spoons and three slices of bread.*

GRANDMOTHER (*to* AGUSTINA). Where're you from my dear?

AGUSTINA. Estarobon. You wont know it, its only a little

village. This is my daughter. We're both visiting our husbands. We havent seen them for a year!

ANTONIA. Rice with peas in it. Rico's coming to eat with us.

GRANDMOTHER. Antonia married my grandson.

ANTONIA (*to* AGUSTINA). There's food in the canteen if you hurry. (*She puts a bowl and spoon in* GRANDMOTHER's *hands.*) Take your spoon.

TINA. D'you work here?

ANTONIA. I started in D shed when I left school. Now Im in H. I met my husband in the explosives block.

GRANDMOTHER. I'm seventy-one. When I was born only birds and insects flew. And a few saints they say. Now men fly about dropping bombs on us. I cant find any peas. The rain makes the glass roof green. Where the stain runs out of the metal, see? This is like a conservatory. When I was a maid the doctor and his wife had breakfast in the conservatory.

ANTONIA. At night you can see the moon through the glass. Its like looking into a river. When we were both on night shifts I used to come here for five minutes with my husband.

TINA. Why is the factory so crowded?

GRANDMOTHER. They're people from the working class area. If we dont surrender their houses'll be shelled.

ANTONIA. They cant get out of the city. The roads are blocked by convoys. Franco wont bomb the factory – its as safe as a bank. Private property. Besides he needs the shells.

AGUSTINA. I've never seen such a busy place. The machines are working and they're stacking shells in the loading bays. But one shed's been turned into a nursery: children playing in circles, babies at the breast, toddlers with rattles. There's a laundry in the basement. They hang the sheets and nappies between the sheds and wheel the shells out underneath them. Some of the corridors have been curtained into sections to give the families somewhere private. Upstairs there's a ward full of patients. Some of them have been wheeled onto the roof for fresh air. There's even a dentist with a barber's chair. And a library. And part of the stores has been turned into a school. The children have taken the chalk they use to mark up batches of shells and they're writing alphabets on the walls. The factory's like a town.

RICO *comes in. He wears military uniform.*

ANTONIA. Is the meeting over?

RICO. As good as.

ANTONIA (*takes away the slice of bread covering his bowl*). Eat this before its cold.

RICO (*eats*). God Im hungry. We'll surrender. No fighting. Our troops move out tonight. The Fascists move in in the morning.

GRANDMOTHER (*to* RICO). You see if you can find my peas.

TINA (*to* RICO). What will you do?

ANTONIA (RICO's *mouth is full*). He'll go with the army.

RICO. In a year or two the whole of Europe will be at war. We can hold out until then. When the allies fight the Nazis they'll have to fight our Fascists.

TINA (*to* ANTONIA). What about you?

ANTONIA. I'll go on working here. They always need trained labour.

GRANDMOTHER (*hands bowl to* RICO, *he empties it into his bowl*). They're good children. They wont leave me.

NANDO *comes in. He wears military uniform.*

RICO (*to* NANDO). I told you it was all over.

AGUSTINA. D'you want to eat?

NANDO. They'll surrender the city. It would cost too many lives to defend. Play for time till the big war. Good. But they wont blow up the factory. It makes shells! No wonder we're not winning! They say they cant get the people out. Turn them out with bayonets! If the city surrenders they'll be safe in their homes. Thy dont *want* to blow it up! They'd lose their jobs! (*He gestures to* RICO.) He'll let his wife go on working here! One of her shells could kill him!

ANTONIA. I've worked in armaments for eight years. I know all the arguments. We need work: we have to live. That's my argument.

RICO. She has to earn so that she can eat and take care of my grandmother. What else can we do? If my number's on it I'll cop it – which'd make some other poor bastard happy. Look, if she didn't make the shell someone else would. So if Im going to be killed at least let her get the benefit of the money. I hope its not a dud so I go quick.

NANDO. If we lose the war that doesnt mean –

RICO. Im going to see if there's any more grub.

RICO *goes out left.*

GRANDMOTHER. Why is the man angry? Does he want to turn us into the street?

ANTONIA. Its all right, Granny. Everything's decided. They'll let the workers stay here. When the Fascists come they'll surround the factory and let us out through a checkpoint. No one will be on their list – if they were they'll have left with the army. The well-off will stand on the pavements and jeer but we'll walk home between them and pretend not to notice.

GRANDMOTHER. Im going to sit with the old people. They cant turn us all out. (*She starts to go left.*)

RICO *comes in left. The factory begins to go quiet as the machines are switched off.*

RICO. There're crowds camping on the streets. The gates are shut. No more are allowed in. The sanitary orderlies say it wouldnt be hygienic – and the food would run out. Go and look! Its like an army. The factory's under siege. Even if they cant get in they feel safe if they can touch the walls.

NANDO. If we lose the war that doesnt mean we've lost

everything. Not if fighting the war made us stronger – freer – more determined. Then even if we lost this one we wouldnt be defeated! But if you help them now we've got nothing from fighting! We've had our chances and we're worse off than before! We had no right to ask our comrades to die!

RICO. How could you move that crowd from outside!

NANDO. This is not just betraying our revolution, its betraying all revolutions! We're chucking freedom back in people's faces!

RICO *holds out his hand to* NANDO. *The* GRANDMOTHER *comes back.*

RICO. Comrade, there's been enough quarrelling.

GRANDMOTHER (*to* RICO). Why're you shaking hands? You're going to let him turn us out! They'll shoot us on the streets!

ANTONIA. No one will turn you out – I told you. Go and sit with your friends. We'll come and see you.

GRANDMOTHER *goes out left.* RICO *still holds out his hand.*

NANDO (*turns away*). There's comrades' blood on it.

RICO (*to* ANTONIA). The troops must leave soon or we wont get out. Let's find somewhere quiet to say goodbye.

From the right a BLIND MAN *pushes in a* CRIPPLED MAN *in a three-wheel bath chair. The* CRIPPLED MAN *guides the wheel chair with a rudder attached to the front wheel. On his lap there is a violin in a case and a flute.*

CRIPPLED MAN. We came in through the little door we used in the old days. The directors' cook was good to us. (*To the* BLIND MAN.) Stop. She gave us her scraps in the evening.

BLIND MAN. We wont be a nuisance.

RICO. You cant stay. The sanitary orderlies –

CRIPPLED MAN. You wont notice two more. Im the Crippled Man who leads and he's the Blind Man who pushes. We're famous. The poets praise us!

RICO. There's a danger of an epidemic.

BLIND MAN. But we had our picture in an American newspaper!

From the right a WOMAN *comes in carrying a full shopping bag and leading a* SMALL GIRL.

WOMAN WITH SMALL GIRL. Im looking after the little girl. Someone tried to snatch my bag and frightened her!

CRIPPLED MAN (*to the* BLIND MAN). Idiot you said you'd bolted it!

RICO (*going right*). I'll bolt it.

RICO *goes out right.*

WOMAN WITH SMALL GIRL. The little girl isnt mine. She lost her people in the war.

CRIPPLED MAN. All this space!

ANTONIA. You can't use it – the roof makes it dangerous!

BLIND MAN. I'll jam the brakes.

CRIPPLED MAN. If I dont lead he cant push! (*To the* WOMAN WITH THE SMALL GIRL.) Mix in with the others. They cant catch you!

BLIND MAN. We'll earn our food and keep your spirits up!

CRIPPLED MAN. Straight ahead!

The WOMAN *and the* SMALL GIRL *go off left. The* BLIND MAN *pushes the* CRIPPLED MAN *off after them. The* CRIPPLED MAN *plays a snatch of a popular tune.*

NANDO. They've switched off the power. The families will sit by their machines till their enemies come and switch them on and then go back to work. They might as well be making their own chains.

TINA. Slaves have to make their own chains. If they saw the owner doing it they'd know what he was and get rid of him. You shouldnt have got angry. If the shells dont kill him they'll kill his friends even if they're fired at his enemies! The owners get workers to fight for them, kill each other for them, orphan each other's children. In the end all weapons are used against the working class. And it wouldnt make any difference if this factory was making sewing machines. They'd be working for their enemies. That means – you said – that all tools turn into weapons they use against themselves. The slave makes his chains. In our society everything is a weapon – so you have only one way of making a living: beating ploughshares into swords. That's why we need a revolution. Then the weapons could become tools again, and we could build instead of destroy. Isnt that what you taught me? I'll come to you in the morning.

NANDO. Walk with us some of the way. I havent seen you for so long.

TINA. My husband's waiting for me. Goodbye.

TINA *kisses them and goes out left.*

AGUSTINA. Can you stay the night?

NANDO. Yes. I'll go early in the morning before its light.

AGUSTINA. I shant go straight back to the village. I'll try to get work here. I can organise the factory girls. We must eat. If I cant find something to cook in this city I couldnt bump into a dark wall at night with my eyes shut.

NANDO. I'll take you back to my place. Its over a cinema. Guess what? Its got a dome. And a wide window ledge – you sit out there with all the statues on the roofs round you and look down at the streets.

AGUSTINA.
The poor dont ask the shopkeeper to give his food away
The prisoners dont ask the governor to set them free

Students dont ask to be taught understanding in an hour
No one tries to pick the fruit while the blossom's on the
   tree

Howling in the desert will not bring one drop of rain
And weeping over dead men will not make them live again
Yet you cry aloud for peace as you hand the knife to Cain
And peace to the war dogs who are pulling at the chain

Nation will fight nation till there is justice between nations
And that will not be till there is justice within nations!

Till then the workers will make guns and quietly eat their
   bread
And will not see the marks of Cain and Abel on their head
The warlords will praise peace by the war graves of their
   dead
And madmen will be rulers in the land of the insane
And the world will call for peace and the call will be in vain

Four: The Gunnery Lesson

Factory yard.

75 mm gun and a sentry in Fascist fatigue uniform.

AGUSTINA *comes in from left.*

AGUSTINA. You'll be glad when the war's over, soldier.
JUAN (*bored*). Hop it.
AGUSTINA. I work here. This is my lunch break. Before you
   liberated us we couldnt stroll in the sun after lunch. Had
   to work for the officers. Wash shirts, clean boots. When
   you moved in it was like watching Lazarus come back to
   life.

JUAN (*bored*). Funny no one you speak to was on the reds'
side.

AGUSTINA. That uniform suits you.

JUAN (*bored*). D'you want to be run in?

AGUSTINA. Its the truth. You take care of yourself. Dont
waste it on the first skirt that comes along.

JUAN. Chance would be a fine thing.

AGUSTINA. There's more rooms in a house than a bedroom.
You want a woman who can cook and look after you.

JUAN. Scram you old cow.

AGUSTINA. Im not doing any harm. You're from the south.

JUAN. How d'you know where I'm from?

AGUSTINA. All the real Spaniards come from the south. Its a
long time since I talked to a man who wasnt complaining
about the mud on his boots. Your people are farmers.

JUAN. Wrong – not our own land. The estate hires us. For
the harvest. Then no work till next year.

AGUSTINA. Will you leave the army after the war?

JUAN. Men and flies. No machinery. Took six weeks. I'll
stay in the city when Im demobbed.

AGUSTINA. There'll be a lot looking for work.

JUAN. I'll be all right. I've got a training.

AGUSTINA. What as?

JUAN. Motor mechanic. Surprise you?

AGUSTINA. No I knew you were clever.

JUAN. Guess where I learned?

AGUSTINA. Some university. Madrid.

JUAN. Self-taught.

AGUSTINA. Motor mechanic? You cant be!

JUAN. Watched the proper mechanics. Looked in an engine
every time I got a chance. Fix my officer's when it breaks
down. Its all right for him: he doesnt pay. I dont mind: its
the best way to learn. He says I was born with a spanner in
my hand.

AGUSTINA. I bet your mother's proud of you.

JUAN (*shrugs*). My brothers'll never get off the land, I'll be able to send her good money from the city. She's had a hard life. When she's washing up her hands are all crinkles. I used to think you're too old to be my mother.

AGUSTINA. You can pay her a visit when you've settled down.

JUAN. We'll see. It's a long way.

AGUSTINA. I know you lads like a bit of fun – you've earned it – but if you ever feel like a quiet evening with a good meal, you're welcome at my place. My husband was killed in an air raid. We had no children. The house gets a bit lonely. I mustn't bother you.

JUAN. The war hurt a lot of people. Thanks for the invitation. We're not allowed out on our own.

AGUSTINA. Bring a mate.

JUAN. We'll see. Well you'd better move on.

AGUSTINA. Yes, thanks for talking to me.

JUAN. That's all right.

AGUSTINA. One day you'll have your own garage.

JUAN. I dont know about that – costs money.

AGUSTINA. Im not often wrong. Anything's possible with a lad like you.

JUAN. I might take up flying.

AGUSTINA. There you are – you're clever! That's why you knew which side to fight on.

JUAN. To tell you the truth they just lined us up on the square and marched us off to be kitted out. You have to hand it to them, they've got it organised. When the reds get an order they vote on it. Our officer said when you reach their lines they'll have one hand up voting on whether you're coming. Soldiers shouldnt have opinions, they're just a liability in war. If our officers changed the enemy they wouldnt bother to tell us thank god – I've got enough to think about. Today its the reds, tomorrow it could be the blues. Its got nothing to do with me who we're fighting. Kill or be killed, that's all it is. Discipline not bloody opinions.

AGUSTINA. I can see you've got it all worked out. What would you do if there was an attack?

JUAN. Now? Blow the whistle and cock this.(*Rifle.*)

AGUSTINA. Wouldnt you fire that? (*Cannon.*)

JUAN. No shells. Only issued in an emergency.

AGUSTINA (*looks at the cannon*). Yes you'd have to be specially trained to fire that. Not easy like a rifle.

JUAN. I can fire it.

AGUSTINA. Dont be ashamed, you cant know everything.

JUAN. Im not ashamed!

AGUSTINA. I couldnt fire it and I'm not ashamed.

JUAN. Well you're a woman. Look you'd better get back to your girlfriends. You'll get a reputation talking to soldiers.

AGUSTINA. I can stay a bit longer, Im not due back yet. (*She looks at the cannon.*) All those knobs. I'd forget which end the shell went in.

The Gunnery Lesson

JUAN. You know the difference between your back door and the front door dont you? Well the shell goes in the front door – and you close it after you. (*He opens and shuts the breech screw.*) That's what the LBM's for: loading breech mechanism. Shut LBM – then turn till grooves on screw lock with grooves on ring.

AGUSTINA. The front door! You'd make a good teacher. If you stayed on after the war they'll make you an officer.

JUAN. Its just a question of finding the right language.

AGUSTINA. What's that?

JUAN. Elevation gear. To aim with. You dont aim at the target, you aim beyond it.

AGUSTINA. Beyond it?

JUAN. Because of the parabola.

AGUSTINA. What's a parabola?

JUAN. Well you have to know a bit of theory. Suppose you

hang your washing on the line. You dont start in the middle and work outwards do you. The rope'd sag. Then your sheets drag on the ground and you have to wash them again. So you start at the ends and work to the middle. That's taking a parabola into account. Only with shells its the other way up.

AGUSTINA. Imagine I've been doing that all these years and didnt know!

JUAN. Now you see that? That's the sights. Mostly you cant see the target. So you aim at something you can see – you call that your gun aiming point – and someone who can see your gun aiming point and the target tells you the difference between the two. You feed the difference into the sight (*Demonstrating*.) but turning it the opposite way from the target. The barrel doesnt move. Then what d'you do?

AGUSTINA. . . . Turn the sight back to the aiming point but this time move that barrel-thing with it.

JUAN. Brilliant! And then the barrel's laid – that means aimed – on the target.

AGUSTINA. Suppose I want to hit those gates. I'd aim at the window.

JUAN. No they're close. You can aim straight at them.

AGUSTINA. That would be easier.

JUAN. You'd use the telescope. You know about your elevation gear. But you could still go wide. So you use your traversing gear. Suppose you want to hit the tower on the Police HQ. (*He points at the telescope*.) Look through that. Go on, it wont hurt you. (AGUSTINA *looks through the telescope*.) See the laying mark in the centre of the glass? Ignore all that grid for the time being. Now align it so that the laying mark is on the base of the tower – then you'll pull it down on top of itself and not just blow the lid off. Use your gears. Go on. (AGUSTINA *operates the gears. He takes her place at the telescope*.) Bit more left. (AGUSTINA *looks through the telescope*.) Turn the traverse gear (AGUS-

TINA *turns the traverse gear.*) – there you go. (*He takes her place at the telescope.*) You're on target.

AGUSTINA. This morning all I could do was thread a needle. Now I can fire a gun!

JUAN. Wrong. Load and aim it. Not fire it.

AGUSTINA. I knew it'd be too hard for me.

JUAN (*indicating*). That's the firing lock. You put the firing tube in the breech screw. Inside the lock there's a striker. When you pull the firing lever the striker strikes the tube – the tube fires gunpowder at the shell – and you're off. As easy as striking a match. See the angel on the church?

AGUSTINA. You mustnt, its sacrilege.

JUAN. Its not loaded. (*He looks through the telescope and turns the gears.*) Target laid. Open breech screw. Insert shell. Close LBM. Turn LBM. Insert firing tube. Close lock. Release firing lever. Bang. Angel sees it coming and flaps off.

AGUSTINA (*laughs*). I bet you're a laugh in barracks.

JUAN. You try.

AGUSTINA. Shall I?

JUAN. It wont bite you. (*He spins the elevating and traversing gears at random.*) You're on your own now. If I keep telling you what to do you'll never learn. Just say to yourself its no harder than remembering what order you put in the ingredients when you're cooking. Now we'll see if that meal's worth coming round for.

AGUSTINA (*operating the cannon*). Target laid. Open that thing. Put the shell in. Close it. Bugger's stiff. Put in the firing tube. Close lock. Release lever. Bang.

JUAN. No.

AGUSTINA. What did I do wrong?

JUAN. You didn't turn the LBM.

AGUSTINA. I told you I was stupid. (*Operating the cannon.*) Open screw. Shell in. Close LBM. Remember to turn it. Put in the firing tube. Close lock. Release lever. (*Quiet contentment.*) It clicked . . . I heard it click . . . it fired.

Open screw. Shell in. Close LBM. A good turn. Insert
firing tube. Close lock. Release firing lever. Click . . . it
fired again. Open screw. Shell in. Close LBM. Remember
to –

JUAN. We wont do it any more. You can damage the lock
without a round. You could go on to study ballistics,
artillery strategy – there's a lifetime of study in it.

AGUSTINA. You could teach anyone anything.

JUAN. You dont have to fawn on people. Its not nice for a
grown woman. Respect yourself like a real Spaniard. Your
husband was from the south wasn't he?

AGUSTINA. Yes.

JUAN. If I can get out one evening. I'll come round for a
meal. I need a change from canteen food. My corporal
might even come.

AGUSTINA. I'll write my address and give it to you next time
I see you. If you need any socks darning just give them to
me. I enjoyed my lunch break today. (*Going.*) If your
officer caught you chatting at me you'd be for it.

JUAN. *You* were chatting at *me*. According to Regulations
I'm entitled to run you in just for saying good morning.
(*Calls after her.*) And what about the recoil? You didn't
stand off when you fired. You'd be broken in half by now.

AGUSTINA *goes off left*.

ANTONIA. From time to time Agustina spoke to the lonely
soldier. Not every day, to arouse his suspicion. Sometimes
she only nodded. At others she gave him his darned socks
neatly folded round a bar of chocolate. She didnt speak
again about the cannon. Many distinguished visitors came
to the factory to gaze at the workers or demand more
shells. Agustina said: They shall not sleep in their beds,
they shall hurry through the streets like criminals fleeing
from their crime, their possessions shall not give them the
joy of use but the fear of loss. And she waited.

Five: The Shot

Factory yard.

75mm gun and sentry in Fascist parade uniform.

AGUSTINA *comes on with a bucket of water with a yard broom in it and a bucket of polishers and rags with a yard broom laid across the top.* TINA *follows her.*

JUAN. Agustina hop it. You cant come here today.

AGUSTINA. Its all right the foreman sent me. (*To* TINA.) The top brass is unveiling a plaque inside. The factory's role of honour in the struggle for fascism. (*To* JUAN.) The bishop loves soap next to Jesus. I washed this floor till its clean enough for him to celebrate mass on. Now I've got to do it again.

JUAN. Who's the girl?

AGUSTINA. My lodger.

JUAN. Well get on with it and no chatter.

AGUSTINA *and* TINA *go to one side and clean.*

AGUSTINA (*quietly to* TINA). Antonia will go by when they're leaving.

TINA. Sh, dont speak.

AGUSTINA. He expects women to chatter. If we dont he'll get suspicious. (*To* JUAN.) You polish your buttons as well as I clean this floor and they'll make you a general. (*Quietly to* TINA.) Leave him to me till I rattle the pail. Then you start. (*To* TINA *loudly*.) That's Juan.

JUAN (*to* TINA). Hello lovely.

AGUSTINA (*to* TINA, *loudly*). Watch him he's got hot blood.

TINA *goes on working.*

JUAN (*to* TINA). Where've you been all my life? (*No answer.*)

AGUSTINA. She's not shy when she talks to me. You should

have heard her just now. (*To* TINA.) You're as bad as the
girls on the bench. All they talk about is soldiers. (*To*
JUAN.) I thought I was normal but they make me blush.

JUAN. Agustina dont go on. You're embarrassing.

AGUSTINA. Lovely isnt he? I have a job to keep my hands off
him.

JUAN. Agustina. (*Aside to* AGUSTINA.) I can do my own
chatting-up.

AGUSTINA (*to* TINA). That's what I call a real Spaniard. And
he knows it.

JUAN. Not in front of her.

AGUSTINA (*gestures at him with her broom*). Shoosh! She's
only blushing because she fancies you. Dont you Camilla?

JUAN. She hasnt said so.

AGUSTINA. You havent said you fancy her but you do. Look
at him drooling over your breasts. In the evenings she
strips and stands on the towel and washes herself in my
kitchen. You should see the water running off her breasts.
I stop and have a look. I had a pair like that when I was her
age. All the men trying to touch them. (*She smacks his
rear.*) The army's bulging on the centre front.

JUAN. D'you sleep with Agustina?

AGUSTINA. O she's got her own room. Everything private.

JUAN. Why dont I come round for that meal Agustina? My
corporal's a pal. He'll let me out if I slip him something.

AGUSTINA. There you are! I've been inviting him for weeks.
Always tomorrow. Now he's drooling, and not for my
paella. Will your corporal let you out all night?

ANTONIA *walks from left to right.*

JUAN (*to* AGUSTINA). Get a move on and less lip. (*He points.*)
Look at that dirt.

AGUSTINA. Where?

JUAN. There. I want that spotless.

ANTONIA *goes out.*

JUAN. What about Wednesday?

AGUSTINA. Too late. You've just liberated her village and she's off to nurse her grandfather. Good thing too. Now she's seen you she'd soon be in trouble. You wont get anything off her. So enjoy looking.

JUAN. Does she have to go?

AGUSTINA. He wont sleep for thinking about your tits. You should see the water running off them. Since the young men have been away the poor girls dont stand a chance: breathe down their necks and they're yours. You'd have added her to your list Juan. They're all different inside, they say. You'll never find out what she's like. She might have been the best. (*She laughs.*) It doesn't bear thinking about. (*She sweeps.*) At my age you take it or leave it. But look at you two: standing there shivering and looking at each other like two herds of cattle. (*She goes to one side, rattling her pail.*)

JUAN. Where's your village?

TINA. Near Vigo.

JUAN. Christ. Cant you put it off for a few days?

TINA. I've got a lift on a lorry. Everyone wants to get home. I darent let the chance go . . . Agustina's always talking about you. That's why I came.

JUAN. If it wasnt so open.

TINA. I know.

JUAN. Put it off one day.

TINA. Its the lorry.

JUAN. I'll get you a lift on an army truck.

TINA. I couldnt risk it. The lorry driver's from our village, he'll look after me.

JUAN. Christ woman dont stand like that.

TINA. Couldnt you – (*She stops.*)

JUAN. Yes! What?

TINA (*points*). Behind there.

JUAN. Im on sentry duty.

TINA. Agustina will keep watch.

JUAN. All right. But wait till they go.

AGUSTINA. Dont be long Camilla. If they catch you here there'll be hell to pay.

TINA. The girls say some of the sentries . . . in the sentry box.

JUAN. I've done that lots of times. Its – there's a general inside.

TINA. You could say you went to look at something suspicious.

JUAN. I have to blow my whistle first.

TINA (*turning to go*). Pity.

JUAN. Wait.

TINA. I shouldnt have come. I cant go home like this.

JUAN. Look – if we're quick, behind the wall. I'd be fantastic with you. (*He changes his mind.*) No – its mad. I'll tell you what: I've got some leave money due. I'll pay your train fare. Take a week's leave and we'll spend it in bed.

TINA. Its poor grandfather you see.

JUAN. Oo you little darling. All right then – the wall. Look – I'll stand on the corner – you go behind the wall – and do me with your hand.

TINA. There's no satisfaction in that for me Juan.

JUAN. Goddam you bitch! Sod you. But be quick.

AGUSTINA *gestures to indicate that she will keep watch: looks over her shoulder at them and jerks her right fist forward with the thumb raised.* JUAN *and* TINA *go behind the wall.* AGUSTINA *waits.* JUAN *comes back.*

JUAN. Christ this is lunacy! I've gone mad!

TINA *comes round the corner with her blouse undone.*

JUAN. Jesus woman there's a bishop inside! Do your blouse up! He'll crucify me! (*Pause. He goes to her.*) Sod you. Sod you. You cow.

TINA *and* JUAN *go behind the wall.* AGUSTINA *picks up her buckets and brooms and goes to the cannon. As she talks she aims the cannon, takes a shell from under the rags in the bucket and loads it.*

AGUSTINA. A woman with a bucket and mop is invisible. Today I ply the ancient trades of whoring and cleaning. The soldier follows his ancient callings of fornication and war. Inside his general unveils a plaque to the fallen. A paper-thin tombstone on a wall. My daughter will be shy. The soldier will be anxious. She'll say Agustina's keeping watch. And soon he'll forget time. In their passion men are like victims running in burning clothes from a fire: they cant see where they're going for the flames they bring with them.

From the left come the GENERAL, *the* BISHOP, *his* CHAPLAIN, *the* FACTORY MANAGER *and his* ASSISTANT. AGUSTINA *cleans the cannon.*

GENERAL. They didn't cheer.

CHAPLAIN. My Lord Bishop has a sobering presence.

GENERAL. Cheering's good for morale.

ASSISTANT. We told them not to take time off to cheer.

MANAGER. We're on target to double production by the end of the first period.

BISHOP. Our workers are still bewildered. We must be patient and strive for their understanding. Words count for little. When they are fed and clothed and cherished they will cheer us.

CHAPLAIN. Thank you for those words of wisdom father.

GENERAL. You can cheer and work.

They go out right. AGUSTINA *is alone. She adjusts the aim on the gun.*

AGUSTINA. What will the soldier do? Run back pulling up his trousers, turn and run up and down between the sheds cursing and roaring like a wounded animal, like a fish threshing on top of the basket trying to find the hook to show why he was tempted. Soldiers will surround him as he stands there shouting and pointing with his trousers round his ankles. He'll be court-martialled and shot. His owners take their time: the managers bow, the general salutes, the chaplain rubs his hands and the bishop gives his blessing. In a moment some of them will be killed or lose a leg or an arm. Or they may all be killed. By a shell that didnt leave the factory in which it was made.

AGUSTINA *fires the gun: there are two detonations, the firing of the gun and the explosion of the shell.* AGUSTINA *goes out left.* JUAN *runs on. His trousers are round his ankles and he is trying to pull them up. He waves his rifle and blows his whistle. He stops for a moment and stands in the smoke and roars like a wounded animal. Then he turns and runs off.*

PART TWO

Six: The Trap

The Ruiz's house.

A trap door in the floor is open with the stone cover beside it.

AGUSTINA.
    The Marquis and I have returned to Estarobon
    The people took back the loot: not to the house
    Instead they left it along the road
    Strange sight! As if the countryside were the Marquis'
        house
    In a field a circle of *quinze* chairs: empty when the sun rose
        and when it set
    Tapestries and curtains hung on rocks: no hand or breeze
        parted them
    Pots and pans on a tree: as unused as in a painted kitchen
    A woman returning from work drank from her cupped
        hands not the crystal glass by the stream
    Children sang but the lid of the portable organ with the
        marquetry cherubs was as shut as a lid in the grave
    The owner drove back to his house and sent out his gangs
    They returned with his loot: he checked each item against
        his lists
    He charged the community for what was missing

    NANDO *comes out of the trap.*

NANDO. I can hide here for a few weeks – I'd be safe for
    years.

    As NANDO *and* AGUSTINA *talk he goes in and out of the trap
    taking down pillows, blankets, food, utensils.* AGUSTINA
    keeps watch at the window.*

AGUSTINA. They've searched some houses ten times. They wont find you. The stone's too thick to sound hollow. I can only buy food for one: the police have told the shopkeepers to report anything suspicious. Dont worry, I'll feed us. And no reading: the smell of a candle would give us away.

NANDO. What'll you do when I go?

AGUSTINA. Carry on as before. The cellar can be used again. You'll need to organise an escape route to the mountains. If any –. The priest on the path.

NANDO *goes down the trap and replaces the cover, using the iron handle on the underside.* AGUSTINA *fetches a broom, sweeps dust round the edge of the cover and treads it in. She puts the broom away and works in the kitchen. The* PRIEST *comes in.*

PRIEST. Good day. (AGUSTINA *nods.*) Have you heard from your husband?

AGUSTINA. No.

PRIEST. I expect he managed to cross the frontier. Is your daughter coming to live with you?

AGUSTINA. She's better off at her in-laws. They can feed the child when it comes. This place is so run-down it hardly feeds me.

PRIEST. You know the army's investigating everyone in the parish. You were one of the group considered today. Your husband and your son-in-law were rebel officers and your views are well known. I had an excuse to speak on your behalf because you defended me at my trial. However there was little I could say. This house and the land were confiscated. You're free to live anywhere else in Spain. Go to your daughter.

AGUSTINA. They cant support me.

PRIEST. Let me finish. They've dealt with you less harshly than they have with many others. No doubt there'll be complaints. It's better for your own sake if you go.

AGUSTINA. Where to? God knows I'm out of their way up here.

PRIEST. That was the decision.

AGUSTINA. I cant go.

PRIEST. Agustina you accept nothing unless its what you want. In a month you'd have the village seething. Organise meetings –

AGUSTINA. I've finished with all that.

PRIEST. Even if that were true you'd be blamed for everything that went wrong. It's better for the community that you go.

AGUSTINA. That's christian charity!

PRIEST. I saved your life. The truth is there's already been a complaint from the mother of the man who was shot in the hut.

AGUSTINA. I didn't shoot him!

PRIEST. When blood is spilt it calls for reckoning in its own kind. I cant protect you. You have to leave now.

AGUSTINA. Now?

PRIEST. Your house has been given to Jose Albana. He's bringing his things up in a cart.

AGUSTINA. I cant leave now.

PRIEST. Realise how fortunate you've been. I asked to be allowed to tell you so that you could leave quietly. There could be a squad of soldiers here!

AGUSTINA. Its tyranny – to turn me out like this! I need time to arrange things. Just a few days.

PRIEST. What is there to arrange? Everything was confiscated.

AGUSTINA. My personal things. Photographs, letters –

PRIEST. Private Albana will put your personal things in a box and the army will mind it till you send for it.

AGUSTINA. I wont go! I have to let my –. Cant I walk round my own field once! Of course I'll go. Thank you for speaking for me. Let me stay one night. One night. On my own.

PRIEST. Nowadays everything's done quickly. Perhaps that's god's kindness: it may be better if we dont have time to think what's happening to us.

JOSE ALBANA and his wife MARIA wheel on a small handcart holding a few possessions: utensils, a holy picture, bedding, clothes and so on. MARIA starts to unload.

JOSE. Agustina. We're really appreciative. You're not leaving the place to vandals. Maria will keep it as spotless as if you were liable to pop in at any moment to inspect us. It ran down during the war . . . With a young couple to get it going . . . I had a look round the other day when you were at the village. We'll have our work cut out.

MARIA (*hands JOSE a box of cutlery*). Put that in the table drawer.

PRIEST (*taking a case from the bottom of the wardrobe*). Agustina's clothes can go in this.

MARIA takes clothes from the wardrobe and drawer and packs the suitcase. JOSE goes on unloading the cart and bringing things into the house.

AGUSTINA. Maria let me have the house for one night. I came here when I was married. My daughter was born here. Five minutes' notice. Its cruel. Come back in the morning. I'll cook breakfast for the three of us. Then you'll come in as friends. Not like this.

MARIA. Agustina let's get it over for everyone's sake. We all have to start from the beginning again.

AGUSTINA. You can wait one night.

JOSE (*coming in with his gun*). No its an order.

MARIA shuts the case and gives it to the PRIEST.

PRIEST. O Jesus who dwelt in the abode of the simple carpenter, bless this house and all who dwell here. O Jesus who had nowhere to lay his head, take the homeless into thy care. Amen. (*To AGUSTINA.*) You can take your coat.

AGUSTINA *takes her coat and holds it in her hand as she goes out with the* PRIEST. *He carries her case,* JOSE *and* MARIA *finish unloading their things and wheel the cart to the side of the house.*

MARIA. If she does something silly it'll bring us bad luck. What if she –

JOSE. Dont start! Im not quarrelling on our first night! For god's sake if you dont like it go somewhere else! (*Pause as they work. Consolingly.*) We'll talk about it tomorrow. She wont do anything silly. That one's tough.

MARIA. Be careful with the blankets.

JOSE. Its our house now. We were ordered to take it. There arent many hands as clean as ours. You've got a good kitchen. You always said the other one was too small. I hope now there'll be some decent grub. I'm sorry I shouted.

MARIA. Its so cut off.

JOSE. Who wants to live under their neighbours' noses?

MARIA. If only it was nearer the village. I wouldnt –

JOSE. Things'll be quiet now the army's in charge. I dont want to hear another word.

MARIA *prepares a small shrine: portable reredos and idol. She lights a candle at the shrine and kneels before it.* JOSE *sits on the edge of the bed and takes off his boots.*

JOSE. They had all the speeches. They'd do this, they'd do that. The big shareout. Boots would polish themselves. Now what? He's dead and she's on the street. I should have written their speeches: 'Brothers things have got to change. But not in our lifetime. Admit it and enjoy what there is. A bed, roof, food in the cupboard, a winter coat. Who wants the freedom to be shot?'

When the shrine is complete he perfunctorily crosses himself in front of it.

AGUSTINA.

The Curse (*Song*)

You set each man against his brother
You hire the father to fight the sons
You drive the daughters from the mother
The workers live by making your guns
You teach the child to walk in darkness
Your city is the gate of hell
You price men by their heap of money
Or by the blood they have to sell
    The earth groaned when you sat on your thrones
    And it will still groan when you are dead
    Because it must find you a place for your bones
    May the stone lie heavy on your head!

JOSE *and* MARIA *are in bed in the darkened house — only the candle is lit.* NANDO *comes from the trap and goes towards the door.* JOSE *gets out of bed and reaches for his gun.* NANDO *sees him and takes the gun.*

NANDO. Dont move.

JOSE. Is there a tunnel?

NANDO (*half to himself*). Why didnt he sleep?

JOSE. Nando. I wont say you were here. Your friends would kill me.

NANDO (*as before*). Why? Why? I couldnt wait any longer.

JOSE. Nando. You went to school with my father. You're like my uncle. Talk to me.

NANDO (*as before*). Why didnt he sleep?

JOSE. I tried to. It was the excitement. I was planning our future. I owe the house to you Nando. Now I'll owe everything.

NANDO (*as before*). Why, why is it always the same? (*To* JOSE.) Is Maria asleep?

JOSE. Yes – she wont be any trouble. She does what I tell her.

NANDO. I'll take you behind the rocks. The noise will wake her but she wont see me. She wont have to suffer.

JOSE. Nando for god's sake!

NANDO. Quiet! I cant trust you, you're a civil guard.

JOSE. I needed the job.

NANDO. I went through everything while I waited. Backwards and forwards for hours. Give me one reason to trust you.

JOSE. Im a worker like you. I wont say a word, I'll be so grateful. Nando you said when I was little: 'an honest boy'. Uncle Nando please. O why didnt I pretend to sleep?

NANDO. Give me one reason.

JOSE. Let's think quietly. Now – take me on the path. Tie me up. Gag me. I'll say I heard a prowler. Went out. Didnt see who it was.

NANDO. That's not the point! I need a reason to trust you! Hurry. I must be in the hills before its light.

JOSE. O yes! Shoot me! Like the men in the hut!

NANDO. Jose, I dont want to kill you! Give me a reason! Help me!

JOSE. Of course, of course! What a fool! Why didnt I see it? No one knows you were here – so you *werent* here! There is no problem!

NANDO. There is! I cant trust you!

JOSE *throws a chair at* NANDO *and runs for the door.* NANDO *shoots him. He falls.* MARIA *sits up in bed.*

MARIA. Jose!

NANDO. Turn to the wall.

MARIA (*gets out of bed; she is naked*). What is it? (*She goes to* JOSE.) O! He's not – he's breathing!

NANDO. Don't look at me.

MARIA. Help me Nando!

NANDO (*lowers gun*). He's dead.

MARIA (*cries quietly*). O god.

NANDO. Maria I'll trust you, you dont need to betray me.

MARIA (*after crying quietly for a moment*). I'll betray you! You shot him! Animal!

NANDO (*quietly*). Look at this gun that killed your husband. Now listen. He said he wouldn't say I'd been here. But tomorrow? To please his CO? Promotion? A bigger house? He worked for the Fascists, how could he be trusted? They dont even know Im alive. If he talked they could have followed me to my friends. Shot my wife for hiding me. It was her or him. You understand?

MARIA. What?

NANDO. Listen. A man came in from the yard. He didnt speak. Scarf on his face. Shot Jose and left. Give me your word.

MARIA. I promise. (*She takes the idol from the shrine and holds it to herself for protection.*) I promise Nando.

NANDO. Good. Get into bed. (*She gets into bed, still carrying the idol.*) Cover your head with the blanket. Pretend to sleep. Wait till its light. You were too afraid to go for help before.

NANDO *replaces the stone cover, fetches the broom, sweeps dust round the opening and treads in it.*

MARIA (*under the blanket*). What are you doing?

NANDO. Pretend to sleep.

MARIA (*under the blanket*). I told him not to come to this house.

NANDO *puts the broom back in its place. He hesitates.*

MARIA (*under the blanket*). I wont tell them it was you.

NANDO *goes to* MARIA *and shoots her through the head under the blanket. He leaves the house and goes out left.*

NANDO.
The priest put my wife on a train

A soldier waited on the platform till the train left
She looked out of the window at the darkness
There were no lights in the countryside
She might have been looking into the eyes of a skull
Rain slanted over the window
The skull was weeping

At Zaragoza she sat on the platform
And waited to be told I was dead
In the afternoon soldiers came and she was arrested
The station master had telephoned the barracks
She said she knew nothing
After six months they let her go

Seven: The Vendors

Mountain road.

From the left, marching in loose order, come CAPTAIN MANI, *a squad of* SOLDIERS *and two* PRISONERS. MANI *wears a pistol, the* SOLDIERS *carry rifles and the two* PRISONERS *carry a machine-gun, its tripod and an ammunition case.*

MANI *is short, thin and dark with a thin black moustache. He wears a képi with a small crucifix in place of the crown stud.*

MANI. The mountains of Spain. The sun rises out of the mist like the host being lifted up in a glass hand.
CORPORAL. Men fall out for a smoke Captain?
MANI (*shout*). Smoke!
CORPORAL. Fall out!

The SOLDIERS *fall out and smoke. The* PRISONERS *stand by the machine-gun. A* SOLDIER *smokes and guards them.*

MANI. Die here! – in all this space you cant think of death:
not in a wet cellar or on a municipal wall where everything
tells you you're dying.

From the right comes a PORTLY MAN, *his* WIFE *and* SON
and two English businessmen.

PORTLY MAN. Captain is this the right road?

MANI. Its over. We're on our way down to the truck.

PORTLY MAN. Over?

SON. I said it was shooting.

PORTLY MAN (*to* HARRISON-LEIGH *and* FAWCETT). Its
over! What a nuisance! We got up so early!

FAWCETT. The walk did us good. What a view! Worth
getting up for that. Really.

WIFE. And I hurried you out with no breakfast.

FAWCETT. We werent in the least bit hungry.

MANI. Come tomorrow.

PORTLY MAN. Our English visitors go home tomorrow. (*He
sits and fans himself with his hat.*) Now the war's over we're
working to regain the confidence of our foreign friends.
Low wages, people weary of politics and queueing up for
work: we have all these advantages to offer. But they wont
invest in us if they think there'll be another round of
confiscations. I wanted to show them how the new Spain is
ridding itself of its enemies once and for all.

HARRISON-LEIGH. Have no fears, we've seen enough to
have every confidence.

PORTLY MAN (*to* MANI). I should have arranged it with your
colonel. These gentlemen are the proprietors of the
Windsor Accumulator-Battery Company. We intend to
manufacture their modern Accumulator-Battery under
concessionary licence. The government likes wirelesses.
They keep them in touch with the people. As the economy
leaps ahead every home in Spain will have its set. (*He fans
his face.*) Its hot so early.

From the left a VENDOR *wheels on his stall. It has a tarpaulin top and paraffin burners. He stops and busily rattles cutlery and glasses as he pretends to clean his counter.*

PORTLY MAN. I was hoping to sign a contract this afternoon. I thought that seeing this – they're not used to war – would give them a jolt. Might get better terms. D'you know my factory? Vacancies at all levels. If you have any relatives . . .

VENDOR. Beefburgers.

SOLDIER 1. Dont get settled, we're going back.

SOLDIER 2. At least he could let us finish a fag.

SOLDIER 1. Christ hasnt crucified enough poor buggers this morning.

MANI. I've got two more prisoners.

PORTLY MAN. No no I couldnt bother you like that.

MANI. They're condemned.

PORTLY MAN. No no not at all not at all.

WIFE (*to* HARRISON-LEIGH). I do hope the concession goes through. My husband tells me our son will study in your factory. It would be so good for his English.

VENDOR. Wine.

PORTLY MAN. Is it those two?

MANI. They should have been shot last week. I let them carry the ammunition. Its not good to keep them too long. They learn the routine and work out how to escape.

PORTLY MAN. If you're sure. It sounds almost like doing them a kindness.

MANI. On your feet!

Subdued murmurs of protest from the SOLDIERS.

SOLDIER 2. Sun's up, Captain. It'll be like an oven before long.

MANI. Corporal! We're taking the English visitors to see the bodies.

SOLDIER 2. They dont need a guide. Even the English couldnt miss them.

PRISONER 1. You don't need the gun Captain.

MANI (*to* CORPORAL, *indicating the* PRISONERS). And them.

CORPORAL (*to the* PRISONERS). And you!

FAWCETT. Dont go to this trouble for us. (*Aside to* HARRISON-LEIGH.) O lor', old Ramiro's fixed something up with the little captain. Just a moment –

The PRISONERS *try to run away.* SOLDIERS *stop them.*

SOLDIER 2. All right Sonny!

PRISONER 2. No!

SOLDIER 3. Bastard!

MANI. Your comrades didnt run. The dogs stood and cursed us. (*He points left.*) That's your road! We only borrow our lives! The time comes to hand them back!

PRISONER 1. Captain I want to see a priest!

PRISONER 2. The priest!

MANI. Infidel lies! You think you know how to dangle me on a little string. If you havent prayed this week you dont know how to pray!

PRISONER 2 (*to* HARRISON-LEIGH *and* FAWCETT). Englishmen – sirs – its cruel to treat us like this!

PRISONER 1. We're not animals.

CORPORAL (*detailing* SOLDIERS). You: gun. You and you: ammo. (*He gives the tripod to another* SOLDIER.) Carry that.

FAWCETT (*to the* PORTLY MAN). Look we dont want to distress anyone. Thank the little captain but tell him we –

HARRISON-LEIGH. Bambury please.

MANI. Corporal get a grip on your men.

CORPORAL. At the double – run!

PRISONER 2 (*to* HARRISON-LEIGH *and* FAWCETT). Give that to my wife. Please. (*He throws an envelope on the ground.*)

HARRISON-LEIGH (*to* FAWCETT). Dont make things awkward for our host. This is just the sort of sensitive area the Foreign Office man spoke about. (*He picks up the envelope and hands it to* MANI.) We observe the same strict neutrality as our government.

SOLDIERS *double out with the* PRISONERS. MANI *follows them.*

VENDOR. Beefburgers. Wine.

PORTLY MAN (*to* HARRISON-LEIGH *and* FAWCETT). They're murderers. The officer explained to me they'd have been shot anyway when they got back to barracks. (*To his* SON.) Aurelio order some iron rations to fortify us on the way. (*To* HARRISON-LEIGH *and* FAWCETT.) Imagine that spectacle every morning, knowing its going to happen to you. Doesnt bear thinking about. And the ammunition weighs a ton. (*He calls to his* SON.) Wine too. (*To* HARRISON-LEIGH *and* FAWCETT.) This early just once: then you can tell your wives you misbehaved in Spain.

SON (*at the stall*). Mother, anything?

WIFE. Certainly Aurelio, our guests cant eat on their own.

SON (*to* VENDOR). Five.

WIFE (*to* HARRISON-LEIGH *and* FAWCETT). In the war we took refuge in our convent. The nuns told them no one was hiding there. The shutters werent opened for three years. The cellars were crowded with poor wretches. At any moment the mob might have broken in.

PORTLY MAN. Dont distress yourself darling.

WIFE. We must never forget it. It was the Buddhists' Nirvana. We ceased to exist, we were shadows. When my daughter went out after the incarceration she'd forgotten there were streets between houses. Can you imagine? It was on her doorstep but she might have come from another world. We should ask why such things are possible.

PORTLY MAN *and* WIFE *go to watch the food being prepared.*

FAWCETT. Will we give him the concession?

HARRISON-LEIGH. No. Its cheaper to make them in Lagos in spite of the cost of freight. And safer.

FAWCETT. Shouldnt we tell him?

HARRISON-LEIGH. No the rest of the day would be embarrassing for all of us. We'll put it off till we leave. Dont worry, Tubby has other irons in the fire. He'll make a fortune out of trinkets for tourists.

SON (*to the* VENDOR). Good meat. Not scraps. The police watch standards now.

VENDOR. Its a pleasure to serve a discriminating young sir. I enjoy it more than eating myself. A double for the Englishmen, yes? Those rumours about food shortages. Let's show them!

PORTLY MAN. Two bottles of red.

SON. Wipe the glasses.

The VENDOR *uncorks two bottles of wine and puts the corks back loosely in the necks of the bottles.* AGUSTINA *comes on right. She uses a walking stick and has a pear-shaped knapsack on her back. The* VENDOR *glances at her.*

HARRISON-LEIGH (*to* FAWCETT). Spain is a land of Tauromaquia and guerrillas. Those two didnt expect anything better. Its the way they do things here.

VENDOR (*to* PORTLY MAN). There's brandy for the Englishmen when you come back. (*He points.*) Excellent Valadamos.

PORTLY MAN (*calls to* HARRISON-LEIGH *and* FAWCETT). They should be ready for us.

PORTLY MAN leads the way out left with a tray holding glasses and two bottles. The SON *follows with a tray of food.*

WIFE (*to* HARRISON-LEIGH *and* FAWCETT). Arthur, Bambury, each take an arm. The last few steps are steep.

HARRISON-LEIGH *and* FAWCETT *each take one of the* WIFE'*s arms and go out left.*

AGUSTINA. I come round the side of a mountain and there's a street vendor!

VENDOR (*without looking at her*). I know about gypsies who ask for dog scraps and eat it themselves. Shove off from my counter. The English are fussy. Came in my shop before the war, if they found a spot of dust you'd think they'd won Waterloo again.

AGUSTINA. Your grub smells good. I'll have one. (*Money.*)

VENDOR. O sorry. (*He prepares a beefburger.*) You meet the cream of the riffraff up here. Beggars. Children thinner than half a matchstick. Cut your throat to lick the knife. First your heart breaks, then you feel the bits sticking in you, then you dont feel anything any more. (*He uncorks a bottle.*) Wine?

AGUSTINA. If its on the house.

VENDOR (*corks bottle*). There's water in the stream. Take it from further up. Its contaminated down here. I call this pitch my branch shop. I was lucky to get it. They wanted their cut: not just the captain, the colonel. Its worth it, thank god: I've got to pay off the bank loan. The crowd come up here to put the lid on the war. They want to celebrate with a drink. Before the war I had a bakery. My cakes were famous: pistachios and chocolate. The nobs sent taxis from the other side of town for them. Then the reds took it over. Asked me to stay on as manager. Same wage as the oven boy. I said fine, now I can keep an eye on it. Then they closed me down. No pistachios, no chocolate, no flour. (*He gives her the beefburger.*) Bon appetit. I took the family south. My boys fought for Franco. One of their officers said work in our mess and you can bake your famous cake. One evening I was serving and he said your sons are dead. Land mine got both of them. I went on handing round the cake – what else? Their mother cried for a week. Women cry better than men. With them its music. So she cried for the two of us and I listened.

Off, a burst of machine-gun fire. It rattles on the rocks.

AGUSTINA. An execution. (*She puts down her beefburger.*)

VENDOR (*astonished*). Woman where have you been for three years?

AGUSTINA. You sell food here?

VENDOR. A baker doesnt ask who eats his bread. At least when they're eating they cant do much harm. Eat. You paid.

AGUSTINA. How many?

VENDOR. Today? Fourteen, not counting those two. At the start it was forty and fifty a time. Real hard cases. Marched. Clenched fist.They could have been parading for their dead comrades. (*He wipes the counter.*) God death can be dramatic! I was worried the crowd might get fed up. Ha! They became afficionados, bet on who'd shout slogans. Dressed up like a holiday crowd. The prisoners die in rags. Leave their good stuff to the others still in prison. Spain must have the best dressed prisoners in the world. Eat. It'll get cold. When the troops aimed the crowd shouted fire. You cant blame them, they'd lost family and friends. Once they shot seven women. When the troops aimed they threw their skirts over their heads. Some insult, cover their eyes – dont know why. Anyway I always remember it: that was the best day's business I've done. Soon they'll do it in the barracks and no one'll know. He'll garotte. He's mad. First shooting he did sent him potty. Off his head ever since. (*He pours wine for her.*) Drink. Eat. (*Off, two pistol shots.* AGUSTINA *doesnt eat or drink.*) You think its wrong to trade here. If I sold to the same people in town would that be different? Do investors – or workers – ask what the company makes? They ask about money. The town goes about its business and down the road or up the hill they're stock-piling bombs: one day they'll blow kids' heads off. The town doesnt come to a halt. All you see here is yourself.

HARRISON-LEIGH *and* FAWCETT *come on from the left.*

FAWCETT. We shouldnt have left so soon. Old Tubby'll gloat.

HARRISON-LEIGH. We did our duty. If we'd stayed any longer it might have looked as if we took an unhealthy interest in that sort of thing. Then they'd all gloat.

VENDOR. Good wine, sirs – no? (*They ignore him.*)

FAWCETT. Wait till I tell the old man. Stared straight in front of them like people waiting on a railway platform. I wouldnt have imagined that at all. Usually onions are – well, arms all over the place. Really Arthur it was just like when I had to put Roger down. Fell over and wriggled a bit and then sort of shrank. Only he wagged his tail, poor bugger. Wouldnt do to have missed it though. A very important thing.

PORTLY MAN, *his* WIFE *and* SON *come on from the left.*

VENDOR. Gentlemen now for our choice Spanish brandy – to improve the view. (*No response.*)

MANI *comes on from left.*

PORTLY MAN. It would have been silly to waste the climb. The *jeunesse dorée* comes up here in their open Bugattis. More money than sense.

WIFE (*to* HARRISON-LEIGH *and* FAWCETT). This afternoon I shall take you shopping for gifts. Next time you must bring your ladies with you to Spain. I insist.

PORTLY MAN. Gentlemen, brandy to drink to the Windsor-Toledo Accumulator-Battery.

HARRISON-LEIGH (*slightly cocking his head to the right and gently raising his right hand to hold it a few inches from the side of his face with the tops of his fingers in line with his eyebrows and the palm facing forward*). Bit early I'm afraid.

SOLDIERS *come on from the left with the machine gun, tripod and ammunition case.*

MANI. Gentlemen. When the prisoners asked for a priest they slandered the regime. Its true that at the start we werent organised and once or twice a priest couldn't see the prisoners in time. But the prison was paraded and the priests absolved all the prisoners together. Perhaps dying in terror makes brutes like these repent when otherwise they wouldnt. We shorten their lives but give them eternity.

AGUSTINA (*eats*). Baker you can cook! This meal will get me over the mountain!

VENDOR *smiles and goes out left.*

HARRISON-LEIGH (*to* MANI. *Handshake*). Well turned-out body of men.

FAWCETT. Very interesting thing. Very important.

MANI (*clicks*). Thank you. I vowed that if I fell into my enemies' hands they'd throw their hats in the air when I told them my name. Soon I'll go into a monastery. A simple place where they grow vegetables in the cloisters and there's one bell. Then I can read and become a monk. I've done my duty for eight years, but that's what I've always wanted. O I dont want to forget: I carry all those we shot in my head all the time so that when I go to heaven and stand in the little crowd that's waiting to be welcomed, my maker – who sees all – will see the dead in my head and smile at me. Long live death!

SOLDIERS. Long live death!

MANI. Christ the king!

SOLDIERS. Christ the king!

VENDOR *comes in from the left with the trays and empty bottles and glasses.*

VENDOR (*to the* PORTLY MAN *as he pockets the tip from the tray*). Many thanks.

MANI (*to* SOLDIER 1). Check her.

MANI, SOLDIERS, PORTLY MAN, *his* WIFE *and* SON,
HARRISON-LEIGH *and* FAWCETT *go out right. The*
VENDOR *follows them, pushing his stall.*

SOLDIER 1. Where d'you think you're going?
AGUSTINA (*eats*). Valencia. I've come from Urgel.
SOLDIER 2 (*takes her knapsack and looks into it*). Why?
SOLDIER 1. Pass.

SOLDIER 2 *takes* AGUSTINA's *pass from the knapsack and
hands it to* SOLDIER 1.

AGUSTINA (*eats*). To join my daughter. My husband disap-
peared in the war. Sat on a mine or ran off with a woman.
SOLDIER 1 (*giving the pass back to* AGUSTINA). Whats wrong
with the trains? They run on time now.
SOLDIER 2 (*giving the knapsack back to* AGUSTINA). But she
cant afford the ticket.
SOLDIER 1. Watch out for the guerrillas on top.
AGUSTINA (*shrugs*). They wont bother me. Wouldn't be
worth their while.

SOLDIERS 1 *and* 2 *go out right.* AGUSTINA *goes out left.*

Chorus

You who smile and live well
Hear what the outcasts can tell
You keep watch from the ramparts on your walls
But you have locked your enemies inside your gates
No one is free in your cities
Fires will ignite on the empty streets
Your cities will burn and you will fall
You who smile and live well
Remember what the outcasts can tell
The ring of your coins as you buy and sell

Tolls like the notes of a funeral knell
And your cities will turn into hell

Eight: A Discussion

Mountain guerrilla post.

NANDO *and* MARCO. *They have rifles.* MARCO *keeps watch.*
NANDO *reads a book.*

MARCO. The allies are fighting Hitler at last – but Franco's
safe. Democracies fight for their interests – not ideas.
They live without ideas at home so why should they fight
for them abroad?

NANDO (*looks up at the sky*). Fokkerschmidt. Reccy.

MARCO. He might see the tracks to the camp.

NANDO. Sheep.

MARCO. Too high for sheep.

AGUSTINA *comes on left. She has a rifle.* NANDO *closes his
book.*

AGUSTINA. He'll circle for hours.

*They hide against the rock. After a while the plane's engine is
heard.*

NANDO. They've rebuilt our village church. Big service to
reopen it. One of the masons worked for us: he put a bomb
inside the wall. Under a stone. Set in thin plaster so you
could lift it out and time the bomb to go off in the service.
Now it'll stay in its little niche till the church falls down.

MARCO. The mason was arrested. Police raided a café in
town and he was at a meeting.

AGUSTINA. Cant someone else set it?

MARCO. Village full of police.

NANDO. Never get near it. Fascists believe only the brutal

are capable of happiness. Once some of them trapped one of our comrades at the bottom of a cliff. He started to climb. They sprawled on the grass and smoked and jeered at him. Threw stones to dislodge the rubble onto his head. When he'd climbed sixty feet their officer shouted up 'Let's have some fun. If you fall we'll be satisfied. If you get to the top – we're down here.' He didn't believe them but he went on climbing. What else could he do? There were tears on his face. Sitting on the top – back where he couldnt see them – was another squad of Fascists. When he reached them they hauled him over the edge, took hold of his hands and feet and swung him in time to a Fascist tune. Then they threw him down to the others. When you hear of these things you realise we're all in danger. So you fight as naturally as you would if you were drowning. But you dont fight on your own. You have the strength of the others who're drowning. It makes each one of us as strong as a crowd. That's why we can fight against these odds.

The plane passes over them: noise and a shadow.

MARCO. After I buried Tomaso when he was shot in the hut I thought now I have to do the fighting of two men. Im not a coward. Thanks for the lesson. But we're throwing our lives away up here. Go back to the cities – live with the Fascists – attack from the inside. Up here I feel like a fly crawling over a tank.

AGUSTINA. You should mend your jacket. It looks shabby.

MARCO (*puts his arm through the rip in the flap of his jacket*). Brings me luck. Bayonet went through that. Im the unkillable soldier – both sides have tried.

AGUSTINA. I could get in the church. If they stopped me I'd say I'd heard the couple had been shot in my house so I thought I could move back – I didnt think anyone else would move in.

NANDO. They'd never believe you.

AGUSTINA. That doesnt matter as long as it sounds plausible. I wont carry a gun or anything suspicious and they wont know about the bomb. We could turn their celebration into a disaster. That's how their victories ought to be celebrated. If the bomb's there the rest is easy!

NANDO. What if they've found the bomb and are waiting for you?

AGUSTINA. That's a risk.

MARCO. She's the only one of us who's got an excuse to be there.

NANDO. How'd you get away? There'd be road blocks and patrols everywhere for the service.

AGUSTINA. I'd hide in our cellar.

NANDO. That's lunacy!

AGUSTINA. No – the house is empty now – if it isnt they'll all be in church. I'd have to hide somewhere quickly. And who'd think of looking there? I could hide for days and then come back through the hills.

MARCO. They might have found the cellar.

AGUSTINA. It would have been all over the papers. I can sleep under my own roof again – under my floor!

NANDO. I didnt go to my daughter's wedding. She's having a baby but I'll probably never see it. We've lost our home. We were apart for years. Now you've been here a few days and you're going away. War takes everything. I shant try to stop you. Be careful.

MARCO. When the gun sentry tried to describe you at his court martial they said you sounded like half the women in Spain. The factory girls are supposed to believe there are no shadows on your face – not even from your nose! And when you left the city it was night but a patch of daylight followed you so that you didnt bump into police: a searchlight shining from the sky.

AGUSTINA. What use is a legend? People hear them and say: they're the big ones, we're ordinary. What do I want? A dry roof over my head and a warm blanket. Isnt that ordinary? And that no one blows up my world – that ought

to be the most ordinary thing of all. People used to make
revolutions to get bread – isnt it ordinary to want to eat?
Now we have to make a revolution to stop them blowing
the world to bits. We cant live with ignorance any more.
We must fight everyone who stops us trying to understand
ourselves. Today we have the power of god and so we must
finally become human beings. To keep the ordinary things
– the dry roof, bed, table – we must make a revolution. If
we dont, everything will be blown to bits. Dont tell me
about legends. The gun was there. My enemies walked in
front of it. I fired. It was the most ordinary thing I've ever
done. I did it for the same reason I lay the table or sweep
the floor. If Im a legend my life is wasted.

They go.

AGUSTINA.
 It is my Spain!
 Mine!
 The fertile coasts and the rocky enduring heart are mine!
 The red earth and apple orchards of Asturias
 The cheese and butter pastures of Santander
 The scallop road to Compostella
 Are all mine!
 Galicia where four sons each own part of one chicken
 The desert below Madrid where the air is like a wolf's
  breath
 The storm city of Toledo and its rapiers as deadly as
  lightning
 The plains of La Mancha empty but for ghosts and the
  grim lakes
 Estramadura raped by Latifundia
 Andalusia where the sun comes to warm itself
 And where olives, the fruit of poets, are grown
 Cordoba the city of horses and silver

Sierra Nevada with its snows and sugar cane
Grenada where two rivers meet and the whole year is
    harvest
The rice fields of Valencia
The lost worlds of the Pyrenees where Hannibal's eleph-
    ants left their bones
Monserrat the mountain of teeth and the holy grail
And where the earth lies like a giant on its back tearing at
    the sky
All these are mine!

In the mountains there are deer and goats and strangely
    swift boars
There are the eagle of Sierra de Cazola and the bone-
    breaker vulture
The storks that teach us fidelity
Scented deserts of thyme and tarragon
Roadsides thick with Prometheus' fennel
Bay and wattle
The rockrose from which came myrrh
The dark sweet myrtle and and mandragora, the plant that
    shrieks
Pines and junipers and Spanish oaks
All mine!

It is a country of fools' churches and cretins' palaces
Where for each throne they built ten thousand cells
But all countries are like this

It is also a country of towns crowning hills
Of white walls as big as the paper giants write on
Of city pavements as graceful as crafted bowls
And everywhere steps and lanterns
There are the factories and mines of the north
The harbours at Cartegena
The Ramblas as wide and beautiful as the sea from which
    it rises

The chatter and laughter from darkened cafés
The frowning children at desks
And the two seas!
All these are mine
Who would not be happy in such a land?

Nine: The Arrest

The Ruiz's house.

AGUSTINA *comes on wearing her knapsack.*

AGUSTINA.
 I have been to the church
 I counted the fissures
 I inserted the blade into the plaster
 I took out the stone
 The wires grinned at me
 I set the hands of the wristwatch to ten
 And put back the stone

 Now I return to the house that stands like a cairn of stones
 In the field from which they were taken
 When the house needed protecting in storms and frost
 More stones were taken and new ones rose to take their
    place
 The field bore stones in all seasons
 It was its richest crop

 New people live in my house
 Curtains – our windows were bare –
 And the door my husband left plain is painted
 A bike leans on the wall
 Signs that the house has prospered
 I've stood here five minutes
 If anyone was inside they'd have come to ask

Why I stand here
A proud housewife
Lace mats on the table
Rugs on the floor
By the sink military boots
The man is a civil guard
I go to the rug that covers the trapdoor to push it aside
And perhaps because there is so much new to see
And so much old to remember
I do not notice at first
Although it is light
That the whole floor is buried in six inches of concrete!

God! Not time to get in the hills! Troops – planes – all day
to find me! O god . . . the bomb explodes in an hour. The
shed! He's a civil guard! They might not even search here!
(AGUSTINA *stands in the open doorway of the shed.*)

I watched the black smoke rush into the sky
Then heard the thud – as if it wished to make sure I knew
    the bomb had exploded
In the distance the voices sounded like children's
Cars hooted then silence
The smoke drifted over the village till it was a thin black
    veil draped in the sky

AGUSTINA *goes into the shed – there is no door.* GUADALUPE
and ROSITA *come on from right.*

ROSITA. They'll look for you.
GUADALUPE. For god's sake give it a rest! We must take
    them up to the hills! Drop them in a ditch! Cover it with
    old branches! They could have been there months. If they
    find them they're nothing to do with us – the whole village
    is as crooked as –
ROSITA. God you're a fool! They'll know it was you!
GUADALUPE. Its all we can do!
ROSITA. What if we're seen with them?

GUADALUPE. We wont be if we're quick!

ROSITA. You should never have taken them!

GUADALUPE *goes into the shed.*

GUADALUPE (*in the shed*). You wouldnt have come here if I hadnt! How could I afford what you expect on my salary?

ROSITA. I knew it'd be my fault!

GUADALUPE (*in the shed*). New curtains! New chairs! There's no end of it!

GUADALUPE *comes out of the shed with three petrol cans. He stands them by the door.*

Get the bike! (*He goes back into the shed.*) They wont miss a few cans of petrol. God knows what they waste driving their tarts round. Hurry. I've got to get back. I'll say I got knocked down in the stampede. Passed out. (*He comes out of the shed with three more petrol cans.*) Where's the bike? For god's sake dont stand there! Tie them on the bike or you'll need six journeys!

ROSITA *goes into the house.*

GUADALUPE *puts the cans next to the others.*

GUADALUPE. You're worth more than mother's milk. All goes well, I'll flog you in a few weeks.

GUADALUPE *goes back into the shed. After a few moments* AGUSTINA *comes out.* GUADALUPE *follows her pointing his gun.* ROSITA *comes from the house with the rope.*

ROSITA. Agustina – what is it?

GUADALUPE. Under the feed box. Tie her legs. You've got the rope. (ROSITA *ties* AGUSTINA's *legs.*) Made a fine mess down there you sow.

AGUSTINA. What d'you mean? What happened? I heard the explosion. Why're you doing this?

GUADALUPE. Leave enough slack so she can walk. Pour it away and lose the cans. (ROSITA *finishes*.) Now walk, pig.

GUADALUPE *follows* AGUSTINA *out right*.

Chorus

You who are clothed and fed
Hear what the hungry have said
The hunger of the body is great
But the hunger of the mind is greater
The belly may be replete
But the sharp tooth of reason is not satisfied
You who sleep in bed with a pillow under your head
And dream the dreams of those who are fed
Remember what the hungry have said
Or you would be better off dead

Ten: The Soldier's Training

A clearing in the mountains.

NANDO *comes on*.

NANDO. In five minutes I shall be dead. I cant kill myself.
Not because of the pain. I cant end my mind.

NANDO *takes a flag from his knapsack and drapes himself in it*. MANI *comes on with his* SOLDIERS.

MANI. Why?
NANDO. Our comrades were buried in it.
MANI. Bravo. (*To a* SOLDIER.) Pio you aim to miss when you're in the firing squad.
PIO (*unsure protest*). Sir.
MANI. I noticed. Dont worry, we're all cowards till we do

something about it. (*Some of the* SOLDIERS *laugh*.) Shut up scum! You're not fit to fight with! Respect the boy! Here's a soldier who's afraid to kill. What use is he to you in a fight? Well scum? (*No response*.)

PIO. Sir –

MANI (*turns to* PIO). Dont speak. It will be like a conversion. Tomorrow you'll shave a different face. (*To the other* SOLDIERS.) Sit. (*The* SOLDIERS *sit cross legged.* MANI *kneels*.) Pio is going to do his first killing. (*To* NANDO.) If you want a priest I'll wait. (*No answer. To* PIO.) That flag is an insult. Lower it. (*To* NANDO.) Right hand – out. (NANDO *holds his right hand a foot away from his side*.) Out! (NANDO *lifts his right hand out at right angles. The flag hangs from his right hand and his shoulders*.) Aim at the right hand.

PIO *aims at* NANDO's *right hand*.

MANI. Breathe easily or you'll snatch at the trigger. Fire!

A long pause. PIO *shoots. Misses.*

MANI. Was that on purpose?
PIO. Sir.
MANI. Aim. (PIO *aims*.) Your rifle wont fire till its cocked.
CORPORAL. What a mess.

PIO *cocks his rifle and aims*.

MANI. Fire!

A long pause. PIO *shoots. Hits. The end of the flag falls from* NANDO's *right hand. The hand bleeds.* NANDO *sways.*

NANDO. There is no god . . . god wouldnt let you breathe.
MANI. Its easy to drape yourself in a flag. Teach our simple Spanish soldier to endure with patience. Left hand. (NANDO *cant move*.) Look at the blue sky: so empty. The quartz shines in the rock. The smell of the dark pine wood below us. Even a running stream – and no fisherman's shadow on the water. God is good: he's given you all this

and five minutes to enjoy it. I could have already shot you like a dog. We could be dropping your corpse over the cliff. Left hand.

NANDO *holds out his left hand, the flag hangs from it and his left shoulder.*

MANI. Fire!

Shorter pause. PIO *fires. Hits. The flag falls to the ground. Both hands bleed.*

MANI (*to* CORPORAL). Dont let him fall on the flag. (*The* CORPORAL *removes the flag.*) He's in a state of shock. He wont feel the wounds he dies of. You'd have thought he'd have felt them more than most wounded people. He doesnt feel any more than a potato does when you peel it. He cant even hear us now. Finish it off. (PIO *promptly cocks his rifle and aims.*) Fire!

PIO *fires immediately. Hits.* NANDO *falls dead.*

MANI (*dangling his pistol in his hand*). Good. That was the lesson: now the soldier fires on target to order.

PIO *marches to* MANI, *takes his pistol, marches to* NANDO *and shoots him in the head.*

MANI. Amen.

MANI *gets to his feet and* PIO *marches to him. The other* SOLDIERS *scramble up quickly.*

PIO (*returning pistol*). Pistol sir.
MANI. Long live death!
SOLDIERS. Long live death!
MANI. Christ the king!
SOLDIERS. Christ the king!
MANI. Throw him to the buzzards. (*To* PIO.) You'll make a good shot. A surprise.
PIO. Yessir.

SOLDIERS *take* NANDO *out right.* MANI *follows them.*
SOLDIER 1 *and* PIO *are left.*

SOLDIER 1 (*offers* PIO *a cigarette*). All right? The boys'll have
a whip round. Tonight we'll get you stinking drunk and
carry you down to the whorehouse. You must have had a
rough time these last weeks. That's all over now. Tomorrow you'll be a new man.

PIO (*irritation, refusing the cigarette*). All right!

SOLDIER 1. Dont mind Jesus. First man he shot, he was
drunk a week. You're better off with him than a lot of
them.

PIO. Its all right – Im okay.

SOLDIER 1 (*lighting his own cigarette*). You're doing fine.

PIO *goes out right and* SOLDIER 1 *follows him.*

Song of Agustina Ruiz known as The Human Cannon

The fire will consume itself
The tempest will exhaust itself
The flood will return to the still deeps of the sea
But I will ride the world with my two talking horses
Till the generations of the earth are free

I do not ride in greed or scorn
I do not fight in rage or hate
Such passions as these are too brief and weak for me
But I will ride the world with my two talking horses
Till the generations of the earth are free

The seed that falls on stony ground
Shall turn the stones to fruitful earth
A garden will grow in the wastes of tyranny
And I will walk beside my two talking horses

As they gently bow their heads and graze the fields of
   liberty

For when the human will is weak
The laws of change shall still be strong
My womb and the earth shall give birth to liberty
And I will ride the world with my two talking horses
And you'll never never never conquer me

Eleven: Human Cannon

A town hall.

*A large white room. On the right a desk, chairs and double doors
to the street, on the left benches and a single door to the basement.
The furniture and doors are dark oak.*

The PRIEST *and the* INVESTIGATOR *stand at a large arched
window right. The* CLERK *sits at the desk and writes on forms.*

The INVESTIGATOR *is middle-aged, tall, big-chested, a bit
flabby – sensual and intellectual.*

The CIVIL GUARDS *wear uniform. The others in the room wear
black.*

INVESTIGATOR. I stopped my car on the road here to relieve
   myself. The middle of nowhere. Rocks and sand and a
   dead tree by an empty river. There were scraps of poster
   nailed to its trunk. Curled up like a dead animal. Unread-
   able. (*He picks up fragments from the desk. Reads.*) . . .
   'When you use' something . . . (*To the* CLERK.) Find
   where it was printed.
PRIEST. They've taken hostages from the village. I suppose
   you know?
INVESTIGATOR. I asked for it to be done.

PRIEST. Ten. (*Half-question.*) It must be necessary . . . ?

INVESTIGATOR. I hope to let them go.

PRIEST. Its an ordeal.

INVESTIGATOR. They were kept overnight in a cell with Agustina Ruiz. Perhaps they've moved her to pity – though she must be made of stone. She denies placing the bomb. It would be better if she confessed. Then we'd be quite sure. Its not pleasant to think of a terrorist wandering round with another bomb. Confess or not she'll be shot. It should have been done before.

PRIEST. Local people respect her in spite of her politics.

INVESTIGATOR. All the more reason.

PRIEST. Why are the hostages women? Its made a bad impression.

INVESTIGATOR. Estarobon is a village of women. Most of the men died in the war. The Marquis cant lose any more labour. He has enough difficulties as it is.

The door, left, opens. CIVIL GUARDS *bring in* AGUSTINA *and ten other* WOMEN. BERTA TORBADO *is supported by one of the others. All the* WOMEN *are in black.*

GUARD. Against the wall.

PRIEST (*to the* INVESTIGATOR). Goodbye.

INVESTIGATOR. Stay.

PRIEST. It would be better –

INVESTIGATOR. You will reassure the innocent.

The WOMEN *stand in a line against the wall, left.*

INVESTIGATOR. It is not government policy to take hostages. All you women are suspects. (WOMEN *murmur in protest. He looks at a document*.) Gloria Vergara you were on the square the night before the bombing.

GLORIA VERGARA. I work at the Post Office. Its on the square.

INVESTIGATOR. Margarita Arrance you were on the square.

MARGARITA ARRANCE. I lost my cat. My neighbours will tell you. She was –

INVESTIGATOR. Renata Ortiz you were on the square. Seen by a Civil Guard, your nephew.

RENATA ORTIZ. I went to pray.

INVESTIGATOR. And so on. (*He lowers the document.*) Any of you could have entered the church when it was dark.

BERTA TORBADO (*timidly*). My mother's ill. Father ask them to let me go. I havent done anything wrong.

PRIEST. The neighbours are caring for her. You know Berta . . . she doesn't really recognise you any more.

BERTA TORBADO. She might have another attack. They wont know what to do.

INVESTIGATOR. Father Roberto will visit her when he leaves.

NINA MIRAN. I was on the square. I go –

INVESTIGATOR. Your name?

NINA MIRAN. Nina Miran. I go every evening. My friend lives there. We've known each other since we were girls. Now she cant leave her house. We have a glass of wine together. Berta is sixty-nine. How could she get a bomb?

INVESTIGATOR. I dont think any of you did: it was Agustina Ruiz. The evidence is strong but circumstantial. I believe it satisfies justice. But it doesnt satisfy the army – nor should it. Justice can afford to make mistakes. Men are fallible but in time god corrects our errors. If the army fails no one corrects it. None of you should be in any doubt about what I say. If I cant be sure who committed this atrocity then everyone who could have committed it – you women – must be shot. You are a silent jury and the accused will pass the verdict – one way or the other – on you. Agustina Ruiz did you place the bomb in the church?

AGUSTINA. No.

INVESTIGATOR. Its coincidence you were hiding on the outskirts of the village just after the explosion?

AGUSTINA. I hoped to be allowed back in my house. After

the shootings I didnt think anyone else would want to move in. When I heard the explosion I thought it was an air-raid so I hid.

INVESTIGATOR. You'd condemn these innocent women to death?'

AGUSTINA. Who condemns them? They were on the square buying bread. Visiting friends. Going to church. It was their daily life. You arrest them. One is nearly seventy. Yes, father: last night they tortured people so that we could hear their screams. What sort of life d'you offer them anyway? Whenever you're goaded into frustration you drag them here off the street.

INVESTIGATOR (*to the other* WOMEN). I will give you a last chance to save yourself. The army will be satisfied with one witness to accuse her. If you tell me the truth you neednt stay in Estarobon. The government will pay you the amount of a war widow's pension. (*He looks at the list.*) Teresa Martin. Who put the bomb in the church?

TERESA MARTIN. Yesterday my children washed and put on their best clothes and walked to the barracks. They didnt cry – they held hands. The whole town's talking about it. The soldiers must listen to them when they see their faces. They'll send a message to let me go. Dont make the children suffer.

INVESTIGATOR. Children have suffered. The Marquis Don Roberto Palmes De Serosan, Colonel Abrantes, Sister Anna and a farmer have been killed. Three children are among the wounded. One lost a leg. One will have a face hideous for life. And others may die. Who put the bomb in the church?

TERESA MARTIN. Estarobon.

INVESTIGATOR. No, who placed the bomb in the church?

TERESA MARTIN. Estarobon.

INVESTIGATOR. The village? The village placed the bomb? Nina Miran who placed the bomb in the church?

NINA MIRAN. Estarobon.

INVESTIGATOR. I see. And that is the answer of you all? Clerk put the question to the others and note their answers.

CLERK. Maria Barrios who placed the bomb in the church of Saint Vincent of Ferrer?

MARIA BARRIOS. Estarobon.

CLERK. Renata Ramones who placed the bomb in the church of Saint Vincent of Ferrer?

RENATA RAMONES. Estarobon.

CLERK. Maria Corves who placed the –

PRIEST. This is monstrous! Stop it! You dont know what you're doing! Why ever you were brought here, this is a crime! You could be shot! Berta I've taken the sacrament to your mother all the years she's been bedridden. I know you to be a devout christian. I ask you to tell the truth.

BERTA TORBADO. Father they say it was Estarobon. Estarobon.

INVESTIGATOR. Clerk, go on.

CLERK. Maria Corves who placed the bomb in the church of Saint Vincent of Ferrer?

MARIA CORVES. Estarobon.

CLERK. Gloria Vergara who placed the bomb in the church of Saint Vincent of Ferrer?

MANI *comes in through the doors, right, and sits at the desk.*

GLORIA VERGARA. Estarobon.

CLERK. Renata Ortiz who placed the bomb in the church of Saint Vincent of Ferrer?

RENATA ORTIZ. Estarobon.

CLERK. Junita Murciano who placed the bomb in the church of Saint Vincent of Ferrer?

JUNITA MURCIANO. Estarobon.

CLERK. Agustina Ruiz who placed the bomb in the church of Saint Vincent of Ferrer?

AGUSTINA. I dont know. I wasnt there.

PRIEST. What about the children in hospital?

AGUSTINA. The children in hospital. There are no more innocents. Not since you bombed cities. Where are the children of Guernica? For you a child is a thing you use as moral blackmail! We fight you for the sake of our children! Dont stand in your abattoir and point your finger at me!

INVESTIGATOR. Let us turn to the murders of Private Albana and his wife.

AGUSTINA. I've already been cleared. I was on a train. Ask the military.

INVESTIGATOR. Where was your husband?

AGUSTINA. I dont know. I havent heard from him for a year.

INVESTIGATOR. He was hiding in the shed. He came out when it was dark and murdered the guard and his wife.

AGUSTINA. My husband wasnt there.

INVESTIGATOR. Where is he now?

AGUSTINA. Father Roberto thinks he may have got into France.

INVESTIGATOR. He's dead.

AGUSTINA (*pause. She shrugs her shoulders. Flatly, as if it ended the matter*). He's dead.

MANI. He kept us running for a whole day. No reason. He couldn't get away. By the time they caught him the soldiers were angry. So. (*He takes out a photo.*) Look at yourself. (*He gives the photo to* AGUSTINA.) From his jacket. There's some blood on the back.

TERESA MARTIN. He's the one who goes to the mountains in the lorry. They tell stories about him. I didnt believe it. Last night we said if we stick together they cant kill us, we're too many. Its not true! He'd kill us – and go on killing till there was no one left! And he (*She indicates the* INVESTIGATOR.) says Jose and Maria who were murdered –

GLORIA VERGARA. Teresa!

TERESA MARTIN. – she didnt tell us about that last night – we dont know what she's done! She put the bomb in the church. Agustina you told us last night.

INVESTIGATOR (*to the* CLERK). Teresa Martin. Strike her out. (*To* TERESA MARTIN.) Thank you. You have saved these women's lives. (*To the* GUARD.) Take her to the side. (*A* GUARD *takes* TERESA MARTIN *right, away from the other* WOMEN.) This defiance is now pointless. I have the witness I need. I ask you again: who put the bomb in the church?

SEVERAL WOMEN. Estarobon.

INVESTIGATOR. Estarobon is already infamous for its double murder and the bomb. Now this. I shall give an example to anyone else who is tempted to obstruct the government when it seeks to protect its citizens. When Agustina Ruiz is shot, one of you women will be shot with her. (*To the* CLERK.) Pick a name.

CLERK (*confused*). How shall I –

INVESTIGATOR. Any name.

CLERK (*drops the list and picks it up, reads*). Nina Miran.

INVESTIGATOR (*to the* GUARD). Take her out.

A GUARD *starts taking* NINA MIRAN *out left.*

AGUSTINA. No!

INVESTIGATOR. You see what misery you cause! You've lost! The fanatics left in the mountains will turn their *friends* against them! *You* placed the bomb in the church!

AGUSTINA. No!

INVESTIGATOR. Look – bits of poster nailed up in the savanna. If you put them in the street they'd have been torn down before they were read! Who read it in the desert? The wind tore it up and threw it away! (*Reads fragments.*) . . . 'teach us' . . . 'teach us' . . .

AGUSTINA.
When you make us weak you teach us to be strong
When you use secret police you teach us to be secret
Its in our heads! You cant get rid of it!

AGUSTINA *moves towards the* INVESTIGATOR. *The* WOMEN *restrain her.* NINA MIRAN *turns back at the door.*

AGUSTINA.
When you rob us you teach us to sabotage
When you exploit us you teach us to strike
When you make laws you teach us to break them

CIVIL GUARDS *move towards* AGUSTINA.

INVESTIGATOR (*to the* CIVIL GUARDS). Leave them.
AGUSTINA.
When you use weapons against us you teach us to arm
When Fascists imprison a country they teach it to be free!

As AGUSTINA *strains towards the* INVESTIGATOR, *the*
WOMEN *hold her and her feet leave the ground so that her body
becomes horizontal. The* WOMEN *stand round her like gunners
limbering a gun. She raises her head to shout at the* INVESTI-
GATOR. *The* WOMEN *exclaim in astonishment.* AGUSTINA
RUIZ *has become the human cannon.*

AGUSTINA. Destroy them! Their world! Cruel! Pull it down!
Lift me! Higher! His head! Point me! His head! Head!
Head! On him! Destroy him! My eyes! Smash! My
mouth! Crush! Higher! Our world! Our hands! Our feet!
The day! Up! Up! Doors open! Hear streets! Our world!
Aim me! Head! Higher! Target! Now! Gun speaks! The
bomb – who put – the church? It speaks! Not Estarobon!
Fool! It was Spain! Spain!

The WOMEN *lower* AGUSTINA *to the ground.*

INVESTIGATOR. Open the doors. (*A* GUARD *opens the double
doors, right.*) The eight may go.

The eight WOMEN *start to leave. A* GUARD *takes* NINA
MIRAN *out left.*

INVESTIGATOR. Father, the nuns will give Teresa Martin a
room for the time being. Put her children in a home till the
village is quiet. (*The* PRIEST *nods.*)
MANI. Excellency.

MANI *goes out right.*

INVESTIGATOR (*to the* PRIEST). Go to that woman.

PRIEST. When she's ready. Let her grieve first.

WOMEN (*turning at the door, to* AGUSTINA). Goodbye. We didnt disgrace ourselves. We'll tell the village about you.

The WOMEN *go.*

TERESA MARTIN (*to* AGUSTINA). My children are so little. I tried to give them a good life. It was so hard. They'd have taken them away and beaten them for having a wicked mother. I cant let anyone hurt my children.

AGUSTINA. It doesnt matter.

The PRIEST *and* TERESA MARTIN *go out right. Two* GUARDS *are left. One shuts the double doors. The other places a chair for* AGUSTINA *to sit on. She stands.*

INVESTIGATOR. Our era has begun. Fascism is normality protected from change. Most people will hardly notice. The streets will be cleaner. There'll be no strikes. And people like you will have vanished. The world you want is a Utopia. I can see your pathetic army setting out for the horizon, each one bowed under the weight of his brick. When they began to fall you'd turn on them with your whips. You'd feel justified, after all you're leading them to paradise. Soon they'd run berserk and you'd have a world of brutes. Life is short. They want to enjoy it. We'll give them food and holidays – and festivals where they can thank their protectors. They'll be content, and that is paradise. What sort of a woman shrugs when she's told her husband is dead? – In paradise the flowers are brighter. Most people wont notice it. To do that you have to bear the misery of journeying to the horizon – and we'll do that for them. They wont know the brightness of paradise – but they'll be spared being brought face to face with their own littleness. Which is hell. That's all you offered them. That's why we get rid of you.

Chorus

Year after year the workers toiled
And plowmen bowed their heads to the ground
Till they were driven to die in war
But the lives they lived have made us strong
And to our children we pass our strength
The fruit they eat will ripen in light
And with joy we eat the bitter fruit
That ripened in the night

Twelve: The Smile

Mountain road.

AGUSTINA, NINA MIRAN, GUARDS 1 *and* 2.

NINA MIRAN *makes a gesture to take* AGUSTINA'*s arm.*

GUARD 1. Prisoners cant touch.

NINA MIRAN (*moving away*). Poor child its easier for me. Forgive me. I sat at home all day till it was time to go to my friend for our evening glass. My life was already over. How many died from our village? Perhaps now the suffering can end sooner.

TINA *comes on left with her baby in her arms.*

GUARD 2 (*to* TINA). Hurry its just starting.

TINA (*shouts, holding out the child*). Mother.

AGUSTINA (*shouts*). Thank you!

TINA. I went to town. They said here. No lift. Ran. (*She looks down at the child.*) All right now. Hold it.

GUARD 1. Prisoners cant touch.

AGUSTINA. Mine.

TINA (*takes a few steps towards* AGUSTINA). Please.
CORPORAL (*off*). Ready!

GUARD 1 *starts to take* AGUSTINA *left.*

AGUSTINA (*bewildered*). What?
NINA MIRAN. Take me first.
GUARD 1 (*papers*). You're down second. All right, say I got it
wrong.

GUARD 1 *takes* NINA MIRAN *out left.*

AGUSTINA. Her face. The shawl. (TINA *lifts the shawl.*)

CORPORAL *comes on left.*

CORPORAL. What's going on?
GUARD 2. Civilian talking to prisoner corp.
TINA (*giving the child to* GUARD 2). Give it to her.
GUARD 2 (*looks down at the baby in his arms*). What?
CORPORAL (*panic*). Search it! The shawl!
GUARD 2 (*panic*). What is – is it? – (*He pulls at the child's
clothes as if they were burning.*)
TINA. Careful!
CORPORAL (*panic*). Pistol! Grenade!
GUARD 2 (*panic, throws the shawl to the* CORPORAL). Empty!
CORPORAL (*panic*). Nappy! Vest! The back!

GUARD 2 *searches the baby. The* CORPORAL *holds the shawl
out like a magician's square: turns it round to show its empty
both sides. Off, a burst of machine-gun fire. It rattles on the
rocks.*

CORPORAL. Not to be trusted.
GUARD 2 (*finishes searching*). Nothing.
CORPORAL. All right let her look.

GUARD 2 *holds the baby up in front of* AGUSTINA *for her to
see.* AGUSTINA *makes a slight step towards the baby.*

CORPORAL. Stay!

AGUSTINA (*looking at the child*). Its father . . . ?

TINA. I dont know.

AGUSTINA. He'll be safe. You came. So far. Im glad. Dont cry. It doesnt help. (*She smiles at the child.*) There: all these years from now it will remember me smiling.

Off, a single shot. AGUSTINA *doesnt take her eyes off the child.*

(*Smiling.*) She doesnt mind the shooting. You'd better go.

TINA *takes the child from* GUARD 2 *and starts to leave.*

AGUSTINA (*smiling*). Her face.

TINA *hurries right, turns the child on her shoulder so that it faces back to* AGUSTINA.

AGUSTINA (*smiling*). Higher.

TINA *lifts the child higher.* GUARD 1 *comes on.*

AGUSTINA (*gesturing to the* SOLDIERS *to wait. Smiling*). A little longer.

TINA *goes out right with the child.* AGUSTINA *stops smiling and turns to the* SOLDIERS. *She goes out with them.*

The Bundle

or

New Narrow Road to the Deep North

A Note on Dramatic Method

Human consciousness is not an innate quality that creates itself. We have an innate capacity for consciousness. How we become conscious is largely decided by our society and its institutions – the family, schools, courts, media and so forth – and by the organization and practice of our work, the means by which we live. Human consciousness is a creation of society and takes historical forms. The nature of human consciousness at any time is a consequence of the particular society in which it is created.

Societies change and human consciousness changes with them. Change originates from technology, which constantly changes the way in which people work, in which they sustain their life. This provokes changes in human consciousness and subsequently in social institutions. Changes in human consciousness begin before changes in social institutions because, although working people have the first experience of using new technology (in this connection working people must be thought of as workers and consumers), they are not usually in control of social institutions. And furthermore, social institutions usually resist change. There are at least two reasons for this. Firstly, in order to function efficiently society must observe certain instrumental values. Cars must normally be driven on one side of the road, promises kept, rules of hygiene respected and so forth. These rules or regulations are not in themselves moral values. You can keep a promise to kill an innocent person, or swerve across the road to miss a pedestrian. But it is morally valuable that they should normally be kept. Without them society is not possible. Secondly, social institutions represent the interest of the ruling class. They developed when technology was simpler than it is now and they represent a social order – a relationship between social institutions, technology, environment and human consciousness – which technology has made obsolescent. Our social institutions do not represent the interests of those people who by experience as workers and consumers are creating developments in human consciousness, new ways of understanding and interpreting the world, and so making necessary new ways of organizing it. But when the ruling class defends its interests it can claim it acts for the good of everyone because it controls the administration, the mechanical efficiency, of society (keeping to the right side of the road and so forth) – and this claim has an obvious plausibility.

Social institutions control law, education, civic force (police and armed forces), scientific research and so on – all the machinery and knowledge we need to live together and create a common life. But the control is deeper. It permeates the ordinary use of language, mores, customs, common assumptions and unquestioned ideas. Together these things – institutions and their social reflections – make up a tacitly accepted view of life, a consciousness of the world which is also in large part a self-consciousness. It is not the whole of self-consciousness because, as I've said, that is partly created by experience as worker and consumer. This experience brings the tacitly accepted, ruling-class, institutional values into confrontation with moral values. Moral values originate in the relationship between men, their technology, their environment and their mutual interdependence. They are not, therefore, necessarily embodied in the structure of any particular society. We can talk of a tacitly accepted view of the world because although this view is often rejected – in industrial strikes for example – it remains powerful unless experience as worker and consumer is transposed into concepts, and then into customs, mores and so forth to make up a radically changed view of the world. Social institutions control the tacitly accepted view by means of education, the selection of information, economic sanctions and if necessary naked force. Above all they control the tacitly accepted *moral* code – and social living requires a moral code (or a reactionary substitute for it) as well as a set of rules. But social institutions do not create culture. Ultimately culture derives from our experience as workers and consumers; and a culture is created by working people bringing social institutions, economic and political organization, into line with their experience and needs as workers and consumers. When that isn't done society is not an agent of law and order but of regulation and force; it is not a guardian of morality, it merely administers (or rather struggles necessarily unsuccessfully to administer) mechanical efficiency. For a society to administer moral law, its institutions, and their reflection in mores, language, expectations etc., must work in harmony with the new self-consciousness developed by working people as workers and consumers. Society requires its members to have certain attitudes to its institutions, to understand the justification for them, to respect and consent to them. Otherwise, instead of relying on understanding, the institutions must rely on lies, force or reaction. Yet a changing technology creates new attitudes and knowledge in those who use it and benefit from it: self-autonomy in place of servitude, a technical interpretation of the world in place of a mythological one, a new image of the self. These attitudes cannot work efficiently, harmoniously, with obsolescent institutions. When technology, social institutions and human consciousness reflect each other's exigencies and possibilities in a rational way, then there is harmony in the organization of life, difficulties are solved rationally, and society can be said to administer moral law. The effort to create such a society, to derive concepts from experience and to develop mores and habits that go beyond immediate, opportunistic, individual interests, is the practical work of creating culture – and this itself brings further changes in human consciousness. Culture is not a static condition administered by social institutions that are its permanent repositories. Culture is provoked by technological change and achieved through the need human beings have to harmonize their experience of sustaining their life with their experience of society, so that a new form of self-consciousness is created.

When a new human self-consciousness, adequate to living in the present and preparing the future, is not being created, human self-consciousness becomes reactionary. Then there are calls for a return to the past in attitudes and organization, and in the imagery (uniforms, architecture, art and so forth) which give social institutions prestige and authority. In the ruling class this is a desire to return to the mode of the eighteenth-century gentleman of enlightenment or to some even more remote historical-mythological birth of the nation. For the working class it means Disneyland or Cloud Cuckoo Land. Then human beings become increasingly barbaric and aggressive. This is partly because they have emotional attitudes to what they think and partly because the organization of their lives has physiological consequences. In conditions of tension people are more readily aggressive and credulous. Usually we assume that when people are destructive that is because they are motivated by unconscious emotional attitudes which make them behave atavistically. But I think they behave like this because of the conditions society allocates to them and because of the tensions of holding an absurd society together. A society which tries to create a self-consciousness based on imagery, organization and attitudes from the past will cause emotional crises in its members that must result in violence and aggression. They either struggle to resist, as any prisoner might, or become dangerously apathetic so that they do not protest at the inhumanities of their reactionary regime, or even become its brutal accomplices. That is the sum total of the forces of human darkness, the original sin or natural aggression, which the ruling class seizes on so avidly and teaches so assiduously.

Self-consciousness is created in the process of understanding the world and our own behaviour. It is necessary to create a new human self-consciousness for our own time, our technology, our society, ourselves. This self-consciousness must be based on a consciousness of the world and an interpretation of it. One can say that socialist consciousness is equivalent to moral self-consciousness in that it is a viable knowledge of the self in relation to practical involvement in the world; this self-consciousness contains not merely experience but unites it with an interpretation of the world and self that restores moral action to our lives. Perhaps one should not even use the concept 'self' in connection with reaction because the reactionary self is only a neurotic or opportunistic parasite on the past: it is ghost-like. A valid self-consciousness is not this ghost-like, wraith-like experience; it has the feel of the world. It is not sufficient for someone to be told that someone else is good or bad and to understand this in terms of reward or punishment. Morality cannot be conditioned because it involves free choice. The practical realities of goodness and badness must be apparent, discernible. If an apple is to be eaten it must look, smell, taste, feel and (when tapped) sound good. And we must know, through our conceptual understanding of the world, that eating it will not destroy moral social relationships (in the metaphysics of christianity, that it is not interdicted by god: the original crime was not murder but theft of the master's property – Cain slew Abel *after* the apple was stolen). Human consciousness, to be practical, requires a wholeness of understanding that has many similarities to this. Conceptual ideas alone cannot create this wholeness. The elements of a man's understanding must relate to one another so that he has a sound, reliable interpretation of the world not merely in terms of concept but also in justified expectation. His experience must be the ground for sound judgement and hope. In this way he can live without absurdity or too much tension and can interpret himself in terms of the world and his society.

Art is one way of creating this wholeness of understanding, and theatre is one of the arts best suited to do this. Theatre can validate human standards, ways of living, ethical decisions, understanding, by demonstrating the relation of cause and effect in practical human life and not merely in concept or theory. This is ultimately a demonstration of the soundness or unsoundness of these standards, methods, interpretations and decisions. In this way experience is not merely recorded randomly but is set in a moral order of reason and judgement. An audience can then see what human beings are and what are the standards, practices and concepts by which they should live. In this way human consciousness is changed.

Art is sometimes said to be a reflection of the ideal. This could mean it is not a guide to action. Yet when in a sense art makes the ideal concrete for the present it must also be a guide to present action. It is not a narcotic or dream. Art portrays present-day human beings who are conscious, or potentially conscious, of a utopian society – and who desire to achieve it. It shows the desire, the possibility, the action necessary to achieve it, and the practical standards that can be used to assess this action and the moral standards that can be used to judge it. These standards are one assurance that the possibility is real. Art doesn't create a void between our world and a rational world. Sometimes the act of trying to achieve this future may cause immediate unhappiness, but this is certainly the only form of cultural action possible in our time. That is why socialist art is not superficial or merely programmatic, but includes the whole of human experience, tragic and comic. And in our time only socialism can produce art because it unites experience of the world and society with the rational understanding of them and with an optimistic interpretation of our present condition. It interprets the world, it does not merely mirror it. The alternative is the despair or dreary cynicism of the theatre of the absurd, which still passes for culture in our schools and universities.

Why is theatre so well suited to help to create self-consciousness? It does not use aspects of human beings in the way painting and novels do, but puts human beings themselves on stage. Audiences judge not merely by what actors say but by how they say it, how they move, how and where they look, gesture, interact. Human acts are then not judged by their theoretical correctness, nor oddly enough by their putative inevitability, but by their concrete plausibility to the audience, who are after all actors in their own lives. The stage does not go inside the mind as easily as novels and music can, but it can demonstrate social relationships between people more concretely than other arts. All theatre is political –

Coward's as well as Brecht's – and theatre always emphasizes the social in art. The audience judges in the same complex way that it judges in ordinary life. But it is given this advantage: it may look at things it would normally run from in fear, turn from in embarrassment, prevent in anger, or pass by because they are hidden, either purposefully or innocently. So audiences respond with all the faculties of their consciousness to the things that determine their social and private lives. They judge and in judging extend their self-consciousness because they have not merely responded to a situation or character in the socially prescribed way (as conditioned by institutions and tacitly accepted mores) but have been made to see aspects of the situation or character which the socially prescribed response blots out. If we say some soldiers behaved in a certain way we show them to the audience behaving in that way. The audience will not judge this as they would an account or description or claim. They will judge with the total involvement they use in their daily lives, with all their senses, with the subtle apprehensions with which they go about their daily business, the consciousness of the world which they validate with their self-consciousness. We shall give them tools of historical hind-sight and access to what is usually hidden, distorted or blurred. This can result in a development of understanding, an improved interpretation of the world, and so in a development of self-knowledge and self-consciousness. The audience cannot repeat itself. It is forced to reassess itself. Of course a dramatist can't prevent an audience from hardening its reaction. That's one reason why theatre can't by itself change the world. But if the audience decide that what we thought was true is false they will still have been changed, not merely for themselves but for society. Their views will have been increasingly identified and defined. So theatre can co-operate with all those who are in any way involved in rationally changing society and evolving a new consciousness. It may initiate the change in some people. What an audience says when it leaves a theatre is less important than what it thinks six months later. Some people angrily walk out of a theatre but six months later know that the play was voicing views they had already started to accept.

Plays should deal, either comically or seriously, with situations, accounts and characters, which concern the audience in their daily life. But a dramatist need not always deal with the present. The past is also an institution owned by society. Our understanding of the past will change with our developing self-consciousness. This is not a partisan rewriting of history but a moral discovery of it. Our account of the past will be compared with other accounts. But the audience's comparison will be made in the sensitive way I have described. We cannot merely say that our account is correct. We must demonstrate it and prove it in the rationality of the stage.

Often the received image of the present, the consciousness of it, and so the corresponding self-consciousness, will not be a true interpretation of reality. Often the received interpretation is influenced, subverted, by the overt teaching and subtler persuasions of social institutions administering to the philosophy and needs of an obsolescent ruling class. Even if this were not so, human beings would still have to become involved in the active creation of their nature, since technology would always be disturbing their relationship to the environment and society. Certainly, in the present, we see ourselves and the world through class eyes: and the working class either sees the world and itself through its own class eyes (which means it is free to create a new culture and not merely produce the condition that requires a new culture) or it sees through the eyes of its masters, judges and other institution-alizers. Because of this, merely recounting an event or telling a story on stage will not provide the opportunity for a correct interpretation of the event or story or the people involved. These things may be misinterpreted, and often will be, because many of the audience will not be politically conscious and so will not understand the event or story or even the moral content of the language in which it is described or played. As we cannot merely tell stories or record events we have to handle punctured myths or broken stories. Effect no longer follows cause, judgement no longer assesses deed, as they did in the past. Not even imagery works for us as it did in the past. Above all, moral language is caught in the same trap. So it is not easy for contemporary writers to contain experience and moral teaching in myths and stories in the way a more secure, settled society could. The way of telling a story, and the normative use of language, no longer contains an implicit interpretation. While we remain part of our present institutional societies our lives have no meaning and therefore stories about them have no meaning. Stories cannot present their own interpretation, can no longer teach us how they should be understood. The dramatist cannot confront the audience with truth by telling a story. The interpretation is counterfeited by society. Even the normative language we use to survive in capitalist society cannot be used to interpret it, our language is fouled by its involvement in that society just as morality is fouled by religion. This means that our moral sanity is at stake. Nor will a technical language of politics or sociology solve the problem because, although it can analyse realism, it cannot reproduce the appearance of reality on stage. And we certainly do not live in a society where the institutions are strong enough to criticize themselves – or rich enough. We are not like American capitalism, which could finance and profit from films on the wickedness of lynching blacks. It is simply that we have to rewrite human consciousness.

This is not a new problem in art – it has always been the task of art, but it has become a more urgent problem because changes in the technological basis of society and consciousness have become so extreme. When one considers the uproar, the sound and fury, of so much twentieth-century art, it is as if a child were trying to speak a new language. All art is a record of reality and an interpretation of it. If the interpretation is valid it changes naturalism into realism and so into art. Art does not consist in the recording or reproduction of a thing (that is merely one sort of skill) but in analysing what is recorded or reproduced. If we look at a painting of a bowl of flowers and ask what part of the painting is art, the answer is not that art is the recording of the bowl and flowers, but is in the way they are recorded – that is, in the analysis or interpretation of them. This means, finally, that art is created by the human, social need to interpret experience and not merely passively submit to it. The equivalent of this in human consciousness is experience and the valid interpretation of it. A person of whom this is typical is cultured, and a work of art is something which helps to create this culture.

A human being incorporates his analysis of experience as part of his experience, and art which demonstrates its analysis in terms of what it records, rather than in externally originated comments on it, proves itself, and is usually more effective in deepening and strengthening human self-consciousness. Of course the artist may not always be able to choose. In a society that incorporates so little truth in its institutions and mores that it cannot reveal itself to itself in any way, how can an artist incorporate true conceptual knowledge into a *record* of that society? If he portrays the suffering of a beggar he may be told that thrift is a higher form of morality than pity. It might seem that the artist could then only comment from outside, in propaganda, and not reveal from within, in art. But there is always a working class which by its experience creates moral values and so this situation can never last long. Perhaps technology *could* be used to make it permanent, but this could only happen if the working class had been made hopelessly robot-like in its experience and responses, and history would then stand still.

It is useful to consider some of the techniques Brecht and other theatre workers used to overcome this difficulty. A scene can be interrupted by displaying placards that explain or comment on what happens in that scene. This helps the audience to understand what it is being shown and to see itself in a new light. And apart from the concepts or slogans on the placards there is also the vitalizing experience of seeing physically demonstrated the truth that life need not be an ungraspable flow of experience (to be understood only through pastiches of the past – as in Joyce's epic

Ulysses) but that new interpretations can be drawn from it. The physical demonstration of this in the theatre helps to create a new way of approaching experience outside the theatre. (At its simplest many people now even stick placards and posters on the walls of their homes.) But there is a limit to what this can achieve. It merely says that something is so and, even though it is in fact true, saying it does not test or prove it in the laboratory of art, in the rationality of the stage. If this were sufficient there would be no need for theatre.

Brecht also paid attention to the method of acting. He believed that a character should be shown not so much as an individual but as a class function. Perhaps there should be a difference between the way members of the exploiting class and the way others are shown. Members of the exploiting class deny their moral function, in practice, while claiming it institutionally. They have merely eccentricity – eccentricity is an attribute over-prized in dying cultures – taste, discretion, etiquette, style, collections of pictures, libraries and so forth. But working-class people create their humanity by daily experience of resistance or impulse for change. Their acts when they do this consciously are moral – and, incidentally, truly individual though united with others. But if a difference is made in the playing of the ruling class and this difference is merely a stage technique (caricature or masks, for example) and is not recorded from reality, then again the play's moral statements may not have been tested and proved – that is, turned into art – but merely assumed. The analysis of an event must not swamp the recording of it. We have to show the mask under the face not the mask on it. Perhaps we should show members of the ruling class in the way they see themselves: it is this good light which is so corrupting, so destructive in Western democracies, not least because it appropriates moral language. Of course, in open class war the role of the artist is clearer. The situation polarizes roles for everyone. But at the moment, in our society as it is, the truth is more terrible than the caricature of it. To show this truth, just as to show the mask under the face, we need a new way of acting, one that will not simplify the complexities of experience by abstracting from it but will let us make the total complexity of a character simple and understandable. After all, that is what self-consciousness does when it develops into political consciousness, into class consciousness, in working people. Self-consciousness then becomes self-manipulative because it has then become a body of concepts, ideas, precepts, tests and experience which have been shown to be valid in critical, defining situations. If this insight and understanding could be used to develop a form of acting that could demonstrate truth to the audience, that would be the most important advance our theatre could make.

The dramatist can help to create a new theatre by the way he writes. He should dramatize not the story but the analysis. He will still have to present the story coherently, just as the painter must achieve a likeness, because that represents the experience, the anecdotal autobiography the audience brings to the theatre. But the scenes will not present the story in the way that is traditionally thought to be satisfying or coherent. In *The Bundle* I tried to find ways of dramatizing the analysis. The play is not best understood as a story of hero Wang but as a demonstration of how the words 'good' and 'bad', and moral concepts in general, work in society and how they ought to work if men are to live rationally with their technology, with nature and with one another. These are some of the moments in *The Bundle* when the analysis is dramatized: in scene seven, when Wang speaks calmly as the blood flows down his chin; at the end of scene five, in the play-within-the-play; in scene nine, the merchant's sudden animal shouts of 'Yu!' (these are shouts of terror, not abbreviations of 'You!'); at the end of scene three, Wang's choice of the word 'buy' when he shouts; in scene eight (c), the mother's struggle to move and her scream; and in scene eight (a), the use of the water bowl – at first this is an object in the story and then it is abstracted from the story and put into the analysis, when the ferryman with a calm, simple gesture places it on the ground and offers the audience an elucidation, just as earlier he had offered Tiger the clear water. The changing of the bundle by the river from a baby in scenes one and four to rifles in scene eight (b) is also a dramatization of the analysis. The director, designer and actors must use such moments as dramatic high-points. They are not 'bits of business'.

The way a play is performed and the mise-en-scène designed teach the audience how to respond to the play and analyse it. Consider the man-handling of the boat in scene three. The boat not merely arrives, it is also removed. This man-handling would be clumsy in a well-made play. The well-made play deceives the audience into believing that the story will itself teach them how it should be interpreted. Instead, in this play the boat is carried out neatly and efficiently by the keepers (helped by the passengers if need be) so that it marks a pause in the play, preparing for the incident that must follow. It does not stop the play or become an incident interesting purely for itself (as Brecht might have been tempted to see it) but with tact and discretion it moves the play forward and teaches the audience their freedom in interpreting the play. Remember, the story will no longer interpret itself, as a joke can, or absolve the audience from the need to interpret it, as a myth might once have done. So the way the performers interpret the problems of performing the play can involve the audience in the interpretation of the meaning, the analysis, of the play.

Brecht sometimes suggests that each scene can be complete in itself and that this isolation of scenes can be used to interpret reality. But the connection between the scenes is essential because it is part of the analysis. Scenes cannot, it is true, relate to one another merely for the purposes of the story, because audiences can no longer passively interpret stories and so the dramatist cannot confront the audience with truth in this way. Instead, the choice and ordering of scenes is decided by the analysis – that is, the analysis will dictate the structure of the story; but care must be taken, as I have said, that it does not swamp it. Azdak the judge, in *The Caucasian Chalk Circle*, vanishes like a deus ex machina after showing that it is possible for judgement to be wise. This is done by incidents in a scene. He does not stay to show that wisdom is practical. In *Cymbeline* a god descends so that we may understand (he tells us not to ask questions), and Azdak seems to vanish so that we may believe! For all his earthiness he is a voice shouting from an upper window, not someone we met in the street. Practicality can only be shown by the ordering of scenes, not by incidents in scenes. The epic's structure must have meaning – it is not a collection of scenes showing that meaning is logically possible. The epic must have a unity based on practical truth, just as once it was based on mythological coherence. This unity comes from the analysis, which demonstrates, embodies cause and effect in a coherent way. The scenes in *The Bundle* were chosen and ordered for this reason. Obvious examples are the parallels between scenes one and four; the placing of scene seven between scenes six and eight, where it interrupts the story, instead of before scene six; the decision to dramatize the preparation for the fight and the consequences of it and not the fight itself – which the traditonal story would have required (some critics were so confused by this that they thought the rifles were not used, although scene nine makes it clear they were).

The 'dramatization of the analysis instead of the story', in both the choice and ordering of the scenes and in the incidents dramatically emphasized in the scenes, is a way of reinstating meaning in literature. It may seem cold and abstract but it is not. The analysis can give us the beauty and vitality that once belonged to myth, without its compromises and intellectual reallocation of meaning. It can be the most exciting part of the play, dramatized through powerful images and dramatic confrontations between appearance and reality. But these dramatizations must not exist in their own right as dramatic effects. They demonstrate those crises in a story when the audience are asked to be not passive victims or witnesses, but interpreters of experience, agents of the future, restoring meaning to action by recreating self-consciousness. At these moments the audience are superior to the actors: they are on the real stage.

I have touched on several matters and not had time to discuss them fully. And it might seem that some of what I've said is too theoretical to be a guide to practical performance – but *this* is something I do not apologize for. We cannot know how to write, direct, design or act till we know why we have a stage. As a species we need an image of ourselves. Other animals are guided by instincts and protected by limited needs. We make decisions, and to do this wisely we need an image of ourselves, a human image. Our biology prepares us for this and if we do not create such an image we cannot use the opportunities of our technology without destroying or corrupting ourselves. Culture is created by a rational, self-manipulating self-consciousness. One of the means of creating this is art. All societies have used art. It is a biological requirement of the orderly functioning of human beings. But other societies have used art not in the way tired business-men want to use our theatre, to escape from labour which denies them self-respect and self-knowledge, but in order to learn how to live and work so that we may be happy and our moral concern for one another is not wasted.

EDWARD BOND
1978

The Bundle was first performed by the Royal Shakespeare Company at the Warehouse Theatre, London. The production opened on 13 January 1978 with the following cast:

FERRYMAN	Bob Peck
BASHO	Patrick Stewart
WANG	Mike Gwilym
FIRST KEEPER	Rod Culbertson
SECOND KEEPER	Alfred Molina
OLD MAN	Clyde Pollitt
OLD WOMAN	Judith Harte
FERRYMAN'S WIFE	Margaret Ashcroft
PU-TOI	Kevin O'Shea
LU	Lynda Rooke
KUNG-TU	John Nettles
WOMAN	Meg Davies
TIGER	Paul Moriarty
SHEOUL	Francis Viner
KAKA	Greg Hicks
TOR-QUO	Martin Read
WATER SELLER 1	Kevin O'Shea
WATER SELLER 2	Greg Hicks
CRACKER MAN	Martin Read
SOLDIER 1	Rod Culbertson
SOLDIER 2	Alfred Molina
SOLDIER 3	Christopher Whitehouse
HUSBAND	Christopher Whitehouse
TO-SI	Christopher Whitehouse
SAN-KO	Alfred Molina
GOW	Rod Culbertson
TUAN (Corpse)	Michael Townsend

Directed by Howard Davies
Designed by Chris Dyer
Lighting by David Boshell

Part One
One: River bank
Two: River bank
Three: Grave mound
Four: Another part of the river
Five: Marsh

Part Two
Six: Ferryman's house
Seven: Road between villages
Eight: (a) Ferryman's house
      (b) River bank
      (c) Ferryman's house
Nine: Room in Court House
Ten: River Bank

PART ONE

One

Fenland. A river and a river bank in the fens. A bell on a post. A baby left by the river.

FERRYMAN. I ask why the reverend sir sets out so early in the morning. He is not a soldier or a tax collector.

BASHO. The landowner wanted to make me judge of the fenland villages. I answered: not worthy. I have seen the darkness of human life – murder theft death. The *truth* when it is dark corrupts. First I must find enlightenment. Then I will judge. The landowner said: when the old judge dies our court will be empty. Don't seek enlightenment too long. I said: I seek till I find.

FERRYMAN. Will the reverend sir now say what enlightenment is?

BASHO. All creation seeks enlightenment as this river flows to the sea. Does the river ask: what is the way? Men are a dark river. We get and spend, fret and eddy, twist into whirlpools till the water seems to devour itself in its frenzy – we delay. See where the river flows to its mouth and enters the ocean, where the great earth sees the vision of itself in the sky and turns to water. (FERRYMAN *helps* BASHO *from the boat.*) May your life prosper.

FERRYMAN. The reverend sir hasn't paid the ferryman.

BASHO. I go to be reborn. Does the midwife charge the child? Is your life so useful, your soul full of such brightness, your trade done with such courtesy – that you can charge enlightenment a penny on its journey into the world?

FERRYMAN. The reverend sir knows our life is hard, there are so few travellers –

BASHO. For those who suffer there is grace.

FERRYMAN. Grace without food won't help me to row my boat.

BASHO. Not one penny. Will you tell the keeper of heaven: 'Yes, I charged the saints a penny to travel in my boat. I come empty-handed, clothed in sin. Let me enter.' You ask me to damn your immortal soul. (*Sees child.*) A child. Left by the river. These villages are in hell! You see why I seek enlightenment. (*To child.*) Why were you left here?

FERRYMAN. The parents were too poor to feed it.

BASHO. They threw you out to die.

FERRYMAN. They laid it by the river and prayed to heaven that passengers would take pity on it. Take the child on your journey!

BASHO. Take the child! I have to cross mountains where there are tigers. Crawl through swamps – unless someone loves knowledge enough to carry me on his back. Beg – and go without. You take it.

FERRYMAN. We're as poor as its parents. And our house is an ignorant place. With the reverend sir the child would grow wise and good. People will take pity on him if he has a child.

BASHO. Ah . . . No. Knowledge must be loved for itself. I would be like an organ grinder with a monkey on his back. If the child had been big it could have carried my bundle. Then heaven's purpose would have been clear. No, it was put here to tempt me at the start of my journey. Shall the sage turn back and never get further than his doorstep? Child, I am Basho the great seventeenth-century poet. I brought the haiku to perfection. Listen!

> The saints' feet are hands
> Washing the dusty earth
> On the narrow road
> That leads to enlightenment

I am often asked to recite that. Of course you understand nothing yet. But my words are a blessing. Child we are both by the river at the start of our journey. Yours may end at this river. I shall cross many rivers. Neither you nor I has a coin to pay the ferryman or lay on our eyes. Learn to be patient. Would the sky alter by one tear if I took you with me? Does the ant on the mountain ask the pines why they sigh? One can take nothing into the mirror of eternity but the vision of oneself.

BASHO *goes. The* FERRYMAN *stands by his boat and looks at the child.*

FERRYMAN. In my house you'd be hungry. Wake up at night with the cold. And I'm not a good man. My wife wouldn't be able to save you from my wicked temper. Wicked. Sometimes I wait all day and no one comes. On those evenings I couldn't stand your crying – though I was crying myself. If you'd dropped off the back of a carriage the lackey (*Starts poling.*) would have been sent to pick you up. The coachman would have been flogged for jolting. You're a poor man's child – you must learn to understand. Be grateful to your parents. Look at the good cloth you're wrapped in! They could have sold that and lived like lords. Your mother didn't have a cloth to dry her eyes. She looked down at you and said: 'Now the cradle clothes are a shroud.' Yes, well. You have much to understand and forgive. The poet was right: patience.

A curlew calls. The FERRYMAN *stops.*

There'd be no harm in making sure you're properly wrapped. (*He starts to punt back to the child.*) You could have kicked your clothes loose. Or they could be too tight. Your parents didn't want to hurt you. I owe it to them to look. You're not crying. It can't be too bad. Perhaps the worst's already over. It would be wrong to wake you. I'll just straighten your clothes.

The FERRYMAN *gets out of the boat, goes to the child and arranges its wrapping.*

I won't pick you up. Better not. I'll tell my passengers: a little boy. A mouth to feed now, two hands to work later. Sow in spring, eat in winter. (*He goes back to the boat.*) Whoever gets you's in luck. They'll fight over you. Heaven must have meant you for someone better than me. If I took you I'd be stealing from the gods. This is the passenger bell. (*He rings one note on the bell.*) They ring and I come. I help them into the boat. Young and old, rich and poor, innocent and some so guilty the river couldn't wash them clean. I take them all across. That is the bell.

The FERRYMAN *gets into the boat and begins to pole.*

We have no children. Heaven was kind. It knew we couldn't feed them. When you welcome us to heaven you'll understand why I left you. You'll be young and happy for ever, we'll be old and soiled.

The curlew calls. The FERRYMAN *stops rowing.*

Terrible to be poor. We have nothing and the world is a mouth wide open saying: 'Give!' We must be hard to live. Yet at any moment a curlew can call and we are lost.

The FERRYMAN *poles back to the child.*

God knows what my wife will say. I'll leave you outside the door where she'll find you. Then she'll be guilty. Or say a god came walking over the water as brazen as anything and when I lifted my hands to cover my face – you were dropped in them – Tch! She'd box my ears! No supper tonight. She'll say: 'If I feed this I can't feed you.'

The FERRYMAN *picks up the child.*

This is a bad thing. Not a wise one. We throw kindness around as if we were kings. Yes, I shall eat tonight – I must be strong to work. So I have taken my wife's bread. She'll go without every night. Soon she'll grow weak. Her life will be half a life. She's shared my sorrow for years. I love her. Yet I betray her for love for you. I kill her. (*Poles.*) Where is the wisdom in that? If you understood you'd be shocked. Look, I row gently so that you sleep there on the floor of my boat. Your fingers lie on your chest like chips from a gravestone. I must hope you're dead. Or you die in the crossing. Then all I need do is dig your grave. That would be best. We'd be spared the results of this folly. Where is the wisdom in that?

Two

The same. Night. Fourteen years later. The FERRYMAN *fishes from the boat.* WANG *sits by the shaded lamp.*

WANG. It's not our boat.

FERRYMAN. Not now.

WANG. Why not?

FERRYMAN. It went in taxes.

WANG. Why?

FERRYMAN. No money. So few passengers.

WANG. Why?

FERRYMAN. Robbers. People don't like to travel.

WANG (*after a slight silence*). The wind ruffles my sleeve like the water. What are taxes?

FERRYMAN. Taxes make sure the country's well run.

WANG. Father –

FERRYMAN. Sh!

WANG. But . . .

FERRYMAN (*after a slight silence*). I'll try to explain. It's true: the other day I got this cut on my head. I took two hefty young men in the boat. They said they were going to join the emperor's army. What a pleasure for an old man to row two strong young men to their glory. In the middle of the stream they laughed and said: 'Give us the takings.' I said: 'Boys, you're my only passengers this week and so far you've given me nothing.' Then because they were angry and because they wanted to amuse themselves, they said: 'Let's sink the boat.' I said: 'Boys, this boat is the landowner's.' Their whole manner changed. If the boat had been mine they'd have sunk it. With so many robbers about the police have many more important things to protect than us. But if they'd sunk the landowner's boat they'd have been hunted down to the ends of China. So, that's taxes: the soldiers left me the boat and only cracked my head . . . Sh.

WANG. No insects on the lamp. Cold.

FERRYMAN (*half sighs*). I wanted to catch a fish for your mother.

WANG. Who owns the river?

FERRYMAN. You're keeping the fish away.

WANG. Who owns the fish?

FERRYMAN. What fish?

WANG. Why do we fish at night?

FERRYMAN. The landowner owns the river and the fish. We can't afford a licence to fish.

WANG. So we steal the fish.

FERRYMAN (*slight pause*). I will try to explain. The landowner owns the boat and the river and the fish. You could say he owns us – he owns the only way we can live. In return he keeps us safe. (*Wang moves as if to interrupt.*) Wait! You sit on the bank in the sun and wave your arms to keep off the insects. Some still bite – but not many. Well, if the landowner didn't keep the robbers away they'd come down the chimney and take the food out of your mouth! We're his property. It's in his interest to look after us. There.

WANG. We steal the fish to stay alive to pay taxes so that there'll be no more stealing and the –

FERRYMAN. I often wonder who your father was. A priest – or philosopher – or a footpad. I think you –

The ferry bell rings, sharp and clear in the dark. Immediately WANG *douses the light.*

FERRYMAN (*faking his voice to sound as if it came from the far bank*). Who's there – so late?

BASHO. Basho.

FERRYMAN. Basho? . . . O reverend sir, one moment!

> *Splashing as the boat is poled towards the shore. The lamp is lit.*

Is it really the reverend sir?

BASHO. Am I known? My fame goes before. I've walked through a thousand valleys and climbed to the top of the world, crossed so many rivers and watched the pole strike the water a million times. My journey has lasted fourteen years. They seem like fourteen lifetimes.

> *As the boat approaches the light falls on* BASHO. *He is old and tired and dirty. His feet are bound in lumps of rag.*

Tap tap tap through China. I've worn out seventeen walking sticks. My feet are bound with rags! I picked them out of the rubbish in the corner of a grave-yard. They'd been used to bind corpses' mouths. Ferryman, is this the way to the deep north?

FERRYMAN. This is your village.

BASHO. My village?

FERRYMAN. Yes reverend sir.

BASHO. My village? This is my village?

FERRYMAN. Yes reverend sir.

> *The* FERRYMAN *steps from his boat and goes to take* BASHO's *arm to help him into the boat.* WANG *holds the light so that it falls on the* FERRYMAN's *face.*

Welcome!

BASHO. This is a dream!

FERRYMAN. No reverend sir, I am the ferryman –

BASHO (*turning round in a circle*). I've taken the wrong road. Walked in a circle. I must go back. Where is the road to the deep north? (*Faces the* FERRYMAN *again.*) Where? Where?

FERRYMAN (*goes to help him, takes his arm to lead him to the boat*). But reverend sir, be comforted!

BASHO (*striking him off*). Get off! A vision sent by the devil! Get off! This is the king of the dead!

> BASHO *falls in a faint.*

FERRYMAN. Water! He's fainted! The poor old man!

> WANG *sets the lamp on the ground, fetches water from the river and throws it in* BASHO's *face.* BASHO *comes round spluttering.*

BASHO. . . what? . . .

> BASHO *faints again.*

FERRYMAN. He's fainted again! Water! Quick!

> WANG *fetches water from the river.*

WANG. Who is he?

> WANG *throws water in* BASHO's *face.* BASHO *comes round.*

BASHO. The water! Enlightenment!

FERRYMAN. Sir?

BASHO. Enlightenment. The water on my face . . . Enlightenment! I have enlightenment! The meaning of my journey! – heaven has shown me the mirror on my doorstep! Enlightenment!

WANG (*to* FERRYMAN) . . . What is enlightenment?

BASHO (*kneels*).

> I travelled the earth
> To the gateway of heaven
> Who kept the door? Doubt!
> How many turn back
> At the last

Help me.

> FERRYMAN *helps* BASHO *to his feet.* WANG *watches.*

WANG. What is enlightenment?

FERRYMAN. Yes, sir, teach us!

BASHO. I crawled over China like a fly on the back of a mirror. I reached the bright silver river at the edge. The glass cuts. That is the moment the crowd turns back. I crossed the river. Now I am on the other side, on the mirror of eternity. Every pillar in the temple sees the altar from its own angle. The sun dazzles from afar, those who live on it see by its light. I have found the little stone that holds the laws of the world in your hand.

FERRYMAN. Sir –?

BASHO. Do not ask for enlightenment till you're ready to lose all. I look into the mirror of this river. If this mirror appeared in your boat – a little round hole in the bottom – you would block it out –

FERRYMAN. Sir!

BASHO. You do not seek enlightenment.

FERRYMAN. But for Wang? This is the boy who was left by the river.

BASHO (*not remembering*). Left by the river . . . ?

TWO KEEPERS *jump out of the darkness.*

SECOND KEEPER. Ha!

FIRST KEEPER. Ho!

SECOND KEEPER. Got you!

FIRST KEEPER. At last!

SECOND KEEPER. Red handed!

FIRST KEEPER. Where's the fish?

SECOND KEEPER (*going to search*). In the boat!

FIRST KEEPER (*grabbing* BASHO). What's this?

SECOND KEEPER. Three! Buyer from town!

BASHO. Leave me alone!

FERRYMAN. Sirs this is Basho the poet.

BASHO. My arm!

FIRST KEEPER. Where's the fish?

SECOND KEEPER. In the bush.

FIRST KEEPER. I'll arm you!

FERRYMAN. Sirs this is the poet from our village. (*To* BASHO.) Reverend sir don't be angry. They were boys when you left.

SECOND KEEPER. Is he a poet? Throw him in the water and see if he shouts alas!

BASHO. At the moment of enlightenment
      The devil springs
      What is knowledge
      Except that the world is evil!

The landowner's made me a judge. If ruffians like you protect the law – it's time I came back.

The TWO KEEPERS *go a little to one side.*

FIRST KEEPER. Poachers don't talk like that.

SECOND KEEPER. There's nothing in the bush.

FIRST KEEPER. No harm in stepping careful.

The TWO KEEPERS *go back to the others.*

FIRST KEEPER. Sir, we're sorry we frightened you.

BASHO. My arm!

SECOND KEEPER. There are a lot of bad people in these parts.

FIRST KEEPER. In the dark – we can't take risks. The floods are bad. Every harvest is spoiled. The young men run off to the swamps and turn into bandits and poachers.

BASHO. It's almost broken!

SECOND KEEPER. We try to do our duty and carry out the will of heaven, as it says in our oath.

FIRST KEEPER. Not easy these days. A judge will understand.

SECOND KEEPER (*picks up the rod from the ground*). What's . . .! A fishing rod!

WANG. Walking stick. I cut it for the poet. His is worn out.

FIRST KEEPER. So! We meet a poet and a saint all in one night!

FERRYMAN. We heard the bell. So late – we knew it would be urgent. So we hurried.

BASHO. Take me home.

The TWO KEEPERS *watch* WANG *and the* FERRYMAN *help* BASHO *into the boat.*

Three

The village burial hills. Refugees camp among the gravestones. They are near the limits of exhaustion. They wear rags. On the ground : bundles, and a cooking pot over a dead fire.

FERRYMAN, *his* WIFE, LU (*a young girl*), PU-TOI (*a young farmer*), KUNG-TU (*a middle-aged shopkeeper*), *an* OLD MAN *and an* OLD WOMAN.

> *Quiet.*

OLD MAN. It's six days.

OLD WOMAN. The flood should have gone down.

OLD MAN. It always goes after six days.

OLD WOMAN. Even four.

OLD MAN (*cries*). That's all the rice we could bring. No one could help us.

OLD WOMAN. The landowner won't let us starve, brother.

> *The* OLD WOMAN *beckons the* FERRYMAN *to one side.*

OLD MAN. All this water.

PU-TOI. That'll take days to go down.

OLD WOMAN (*aside to* FERRYMAN). Did you get the rice?

FERRYMAN (*shakes his head*). I have to steal it from our bundle in the night. Wang was awake.

OLD WOMAN. You promised.

OLD MAN. The water's been on the edge of Kan's grave six days. Just by the little hole. Like a cat waiting to pounce.

OLD WOMAN. We'll starve.

FERRYMAN. We're all hungry.

OLD WOMAN. Our rice won't last two days.

FERRYMAN. I'll try tonight. Wang would be angry if he knew I'm feeding you. His mother's weak, she needs the rice . . .

OLD WOMAN. See my wrists! So thin.

FERRYMAN. He sleeps with the bundle by his head. Please – don't cry, my dear. I'll try.

LU. We shouldn't camp out here on the graves. I have a bad dream.

PU-TOI. This is the only high land.

WANG. There's the landowner's hill!

OLD WOMAN. What d'you dream?

LU. I'm asleep on our grave. I fall in – and there's my house! The room, the mat, the bowl with the copper rivets, even the broom in the corner. But no window or door. Then a fly comes in through the wall – and I know I'm dead: flies are buzzing in and out of me.

> OLD WOMAN *groans*.

WANG. A boat!

> *They all look off.*

OLD MAN. A boat!

LU. Look!

PU-TOI. They're coming to get us.

FERRYMAN (*to his wife*). Our boat's coming.

OLD MAN. Hush! We mustn't shout.

> *They wave, collect their bundles and form into a queue on the edge of the water.*

OLD WOMAN. Our houses are still under water.

OLD MAN. The landowner will take us in.

PU-TOI. He'll let us sleep in the compound.

VOICES (*off*). Here! Here! Here!

LU. They're all shouting!

OLD MAN (*yells*). No respect for the dead!

PU-TOI. We'd better shout! (*Calls.*) Here! Here!

ALL. Help us! Help us!

LU (*calls*). Old people here!

PU-TOI (*calls*). And a sick woman! Help!

KUNG-TU (*calls*). Us first! Us first!

VOICES (*off, calling*). Us first. Here. A woman's giving birth. Don't let her bear her child in the graveyard. She'll defile the graves. Help! Help!

OLD MAN. No use shouting. They'll go where they want. Kneel. (*He, the* OLD WOMAN *and* LU *kneel.*) Ancestors I thank you for sharing your resting place –

VOICES (*off, calling*). Help. Help.

OLD MAN. We hope we haven't troubled your sleep –

WANG (*calls*). Here!

OLD MAN. My dear wife . . .

OLD WOMAN (*to* OLD MAN). Sh now.

OLD MAN (*in tears*). I've slept by you again with my head on this ground . . .

OLD WOMAN. Hush.

OLD MAN. Every year I pay the interest on your medicine. I don't begrudge it. It's a happiness to me to pay for what you had. Soon I'll be too old to live. I'll come and sleep by your side. What happiness . . .

OLD WOMAN (*weeps silently*). My brother's an old fool. Crying when the boat's coming!

VOICES (*off, calling*). Over here! Us! Help!

PU-TOI (*to* FERRYMAN). It's your boat! (*Calls.*) Us! It's our boat!

FERRYMAN. When the water rose the landowner commandeered it. It's coming here first.

PU-TOI (*calls and waves*). Here! Here!

WANG. Mother. They'll take us to the landowner's compound. We'll build a shelter against the wall. His stone wall's so high the floor's dry even when it rains. If we lived here instead of letting the dead have it –

OLD MAN (*to* FERRYMAN). Keep your boy quiet! We only live a short life. Even at my age after all I've seen it looks short. When we die we're here for ever. What respect is it when we can't house the dead – who need it most! No wonder the flood's lasted six days. Our village! – swearing, lying, profaning, thieving! – no wonder heaven's not kind! You young people – I shudder at what will happen to us when we're dead. You'll throw us out on the fields.

FERRYMAN (*calmingly*). The boat's coming.

OLD MAN. The village saint speaks!

OLD WOMAN (*waving to the boat*). A grandmother blesses you!

PU-TOI (*to* LU). Ask Kung-tu to pay your fare. He sleeps on his bundle at night. Not comfortable – that hard lump in the back.

KUNG-TU. If I had money would I be on this pauper ground? I'd be buried higher up. With trees.

    OLD MAN *and* OLD WOMAN *giggle.*

PU-TOI (*laughs*). Kung-tu scrimps and saves but he has to come and pay his respects with the poor where his ancestors are.

OLD WOMAN (*giggles*). Paupers' graves.

OLD MAN. When he's very rich he'll dig them up –

OLD WOMAN. Dig up the bones!

OLD MAN. – and bury them in rich ground. He can't afford to yet.

OLD WOMAN. The priest would want a lot of money.

OLD MAN. You might need a bishop for that.

    They giggle.

KUNG-TU. I work – and you sit and jeer –

    The others laugh.

Till you're in trouble! Then you know the value of money!

    The TWO KEEPERS *pole in the boat.*
    All the people on the mound bow. The KEEPERS *land the boat on the hill. The* SECOND KEEPER *ties it up to a gravestone. The* OLD MAN *and* OLD WOMAN *come forward.*

OLD WOMAN (*crying as the boat arrives*). Bless them. Bless them. I couldn't have come through another night. At my age you –

FIRST KEEPER. The dead must have thought this lot were ghosts come to haunt them!

SECOND KEEPER. How much?

OLD MAN. We left our money behind.

OLD WOMAN. The flood came so fast. We ran to the graveyard. The water was –! (*Points to her waist.*)

SECOND KEEPER. That bundle.

OLD MAN. It's all we've got. The rest was washed away.

OLD WOMAN (*undoing the bundle*). Two mats, three bowls, chop sticks.

SECOND KEEPER. That!

OLD MAN (*pretending not to understand what the* KEEPER *wants*). This leather belt? It'll last me out. It stays on me because I'm old. Young man on the go like you: snap straight away.

SECOND KEEPER (*bored at the* OLD MAN's *pathetic attempts at evasion*). No, that!

OLD MAN. Take the belt and leave me the padded jacket. At your age you don't know how cruel the wind is. I must keep my jacket.

OLD WOMAN. I share it with my brother at night.

KUNG-TU. They'll go on to the next hill!

OLD WOMAN. Brother?

OLD MAN (*takes coins from the jacket lining*). All I've got. Don't drop it, it's slippery with years of sweat.

The SECOND KEEPER *takes the coins.*

FIRST KEEPER. And the coat.

OLD MAN. No.

SECOND KEEPER. Two fares! We can take a trip round the grave-stones while you think.

KUNG-TU. You old fools! They'll take the lot if we freeze to death!

The OLD MAN *hands over the coat. The* OLD MAN *and* OLD WOMAN *get into the boat.*

OLD MAN. May your ancestors judge.

SECOND KEEPER. Old people fall out of boats like babies falling out of cradles.

OLD WOMAN (*to* OLD MAN). Hush. (*To* SECOND KEEPER.) You'll get old too.

FIRST KEEPER. Too wicked. Our throats'll be cut long before. Don't begrudge us. You've had more out of life than we'll ever get.

SECOND KEEPER (*to* FERRYMAN). For three.

FERRYMAN (*bows*). I know that ferrymen have to live. (*Gestures off.*) Look at the crowd! The boat will be heavy. How many trips? Let Wang and me work our passage.

VOICES (*off, crying*). What's happening? Get in the boat! Help! Be quick!

    KUNG-TU *steps forward.*

KUNG-TU. These fools will argue all day. I've got nothing here. Between us: I'm half-way into a deal. Rape seed left over from my neighbour. Safe in the waterproof jars. The moment the town merchant pays up I'll see you're –

FIRST KEEPER. Did he keep you awake counting coins?

SECOND KEEPER. No – his gold teeth were chattering.

FIRST KEEPER. If this water ever goes down you'll be crawling home with your arse in the mud. We'll be there first – and dig up your floors.

SECOND KEEPER. His face is so blank it could be on the side of a coin.

KUNG-TU. Bandits!

VOICES (*crying, off*). Us! Us! Us! Us! Us! Us!

FIRST KEEPER. Don't call us names. You're not so rich – yet – you can make the laws. Between us: you'll get your money's worth. Think of your mud floors tomorrow. You can't arrest everyone with an ugly face and a spade. We can. (KUNG-TU *hands over a roll of notes.*) Give him the chair!

KUNG-TU. No, no. That sort of show isn't –

SECOND KEEPER. The chair! He paid!

FIRST KEEPER. Respectable people must be respected.

> KUNG-TU *sits uncomfortably in the chair in the middle of the boat.*

Pu-toi, farmer by day, by night fetches and carries for merchants in town. We haven't asked what. But it must pay – at those hours!

> PU-TOI *hands over money and steps silently into the boat.*

(*To* KUNG-TU.) That's how the town merchants get on. They employ deaf and dumb.

LU (*hand out to* KUNG-TU). Please. My money's at –

KUNG-TU. Don't ask me! They've got it! – Ha! They'll pay *you.*

FIRST KEEPER. That sort of brute would hit her with this (*fist*) and drag her behind the graves where your latrine is.

> (FIRST KEEPER *takes the hat from* KUNG-TU.) That pays for her.

> LU *steps into the boat. She's unsure who to thank.*

LU (*to the* KEEPERS). Thank you. (*To the* OLD MAN *and* OLD WOMAN.) Thank you. (*To* KUNG-TU.) Thank you.

FERRYMAN. We have these clothes –

WANG. It's our boat!

FERRYMAN. Quiet.

VOICES (*off, crying*). Help. Help. Quick. The woman's giving birth. The hill's slipping into the mud. The gravestones are falling over.

> *The* WOMAN *is heard in labour. Slowly during the scene the shouting, moaning, and sobbing increase to a climax and then fade into the hum, whimpering and stray cries of a desperate crowd.*

FERRYMAN. – three rice bowls, a cooking pot, a kettle, two mats, a mattress and cover for my wife. She rests her head on my legs. Leave us something to live on.

SECOND KEEPER (*pokes at bundle*). Soiled. Dirty old rubbish.

FIRST KEEPER. That cow's ratsbane will be into everything. Don't touch them.

SECOND KEEPER. Their rags peel off like paint.

KUNG-TU. I've paid for my trip. Let's go! Isn't there anything you want?

FIRST KEEPER. Yes.

WANG. Then what?

FIRST KEEPER. We need consent.

FERRYMAN. What is it?

FIRST KEEPER. The son.

FERRYMAN. My son?

FIRST KEEPER. A proper indenture. Drawn up in a lawyer's office. A form of a loan. You get him back.

KUNG-TU. I did it to help my neighbour who went bankrupt. (*To* FERRYMAN.) Do your boy good. Needs controlling.

FERRYMAN. But who'll work the ferry when I'm old? We invested so much in him. If you take him away our lives have been wasted!

SECOND KEEPER. You'll survive. You have so far.

WANG. We'll live out here on the gravestones. Let the landowner be ashamed!

FERRYMAN. Quiet.

FIRST KEEPER. He couldn't keep quiet at his own funeral.

SECOND KEEPER. Nasty little bastard. Insulting, stealing . . .

VOICES (*off, crying*). Help!

SECOND KEEPER (*shouting off to the crowd*). Tell her if she drops the kid we'll charge the fare.

FERRYMAN (*to* WANG). You owe your life to us. Your mother can't stay here another night. Give her a little time.

WANG. I'm not a slave.

PU-TOI. I am. I slave day and night. We all do. What's it matter if they call us a slave for once? That old woman's not worth taking. She'll be back in a few weeks. Let them stay – they won't have to pay for the trip to the grave-yard.

KUNG-TU. Confucius placed filial piety over all virtues. I shall remove my ancestors. They're not staying in this company.

WANG. He's not my father.

PU-TOI. All the more reason to thank him.

FERRYMAN. A year.

SECOND KEEPER. Ten.

FERRYMAN. No, no. Too long. I won't ask that. We'd never see him again. No not ten years.

OLD MAN. Who knows the wheel of his fate?

WANG. Two years.

FIRST KEEPER. Ten.

WANG. Three. No more. I'm fit. I'll do ten years work in three.

WIFE (*crying and holding* WANG's *hand*). It's wrong to take a young life, but I don't want to die and leave your father without me. (*She strokes his hand.*) Wang forgive me. You men in the boat: four. No more.

VOICES (*off, crying*). Help. Help. We're drowning. The graves are falling into the water.

SECOND KEEPER. Ten.

FERRYMAN (*squats*). It's over. We stay. The water will go down soon.

SECOND KEEPER. Why d'you think we're here? (*Points.*) Look!

LU. That uprooted tree. The water's started to flow.

PU-TOI. Yes! The water's running in white lines!

FIRST KEEPER. Would we waste time collecting you garbage if the water was falling and you could crawl home? The banks higher up have broken! The water will rise!

KUNG-TU. He's right! It's running into the hole by Kan's grave.

OLD WOMAN (*points off*). Look, it's stirring the branches of the trees.

OLD MAN (*trying to see*). My eyes!

OLD WOMAN. There!

LU. I thought they were hands coming out of the water!

OLD MAN. Where?

The shouting increases again, off.

PU-TOI. The whole landscape's moving – running –

KUNG-TU. Pushing the trees and the debris along with it.

The people in the boat suddenly lurch.

OLD MAN. The boat's beginning to move.

OLD WOMAN (*whimpering*). Brother! I'm frightened!

KUNG-TU. Pu-toi, you've got money. Ten years: six to one. Nine: five to two. Lu, you've got money at home. Five years: evens.

PU-TOI (*passes money*). Eight to three.

KUNG-TU. What it is to be young.

VOICES (*off*). Help us!

OLD MAN. Could you accept this bowl?

OLD WOMAN. Brother!

OLD MAN. It's a certainty. (KUNG-TU *takes cup. To the* OLD WOMAN.) It'll help us so much later on.

FIRST KEEPER. Wang, your last chance.

KUNG-TU. If only I hadn't worn my hat! Dressing up for a flood! I get these colds in my head.

FIRST KEEPER. It's wrong to force a bargain in hard times. Nine years. Not a second less.

WANG. No.

FIRST KEEPER. I once saw a herd of cattle outside a slaughter-house shoving to see who got in first.

The SECOND KEEPER *unropes the boat from the gravestone.*

OLD MAN *and*

OLD WOMAN. Goodbye.

PU-TOI (*to* KUNG-TU). It's not over.

The boat goes. FERRYMAN *holds his wife.* WANG *stands a little apart from them, rooted to the spot. The* WIFE *cries quietly.*

FERRYMAN. Don't cry my dear. We knew our lives would end. We have each other. Wang, swim.

WANG. No.

FERRYMAN. What is the use? Swim!

WANG. I'll stay.

FERRYMAN. These aren't your graves! You have no ancestors! Swim! Leave us together.

WIFE. If only . . .

WANG. I'm not a slave!

FERRYMAN. Swim! I order you!

WANG. The water will go down.

FERRYMAN. It's rising.

VOICES (*crying off*). Help. Help. The woman has given birth! I'm up to my neck in mud. Bodies are being washed out of the ground. The dead are floating round us. The landscape is moving.

FERRYMAN. You owe us nothing. We're not your parents. I was wrong to ask. I took you from the water: now you can swim!

WIFE. If only . . . If only . . .

WANG. Mother!

FERRYMAN. She's too weak to answer!

WANG (*stands stiffly, rooted to the spot. Yells*). Buy me! Buy me! Buy me!

The FERRYMAN *embraces his wife with one hand, reaches with the other towards* WANG *and then reaches it up as if holding off the sky. He cries. His wife embraces him.*

FERRYMAN. We're going to be saved! Saved!

WIFE. Our son. He saves us.

FERRYMAN. Our son.

WANG (*as before, yelling desperately*). Buy me! Buy me! Buy me!

Four

Another part of the river and the bank. An abandoned child.

BASHO *comes on and glances briefly. Calls back off-stage left.*

BASHO. It's quiet by the river. Here, in the shade of this tree. Fetch my court list from the carriage.

> BASHO *lays his cushion on the ground, sits, unfolds his travelling desk and writes.*

> Bamboos flutter by the moorhen's nest
> Army banners!
> She does not ask
> Where the river goes
> Nor where the arrow flies

Slight pause. BASHO *glances surreptitiously off left and then writes again, slightly raising his voice so that it can be overheard by someone waiting quite near.*

> The poet's brush
> Made from hair tugged from his beard
> Is dipped in black ink
> He writes
> The ink drains on the page
> The brush turns grey

(*Calls left.*) Wang.

> WANG *comes on. He wears a servant's coat.*

Thank you. (*He takes the court list from* WANG. *Reads it.*) I called for water in the night. You were not there.
WANG. I visited my home.
BASHO. Is your mother well?
WANG. Better.

BASHO. You took her more food.

WANG. Yes.

BASHO. And the man you call father?

WANG. He's glad my mother's better.

BASHO (*reads the court list*). Mrs Su-tan broke her neighbour's arm because she stole her thatch – and sang at night. The neighbour came round, screamed in the street and threw stones through Su-tan's door. Su-tan's husband held the neighbour's broken arm while Su-tan broke the fingers on it. Such acts of human nature are so bestial, the times so dark, that it is not possible to see what we can do to help ourselves or change the times. They say your father is good.

WANG. He shelters travellers at home when they're too poor for the inn. He lets the sick cross for nothing, even in famine. He saved me from the river.

BASHO. A tree has one good fruit on it. Heaven smiled when he was born. You were there when I went to seek enlightenment. You were there again when I found it. The landowner gave you to me for a servant. We call the plans of heaven coincidence. Your nine years end today.

WANG *is silent.*

> The arm of the woman who sang at night
> Was broken by angry neighbours
> She stands in my court
> And I wonder:
> Why do the poor sing?

Wang, I have taught you to write and how to study the classics. Your hands are pale from holding a pen. You stand behind my chair in court. You sit by the wall while poets sing to the koto. How can you work in the fields – or the shops? You can't live on the ferry. That supports two at most. Stay in my house. (*Pause.*) No gratitude?

WANG. Thank you. I can't stay.

BASHO (*writes*).

No bird flies as fast as the arrow
No fruit falls as straight as the axe
No man escapes his end
Or the road to it

Not as a servant the master's so used to he treats him as a friend in order to keep him as a servant. What torments you? The past? Even your parents couldn't say you were their child. So many babies are left by the river. How could they know even the day they left you? All trace is gone.

WANG. I don't ask those questions. It would be foolish.

BASHO. Then stay and seek peace.

WANG. No.

BASHO. The father first learns he has spoiled his child when his child tells him. Why did the woman break her neighbour's fingers? You forget that your eyes can ache with cold, the grit that comes in your mouth when you starve, the thin dirt on the rice bowl, filth decaying in corners, the smell of unwashed clothes. You can be too tired to clean and too hopeless to think. Such people are always lost, even at home. One day you may scream on the street and break your neighbour's bones. Ignorance destroys from within. Nothing is seen, but one day you collapse – mind and body.

I turned away from this world. I administer law for the good of heaven not the good of man. There's no help I can give to those so poor they can only seek self. They must live in ignorance – just as a stone must fall. You shared my house for nine years. If I could care for anything in this world it would be you. Stay.

WANG. No.

BASHO. Madmen take pleasure in destroying themselves.

WANG (*he has already seen the child upstage. He points*). Look, a child left by the river.

BASHO *turns his head to look.*

BASHO. Every day now. More and more. A whole generation left by the river. Dead?

WANG. No. It stirred a moment ago. Take it.

BASHO. How strange. For a moment I see into heaven. Once before – a child by the river. I left it to seek enlightenment. Now this child. What should we seek this time? Always enlightenment. Heaven has done this. You take the child. Live with it in my house. Then you will find the way.

WANG. There's no argument I can use. I've waited behind you in court and heard the innocent and the guilty plead. Living women with fingers twisting like ghosts, old men staring like lost children, murderers who laughed over corpses. I marvelled at them as they talked. How subtle the human mind is. Each told the truth in his way, even against himself. How strange their lives, the stories of the little things that shaped them. You can go for a walk, and come back another man. But you talk of the way as if it was laid down in an iron map. You must leave the road from time to time – to ask if it's the right road you're on. Take the child.

BASHO. If you had asked yesterday –

WANG. It's easy for you.

BASHO. – I might have listened –

WANG. You have a house! Food! Take it!

BASHO. – and made this mistake. Heaven has chosen to show me how to save you. The child alone: no.

WANG. I'll take it to the temple.

BASHO. The ordinance is against that! The priests take too many infants. The old suffer. The pediment is crumbling. When the temple is neglected, its image no longer works with the people. Then no infants are taken in! (*He points to the stool, desk, and umbrella.*) Bring these things to my carriage.

BASHO *goes out.*

WANG. How still! You face the sky. Your eyes are closed and your life is decided. (*He sits by the child and touches it.*) My father said

there were curlews once – and one called. (*He picks up the child.*)
How light. No don't smile. I must put you down. (*Still holds the child.*) You're fit and strong. You won't die.

A WOMAN *comes in, looking at* WANG. *She stops abruptly.*

WOMAN. O have I taken the wrong way? I must find the ferry.
(*She turns to go.*)

WANG. Look, a child left by the river. Often they have no limbs or they're blind. This is a fine child.

WOMAN (*looks at the child from where she stands*). Is it? I must get to the ferry.

WANG. Take it.

WOMAN. No, no.

WANG. It was left to die. Women know how to care for a child –

WOMAN. My husband is waiting.

WANG. It will die!

WOMAN. I must find the ferry –

WANG. Its hands are clutching the cover – as if it was the edge of a cliff or the side of a plate. Take it!

WOMAN (*going*). No! You!

WANG. Its eyes opened! When you spoke! Look!

WOMAN. You woke it!

WANG. Why? (*He goes with the child to the* WOMAN.) Why?

WOMAN. My husband is waiting for –

WANG. Why?

WOMAN. I'll report you to the –

WANG. Bitch! (*Hits her face.*) It could have died!

WOMAN. No. Someone would find it. You found it.

WANG. Take it!

WOMAN. No! My husband –

WANG. Your child!

WOMAN (*angrily*). You hit me! Will that make me take it? My husband hit me harder to get rid of it! It was torn from me! You think – one hit and you change the world?

WANG. It could die!

WOMAN. It was meant to die!

WANG. No!

WOMAN (*angrily*). What can I do? Our other children – it steals their food. Their stomachs are swollen. Have you heard them cry? (*She points to the child.*) This was like a disease in our house! O let me go!

WANG. No! No!

WOMAN (*sits wearily: speaks flatly, almost calmly and reasonably*). More anger . . . What is the use? You see how we live. I thought I'd jump in the river. Drown with it. But my husband – my children – I've done what I can. What more? You tell me what more there is. (*Slight pause. Still calm.*) I came back to give him water. Stupid. When I saw you holding him I was jealous. I wanted to shout 'My child!' and take him away. I was glad. You were clean and fed. The child had been lucky at last. He'll serve in a good house. (*She touches her face.*) My face is red where you hit it. I'll tell my husband I cried. (*Stands.*) I must go or he'll be suspicious.

WANG. I can't keep the child.

WOMAN. You have a dry roof! I can see that.

WANG. You don't understand.

WOMAN. And look at your coat! You have everything. Yet you ask me to take the child! I have nothing – I must even give the child away. You'll find him a corner in the house. You have a good face. You come from a good family. (*She becomes almost happy.*) My child will have a good life. Better than we could have given it. You'll teach it to be polite and bow –

WANG. This isn't the first child you've left.

WOMAN. No.

WANG. How many?

WOMAN. What's the use?

WANG. When did it start?

WOMAN. I don't think of them.

WANG. How long ago?

WOMAN. I don't know.

WANG. How did you make yourself –? Ha! it's a habit now! But the first one.

WOMAN. I didn't choose my life. These things happened to me. I don't ask anymore. I'm an animal.

WANG. You don't know what I . . . I was going away . . . Tell me . . . tell me . . . how I should live?

WOMAN (*stares at him in fear*). I didn't mean any harm.

WANG. Take this! (*He gives her* BASHO's *equipment*.) And this. All of it.

WOMAN. No! I'd –

WANG. For the child!

WOMAN. Yes. Yes. Then it's a transaction. A part of the law. I haven't left my child. I sold him. Into care. Thank you. (*She holds* BASHO's *things. Now that the child has been sold and not left to be found her self-respect comes back.*) Now – I'm a good woman and you're a good man. Tell him when he grows up to think well of people. Say I came back. Remember. I only left when I saw he was in good hands. Thank you. Goodbye, goodbye.

The WOMAN *hurries out left.* WANG *holds the child.*

WANG. Nine years – finished! I can go! Tonight! Through the door. Free. (*He stares at the child.*) What is trouble? – you don't know! Nothing changes here. I get up – I do the same things and pretend they're different. You don't even have to walk. You've been lying there for hundreds of years. I trip over you every time I come out of the door!

Why should I pick you up? Why do I hold you? You're as big as a mountain. My back's broken. I live in his house so that you have a house? Give you the things I run away from? Nine years! I planned – no, schemed, plotted, dreamt! And now you're drowning me in the river? No! No! No! No! No!

He puts the child down.

How many babies are left to die by the river? How many? For how many centuries? Left! – Rot! Eaten! Drowned! Sold! All waste! How many? Till when? All men are torn from their mother's womb: that is the law of nature. All men are torn from their mother's arms: that is the law of men! Is this all? – one little gush of sweetness and I pick up a child? Who picks up the rest? How can I hold my arms wide enough to hold them all? Feed them? Care for them? All of them? Must the whole world lie by this river like a corpse?

He snatches the child from the ground. Holds it up high to show it the river.

Look! You already have a face! Look at yourself in the river! You see your face in the mud? Look! Look! The river is a corpse that goes on devouring even when it's dead! Towns fall in! Whole generations! Their bones pile up under the bridges! You throw us in the river! Your arms are too strong! They crush me like a prison!

He puts the child down.

There's a child! (*Pointing at other imaginary children.*) There! There! There! There! You fight them off with your little hands. There! There! You little killer!

He snatches the child from the ground.

If there was a gun in your hand you'd pull it! You would kill! And you smile! Like a god playing games! As if men were your toys!
No!

As he hurls the child far out into the river he holds a corner of the white sheet in his hand and it unravels, catches the wind and falls to hang from his hand.

The world is shivering – there! Who will speak?

Five

Swamp.
A hand bell rung.
A group of thieves sorting loot. TIGER *and* KAKA *are thin young men.*
TIGER's *right arm ends in a stump.* TOR-QUO *is an older and heavier*
man. SHEOUL *is a dark-haired girl.*

TIGER (*ringing*). Bell.
SHEOUL. All right.
TIGER (*ringing*). Bell. Bell.
KAKA. Mat. Torn. Not bad.
TIGER. Cap. (*Stops ringing to examine the cap.*) Fur.
SHEOUL. Fur?
TIGER. Moths. Huh! Catch! (*Throws the cap to* KAKA.)

> TOR-QUO *is upstage on the look out.*

TOR-QUO. Kaka got a knife.
KAKA. It's in. Catch. (*Throws the cap to* SHEOUL.)
TIGER (*ringing*). Bell.
SHEOUL (*picking at fur*). Fox! Lot still left. Brim's gone.
TIGER. Ding, ding. (*Rings.*) Mat. Knife. Fur cap. Good! Huh!

> (*He puts down the bell to distribute the loot.*)

SHEOUL. My cap.
TIGER. Cap – you. Tor-quo – mat.

> KAKA *rings the bell.*
> TIGER *takes bell from* KAKA.

Kaka – knife. Bell – me. (*Taps his chest with his finger.*) Musical.
KAKA (*grabs bell*). My bell! You had the whistle!
TIGER (*springs up*). Huh!
KAKA (*springs up*). Huh!

> TIGER *and* KAKA *fight violently.*

SHEOUL (*indifferently as she works at the hat*). Kill him. Break his leg. Throw him up and break his arm.

TIGER. Ha! Hoo! Grrrraaaaahhhhhhhhhh!

TOR-QUO (*to* SHEOUL). Keep it? – or make it up?

KAKA. Kill!

SHEOUL (*to* TOR-QUO. *Shrugs*). Pair of mittens? Tie on with a bit of string.

TIGER. Hah!

TIGER *and* KAKA *stop. They are winded. They squat and face each other, breathing heavily.*

TOR-QUO. What's the food?

KAKA (*quietly*). Death.

TIGER (*quietly*). Murder.

SHEOUL (*indifferently, to* TOR-QUO). When I've finished this hat.

TIGER. Ha! Err! Hoo! Aaaghghghghghghgh!

TIGER *and* KAKA *spring and fight.*

TOR-QUO (*reflectively*). They say you lose your appetite as you get old . . . I'm losing my hair. And my wind. And everything else . . . But I'm still hungry. It's not right . . . Look in the lining.

SHEOUL. Have. Nothing.

TOR-QUO. Found silver once.

SHEOUL. In a hat?

TOR-QUO. Boot. In the top. Dirty old working boot.

SHEOUL. Dress like tramps to trick you.

TIGER *throws* KAKA *on his back –* KAKA *twitches senselessly on the ground.* TIGER *picks up the bell, creeps to* KAKA *with it, holds it in front of* KAKA's *face, grins slyly, waggles his stump playfully at him, pauses, grins, and finally shakes the bell – silence. He stares at the bell for a second, violently shakes it, and then looks inside – the clapper has gone.*

TIGER. Clapper! Clapper!

KAKA *groans in contentment, grasps the clapper in his hand, and rolls over to lie with it under his stomach.* TIGER *rings the bell again. It is still silent.*

TIGER (*kicking* KAKA). Clapper! Clapper! Mine!
TOR-QUO (*sudden warning*). Hup!

The others react, hide the loot and kick KAKA *to his feet.*

SHEOUL (*to* KAKA). One coming.

TIGER *lies in the ditch and pretends he has been attacked. The rest hide.*

TOR-QUO. Past the willow.
TIGER. What's he like?
TOR-QUO. Tramp.
SHEOUL. Boots?
TIGER. Kill. Kill all day today. Heeeeee.

Silence. WANG *comes on. He is dirty. His clothes are newly torn and soiled.* TIGER *groans feebly for help.*
(*Feebly.*) Help.
WANG *sits on the ground, doubles over, and cries.*

WANG. I ran through swamps, crying for seven days. I saw the rich prey on the poor. The poor prey on themselves. An old woman. She wore knitted mittens. Her hands were like a squirrel's paws – holding an empty bowl. She knelt by the pilgrims' path and said: 'Give – heaven will bless you.' What heaven would bless such pilgrims when it hadn't blessed her? Now even the marsh calls help!

WANG *hides his face and cries.* TIGER *sits up and whispers to the others.*

TIGER. Mad. (*He begins to rise in fear.*)
SHEOUL (*whisper*). Try!

TIGER *lies down again.*

TIGER (*feeble groan*). Help.

WANG (*looks up*) . . . Is someone in the swamp?

TIGER. I'm hurt. Thieves. Help me.

WANG. Alone?

TIGER. Yes. (*Tries to rise, groans, falls back.*)

WANG. Did they take much?

TIGER. Everything. But my family will pay you.

WANG. You're rich? You deserve to be robbed!

TIGER. No, no. Poor. God knows! Please. Over here. I'm drowning in the rushes!

WANG (*goes to* TIGER). Poor! – and you let yourself be robbed? That's worse! They take your money – and you offer your life! Then cry: 'Help! – pity the poor!' And someone must save you! Let someone else get blood on their hands – so you can be simple and honest and good! You deserve what you got! (*Knocks* TIGER *out with a stick.*) Learn – and next time know! Or you'll go on paying!

> The other THIEVES *have crept up behind* WANG. *They throw a rope over him and bind and gag him expertly: it takes seconds.*

SHEOUL. Murderer!

TOR-QUO. Pig!

SHEOUL. Hold him!

> KAKA *kneels by* TIGER *and feels his head. Roars with laughter.*

Feel that. Like an egg!

SHEOUL. It's growing.

KAKA (*laughing*). Tiger will kill you.

TOR-QUO (*sighs*). O, he'll make a mess.

KAKA (*laughs*). Tiger jabs eyes out with his stump and strangles with his hand. Hoo. (*He rocks with laughter.*) Windpipe comes out of their mouth: plop!

> SHEOUL *puts out food: crackers, salt, vegetables, water.*

TOR-QUO. Food!

> *They eat.* WANG *lies trussed on the ground.*

SHEOUL (*slaps* KAKA *to get his attention away from* WANG, *and points to* TOR-QUO *as he eats.*) He'll eat it all. Hog!
KARA (*wiping his eyes*). Squeeze – one hand.

> TIGER *groans.*

> (*Giggling.*) Kill.

SHEOUL. Save Tiger some. He'll be roaring all day.

> TIGER *groans and rocks quietly. The others eat.*

TOR-QUO (*eats.*) Good.

> TIGER *groans and twists spasmodically.*

SHEOUL. Takes him time. He's worse in the mornings.
KAKA (*eating and giggling*). Kill.
TOR-QUO. Pass the salt.

> TIGER *sits up. Groans. Sees the others watching him and eating.*

TIGER. Food! Ha! (*Stands.*) Who let me sleep! Thieving bitches! (*Stops. Groans. Feels head. Remembers.*) Aaahhh! (*He sees* WANG.) Aaghghghgh! (*Runs round looking for knife.*) Knife!
KAKA. I said you'd strangle him.
TIGER. Strangle. Stab. Chop. Eat. Ha! Hoo! Eat you and spew you up in your face! (*Feels the bump.*) Head cracked. He killed me!
SHEOUL. Not cracked.
KAKA. It wouldn't show.
TIGER. Ha. Hoo. (*Reaches for food.*) Eat. Stay alive till I chop him! (*Chews frantically.*) Better! Ha!
KAKA. Undo his face. Then we can hear.

> TOR-QUO *snicks* WANG's *gag with a knife.* TIGER *breathes in* WANG's *face.*

TIGER. Haaa! Smell: Tiger. Next-time smell: You! Ha! (*He shows his stump.*) Story. How Tiger lost hand. (*The others sigh quietly.*) Ha! True! (*He sits.*) Town. I live there then. Streets. Houses. White walls. People have clean clothes. Walk in street. Children – hola! (*Imitates children's arms.*) Aahh ... (*Sighs. All the thieves eat.*) Man. Dark eyes. In the corner shop. (*Takes more food.*) My share – you started first. (*Eats.*) Man. Bought and sold. Next – town his. Earth his. Everything goes dry. Cloth on window-sill: dry. Fields: dry. No rain: heaven forget. Ha! (*Kicks* SHEOUL *to get her attention.*) True!

SHEOUL (*eats*). True.

TIGER (*eats*). Man came. My house – sold! Walls, roof, garden, tree. Police pull me out on street. Hm. (*Chews meditatively for a moment. He speaks the next line quietly.*) Then I was quiet – before the prey. Walk to corner shop. Stand in doorway. Humble. Ask: job. Man smiles like little window high up on side of house. Beckons. So – I enter. Kow-tow. Rise. Left hand shuts his mouth. Right hand: on throat. Squeeze. Like a bag of beans. (*He holds his stump up.*) Dead. Then walk down street. Still hold. One hand: throat. Lift him up. One hand. Show. Soldiers run. Neighbours. First son. Second son. Number one wife. Number two wife. Third son. Pull. Push. Shout: Let go! I hold him up. One hand. Show. Off to court house. Judge says question: 'Have you murdered?' Hold up corpse. Show. Judge tells soldiers: 'He let's go – or chop!' Hold corpse up! High! Show! Chop! Corpse falls. Hand still on throat. Judge saw. (*Smiles at* WANG.) Ho! Tiger! (*Chews.*) Yum. Ah. Appetite come back! Ha!

WANG (*sneers*). Are you this rabble's leader?

TIGER. Ha!

WANG. There's no look out.

TIGER. Ha! (*He gets up and kicks* TOR-QUO.) Look out! Look out! Eat like pig! Look out! Ha! Fool!

TOR-QUO. I was hungry.

SHEOUL. We could have been killed.

WANG. And I haven't been searched.

TIGER (*to* KAKA). You! Search! Always! Permanent order! (*Points to* TOR-QUO.) You: kill! (*To* KAKA.) Kill! (*Waves at them all.*) Massacre!

> KAKA *and* SHEOUL *search* WANG.

SHEOUL. Nothing.

KAKA. Trousers. Jacket. Nothing.

SHEOUL. Paper.

> SHEOUL *takes* BASHO's *sheets of poems from* WANG's *pocket. The thieves stare at the papers in silence.* TIGER *walks towards them. Stops. Doesn't take the papers. They try to decipher them.*

TIGER. Tor-quo.

> TOR-QUO *comes down. He tries to decipher the papers.*

TOR-QUO. 'Flutter' . . . 'Banners.'

TIGER. Government. Official.

TOR-QUO. '. . . the arrow flies . . .'

SHEOUL (*after a silence*). Shall I undo his rope? . . . A little?

TOR-QUO. 'No man escapes his end.'

TIGER (*to* TOR-QUO). Ha!

TOR-QUO (*reads*). 'Women . . . in court.'

> *They suddenly panic.*

KAKA. A message from the emperor!

KAKA. Declaration of war!

TOR-QUO. Warrant to chop!

TIGER (*backs. Trying to control them*). We don't know! (*After a silence.*) Sir, we don't rob rich – only poor. The emperor comes on foot –

KAKA. As long as he's not in disguise.

TIGER. – and we don't hurt! We respect uniform.

TOR-QUO. And clean face.

SHEOUL. Good people. Only rob poor. To live.

TIGER. Emperor keeps people like this!

He makes a gesture with his right arm. He stares at WANG *for a response.* TOR-QUO *and* KAKA *stare perplexedly at* TIGER. SHEOUL *nudges him.* TIGER *changes the gesture to his left hand : a thumb holding something down. The others sigh with relief.*

Emperor to look on us as helpers. If advisers tell him true.

SHEOUL (*looks at poem. Cries*). It's a pardon for poor criminals.

TIGER (*to* WANG). What does papers say?

WANG. Undo this rope.

> *The* THIEVES *look at each other uncertainly.* TIGER *cuts the rope.* WANG *sits up.*

Sit. (*They hesitate, then sit in a circle facing* WANG. WANG *picks up two stones.*) Two stones. Hard. Dry. No moss. I strike – thus! (*He strikes them.*) A spark! We have met – I will tell the truth. (*The thieves glance away from him and then look back.*) The emperor didn't send me. If the soldiers caught me they'd cook me and eat me. I came to the swamp to find a band of thieves. When I found them I'd join them.

TIGER (*stands swiftly, refuses*). No!

WANG. I won't join you. You're fleas under an elephant's tail.

TIGER. Ha!

WANG. What have you got today?

TIGER. Bell. (*Rings it. It is silent.*) Good brass.

KAKA. . . . Hat.

TIGER. Fur!

SHEOUL. Knife.

> TIGER *hits* KAKA, KAKA *gives him the clapper.*

TOR-QUO. Mat.

SHEOUL. Old woman's mat. Didn't she screech. Held on the end till it tore.

TIGER (*strikes clapper on the side of the bell. It rings false – he is holding it against his chest with his stump*). Bell. We eat. No one catched us.

WANG. You were brave when you taught the judge to see. Now you're blinder than the judge. You have the bravery of a child: when it's angry it does anything. (*The others rise threateningly. He bows.*) Forgive my seeming rudeness. I was the servant of a great thief. He covered his floors, walls, ceilings with loot. It filled his attics and cellars. It grew in his garden. There was so much loot he built storehouses.

THE REST. Ah!

WANG. He carried it on his back. In his pockets. Other thieves guarded his loot – he paid them in loot. His hands were clean. He never raised his fist. Not even his voice. He prayed for those he sent to death. Gave money to orphans and widows. It became the meaning of ambition to follow him.

SHEOUL. That is a great thief!

WANG. I haven't told you how great yet. He had a great servant. (*He takes a bowl of water.*) This. (*He empties the bowl of water.*)

SHEOUL. Careful!

KAKA. Water!

WANG. Every year this servant raids the land. Digs up the dead to steal the coins from their mouths. Eats the fields. Strips trees. Takes men's lives. Then it's the day of judgement every day! – even when it goes back to sleep in its lair its breath stands in the fields like a white mist. What does it take: hope. What does it give: mud, to bury all things. And the people stand in their ruined fields like ghosts. They might as well be buried in them.

TOR-QUO. But the thief you worked for –

WANG. Lives on a hill. (*To* SHEOUL.) You are the poor woman. I am the thief my master. Tiger is the river. The river rises.

TIGER. Ha! Hoooooo!

WANG. I sit and smile on my hill. Where d'you run for protection?

SHEOUL *runs away from* TIGER *to* WANG. *She brings the bundle of loot.*

I smile at the poor and weep at the flood.

SHEOUL *sits by* WANG. *He steals the bundle.*

As I weep the waters go down.

TIGER (*sits*). Ha.

WANG (*to* SHEOUL). Go home. Praise heaven.

SHEOUL *goes. She misses the bundle and comes back.*

SHEOUL. My hat!

TIGER. My chop stick!

KAKA. My knife!

TOR-QUO. My mat!

WANG. Mine. You pay for protection.

KAKA. . . . Why don't . . . the people . . . build a wall round the river? . . . Then they don't need your protection.

WANG. Tor-quo, you are my soldier! Arrest that man.

TOR-QUO (*goes to* KAKA). Sir!

WANG. And hang him.

KAKA. Why?

WANG. You stole from the woman.

KAKA. What!

WANG. Her innocence.

TIGER. Ha . . .

WANG. You see how well the landowner works. Everyman must open his mouth and drink to live. He uses the means by which men live to fill them with ignorance. They live by being condemned to death. (*Picks up a poem. As he reads the house lights come up.*) It says:

> The great thief
> Like little thieves
> Works in darkness
>
> The poor are ignorant
> They live in darkness
> What is enlightenment?
> Understanding who is the thief
> And what is the great light

PART TWO

Six

The FERRYMAN's *house by the river. Night. The* FERRYMAN *stands in the middle of the room. His* WIFE *sits in a chair with a cover over her knees. They stare at the door and listen intently.*

WIFE (*whispering*). The path.

> *Silence. A knock. The* FERRYMAN *looks at his* WIFE.

FERRYMAN (*whispers*). He wouldn't knock.

> *Another knock.*

SOLDIER (*off*). Open.

> *The* FERRYMAN *opens the door. The* FIRST SOLDIER *comes in. The* FERRYMAN *bows.* BASHO *follows the* FIRST SOLDIER *in. The* FERRYMAN *deepens his bow.*

FERRYMAN. Sir . . .

> BASHO *looks round.*

FIRST SOLDIER (*points*). The mother, sir.
FERRYMAN. Does the reverend gentleman . . . ?

> *The* FIRST SOLDIER *starts to search the room. He is casual, polite but thorough. The others pay no attention to him: they are used to soldiers searching. Everything in the room is grey except for the clothes of* BASHO *and the* SOLDIER: *they are a little brighter.*

BASHO. It's late.
FERRYMAN. My wife was unwell. It's better if she sits. If the reverend gentleman permits . . . (*The* FERRYMAN *gives his* WIFE *a bowl of water. She drinks.*)

BASHO. Last year your son's head was worth two hundred dollars. Now it's a thousand.

FIRST SOLDIER (*going behind* WIFE, *politely and routinely*.) Excuse me.

The WIFE *stands, holding the cover round her legs.* BASHO *and the* FERRYMAN *pay no attention. They go on talking.*

BASHO. Did he talk of me much?

FERRYMAN. You were kind to him.

BASHO. He only talked of you when I asked. He changed.

FERRYMAN. A child grows up. They ask so many questions. Then one day they're quiet. They start to think.

BASHO. What about? Did he say?

FERRYMAN. No. He sat on the bank and stared at the water. I didn't speak to him then. I was jealous of the silence.

The FIRST SOLDIER *finishes searching. He stands by the door with his hands behind his back and faces the room.*

BASHO. Were you wrong to take him from the river?

FERRYMAN (*carefully*). It was long ago.

BASHO. Would you do it again?

FERRYMAN (*carefully*). I regret what he's become. He gave us happiness when he was young.

BASHO. Where did he sleep?

FERRYMAN. That was his corner.

BASHO. I've brought your wife this.

FERRYMAN (*bows*). Sir.

BASHO. The merchant Kung-tu put his neighbour's cart up for sale. His neighbour owed for last year's seed. Then the money was thrown through the neighbour's door. Tied to a stone. But you've heard this from your passengers.

FERRYMAN. The reverend sir is right: people talk on the water. They like to tell what they think is the truth. At first I listened. I learned that my mother had been unfaithful to my father – and my breath smelt. Then I stopped listening.

BASHO. The people are the emperor's eyes and ears. The judge is his tongue. Commit to memory all that is said in your boat. Bring it to me. You may come to my house at any time. Help me to be a good judge.

FERRYMAN. The reverend sir is renowned.

BASHO. There is a small payment.

FERRYMAN. We will do our duty. As it could lead to the death of our son we should not be paid.

FIRST SOLDIER. Hh!

BASHO. Then you're not poor. Your son will cause great mischief. A few will benefit by a brief happiness. A few wrongs will be righted. Anyone can do that. But those who stand the river on end drown the country. Do not be misled. Better to stop him now. That is hard but true.

> *The* FERRYMAN *bows.* BASHO *goes. The* FIRST SOLDIER *steps forward one pace. He speaks calmly and quietly, almost courteously, almost like an uncle musing over his pipe.*

FIRST SOLDIER. You people are doormats. You wait in the doorway. The street shit is rubbed in till a hole's worn in your centre. The dust collects in it like a puddle. When you're kicked out of the way, you're kicked back. Lift you up, and the dust pours out. Doormats. And soldiers worth fifty of you are dead. They didn't ask to fight for you. They don't know your names. You don't know theirs. The unknown soldiers fighting for the unknown citizens. How I rejoice when a bullet goes astray through your necks. Then I'm content. I shall watch you.

> *The* FIRST SOLDIER *goes out. He closes the door behind him. The* FERRYMAN *and his* WIFE *are alone. For a moment they talk in artificially high voices.*

WIFE. A whole jar.

FERRYMAN. Best honey.

WIFE. You must find out all you can to help the judge.

FERRYMAN. Yes.

The FERRYMAN *goes to the door, listens, turns back to his* WIFE. *She stares at him in fear.*

(*Whispering urgently.*) He wouldn't come – with the soldiers outside.

WIFE. We shouldn't have told him.

FERRYMAN. He must know.

WIFE. It's better to keep it to ourselves . . .

FERRYMAN. Perhaps it's too dangerous to come.

WIFE. There are old grandmothers who walk like girls. If I'd eaten better and kept warm in the wet winters I'd still look young. I went without food till I was so weak I had to hold on to things to stand. The skin shrivelled on my hands. I was grey so soon. He got bigger and stronger. I heard him running on the bank. Shouting. What luck! – to give my life and see him grow. Then I became his mother – I died in this slow childbirth. He fed me later. But the damage was done. Inside. That couldn't be put. . . (*Remembering* WANG *as a child has made her quietly happy. Now her strength goes again. Her voice becomes flat and mechanical.*) I wanted to live and see him come home from work, hold the arms of my chair – so there was a little jolt – and kiss me. I wanted to teach his wife and scold her a little. Mothers-in-law shouldn't be too easy. I learned from my mother-in-law. She'd be a good girl. One day I'd hold their child. It was a dream. Well.

FERRYMAN. He was a good son.

WIFE. Even that man was fond of him in his way.

FERRYMAN. Basho? – When a guttering candle goes out it stinks.

A hand has come through a loose paper window-pane. It lifts the pane cautiously: outside someone is looking in. The FERRYMAN *points to warn his* WIFE. *He sits. The door opens.* WANG *and* TIGER *come in.*

FERRYMAN. Soldiers! –

WANG. They've gone!

FERRYMAN. Is it safe?

WANG. If we're quick. I've got a look-out. (*He embraces the* WIFE.) Good. Good. Yes. (*Embraces the* FERRYMAN.) Father. Good. Is the boat all right?

FERRYMAN. Yes. I think it –

WIFE. You came. You came.

FERRYMAN. I said he would.

WANG. We need your help.

FERRYMAN. Our help?

WANG. You know what a rifle is? We're arming the villages.

FERRYMAN (*blankly*). A rifle? You have rifles?

WANG. From a merchant. A westerner. A lot. In the swamp. You look surprised! Yes – isn't it good! What did you think we did with our money?

TIGER. Ha! Women! Concubines! Wine!

WANG. We loot the big houses. Raid convoys. Kidnap. Blackmail. Take hostages. Now we're rich we don't count our money in cash. We say: 'How many rifles are we worth?'

FERRYMAN (*blank*). Rifles?

WANG. Yes! For the villages!

FERRYMAN (*confused*). Clothes – food – bedding – medicine. But rifles?

WANG. To fight the landowner. We can take over the villages with rifles.

FERRMAN (*turns in confusion to his* WIFE). He's talking of rifles –

WANG. To take to the villages. In your boat.

His WIFE *stands in front of her chair. The cover is round her legs.*

Then everything follows: Food, clothes, bedding, medicine – and more! Understanding, knowledge –

FERRYMAN. You take from the landowner. Good. We get a half-sack of rice! But understanding, knowledge –

WANG. That is a good question, but –

FERRYMAN (*cutting in angrily*). Will heaven like you so much it works miracles for you?

WANG. We'll build the river banks –

FERRYMAN (*shaking his head*). I don't understand!

WANG. We're poor because there's little to go round. Why? Because the river floods. Why? The mouth is silted. The banks are down. There's no cut-off channel for the spring water –

FERRYMAN (*trying to think*). Why doesn't the landowner build banks? Rifles? Rifles?

WANG. Why should the landowner build banks? He's rich. Why? Because we're poor. Why are we poor? Because we're ignorant. Why ignorant? Because the bank breaks and takes away all we have. We're like cattle who live in the mud. Even when the sun shines the people who live on the bank are afraid. They shake and their faces are white. Fear, flies, disease, famine. The landowner needs to do one thing. Only one. Keep us in ignorance. The river does that for him. So take the river and make it ours! That's why rifles are food and clothes and knowledge!

TIGER (*to* WIFE). Rifles! In swamp! Ha!

WANG. You must take them across the river.

FERRYMAN. Did you get my message?

WANG. Yes.

FERRYMAN. Your mother –

WANG. Yes. The message came.

WIFE. The midwife says – a growth (*touches herself*) – I have only a little more time.

WANG. Is the pain . . . ?

WIFE (*after a slight pause; shakes head*). No.

TIGER *gives a slight grunt.* WANG *turns to the* FERRYMAN.

WANG. You'll help?

FERRYMAN. The soldiers watch us.

WANG. They watch everyone. You're called a saint. They'll trust you more than the rest.

FERRYMAN. Make a boat.

WANG. A new boat would be stopped. Especially at night. Hide the rifles under the boards. We hid the fish.

TIGER (*to the* FERRYMAN). See! We make so much trouble –
enemy brings many soldiers – enemy now strong – *we* get
strong – or chop! (*To* WIFE.) See! Too late to go back! (*Points
to* WANG.) Him – me – everyone: chop! (*To* FERRYMAN.) Ha?

FERRYMAN. No.

WANG. Then you're an enemy.

FERRYMAN. No.

WANG. Yes! If you don't help now, you'll make other mistakes!
Listen to their arguments too long. Hesitate. Be patient at the
wrong time. One day people like you will take us to be shot!

FERRYMAN. No. I want to do what is good. Wang – help the poor.
Give them . . . but if I was caught (*He looks at his* WIFE.) . . .
she . . .

WANG. I know.

TIGER (*picks up the jar, suddenly suspicious*). Honey!

FERRYMAN. Basho. My wife. He told me to spy. A sort of bribe.

WANG. Even better! (*To* TIGER.) We'll give him information to
pass on. Nothing to cause real damage. (*To the* FERRYMAN.)
He'll trust you and your boat won't be stopped. (*Slight silence.*)
You picked me up and took me home. A good man! The good
ferryman! The saint who lives by the river! Do the birds sing
when you come through your door? It's not easy to do good.
You pick up one child. What about the tenth child? Or the
hundredth child? You leave them to rot! Drown them with
your holy hands.

The WIFE *sits.*

FERRYMAN. It was hard to bring you up to –

WANG. You saints who crucify the world so that you can be good!
You keep us in dirt and ignorance! Force us into the mud with
your dirty morality! You are the scourge of the –. No, no, I
must understand. I must be patient. I'm sorry. – Father. (*He
takes the* FERRYMAN *aside.*) She'll die *soon* – your message said –

FERRYMAN. Wang!

WANG. It's true!

FERRYMAN (*fiercely, quietly angry*). But not dragged out by her hair – thrown into a ring of soldiers with knives. I love her!

WANG. But you took her life!

FERRYMAN. No!

WANG. When you took me from the river! You starved her – crippled her – she's dying now because you took –

FERRYMAN. I love her!

WANG. And you killed her!

FERRYMAN. Aieeeeeeeeee!

WANG. O we are little men! We love – and think that changes the world! I have done nothing that you have not done before!

FERRYMAN. Aieeee!

A moment's silence.

WIFE. Yes, I will die. But you mustn't speak to your father like that. The night he brought you home I shut the door. He sat with you in the boat. I said: 'Good, let him be cold.' He put up the little canvas awning. It flapped in the wind. You started to cry so he cried too. Sat in the boat and cried with you. You were a greedy child. Always after more. We gave it – when we could. You are right, that's why I've lived like a cripple and can't fight this sickness. And now – strange – you come over the river – hiding for your life – and ask for more – not with a gun – but something stronger – even stronger – as you've shown. Father, do what he wants.

FERRYMAN. Yes. If you'd drowned in the river someone else would have been asked the same question. I'll take the rifles. I've loved and hated. The river kept me alive and almost killed me. Now it will carry the rifles. I shall be careful. Your mother will be safe.

WANG. So we go on. The rifles will come in threes. If anything goes wrong we won't lose many. Leave them out in the boat. Come in the house. Don't look. They'll be taken away. We'll warn you each time we're coming. It'll be finished in six weeks.

WIFE (*to* WANG). Here. Let me hold you. (*She holds* WANG *against her, strokes him and makes soothing noises as if he were a child.*) There. There. My child.

TIGER *talks excitedly to the* FERRYMAN *at one side.*

TIGER. Once a judge said: 'Execute.' (*Points at himself.*) Chop! I escape? How?

FERRYMAN (*blankly*). What?

TIGER. Story! True. Listen. Soldiers take me to town. More people to see chop! Walk all day. Hot. Dust. Girls stare. Children. (*Waves arms like a child.*)

WIFE (*nursing* WANG). There. There. It will be all right. (*She cries quietly as she rocks him.*)

WANG. Mother.

TIGER. Riot in town! Barracks upside down! Drink on sale. Soldiers give me to jailer. True! (*Nudges the* FERRYMAN.)

FERRYMAN (*half listening*). Yes.

WIFE (*nursing* WANG *against her breast. Rocking and crying quietly*). This is our last time. Thank you. Thank you.

WANG. Thank you.

TIGER. Jailer takes me to cell. Iron chain on wall. Ring. Bolt. I whimper like christian. Clasp hands under shawl – hold out to pray – so! Jailer knows nothing. Heaven smiles. Jailer puts ring round right arm. Click. Goes out. Wait. Soldiers drunk. Doors open. Night. Slip arm through ring: hup! Walk home.

FERRYMAN. Home?

TIGER (*giggles*). Ha! They say: 'Tiger has one hand but fights with ten.'

WANG *leaves the* WIFE.

WANG. We must go.

TIGER. God has ten hands. Each side. Good for miracles. But never escape.

WANG (*angrily to* TIGER). Quickly.

WANG *goes out.*

TIGER. Life good. Wise say: 'Give hand in friendship.' Tiger raise stump: Great Friend!

> TIGER *hurries off after him.*

WIFE. Help me to lie down.

Seven

Roadside between the villages. The WOMAN *from Scene Four sits on the ground with her* HUSBAND. *She wears a stone cangue closed with a bolt. Down left, the* FIRST WATER SELLER. *He has a water can, cups, a towel and a picture of snow falling on a mountain. The* SECOND SOLDIER *sits on guard at the back.*

FIRST WATER SELLER. No one will buy anything! If you'd done one good deed – someone would come! The judge was right! You're an evil woman!

> *The* WOMAN *groans to quieten the* WATER SELLER.

I've sat here an hour! Not one cup!

HUSBAND. Is it still morning?

FIRST WATER SELLER. Soldier, you're thirsty.

SECOND SOLDIER. Your wife pisses in it to make it go further.

> *The* FIRST WATER SELLER *doesn't bother to defend himself. The* SECOND WATER SELLER *comes on. He carries a picture of a temple.*

FIRST WATER SELLER. Hey! Clear off!

SECOND WATER SELLER. The road's wide enough for two.

FIRST WATER SELLER. I got them first!

SECOND WATER SELLER (*unloading his equipment*). Pure water!

FIRST WATER SELLER. Clear off! I was here when you were still snoring on top of your woman.

SECOND WATER SELLER. Pure water! Water from the temple well!

FIRST WATER SELLER (*to* SECOND SOLDIER). Arrest him! Hey! Send him off!

SECOND SOLDIER. No law against two.

FIRST WATER SELLER. I was here first!

SECOND SOLDIER. You won't be here last!

FIRST WATER SELLER. It's not justice! He's taking my livelihood! Get out! – or I'll chuck your water out!

SECOND WATER SELLER. Soldier, this tradesman is threatening a disturbance. (*Points to the* WOMAN *and her* HUSBAND.) I've got witnesses.

FIRST WATER SELLER. I'll break your cups! They can witness that!

SECOND SOLDIER. I'll break your heads!

FIRST WATER SELLER. You won't sell water. You'll float in it.

SECOND SOLDIER. A war would be better than rotting here. You're all thieves. I'd hang the lot. I was in a garrison town. Coloured lights in the evenings. The whorehouses had orchestras. Fried rice on the stalls. We had the girls under the trees by the park in the evenings. Then they dragged us here. And you expect us to feel sorry you're –

The WATER SELLERS *see something off stage. They start to call their wares.*

FIRST WATER SELLER.
Water! Sparkling water!
The moon shone on the snow
As it fell on the muses' mountain
I melted the snow at dawn
Sparkling water!
Who drinks speaks truth!

SECOND WATER SELLER.
Water! Pure water!
From the temple well
Of the goddess of truth
I drew it
From the dark cool well
Who drinks sees truth!

The WATER SELLERS *bang their cups on their cans.* TIGER *and* WANG *come on left. They are disguised as priests.*

SECOND WATER SELLER (*aside to the* WOMAN, *pointing to her* HUSBAND, *who is asleep*). Get grandad going! If it's a good sale it'll be worth your while!

FIRST WATER SELLER (*groans*). Ugh, priests! (*Aside to the* WOMAN.) Make the best of it. Put on a good show. I'll give you two cups.

The WOMAN *shakes her husband awake.*

HUSBAND. Water . . . water . . . water . . .

FIRST WATER SELLER. The woman's suffered all her life. A terrible home! They beat her not the mule! The whole village pities her! 'Poor woman,' they say, 'never out of trouble.'

SECOND WATER SELLER. Holy fathers, the woman has this sick husband. Their sons are ungrateful. They ran away as soon as they could. Thirst has tormented her three days. Buy her a little water!

WOMAN (*crying*). The court said I was guilty . . . It was only a crime on earth . . . In heaven the gods would have blessed me . . . I stole for my husband.

SECOND SOLDIER. Strangers?

WANG. Pilgrim priests who travel from temple to temple. Our footprints are in the dust of a hundred shrines.

FIRST WATER SELLER. Don't buy his grandmother's pee holy fathers! It's wrong to sell that even to tax collectors! But to holy fathers – it's sacrilege!

SECOND WATER SELLER. Don't listen to that trafficker in dogs' urine. Taste how fresh my water is! Tears of pity!

The WOMAN *whimpers.*

WANG. We have no money.

FIRST WATER SELLER. Then don't come begging here!

SECOND WATER SELLER. Clear off! Layabouts! We were here before you!

The WATER SELLERS *go back to their pitches.* WANG *and* TIGER *come downstage.*

WANG (*to* TIGER). Ask her why she's punished.

TIGER. The meeting –

WANG. Ask her!

TIGER (*goes to the* WOMAN). Why are you punished?

WOMAN. Stealing.

HUSBAND. Cabbage leaves.

WOMAN. He needed broth.

SECOND SOLDIER. That's what she was *caught* for! Don't pity them. You think they live in ruins? They've all got so much loot under the floor their houses are lopsided.

TIGER *goes back to* WANG.

WOMAN (*to the* SECOND SOLDIER). Soldier, the stone is heavy. Can my husband help me?

SECOND SOLDIER (*shrugs*). Has he got the strength?

The HUSBAND *tries to take some of the weight of the cangue.* TIGER *and* WANG *are downstage.*

WOMAN. The weight off my neck. Yes.

TIGER. The village elders are waiting –

WANG. Sit. (*He pulls* TIGER *down. They sit in the lotus position.*)

TIGER. Ah – kill the soldier and break the stone? Let me get close. He won't suspect priests.

WANG. No!

TIGER. Her husband's tears run down the stone. It's quiet outside the village. One soldier. (*He gestures with his stump.*) My hand itches.

WANG. No.

TIGER. People who did this – they made your parents leave you by the river. Ha! Show them change coming! Tonight their feather pillows like stones. (*Gestures with his stump.*) When this hand itches: means good deed!

WANG. I know the woman. I'd help her before all others. I sit here calmly. I bite the inside of my lip to stop shouting out. Look, there is blood inside my mouth –

TIGER. And my hand itches!

WANG. Too soon.

TIGER. Then buy her water!

WANG. Worse!

TIGER. Hard!

WANG (*there is a sudden fall of blood from* WANG'*s mouth. As he talks it runs down his chin*). No. The ox bears the yoke. Break the yoke. Another yoke is put on its neck. The farmer has fifty yokes in his store. Stop being an ox. What is the use of breaking a window when it has iron bars? The landowner still controls. When he needs soldiers he sends – and they come. So people fear him. If we're kind to the women – he must be crueller to the people. So they say: 'She deserves to be punished.' They act out of fear. That is their morality. The only morality they can have. Learn it: the government makes not only laws, but a morality, a way of life, what people are in their very nature. We have not yet earned the right to be kind. I say it with blood in my mouth. When the landowner is no longer feared then our kindness will move mountains. That is our morality, Tiger. Today we should look on kindness with suspicion. Here only the evil can afford to do good.

KUNG-TU *comes on.*

FIRST WATER SELLER.
   Water! Sparkling water!
   The moon shone on the snow
   That fell on –

SECOND WATER SELLER.
   Water! Pure water!
   From the temple well
   Of the –

   The WATER SELLERS *break off. They smile in anticipation – knowing what will happen.*

FIRST WATER SELLER. Kung-tu.

SECOND WATER SELLER. His nephew owned the cabbage leaves. Be merciful Kung-tu!

FIRST WATER SELLER. Earn remission in heaven!

SECOND WATER SELLER. Don't teach him about earning.

FIRST WATER SELLER. I wouldn't try to cheat Kung-Tu. How could I get mountain water at a sellable price? It's from a clean stretch of the river. I carried it on my back for an hour. It would taste like mountain water to her, so I haven't lied.

SECOND WATER SELLER. That's water from down-river. Mine is up-river water! And cheap at the –

KUNG-TU. Shut up. (*To* WOMAN.) You did wrong.

WOMAN. My husband's ill. Our children left home. They can't beg for us *and* themselves.

KUNG-TU. Did you do wrong?

TIGER (*to* WANG). We must go.

WANG. Watch. Learn.

HUSBAND. She saw from my face I was hungry. If I'd hidden my face from my wife all would have been well. I'm to blame.

> *The* RICE CRACKER MAN *comes in.*

RICE CRACKER MAN.   Rice crackers!
                     The rice crackers lay on the table
                     To cool from the oven
                     The moon passing over the table
                     Stopped at the crackers an hour
                     To taste them: food for the gods!

FIRST WATER SELLER. Get out! He's buying water!

SECOND WATER SELLER. Mouse bait!

RICE CRACKER MAN (*aside to the* WATER SELLERS). They're salty today.

FIRST WATER SELLER. O these are the famous Moon Rice Crackers.

SECOND WATER SELLER. The soldier should try this local delicacy.

SECOND SOLDIER. A starving dog wouldn't howl for them.

KUNG-TU. Two rice crackers. Two cups of water. One from the temple of truth. One from the muses' mountain.

FIRST WATER SELLER. Everyone respects Kung-tu.

SECOND WATER SELLER. His own worst enemy.

RICE CRACKER MAN. They'll name a march after him one day!

> The WATER SELLERS *pour two cups of water. The* RICE CRACKER MAN *puts two rice crackers on the ground.*

TIGER (*to* WANG). The meeting!

WANG. Wait! Learn!

TIGER. It's dangerous here!

KUNG-TU. Fathers, my heart is full of a natural pity. It brims! Shall I give in? Or be stern for the good of the community?

WANG. We're in meditation. Lost in wonder. Deep in thought.

KUNG-TU. I've never studied theology. So I'll have to give in. A man without feelings is a stone.

> KUNG-TU *hands the water and crackers to the* WOMAN *and her* HUSBAND. *They eat and drink.*

WOMAN. Thank you. Thank you.

HUSBAND. Thank you.

KUNG-TU. Look, the woman's lips can't help smiling now they're wet. His hand is shaking for joy.

> THIRD SOLDIER *comes on.*

THIRD SOLDIER. Back to barracks.

SECOND SOLDIER. Another action? I didn't get the regulation sleep last night.

THIRD SOLDIER. The landowner's leaving.

KUNG-TU. Leaving?

THIRD SOLDIER (*raising his voice for all of them to hear*). For a few weeks. To visit the capital. (*To the* SECOND SOLDIER.) He wanted an escort. We're on barrack duty.

SECOND SOLDIER. Better than this.

THIRD SOLDIER (*to the* WOMAN). Squat in the village.

FIRST WATER SELLER. Water!

THIRD SOLDIER. I wouldn't wash a dead rat's foreskin in that.

The SOLDIERS *go.*

KUNG-TU (*panicking*). The landowner leaving. That's why the carts weren't sent out to the fields this morning. He's taking all his stuff. A short visit? (*Shrugs. Tries to reassure himself.*) We've got the soldiers. They're our bridge tower wall in one! . . . When this gets out the shop will be busy. People panic – they're silly enough – and hoard food. (*Uneasily.*) A short visit? I must get back . . . (*Gets a grip on himself.*) And at times like these supplies don't get through.

KUNG-TU *hurries out left.*

WANG. Break the cangue.

TIGER. Now?

WANG. Yes.

TIGER. Ha! Why?

WANG. The landowner's run. We worked underground at the foundations. No one saw. But the walls shook. Now – suddenly – a brick falls from the top! The first sign of weakness. The people see it – a sign of our strength! The wall cracks! Now pull it down!

TIGER *and* WANG *run to the* WOMAN. *The* WATER SELLERS *and the* RICE CRACKER MAN *stop packing their equipment.*

WOMAN. Fathers!

TIGER *and* WANG *kneel by the* WOMAN.

TIGER. Ha!

WOMAN. What is –? Help!

TIGER *takes out his gun.* WANG *takes out an iron cosh. He gently pushes the* WOMAN *over till the cangue rests on the ground.*

WOMAN (*screams*). Help!

TIGER. Quiet! Or –! (*Threatens her* HUSBAND *with his gun.*)

WANG (*struggling with the* WOMAN). Still! We've come to help!

HUSBAND (*bewildered*). Help . . . ?

FIRST WATER SELLER. What is –?

SECOND WATER SELLER. Help!

> TIGER *covers everyone with his gun.*

RICE CRACKER MAN (*sees* TIGER'*s stump and recognizes him*). Look! – the stump!

TIGER. Quick!

> WANG *hits the stone with the hammer. Blows ring out. The* WOMAN *screams.*

WOMAN (*struggling*). No, no, no. Don't kill me.

HUSBAND. Help us . . .

TIGER. Shut up!

WANG. Like iron.

TIGER. Towels! (*He runs to the* WATER SELLERS, *takes their towels, throws them to* WANG.) Quick!

WOMAN (*while* TIGER *gets the towels*). Please. No. (*She is paralysed with fear.*) Don't kill me. (*To the* WATER SELLERS *and* RICE CRACKER MAN.) I didn't ask. You saw. They forced me –

HUSBAND (*terrified*). Please. The soldiers.

> WANG *muffles the stone with the towels and begins to hit it again.*

WANG (*quiet, intense*). Now see – who is the stone – on the people's neck! And who is the stone breaker.

> *The stone falls apart. The* WOMAN *sits up. She doesn't dare to move her neck or even look down. She stares straight ahead.*

SECOND WATER SELLER. Don't shoot.

FIRST WATER SELLER. We didn't see it.

RICE CRACKER MAN. We'd gone.

TIGER (*quietly*). Haghghghgh!

TIGER *and* WANG *go out right.*

WOMAN (*in tears*). Tell the soldiers you saw. I tried to stop it.
HUSBAND (*in tears*). We tried. I'm always too weak.

The WATER SELLERS, *the* RICE CRACKER MAN, *the* WOMAN *and her* HUSBAND *stare at the pieces of stone. The* WATER SELLERS *hurriedly snatch up their towels and hide them.*

FIRST WATER SELLER. What shall we do?
RICE CRACKER MAN. If only the soldiers hadn't seen us!
FIRST WATER SELLER. Say we left.
SECOND WATER SELLER. No – run them to barracks!
RICE CRACKER MAN. No! No! Fool!
SECOND WATER SELLER. Fool? Why?
FIRST WATER SELLER (*gestures off after* WANG *and* TIGER). *They* saw us!

Silence. They realize their situation.

SECOND WATER SELLER (*dull fear*). O god we're between two tigers. My father said: 'Never between two tigers'.

The WOMAN *whimpers quietly as she feels her neck. They all talk in whispers.*

FIRST WATER SELLER. Give them some water.
SECOND WATER SELLER. Give . . . ?
FIRST WATER SELLER. Everything's changed.
RICE CRACKER MAN. And they need water.
SECOND WATER SELLER (*puzzled, unsure*). Give them . . . ?

They still talk in whispers.

FIRST WATER SELLER. Yes.
RICE CRACKER MAN. Yes.

They all stare at one another in amazement. They hardly believe what they're doing.

SECOND WATER SELLER (*observing himself in amazement, watching the running water as if it were the first time he had seen it, handling the water can as if it had just dropped from space*). . . . I pour the water . . .

FIRST WATER SELLER (*staring at his own hand as it moves; almost whispering*). I take the cup and . . .

> The FIRST WATER SELLER *hands the cup to the* WOMAN. *He stares at his hand holding the cup of water.*

RICE CRACKER MAN. Drink.

> *They watch in silent amazement as the* WOMAN *drinks half the water and gives the rest to her* HUSBAND. *She watches the* WATER SELLERS *as her* HUSBAND *drinks.*

FIRST WATER SELLER (*quietly, unsure, amazed, puzzled, calm, without boasting*). We gave her the water to drink.

> *They straighten up. The* WOMAN *and her* HUSBAND *stand. Silence. They become tense and stare anxiously.*

Now . . .

HUSBAND. The soldiers . . .

RICE CRACKER MAN. *Hide!*

FIRST WATER SELLER. And show the stones in the villages.

> *They pick up the stones and hurry out left.*

Eight
(a)

FERRYMAN's *house. Night.*
BASHO *and the* FIRST SOLDIER *have just come in.*
The FERRYMAN *rises from his bow.*
His WIFE *stares from the chair.*

FERRYMAN. Sir.

BASHO. You did not come to see me.

FERRYMAN. I had nothing to tell.

BASHO. No one has used your ferry?

FERRYMAN. They were silent.

BASHO. When did you see your son?

FERRYMAN. Not since he left the service of the reverend –

FIRST SOLDIER (*calm disgust*). Tch.

FERRYMAN. The soldier accuses me? I humbly beg to be believed –

> *The* FIRST SOLDIER *makes a short sound of anger and disgust.*

BASHO. You had the chance to clear yourself. You might have acted from fear. But you speak this to my face. I see how your son was taught.

> *The* FIRST SOLDIER *goes to the door, opens it, briefly looks out, and turns back to the room, leaving the door open.*

You carry rifles over the river.

FERRYMAN (*bows slightly, shaking his head, not looking at the open door*). People denounce their neighbours out of fear. Or spite.

> *The* SECOND *and* THIRD SOLDIERS *come through the open door. They support* TIGER *between them – though he can walk unaided. His hair and face are covered with several patchy layers of dry, faded blood. The upper part of his body is knotted in a sheet.*

BASHO. You meet your son at night. You take the rifles over the water in the bottom of your boat. Then they're taken into the villages. You meet him again tonight. (*To the* FIRST SOLDIER.) I'll be by the window.

> BASHO *goes out. The* FIRST SOLDIER *speaks and acts without salacious violence. He is calm, almost courteous. The* SOLDIERS *are used to their work and too bored with it to enjoy it. Really they act out of fear – amateur mountain climbers: a show of calm, hollow inside.*

FIRST SOLDIER. Once Tiger roared. The roaring got on our nerves. We're only human. We like working conditions to be as good as circumstances allow. After all, a prison's not a zoo. Now Tiger does farmyard imitations. He's lost his tongue. (*Points to the* THIRD SOLDIER.) He's a real tearaway. (*To* TIGER.) Do chicken.

> TIGER *imitates a chicken: a residual noise in the back of his throat.*

Chicken with twisted neck. Now sheep.

> TIGER *makes the same sound.*

Good. Now the big one. Do pig.

> TIGER *makes the same sound.*

(*Reasonably.*) He's not trying. Someone show him.

> *The* THIRD SOLDIER *lifts his foot from the ground and lowers it.* TIGER *goes down on all fours. The* WIFE *quietly covers her head with the cover.*

That's the right posture for well brought up pig. Tiger told a great story – how he lost his hand. A lie, of course. Lost it for pick-pocketing. No more stories. Pity. (*Imitation.*) 'Tiger has true story tell now. How Tiger lost other hand.' (*Points to the* THIRD SOLDIER.) He collects memos of the departed. It was like chopping branches off a tree. I thought he'd get to the roots.

THIRD SOLDIER (*laughs flatly at the bad joke*).

FIRST SOLDIER. As for the present: you take out the boat. Meet the enemy. We lie in the bottom. I look round this room to find something valuable enough to break. Nothing's of value to me. But standards change from the point of view.

FERRYMAN. I wouldn't –

FIRST SOLDIER. You will. That's how it will always be. That's why I'm here. Answering. Not asking for questions.

The FIRST SOLDIER *nods. The* SECOND SOLDIER *goes to window and raps on the paper pane.*

I can't promise you your life. That's out. No pardons. (*Shakes head.*) Not that it's up to me. Or the judge. The government's said it. But there's no need for your wife to be killed. She's senile enough not to know what you were up to. When my word's given it's kept.

BASHO *comes in.*

BASHO. We'll wait.
FERRYMAN (*to the* FIRST SOLDIER, *points to* TIGER). Some water
. . . ?
FIRST SOLDIER. Why bother? Too late.

The FERRYMAN *holds a cup of water for* TIGER *to drink.* TIGER *drinks messily and greedily.*

BASHO (*suddenly very angry*). I said wait! In quiet!
FIRST SOLDIER (*to the other* SOLDIERS). Outside.

The THIRD SOLDIER *takes the bowl from* TIGER's *mouth. The* SECOND *and* THIRD SOLDIERS *take* TIGER *out through the door. The* FIRST SOLDIER *closes it behind them. The* FERRYMAN *still holds the bowl.*

Sorry, sir. Not long. Dark three hours.
BASHO. Yes.
FERRYMAN. The judge is wise. I'm old and foolish. My love for our son made me a traitor. My wife wasn't told. Now all this is known I'm at peace. I don't meet him tonight. (*Points after* TIGER.) He said what you made him. Let me live here under the soldiers' watch till my son sends a message. Then I'll make amends.
BASHO (*to the* FIRST SOLDIER). The staff meeting may last longer now. Your second in command can take charge of the search.

FIRST SOLDIER. Sir.

BASHO. Tell him not to pick the area till an hour before-hand.

> The TWO SOLDIERS *come back, shut the door behind them and wait in the background.*

THIRD SOLDIER. Nothing outside yet.

SECOND SOLDIER. A bit of moon.

FERRYMAN (*simply and calmly, as if he no longer had to struggle with his thoughts but knew what to say. He holds the water in front of him. Close to his chest*). Why are our lives wasted? We have minds to see how we suffer. Why don't we use them to change the world? A god would wipe us off the board with a cloud: a mistake. But as there is only ourselves shouldn't we change our lives so that we don't suffer? Or at least suffer only in changing them? (*Noiselessly, carefully he puts down the bowl.*)

> *The ferry bell in the distance: one stroke.*

FIRST SOLDIER. Outside.

FERRYMAN. I'll light the lamp.

FIRST SOLDIER (*bored and angry*). Outside.

> *The* FERRYMAN, BASHO *and the* FIRST *and* THIRD SOLDIERS *go out. The* SECOND SOLDIER *and the* WIFE *are left. The* SECOND SOLDIER *pokes out one of the window panes with his fist. He peers through the hole for a moment. He turns and goes to the* WIFE.

SECOND SOLDIER. I'll tie your mouth. Then you don't need to shout. That won't help.

> *The* SECOND SOLDIER *gags the* WIFE.

(b)

This scene is played on the front of the stage. The SECOND SOLDIER *and the* WIFE *remain motionless in the* FERRYMAN's *house.*

Far bank of the river, by the bell pole. Dark. WANG, SHEOUL *and* PU-TOI *wait. They are armed with rifles.*

PU-TOI. Listen!
WANG. He's started!
SHEOUL. I wish the moon would go.
WANG. It will.

    They listen in silence.

We wait by the river. My mother came here. And left me. Do you call her a criminal? Perhaps in a month she was dead in the gutter. Perhaps she reached up out of the gutter to put me here. Now we'll help those like her.

    The young set out from this river. The old return to die. Merchants cross day after day till their lives are as soiled and faceless as old money. Orders are sent to buy or sell or accuse. Thieves plot while they wait on this worn-out landing. Soldiers with blood down to their underclothes. Monks without the child's right to innocence, with faces like snakes or pampered old women. They all came here, waited, stepped into the boat and trusted their lives to the dark river that crosses their path even as they pass over on it.

    This time we wait with rifles – and the ferryman comes to meet us.
SHEOUL. I'll fetch the rifles.
WANG. When he's nearer. (*To* PU-TOI.) Keep watch up the bank.

    PU-TOI *moves off in the dark.*

Tie this to a rifle.
SHEOUL. What?
WANG. A note for my mother.

    SHEOUL *takes the note into the bush.*

(*Whispering to* SHEOUL.) There! In the dark against the horizon. – The rifles!

SHEOUL *brings three rifles, bound in sacking to the landing place.*

In the bushes. See it all goes well.

Splash. The sound of the ferry pole falling in the water.

SHEOUL. What –?
WANG. The guns!

SHEOUL *and* WANG *run from the bushes, she takes the rifles out left,* WANG *covers her with his rifle,* PU-TOI *runs in.*

PU-TOI. What –?
WANG. *The pole! He dropped it!*
PU-TOI. The guns!
WANG. Here!

WANG *and* PU-TOI *run out after* SHEOUL. *Subdued whispers from the water.*

FIRST SOLDIER. . . . there . . .
FERRYMAN. . . . got . . .

Slight pause. The FERRYMAN *walks out of the darkness on to the landing place. Calls softly.*

Wang . . . The boat . . .

Turns to the SOLDIERS *hidden in the dark, as if for instructions.*

I . . . ?

Suddenly the SOLDIERS *jump on to the land. They run frantically up and down the bank searching.*

THIRD SOLDIER. No one.
FIRST SOLDIER. No sign?
THIRD SOLDIER. Nothing.

The FIRST SOLDIER *fumbles to light a lamp. He holds it over their heads.*

The landing place is worn flat. Nothing to tell from this.

FIRST SOLDIER. Pig. How did he get tipped off?

THIRD SOLDIER. Or Tiger lied.

FIRST SOLDIER. Pig it. We've killed him. (*To the* FERRYMAN.) Get in.

> *They all vanish in the darkness in the direction of the boat.*

(c)

FERRYMAN'*s hut.* SECOND SOLDIER, *the* WIFE *and* BASHO. BASHO *is nervous.*

SECOND SOLDIER (*looking through the hole in the window*). Them sir.

> *The* SECOND SOLDIER *knocks out the rest of the window with his rifle butt – there is no need to hide their presence any more. The frame falls out neatly, leaving a black hole shaped like a TV screen.*

BASHO. Alone? There was no shouting . . .

SECOND SOLDIER (*peering out*). Too dark to . . .

BASHO. Undo her mouth.

> *The* SECOND SOLDIER *crosses to the* WIFE *to unfasten her gag. Sound of the boat tapping the wooden landing place and the* FIRST SOLDIER *saying 'Hup!' The* SECOND SOLDIER *returns to the window. The* WIFE *is still gagged.*

SECOND SOLDIER (*peering out*). They're back, sir.

BASHO. Who's with them?

SECOND SOLDIER (*peering out*). It's dark . . .

> *Slight pause. The* FIRST SOLDIER *appears head and shoulders in the open window.*

FIRST SOLDIER (*in the window*). No one, sir. (*Pause.* BASHO *doesn't answer.*) Sir.

BASHO. Tell me what happened.

FIRST SOLDIER. We crossed the river. He called as we said. We kept quiet. Even when he dropped the pole.

BASHO. He dropped the pole in the water?

FIRST SOLDIER. Sir.

BASHO. Is he there?

FIRST SOLDIER. Sir.

> BASHO *raises his voice for the* FERRYMAN *to hear. The* FERRYMAN *isn't seen. The head and shoulders of the* FIRST SOLDIER *stay in the window as he turns to look off, left, to the* FERRYMAN.

BASHO. A haiku is made of seventeen syllables in three lines in the order of five, seven and five. These lines are short and clean – like the strokes of a pole driving a boat through the water. You've ferried your boat long enough to know about haiku. You'll understand what I say next. In haiku the lines come to the master complete. Each line enters the head the moment the line before ends. There are no deletions or fumblings, no lines are dropped. For example:

> The ferry pole fell
> Deep in the dark water – poked
> In the eye of god

The ferryman's son knows he could not drop the pole in mistake. Throw him in the river. To warn the rest.

> *The* FIRST SOLDIER *disappears from the window. The* SECOND SOLDIER *goes out. A moment later he's seen crossing the open window.* BASHO *goes out and disappears in the other direction – he doesn't cross the window.*
> *Sounds off.*

FIRST SOLDIER (*off*). Hey!

THIRD SOLDIER (*off*). Up!

> *Off, a splash.*

FERRYMAN (*off*). Ah – I – ah –

SECOND SOLDIER (*off*). Hold him.

THIRD SOLDIER (*off*). The pole.

FERRYMAN (*off*). Ah – ah –

Off, splashing and the sound of a wet bundle being hit. The WIFE *rises and slowly crosses the room towards the window. As she moves she fumbles with her gag. She stops in exhaustion. She does not reach the window. She is silent.*

THIRD SOLDIER (*off*). Hit him.

SECOND SOLDIER (*off. Annoyed*). You do it!

Off, the sound of the wet bundle being hit. More splashing.

FERRYMAN (*off*). Uh – uh –

SECOND SOLDIER (*off*). His hands!

The WIFE *removes her gag. Immediately, as if tuned in on a radio, the weak, persistent sound of her cry, on one note.*

THIRD SOLDIER (*off*). Kick!

FIRST SOLDIER (*off*). Why do they struggle at that age?

FERRYMAN (*off*). Uh –

SECOND SOLDIER (*off*). Cantankerous old sod.

FERRYMAN (*off*). Uh –

Off, a few splashes. The WIFE's *cry ends.*

Nine

BASHO's *house. Night. He sits at the writing table. Paper and other writing materials on the table before him. He is listening intensely.* TO-SI, *his servant boy, waits in fear. In the distance, a shot.*

BASHO (*calmly*). There – again! A shot.

Another shot, off, in the distance. No other sound.

BASHO. To-si, send the chief soldier to me.
TO-SI. Sir. (*Crosses to the door.*)
BASHO. If he can be spared.
TO-SI (*stops, bows*). Sir.

> TO-SI *goes out left.* BASHO *starts to collect manuscripts. He stops in uncertainty.*

BASHO (*calls*). To-si!

> *No answer.* BASHO *hurries round the room with more manuscripts. He stacks them on the table.* KUNG-TU *hurries in left.*

KUNG-TU. Why aren't the soldiers fighting? The village is being attacked. (*Sees papers.*) What are you doing?
BASHO (*calls*). To-si! – I sent my boy for the captain. Keep calm. Official documents.
KUNG-TU. They're poems! Are you leaving? They'll burn my store!
BASHO. How many were there?
KUNG-TU. How could I tell? It's dark! There was shooting. I bumped into people. And a donkey. D'you want me to count the donkeys! Half the people here will join them!

> *The* FIRST SOLDIER *comes in.*

FIRST SOLDIER. The village is being attacked.
BASHO. What are you doing to –
FIRST SOLDIER. Nothing.
KUNG-TU. Nothing?
BASHO. But what –
KUNG-TU. They'll burn my store! Our homes! My family's in –
FIRST SOLDIER. Shut up! I know. (*To* BASHO.) My men went to look. The military beacons have been fired up the river. That means a concerted attack on all villages.
KUNG-TU. Why was it allowed to get so far? I'll complain to –
BASHO. Why aren't you doing –

FIRST SOLDIER. I'm following orders.

BASHO. Preposterous! What time have you had for orders? As judge I order you to hand over to the second in command.

KUNG-TU (*fear*). O god.

FIRST SOLDIER. I came here with orders. The decision was made two years ago. We were to try to contain the situation. If we failed or there was a serious attack: withdrawal to the provincial capital. That must be defended at all costs.

BASHO. Then the government's hollow within.

FIRST SOLDIER (*shrugs*). I must go to my men.

KUNG-TU (*sudden, short, sharp yelps of panic. Pure animal sound*). Yu! Yu! Yu! Yu! Yu!

BASHO. You abandon us!

KUNG-TU. Traitor!

> KUNG-TU *hits the* FIRST SOLDIER *awkwardly. The* FIRST SOLDIER *pushes him off, he won't waste his energy.*

FIRST SOLDIER. I'm sorry, I haven't time.

KUNG-TU. My stocks – rice, corn, oil – well, a little fortune. All cased. Ready to move. Send your soldiers. It'll be worth your while.

FIRST SOLDIER. We're not a baggage train. We must move fast or we'll –

KUNG-TU. Take me. I'm not rich, you know – but there's money in – (*hesitates*).

FIRST SOLDIER. My men will need paying too.

> TO-SI *comes back left. Bursts of distant firing are heard from time to time but nothing is seen.*

TO-SI. They're burning your shop.

KUNG-TU. You have an army outside and you haven't fired a shot!

FIRST SOLDIER (*to* KUNG-TU). I'm going.

> KUNG-TU *produces a roll of notes.*

KUNG-TU (*gestures vaguely, he has an almost sexual embarrassment over the notes*). You see . . .

FIRST SOLDIER. I'll ask the men.

KUNG-TU (*wheedling*). Just a few cases. There's Korean tea. A few rolls of – there's oil –

FIRST SOLDIER. My men get their hands on that – d'you think you'll see any of it? It'll be all I can do to stop them vanishing over the fields – without giving them loot to take!

KUNG-TU. I'll fetch my family.

FIRST SOLDIER (*to* BASHO). And you?

BASHO. My poems!

FIRST SOLDIER (*stares at* BASHO). You'll have to carry them in your head. (*Goes left towards door.*)

BASHO. Why wasn't I warned? The government sent me no instructions.

FIRST SOLDIER (*shrugs*). The landowner must have got them. I expect he forgot to pass them on when he left.

The FIRST SOLDIER *goes out left.*

BASHO. To-si, go to them. They won't hurt you. Tell them I'll receive them. Say there will be an arrangement. Pardons.

TO-SI *goes out left.*

KUNG-TU. You think they'll come?

KUNG-TU *sits uncertainly. More sporadic bursts of firing, off.*

I ought to fetch my family. The children could carry a few sacks. (*Figuratively biting his nails.*) O god it's like an examination. What is it best to do? If we run and get caught – that would be worst! Should I risk it and stay? (*Looks at* BASHO.) If they come, what will you give them?

BASHO (*fingering his poems*). What?

KUNG-TU. What will you –

BASHO (*cutting him short*). I'm not sure.

KUNG-TU. You must be sure! I'm betrayed on all sides. The

moment we're out of town the soldiers will cut my throat. I'll tell them about my – you see, there's a small account in the capital. Not much, but enough for this. If I promise – when we get there –? I wasn't born rich. I'm *not* rich! But I gave my life to my store. Now? Perhaps my wife will bring a few cases. (*Cries.*) She's a good woman. And my son's got a strong back. He could manage two.

Noises outside. KUNG-TU *runs to the door left to listen.*

KUNG-TU. Soldiers leaving. (*Panicking.*) My money!
SECOND SOLDIER (*off*). Light out.
FIRST SOLDIER (*off*). Out!
KUNG-TU (*turns back to* BASHO). Tell my wife. She'll catch us up.

KUNG-TU *goes out left.* BASHO *starts collecting manuscripts again. He puts some on the table. They slither off.*

Ten

River bank. Mid-day. WANG, PU-TOI, SHEOUL, LU, KAKA, TOR-QUO *and others eat their bread. Shovels stacked like rifles. On one side* PU-TOI *mends a shovel. He reshapes the bottom end of the wooden handle and nails the spade back on to it.* SHEOUL *helps him and eats at the same time.*

TOR-QUO. My wife doesn't want to live by the river.
SAN-KO. When the banks are mended?
TOR-QUO. So she says.
SAN-KO. Handy for fish.
TOR-QUO. I told her.
LU (*laughs*).
TOR-QUO. What's funny in that?
LU. San-ko wiggles his feet when he talks.

SAN-KO. No I don't.

LU. You do. Say something.

SAN-KO. No.

KAKA. Coward.

SAN-KO. You're all looking.

PU-TOI (*to* SHEOUL). A bigger nail.

SHEOUL *searches in the nail can.*

WANG. Is she afraid of the river?

TOR-QUO (*shrugs*). Perhaps.

LU. A lot are.

KAKA. The banks won't break now.

SHEOUL (*to* PU-TOI). That do?

PU-TOI. Fine.

TOR-QUO. People remember the river. Young people, it's different
    for them. They don't know what the past means.

PU-TOI (*hammering. To* SHEOUL). Be more careful.

SHEOUL. I was.

PU-TOI. Next time it sticks don't bend it. Lift it out cleanly and
    try again.

SHEOUL. Something to eat?

PU-TOI. Please.

SHEOUL *crosses to* LU.

TOR-QUO. Are you afraid of the river?

SHEOUL. No.

LU. Would your wife move?

SHEOUL. Pu-toi hasn't eaten yet.

LU (*putting food in a bowl*). Anyone else?

TOR-QUO (*nods*). Me.

SAN-KO. Me. See – my feet didn't move.

SHEOUL (*taking a bowl from* LU). Thank you.

LU. Because you stopped them.

SAN-KO *groans in disgust.*

I don't mind them wiggling. I like it.

SAN-KO. It's odd.

LU (*to* TOR-QUO). I wouldn't move. Here's grandad for the bowls. Grandad –!

> *The* HUSBAND, *from Scene Seven, comes on. He carries a stack of bowls. Empty rice cans are looped on his arms.*

HUSBAND. Finished?

LU. – are you afraid of the river?

HUSBAND. I'm not afraid of anything.

SHEOUL (*takes the spade from* PU-TOI *and gives him the food*). Thank you.

PU-TOI. Thanks.

SHEOUL (*looks at the spade*). I couldn't break that if I tried.

PU-TOI (*eating*). We'll see.

LU. Bowls please. (*She collects bowls for the* HUSBAND.) Aren't you afraid of the dark?

HUSBAND. No.

LU. Tigers?

HUSBAND. No.

LU. Landowners?

HUSBAND. I'm not afraid of anything, my dear. I try not to be.

LU. Not even the water when the banks are broken?

SAN-KO. Why should the banks break? We'll build them well. It's for our own sake. There'll be locks. A cut-off channel for the spring tides. The banks will have stone walls. We're changing the river. What's the matter with you? You speak as if the old river was there. We have a –

> *The others roar with laughter.*

Now what?

WANG. Your feet!

LU. They're wagging!

SAN-KO. They're not!

KAKA. They are! They are!

SAN-KO. Of course they are! I'm telling the truth! Your feet ought to waggle when you tell the truth! They're still when you lie! Or you're dead!

LU (*puts an arm round* SAN-KO's *neck*). San-ko I'm joking!

SAN-KO. It's good when my feet waggle! Look!

The others laugh.

HUSBAND. I don't understand you young people half the time. (*Calls loudly.*) Work in five minutes. (*Crosses to* PU-TOI.) Not finished? What's wrong with your appetite? When I was your age –

VOICE (*off, right*). Help!

Immediately GOW *runs across the stage from right to left, shouting as he goes.*

GOW. Quick. Quick. Tuan's in the water.

The others jump up and run out left after GOW. SHEOUL *is left on the stage holding her shovel. The* HUSBAND *stands a little way behind her.*

WANG (*off, running*). How long's he been in?

GOW (*off, running*). Who saw?

WANG (*off, running*). Why didn't he call?

VOICE (*off, still*). Hit his head on the bottom.

Incoherent distant sound. SHEOUL *and the* HUSBAND *stare off.*

GOW (*off, still*). His leg.

Silence. SHEOUL *puts her spade on the ground. The* HUSBAND *doesn't move. The crowd comes back with* TUAN's *body.* TOR-QUO *points to a place on the ground. They lay the body there. They stand in silence.*

TOR-QUO. Dead hours.

WANG. We need a stretcher.

They go. SHEOUL *and* LU *are the last. They stare at the body.*
LU *cries against* SHEOUL. SHEOUL *comforts her as they follow
the others out, left. In the silence* BASHO *comes from the right.
He is old and weak. He clutches a few charred manuscripts. His
clothes and skin are smudged with soot.*

BASHO. Where is the . . . ? . . . I sat in my court . . . After it was
burned . . . I woke. A rat sat in a cobweb on a dead man's head
and watched me . . . (*Goes to the corpse.*) Show me the way to
the deep north . . . I am old . . . respect my age . . . my robe of
office . . . where is enlightenment? . . . where can I find it before
I die? . . . (*Touches the corpse.*) Your face is stern . . . You have
found the way . . . Master, tell me . . . Don't turn away . . .
(*Shakes the corpse violently.*) Tell me . . . The way . . . The way
. . . (*Clambers across the corpse and shakes it.*) I will be told! Tell
me the way! . . . Or I will shake the life from your soul . . .
(*Hits at corpse.*) The way! . . .

The others have come back. They stare. They carry a stretcher.

WANG. Basho . . . the man is dead.
BASHO. What? . . . Who is it? . . . When they burned my court the
light was so bright . . . Since then I see . . . only a few . . . the
skin has fallen over my eyes . . . soft and cold as a bat . . . My
eyes are old . . . Where is the narrow road to the deep north? . . .
Tell me . . . Please . . . I am a lost child . . . Who will show me
the way?

BASHO *gropes down to the audience. He is bent, black and as old
as time. His hands as he walks are near the ground. His stick
reaches high over his back.*

SHEOUL. To do that to a corpse!
LU. It doesn't matter when the living disturb the dead.
WANG. Yes, remember: there is a worse story. Once a man lived
by a river. (*The rest nod silently in agreement. They already know
the story. They go to* TUAN, *lay him gently on the stretcher, and*

prepare to carry him out. WANG *talks as if the story were the funeral oration.*) A king came. He said to the man carry me over the river on your back. The man obeyed –

BASHO (*crying in the audience*). Where is the narrow road to the deep north?

WANG. When he reached the shore the king spoke again. Carry me over the plain to my house. The man carried him for a year. Then he asked the king when they would reach his house. The king said I'll tell you when we are there but I cannot speak till then – I have many things to think of. So the man carried him –

The bearers lift TUAN *on the stretcher and begin to carry him out – not on their shoulders but at the height a medical stretcher is carried. The other people follow them.*

BASHO (*in the audience angrily banging his staff on the ground*). The narrow road to the deep north!

WANG. – for many years and the king did not speak. Each night he laid him on the ground. Each morning he took him on his back. The man did not know that the king had died long ago. So he carried him always and wasted his life. That is the worse story. To carry the dead on your back.

BASHO (*in the audience. Old and as feeble as a child. Cries*). Where is the way ... the way ... the way ... ?

BASHO goes. The bearers and the others have already taken TUAN *away.* WANG *is alone on the stage. As he speaks the lights begin to come up.*

WANG. We live in a time of great change. It is easy to find monsters – and as easy to find heroes. To judge rightly what is good – to choose between good and evil – that is all that it is to be human.

The Bundle Poems

THE TREE

The tree has stood before my house for eighty years
In good years the branches heavy with blossom and leaves
In bad years surviving
The branches bare only in winter
When the tree and the earth sleep

In that time the rule in the local school hasn't changed
The old gods are still worshipped
Most of the dead are buried in their name
Wages and prices have risen
There is no order
On the heath a missile site where the gibbet stood
And the young have been cut down twice

The tree endures the changing seasons
We cannot wait for spring or live long in winter
We cannot
We must change

WHO CAN CHOOSE?

Each man walks out his life in his small circle
Lifted from his cradle by elders
Borne to his grave by sons
And in that small circle
Works and laughs
Argues for or against reason
Loves and mourns
And is made weaker or stronger by neighbours

He is born in his spring and dies in his winter
But his seasons are ruled by other men's lives
Who can choose?

Great storms rock his chair
Or he opens his door to the fury
Avalanches gently push him one step
Or he leaps over cracks as they open in mountains
Seas wash his hands or he swims through them
Armies whisper into his ear
Or he asks who leads them and why they fight
He sleeps in his quiet world
Or goes out to the cry in the street
He waits till the storm batters his house
And crowds stand at his door
Or he asks: what is justice?

He can choose

VERDICT

How shall we judge this man?
By the best he did or the worst?
If we judge by the best
All men are saints

He gave to the poor
Sheltered the homeless
Visited the sick
Fed the neglected
Throw him into the fire!

What did he do to change the world?
How many suffer because he did nothing to change it?
Yet he pitied the suffering because the world wasn't changed!
Into the fire!

CRIMES

The unjust temper injustice with pity
The merciless give mercy
Just as tradesmen to make a profit
Mark some goods down

Those who teach ignorance
Endow libraries
And found great colleges
To teach it in

Barbarians patronize art
Would you expect the rich
To keep ugly whores?

Many shout peace!
Before their armies banners flutter
As if an invisible hand
Was struggling to rip them off
And throw them away

Perhaps this is their greatest crime –
Not the centuries of exploitation and violence
But their occasional use of virtue?

LOVE AND PITY

Men are formed by their rulers
Or in the struggle against them
Our minds are created by fear and obedience
Or by that struggle

What is pity?
To break the yoke on the ox's neck?
The yoke-maker has a hundred yokes in his store
Break the yoke-maker!

You break the glass in the prison window
You have not broken the iron bars
In the prison window
That is harder!
Pity is pitiless to those who serve her!

What is love?
To cry for the hungry and lost?
They can cry for themselves

Let the powerful love and pity mankind
Let the powerless love each other
No one else!

When the calf is seen to weep for the butcher
The time for change has come!

SACRIFICE

You tie the calf to the post
The ropes aren't too tight
You polish the hooves
Nuzzle the crown
Stick flowers behind its ears
Sweep up the dung it drops in fright
Mop the tears from its jowls
With your hanky
Its lips pull back at your touch
You grin at the big teeth
Even your last curse
Begins with its pet name

As it jerks in the ropes
You make your mark in its neck –
    The gash

FIRST WORLD WAR POETS

You went to the front like sheep
And bleated at the pity of it
In academies that smell of abattoirs
Your poems are still studied

You turned the earth to mud
Yet complain you drowned in it
Your generals were dug in at the rear
Degenerates drunk on brandy and prayer
You *saw* the front – and only bleated
The pity!

You survived
Did you burn your generals' houses?
Loot the new millionaires?
No, you found new excuses
You'd lost an arm or your legs
You sat by the empty fire
And hummed music hall songs

Why did your generals send you away to die?
They were afraid of the Great War that was coming
Between masters and workers
In their own land
So they herded you over the cliffs to be rid of you
How they hated you while you lived!
How they wept over you once you were dead!

What did you fight for?
A new world?
No – an old world already in ruins!
Your children?
Millions of children died
Because you fought for your enemies
And not against them!

We will not forget!
We will not forgive!

THE SAMARITAN

A merchant travelling
On business to Sidon
Saw at the roadside
A naked man
Filthy bruised bound
(Words taken at random
From the history books)

He crossed the road
He saw under the trees
Three soldiers

Who said
We're taking him to be crucified
By the port gate of Sidon

The merchant asked what he had done

They said
For six years he robbed merchants on this road
Throwing their naked bodies in ditches

The merchant said I will give him water

Three hands shot out like lizards' tongues
The merchant dropped one silver coin
On each palm
The fingers shut – bars of a trap

The merchant poured water into his bowl
He held it out to the thief
The thief did not open his mouth

A soldier kicked his ribs
A soldier prised open his jaws with his fists
A soldier emptied the bowl into his throat

The merchant took the bowl
Wiped it
And left

POEM

They run the clinic in which you're born
Christen you in their church
Teach you the rules of their school
Examine your minds
Mark them
Donate your playing field
Teach you the rules of their games
Employ you and pay you
Pay you when there's no work
Print your money
Marry you in their church or their registry office
Christen your children
Censor your television
Let you listen to their radio
Share their newspapers with you
Sweep your street
Train your police
Give you medals
Encourage you with bonuses
Punish you when you're a nuisance
Put you in hospital when you're sick
Take you into care when you're old
Burn you in their crematorium
Scatter your ash in their garden

No wonder some of you fight for them
When the rest start to ask
Who the hell they are!

DE QUÉ SIRVE UNA TAZE?

You knock out the teeth
Twist the neck till the skin is taut
As wrinkles on ice
Scorch the hair as you do on a pig
Tie the hands
And break them with a hammer
Dress the body in rags
As if it were a wound
Empty the skull
And stuff it with sheets
Torn from your book
Shoot out the eyes
So the face looks like cracked glass
And now you offer a cup

What use is a cup?

THE WATER SELLER AND THE SOLDIER

On the street the water seller
Meets a soldier and his prisoner
The prisoner asks for water
But has no money to buy it

Though the soldier forbids the water seller
To give the prisoner water
The water seller could bribe the soldier
But he is poor and must sell his water

And though the soldier
Would arrest the water seller
If he smiled to comfort the prisoner
As it is forbidden to fraternize with prisoners
(Unless the water seller had bribed the soldier
To permit him to smile at the prisoner –
An event so unlikely it can be discounted
Even by poets)
It so happens that the water seller
Does not choose to smile at the prisoner
(Or anyone else for that matter)
Because lately many water sellers' water
Was stolen on this very street

Thus the soldier defends the water seller
So that his trade may prosper
And his life be happy and good
But the water seller can't do this good deed
Nor even smile
(Had he chosen to smile)
Because the soldier defends him

So the water seller and the soldier
Smile at each other

Is this the behaviour of rational beings?

VIRTUE

We wish to be kind
To speak gently
To comfort the sufferers
We would walk over continents to feed the hungry
Build shelters for those made homeless by storms
Sit with the aged and talk to the bewildered

It is not time to sit and talk
We have not earned the right to be kind
We have not won the power to do good
In our world only the evil are clothed in virtue
And a good deed arouses suspicion

Then be hard!
Be unforgiving!
Do not be patient!
How else shall we find justice?

CULTURE

What is culture?
The best? – Too vague!

Who owns the tool?
The man with money
Who uses the tool?
The tool user
What does the tool do?
Change the relationship
Between men and the world
Who owns the tool user?
The man with money
What does the tool do?
Change society
What is society?
The relationship between
Owner and user

What is culture?
Taking power from the owner
To give to the user
That is culture
The highest the human mind
Can aspire to!
The passing of power
From owner to user
Creates virtue and art
Nothing else raises
Men over the beast
Whatever hinders this passing of power
Is against culture
Culture is this change

WHAT IS WANTED

I wanted to smile
But I saw how the evil smiled
I wanted to share
But I learned that long after I'd given
All I had
The poor would be poor
I did not want anger
I'd heard of the saint who found freedom in prison
But this only comforts gaolers
Above all I wanted peace
For I knew war

But what I wanted is not yet to be had
Now I want something else:
That one day it will be

For that I would give up
All I had wanted

ESSAY ON THE SELLERS OF WATER

I.

Water sellers sell water to the poor
The groans of the poor are pitiful
Why don't the water sellers give water
At least to the poorest?

In the merchant world everything is priced
A green paper fluttering in the storm
Is scrap or a banknote –
Which is decided by the world of the merchant
Though both flutter like a leaf in the storm

Men too flutter in the storm
And whether they're scrap or worth money
The world of the merchant decides

2.

Every commodity has a price
The price tags are clear to be seen on the counter
But in the world of the merchant all things are priced
Acts thoughts dreams regrets – all priced
Just as all things on earth cast a shadow

It is a law:
When one thing is priced all things are priced
The water seller prays for drought
To keep up the price of water
And so he prays that the world of the merchant stands firm
And therefore that all things shall keep their price

See! the water in the bowl
Creates the water seller
He earns his life by selling water
His life is shaped by the laws of selling
His world lives by the laws of selling
His morals are based on the laws of selling
All his laws are laws of selling!

If the water seller can't give his water
At least he can smile at the poor?
No! – when one thing is priced all things are priced
To give water ruins the price of water
To smile freely destroys the value of virtue
It replaces the law of selling with a new law
But in the world of the merchant
Virtue depends on the price of water
So to smile you must first change the world
The man who smiles does not wish to sell water
The water seller can only simper or grin

3.

The merchant thinks that at evening
He shuts his shutters and goes – leaving the market
No! – the whole of his life is bought and sold
His world is a tree that roots in the market
The topmost leaf and the smallest twig
Grow from its gutter

The merchant is like a boy in an apple tree
When the wind blows his body contorts
His arms stiffen like branches
The apples hang from his hands
The wind blows through him
And he has become part of the tree

He may reach for the highest apple
But the wind still blows or the bough bends
And shapes the boy to the tree

The merchant believes he has hours of peace
And contemplation after takings are checked
No! – even time flows like water from the municipal conduit
In the market square
Guarded by marble statues of commerce and providence
All all! follows the same law
Even contemplation is sold in the market
Even silence and stillness
Religion virtue culture and love
All buying and selling
Bubbling and seething

4.

And one day the spring water rises
And sweeps the merchants and soldiers out to the ocean
Like rubbish thrown behind a mountain

There is also this law:
When one thing is not priced nothing is priced
The water carried to the streets is not changed
But the laws are changed
The powers that force the laws are changed
The men that carry the water are changed

The spring water rises and merchants and soldiers are swept away
Like trash thrown over a mountain
And the value of water is judged
Not by what it earns
But the thirst it quenches
And all things are changed

Jackets

or

The Secret Hand

Jackets was premièred by the Department of Theatre Studies at Lancaster University on 24 January 1989, with the following cast:

Part One: The Village School

CHIYO	Margaret Eddershaw
TONAMI	Amanda Hadingue
KOTARO	Philip Coates
TYGO	Laurie Smith
GAULI	Adam Clayton
CHICO	Tim Meekings
FOOSHI	Richard Bousfield
GENZO	Chas Ambler
MATSUO	Charles Waples
HENBA	John Freeman
NCO	Ralph Ineson
THE MOTHER	Bernadette Hughes
VILLAGERS	Anne Baker
	Ceri Jones
	Robert Knowles
	Patrick Ladbury
	Jane Lindsay
	Nicky Sims
KAN SHU	Matthew Telfer

Part Two: The City

MRS LEWIS	Amanda Hadingue
MRS TEBHAM	Margaret Eddershaw
PHIL LEWIS	Charles Waples
BRIAN TEBHAM/THE OFFICER	John Freeman
THE PADRE	Chas Ambler
THE POLICEMAN	Ralph Ineson

Directed by Keith Sturgess
Composer and Musical Director Kim Baston

Part Two of *Jackets* opened at the Leicester Haymarket on 28 November 1989 with the following cast:

BRIAN TEBHAM	Tom Hudson
PHIL LEWIS	Ross Dunsmore
THE OFFICER	Tom Hudson
THE PADRE	William Whymper
THE POLICEMAN	Steve Ullathorne
MRS TEBHAM	Janette Legge
MRS LEWIS	Maureen Morris

Directed by Nick Philippou
Designed by Anthony Lamble
Lighting by Ian Moulds
Sound by Paul Bull
Music by David Sawer

Note

For this production Kan Shu was omitted from Section [C]. Instead, Brian came on and sat till the Padre came on. The Padre's words '– its the infantryman's best friend' were removed from their position in the printed text and placed after the Padre says 'Rifle, Tebham.' just before Brian leaves.

Note

The play is derived from 'The Village School' scene of *Sugawara* by Takeda Zumo. Part One is set in eighteenth-century Japan and Part Two is set in modern Europe.

The roles in Part One should be doubled with those in Part Two. Various doublings are possible, but in Part Two the roles of Brian and The Officer must be doubled.

Part One: The Village School
The New Pupil
The Show
Chiyo's Narration
The Identification
The Proclamation

Part Two: The City
[A] Mrs Lewis's Kitchen
[B] The Padre's Office
[C] The same – later
[D] The Street
[E] The Canal Path
[F] The Police Station
[G] Mrs Lewis's Kitchen

Songs

In the first production a chorus from the cast sang the songs in the following places in the text.

Children Sit Bowed at Your School Desks before the first scene.

D'You Think I'll Always Carry Your Load? in The Proclamation immediately after Kotaro's body is carried out and before Kan Shu asks 'What d'you want?'. While it is sung the Mother sits alone on stage. It is important that she does not take part in the song.

The Broken Cup immediately after Part 2, [A]. Alternatively it might be sung immediately after Part 2, [B]. While it is sung Brian might come on stage and sit in his chair. Kan Shu might follow him a little later. Both would then wait till the end of the song.

Two more songs were written for the production of the second part of *Jackets* at the Leicester Haymarket. In this production *Children Sit Bowed at Your School Desks* was not sung. The other songs were sung at the following places.

The Broken Cup between Sections [A] and [B], by all the performers except the actor playing Brian.

D'You Think I'll Always Carry Your Load? the first two verses between Section [B] and Section [C] and the last two verses in Section [C] after Brian leaves and before the Padre says 'Fool. Fool. Fool.', by the actor playing Phil.

The Song of Two Mothers between Sections [D] and [E], by the actresses playing Mrs Tebham and Mrs Lewis.

The Padre's Song between Sections [F] and [G], by the actor playing the Padre.

Songs for the First Part

Children Sit Bowed at Your School Desks

Children sit bowed at your school desks
The prisoner's safe in his cell
The rich man rides to his factory
The street traders haggle and sell
The tanks stand guard at the frontier
The sentries keep watch in the night
Children bow low at your schooldesks
And learn to read and write

Children add sums on your fingers
The judge is washing his hands
The soldiers are taught to pull triggers
The officers to roar commands
Are they trenches or graves they're digging?
And why have they cordoned the square?
Children bow low and write at your desks
When you look up the streets will be bare

Children stand straight to salute the flag
That flaps on the hangman's rope
Dont ask what your fathers are making
In the factory outside the town
There has to be food for the table
And a roof to cover your head
And doctors to call when the roof's blown down
And flowers for when you are dead

Children bend low and study
The world will go on its way
The rockets are aimed in their silos
So its safe to go out and play
And when the rockets are fired
And your city burns day and night
You'll be bent very low at the schooldesks
Where you learned to read and write

Children sit bowed and study
Let the world go on its way
Dont ask what your fathers are making
Its safe to go out and play
The wind whistles over the barbed wire
Your enemies live far away
They dont walk beside you as you go home
And watch over you all the day

D'You Think I'll Always Carry Your Load?

D'you think I'll always carry your load?
D'you think I'll always sweat and toil?
D'you think I'll give you my limbs and my blood?
Like the birds of the air! Like the beasts of the soil!

D'you think I'll always come when you call?
D'you think I'll always jump when you shout?
D'you think I'll always bow my neck?
Like a beast in a stall! With a ring in its snout!

D'you think I'll always fight in your wars?
D'you think I'll always give you my breath?
D'you think I'll always march to be shot?
Like the clowns in your court! Like the armies of death!

    The grass will grow on the fields of war
    Rust rot your rockets and radar discs
    Trees will stand where your watchtowers stood
    Your prisons and barracks vanish in fire
    I dont need your pity or fear your fists
    My anger will rise like the sun at dawn
    On the empty world where no one will mourn
    And only wind howl for your funeral pyre

Songs for the Second Part

The Broken Cup

A tear running down the side of a mountain
The heroes chained to the frozen peaks
A paper boat sailing in the whirlwind
Dead soldiers' helmets thrown in a fountain
These are the questions! Who answers? Who speaks?

The lame man holds up the march
But marchers must rest
Let them rest while the lame man dances
His dance will cheer the marchers
Carry him on our backs
We'll manage!

The madwoman cant follow orders
Let her croon to the children
Her shouts will warn the enemy?
So would the children's crying
Let her croon – the kids will be quiet
We need her!

We found a dress in the ruins
Hung from a nail on a door
Don't borrow clothes from the dead
Let the curtain hang over the past
In these ruins we found a cup
Some things can only be drunk
From cups that are broken!

Trees that stand alone must bend in the storm
If a forest bent it'd uproot the earth
Collect bricks from the ruins
To build houses – or prisons for those who steal bricks
Decide!

    We are strong
    We came from the golden city
    We fled from the promised land
    We grow the harvest of plenty
    In the parched fields of rubble and sand
    We are brave – we are wise in measure – we are tough
    People of the ruins who found the cup that was broken
      Its enough!

The Song of Two Mothers

When you were young I told you
To wash your hands before you ate
I should have said sharpen your claws
And nourish the appetites of hate
So that you grow to flourish
In the city of the wolf
Where pity is the burden of the poor
And happiness is wealth

And when I sent you off to school
I should have hired a murderer
To teach you the tricks of his trade
And a butcher to teach you the rules of the game
And to stifle the voice of human shame
So that you grew to flourish
In the city of the wolf
Where pity is the burden of the poor
And happiness is wealth

And when you went into the world
I should have given you a pack
Of traitors to be your guide
And a knife to stick in the back
Of the comrades at your side
So that you came out on top
In the city of the wolf
Where pity is a liability
And happiness is wealth

And when I rocked you in your cradle
I should have hammered into your head
Be hard be hard as the nails
They'll knock in your coffin when you are dead
Instead I said child be gentle
And wash your hands and face
And sent you off to the lair
Where wolfs gnaw human bones
And I hear the human cry
In the groans of the market place
And in the traffic's roar I hear
Weeping and despair and fear
And Im so ignorant I try
To mend the holes in your shadow
And smooth the frowns of the sea
And wash the wounds of the sky

The Padre's Song

One hot summer day
Terrorists shot a soldier dead
He lay in the street
Leeking blood in his khaki
Like a baby messing its pants
They covered him with a clean white sheet
Nineteen and fit till he was hit
And got a hole in his head
His mouth's wide open – but he cant speak
So everyone else said what had to be said

The PM gasped animals
The opposition yelled scum
The colonel roared cowards
Only the dead man was dumb
TV presenters were outraged
Royalty was moved
A thug scrawled on a neighbourhood wall
Cut them up and feed them to pigs – hanging's too good for them
And the gutter press had a ball
And every cabinet minister swore
To give the last drop of the people's blood
And the army yelled more more more
Dont waste your life on the dole lads
Come and get your beret and gun
Have an army career in a hole lads
Funerals are fun

Business is good in the burying trade
The pound will rally round
The flowershops have got it made
Mechanical diggers dig the holes fast
And I've found my niche in life at last
Lowering lads in the ground
I keep clean white surplices ready to hand
The honour guard fire over the grave
And shit bricks – they could be down there – but look brave
And the bugle call sounds grand
There's nothing like a military funeral
To rouse the spirits of the land
Share prices will rise – but boom or bust
Go to your doom with a grin

Yours is to die and not ask why
We'll look after your next of kin
And give them money to ease their pains
And shovel earth on your remains
And pretend the earth is the sky
And at night as you lie and rot in your grave
In the ranks of the silent dead
The nation that said what had to be said
Pulls clean white sheets over its head
And goes to sleep in peace in bed
More more more
Get your beret and gun
Funerals are fun

PART ONE: THE VILLAGE SCHOOL

The New Pupil

A screen across the middle of the stage. Off, occasional shouts of schoolboys playing in the yard.

CHIYO *comes in.*

CHIYO (*calls*). Is the schoolmaster in please? (*Turns and calls off.*) Kotaro – quickly!

TONAMI *comes on from behind the screen.*

TONAMI. The schoolmaster's been called to town by the mayor.

CHIYO . When will he be back?

TONAMI. I dont know. Im his wife.

CHIYO (*calls off*). Kotaro – if the schoolmaster's wife sees you dont come when you're called she wont let him take you as a pupil.

TONAMI (*looking off*). Is he your son?

CHIYO. My husband's a cloth merchant. The war made people too poor to buy cloth. We have to travel far to make a living. It isnt good to take Kotaro with us. He should settle down so he can learn.

TONAMI (*calls*). Kotaro! – He looks a sensitive boy. Im sure my husband will take him.

CHIYO. We would be grateful. I have to go into town on business – may I leave Kotaro here and come back this evening to settle the fees?

TONAMI. Of course.

CHIYO. He's coming now you've called him.

KOTARO *comes on. He doesnt look at* CHIYO.

TONAMI. Good morning Kotaro.

KOTARO *bows to* TONAMI.

CHIYO. Say goodbye Kotaro. Behave so that we can be proud of you.

TONAMI. You may embrace your mother Kotaro. (KOTARO *doesnt move or look at* CHIYO.) Bring his change of clothes this evening.

CHIYO (*starts to go, then turns to look at* KOTARO). Goodbye.

KOTARO *doesnt look at her. She goes.*

TONAMI. Hands out. (KOTARO *holds out his hands.* TONAMI *looks at them.*) Palms. (KOTARO *turns over his hands.*) Good. Most of our pupils are farmers' sons. They have a hard life. You'll learn to survive. That'll help you when you're a merchant and times are so bad they bury people in their cot-blankets.

TONAMI *has rung a handbell. Four schoolboys come on:* TYGO, GAULI, FOOSHI *and* CHICO.

TONAMI. Quickly! Welcome our new pupil from the lowlands. Show him how polite mountain people are.

KOTARO *bows and the other boys giggle.*

TONAMI. Gauli – Chico: desks!

GAULI *and* CHICO *take the desks from a stack before the screen and set them out. The desks have flat tops and short legs: to write at them pupils squat on the ground.*

TONAMI. The schoolmaster set us a task. Fair copies of our alphabets. Fooshi: ink and paper.

Quickly and efficiently the village boys put out desks, ink and paper.

TONAMI. Kotaro's father is a merchant. Kotaro will be able to tell us all about the clothing trade. Kotaro will borrow the headboy's desk: *he's* working in the schoolmaster's study.

TYGO. Crawler.

TONAMI. What did you say Tygo? (*No response.*) Im glad to hear it. Gauli: desks straight please. (GAULI *straightens the line of desks.*) I want to see nice bold letters. Cheating wont help. Im going to get Kotaro's bedding roll and handbasin. Let's show the schoolmaster how well we work when he's away. I dont want to be ashamed when he comes back.

TONAMI *goes out. The boys squat in a line:* TYGO, CHICO, FOOSHI, GAULI *and* KOTARO. *They work in silence. Slowly* TYGO *pushes his desk till it shunts* CHICO's, *then goes on pushing till all the desks are shunted together.* GAULI *giggles briefly and* FOOSHI *gives a short anxious whimper.*

TYGO. Our mountains are steep.

The line of desks reaches KOTARO's. TYGO *pushes but* KOTARO *holds his desk still by pressing one hand flat down on the top. The line of desks stops.* KOTARO *goes on writing with his free hand.*

TYGO. Set stones on our fields stop the land slitherin in the river.

TYGO *pushes harder.* KOTARO *holds his desk down and goes on writing as before. His face is concentrated but without strain.* FOOSHI *jumps up and runs to help* TYGO *push.*

TYGO. Paths so steep they could set a door in 'em!

TYGO *beckons* CHICO *and* GAULI *to help him. They take up handholds along the edge of* TYGO's *desk.*

TYGO. Hup!

The village boys push. KOTARO *writes as before: his desk doesnt move.*

TYGO (*strains. The other village boys stop pushing*). Clever little sod's nailed his desk down.

The village boys laugh at TYGO. *He sits on the floor facing
away from his desk, levers his hands and feet against the floor
and pushes with his back against his desk.*

TYGO. Hed enough of play-acting! – now I'll move him!

GAULI. Ont use nails – we'd've heard the hammerin.

TYGO. Hid somethin under the top!

FOOSHI (*looking under* KOTARO's *desk*). No he ont!

TYGO (*stops pushing*). Well thass a rum un! (*To the other
village boys.*) Ont all gape! – that give him encourage-
ment! (*Pushes again.*)

FOOSHI. He'll break the desks!

GAULI. Ont want no bother!

CHIYO. Not worth it!

TYGO (*stops pushing and walks round* KOTARO's *desk.
KOTARO goes on writing*). Brought magnets into it
somehow . . . thass how thass done!

Suddenly TYGO *dashes to his desk, throws himself on his back
and pushes against his desk with his feet.* KOTARO *writes.*

FOOSHI. Stop it! Stop it! Stop it!

TYGO (*straining*). Push him through the wall an through the
mountain!

CHICO. Goo it boy!

FOOSHI. He'll smash the desks!

TYGO. I'll push the mountain on top of him!

The line of desks breaks and all of them except KOTARO's
scatter – he goes on holding his down and writing as before.

FOOSHI. Done it now boy! My leg's chip!

TYGO. I'll chip his head!

FOOSHI. Yoo know what a tarter she is: come through that
door, point straight at it and say: chip leg!

TYGO. All right boy, you hev a bit of strength. Merchant
buy cheap, sell dear: put our strength in their pocket. No
wonder you're fit! See through yoor tricks boy, only I ont

lettin on: suits me best you think Im ignorant. Tell you what though! – you come tradin round here I'll make dam sure people know all 'bout your tricks. Then we'll see who's smart!

KOTARO *writes as before.*

TYGO. Right! I give him fair warnin'! (*He pretends he's trying to get to* KOTARO *to attack him but the other boys are stopping him: he dodges about behind them, but really pushing them in front of him.*) Hold me back! Thass right boys! Save him from me!

CHICO. Git off!

TYGO (*pretending to struggle to pass the boys*). Stop me Gauli for the poor lad's sake! Devil now my rag's up! I'll turn him inside out! Rip his limbs off an stuff em in his pockets! Let me git at him!

GAULI. Bloody ass!

TYGO. I'll massacre him! Thank god there's a human wall between us!

FOOSHI *screams as* TYGO *pushes him.*

CHICO. Git off idiot!

TYGO (*pretending to calm down*). Thank God! – its pass! The power come over me!

FOOSHI. He damage my arm!

TYGO. There could've bin a massacre! Ont know me own strength! Pat a chap on the head an he goo through the ground! Thass a terrible talent for destruction! God bless you boys for savin the lad!

KOTARO *writes as before.*

FOOSHI. You massacre my desk – that'll be enough destruction for her!

GAULI (*to* FOOSHI). Look what he's up to boy.

FOOSHI *looks at* KOTARO's *script.*

CHICO. Whass he puttin down?

FOOSHI. Lor!

CHICO (*looks at* KOTARO's *script*). What is it . . .?

TYGO. Ont be fox by his squiggles. He'll say thass how they write where he come from! Tell a donkey it cant bray!

> GAULI, FOOSHI *and* CHICO *look at* KOTARO's *script.* TYGO *stands apart.*

CHICO (*to* TYGO). He's writin proper words!

TYGO. Schoolmaster'll catch him out – he know every sort of writin there is!

GAULI. He's writin down what we say!

FOOSHI (*points to* TYGO). You said all merchants cheat! – now they ont trade with our dads an we'll starve!

TYGO. They'll trade! Ont miss a chance t' cheat!

FOOSHI (*scared*). Shut up you ass!

TYGO (*looks at* KOTARO's *script.* KOTARO *goes on writing*). She said write alphabet! – that's a whole dam book there boy! Tent right! This is a school – come here t' learn, not show off what yoo already know! Thass worse than cheatin!

GAULI. Now he'll write that down!

TYGO. 'I'm a bloody fool'! – write that boy! I'll give you plenty of dictation!

CHICO. Stop it Tygo!

FOOSHI. I ont said anythin! – Cant remember what I *hev* said, with all Tygo's rattle!

GAULI. We was only larkin!

CHICO. Give you a laugh help yoo settle down!

TYGO (*reaches towards script*). Whass that?

> KOTARO *spits in* TYGO's *face. His expression doesnt change. He goes back to his writing.*

CHICO. He spit!

TYGO (*quiet, stunned*). No need for such depravity ol' chap! Are you sick?

CHICO (*quiet, explaining*). He's a gentleman. Thass how he learned t' hold his desk still an spit.

FOOSHI. Told him never t' push the desks! Ont my fault I cant read an write! Squiggles scare me – come out my hand like thass sick. Be even worse now he's broke my arm! (*Points to* KOTARO *as he writes.*) Look at that! Ont even got ink on his fingers! Writin so dam clear they'll hev t' read it! Yoo gone too far Tygo, you'll –

CHICO (*warning*). Desk!

The village boys frantically straighten the desks, squat and start to write. Silence. GENZO *comes in.*

VILLAGE BOYS. Mornin sir!

GENZO (*ignores the boys, calls*). Tonami!

GENZO *stands to one side deep in thought.*

FOOSHI (*whispers to* TYGO). Yoo hev the chip boy! See how yoo like it!

TYGO *and* FOOSHI *change desks.* TONAMI *comes in.*

TONAMI. Look how good they are!

GENZO (*to boys*). Home! School's over!

TONAMI. Not now they're working so –

GENZO. Out!

The village boys start to leave.

TONAMI. Desks – desks!

The village boys stack the desks at the screen, bob to GENZO *and hurry out.*

KOTARO (*to* TONAMI). May I be allowed to finish my –

TONAMI. Later.

KOTARO. The master will need an example of my work.

TONAMI (*moment's hesitation*). Take it over there. I dont want to hear you breathe.

KOTARO *takes his desk upstage, sits with his back to the others and writes.* GENZO *doesnt notice him.*

TONAMI. What's the matter?

GENZO (*low*). The message was a trap to get me into town. Henba was there! He's surrounded the town with his soldiers. He asked me four questions. 'Why does a general become a priest?' I didn't answer. 'Why does the priest hide on top of a mountain?' 'Why does he open a school for village idiots?' I started to say 'The wise man withdraws from the world when –' 'Tcha! – and why is his best pupil the son of the emperor my soldiers chopped to pieces and threw in the palace sewer?'

TONAMI. His spies were bound to find us even here.

GENZO. He ordered me to cut off the prince's head.

TONAMI. Ah no! What can we do?

GENZO. I came back through the pass. Rocks full of cracks as if they'd been thinking a thousand years and they dont even know where the path that runs at their feet is going!

TONAMI. Disguise him – smuggle him out through –

GENZO. Henba's soldiers are everywhere. By now he knows these mountains better than a snake with a glass belly. Even if we got the prince out how could he live? He knows how to order granneries to be built but he cant hold a beggar's bowl. He can send armies to die but he couldnt wash a scratch on his leg. He cant breathe without us!

TONAMI. He grew up in the hidden palace. Henba doesnt know what he looks like. Give him another head.

GENZO. Henba's as cunning as the thief who was hanged with the loot in his pockets! He's brought someone who'll identify the head with pleasure – Matsuo!

TONAMI. That traitor!

GENZO. He taught the prince archery. He stood so close to him he's adjusted the string over his face.

TONAMI. Children change! Matsuo hasnt seen him for a year!

GENZO. The prince belongs to the ruling class! That shows in his face! Where could we get a head like that? All we've got are peasants with as much breeding as cattle!

TONAMI. But dead? The face screwed up? Try! – or you'll spend the rest of your life –

GENZO. When the prince is dead we'll kill ourselves on his grave! You think I'd live after I'd killed him?

TONAMI. O god strike Matsuo blind!

GENZO. We asked god to give us victory!

TONAMI. Why are we talking of failing? Kill someone slowly – hack their throat – stamp their living screams in the dead flesh! Nothing's cruel or wrong if it saves the prince! This is the test! Kill one of this rabble! What gratitude do they show when we try to teach them to be human? I soil my hands on them like a washerwoman! We're entitled to their heads – we'll use them better than they can!

GENZO. If I peeled the skin from the prince's head in strips his class would still show: he takes care of his teeth. No matter what pain he dies with he'll look on the world with iron serenity. Does the sun set when you blow out your lamp – or one sort of fruit change into another sort because you bite it? The prince will die as he lived. If that isnt true we have no right to call ourselves leaders. Matsuo knows all this – even a *peasant* knows his dirt looks different when the sun shines on it! We need a boy who'd pass for ruling class – and where could we find him!

KOTARO *has stood. He bows to* TONAMI *and* GENZO.

KOTARO. Sir I hope I shall have the honour to call you master. M'am I have finished the calligraphic exercise.

GENZO. Who's this?

TONAMI. A new pupil. His mother left him. Kotaro you musnt interrupt –

GENZO. A pupil? To live in? Kotaro would you like to study

under me.

KOTARO. Yes sir.

GENZO. Then you shall. Go to the dormitory. Wait there.

KOTARO *bows and goes out behind the screen.*

GENZO. Who is he?

TONAMI. His family are merchants. His mother's coming this evening to –

GENZO. Late?

TONAMI. She didnt –

GENZO. Late enough! Too late! We'll give Henba his head!

TONAMI. We cant!

GENZO. *Merchant's* son? Why not! – monsters are born with two heads! Now a tradesman's fathered a gentleman! You begged the gods to blind Matsuo. The gods are wiser! They've sent us a head to deceive anyone!

TONAMI. But what if – !

GENZO. They say mountains creep forward. You dont notice till one day the path's changed direction or a wall of rock bars the old pass as if the stone floated there like mist! Matsuo hasnt seen the prince for a year – boys change fast! I'll creep up behind him – chop off his head with one stroke! He wont feel the wind of my sword on his cheek – it'll be blown away by his last breath! No disfigurement – a slight look of surprise – the eyebrows raised. Matsuo betrayed us because he thought our class was decadent. He'll take the raised eyebrows on the dead face as proof! O if he looked close he'd see the merchant's eyes narrowed to price up a customer – not a judge's piercing the accused! But he'll pass! *I* fell for him!

TONAMI. His mother will scream all over the mountain!

GENZO. Tell her he ran off because she'd abandoned him! We'll help her to search the – (*Stops.*) We cant, we cant!

TONAMI. Why not?

GENZO. Missing boy – screaming mother: the soldiers'll put two and two together. But the head's in our hands! If we let it go we're not fit to rule!

TONAMI. So the mother –

GENZO. Will be dealt with – if I must. All we live for, our culture, honour – one woman stand in the way of that? Not even a tradesman's wife! A whore! There *is* no husband to come prying! Its the war – an officer away from home. That boy's lucky! He was born above his rank – now he'll die above it: killed by an officer's sword! He came to learn. I'd've taught him to die for his country. Now he'll die before he's taught! Pass the exam without the study! Lucky lucky boy! Such abundance is extravagant! The gods are good to him! . . . Tonami, my officer's sword is under this priest's robe. If Matsuo sees we cheated I'll cut him down – and with luck Henba! – before I kill us both. – Its good we came here. If we'd crossed the frontier the foreigners would have sent the prince back to appease Henba. This village still has the old innocence. The houses and streets are built from stones gathered in the fields. In this bright light the crooked stream seems straight. Cattle and people born under one roof: the old die on one side of the wall, the cattle are slaughtered on the other. The sagas say the mountains give birth to dragons: in this squalor the prince will grow up to take back the riches of an empire.

The Show

TONAMI. Soldiers in the playground.

HENBA *and* MATSUO *come in.* MATSUO *carries a ritual cloth and headbox.*

HENBA. Is it done?

GENZO. I've finished the ritual ablutions.

HENBA. Get it over. He's seen my troops in the yard. Dont make him linger.

Off, villagers' voices.

VILLAGERS (*off*). Our boys! Please! Look their heads in the window!

HENBA (*calls*). What the hell –?

VILLAGERS (*off*). Schoolmaster! Gauli! Tygo! Yoo all right lads?

NCO *comes in.*

NCO. Villagers. Reckon one of their brats going to be killed.

HENBA (*looks at* GENZO). Its a trick! (*To* NCO.) Send one of the mob in. (*To* GENZO.) I'll sort those boys out inch by inch!

NCO *goes out.*

VILLAGERS (*off*). Our boys! Please!

NCO (*off*). Shut it! (VILLAGERS *murmur.*) One of you in there! – Lost your tongue now its your turn t' speak? Pick one of you out quick!

Slight pause. The MOTHER *comes in with the* NCO.

MOTHER (*uncertain who to speak to*). Sir – mister – villagers say one of our boys . . .? They on t' blame if they fail their lessons sir! Ont hev time t' study! Is it the grown-ups? Your war ont hardly reach us – we ont take sides. We're as harmless as our children. (*To* GENZO *and* TONAMI.) Never want their school!

VILLAGERS (*off*). Whass gooin on? (*Wail.*) Fooshi?

MOTHER (*calls to* VILLAGERS). Tellin 'em school ont right for young lads! (*To* GENZO.) Sit there all day till their limbs git distorted.

TONAMI. Be quiet!

MOTHER. We'll jist git our lads out your road. We'll tan 'em if they done wrong. Once I git my stick started I can win a race on a donkey thass bin dead three week!

GENZO. Must the prince die in the bellowing of a cattle market? You send him to the gods with a message of disdain on his face to show them the misery and despair you've brought to this country!

HENBA. Hush hush hush a few simple people looking for their young – and you drag the gods into it!

VILLAGERS (*off*). Gauli we're here! Ont fret lads!

HENBA (*to* GENZO). Fetch their kids out. But dont try to smuggle mine with them. Matsuo: dont be fooled by a few rags and a smear of yardmuck. (*To* GENZO.) One at a time. (*To* NCO, *indicating* GENZO *and* TONAMI.) Any trick, run them through!

TONAMI *and* GENZO *sit on one side of the stage.* GENZO's *hand is near the handle of the sword under his robe. The* NCO *stands behind them with a raised spear.* HENBA *sits alone.* MATSUO *sits with the ritual cloth and headbox by him on the floor.*

TONAMI (*calls*). Gauli.

GAULI *steps from behind the screen.*

HENBA. Stop!

GAULI *stops.*

MATSUO. He is not the emperor's son.

HENBA. Sure? Have his head if there's any doubt.

MOTHER. He's Gauli – Mr Looshi's boy!

HENBA. Shut up! (*To* MATSUO.) *Any* doubt!

GENZO (*disgust*). Doubt that pig's face? (*To* GAULI.) Grunt! (GAULI *stares in incomprehension.*) Grunt boy! – show the gentleman what's in front of him!

MOTHER. Grunt Gauli! Save yourself!

GAULI *grunts.*

MOTHER. He grunted! Can he goo?

GENZO. The prince wouldnt grunt if your army marched over his tongue.

HENBA. Fake priest, fake schoolmaster, fake *clown*: he

throws his voice! (*Stands close to* GAULI *and peers into his face.*) Grunt. (GAULI *backs away.*) He cant grunt!

GENZO. Your army took over the country like a corpse dressing itself up in living skin, and you cant tell the stink of a little gutter-rat . . .

MOTHER. Grunt Gauli! Doo a pig or they'll hev yoor head! (GAULI *squeals, half in imitation and half in fright.*) There! He squeal! Thass a proper pig sir! His family handle pork! (HENBA *walks away from* GAULI *in silence.*) Show the gentlemen how piglet goo when they git sight the old sow's dugs! (GAULI *squeals weakly.*) Help me boy! Ont my fault I hev t' ask such things! Gentlemen hev t' know so's they can run the country. (*To* HENBA.) Yoo heard 'un squeal sir. Poo he stink of pig! – gale ont blow it off 'un! Educated lad yoo're after ont even know pig squeal! Think they fly bout la-ing like a nightingale till they drop on his plate! (*To* GAULI.) Root boy! (*Calls to villagers.*) Gauli hev t' be a pig! Help him!

VILLAGERS (*off*). Pig? How they git a pig in there?

MOTHER (*calls*). No – Gauli hev t' be a pig!

VILLAGERS (*off*). What they want a pig for? Is they hungry woman?

MOTHER (*to* GAULI). On yoor knees boy! Show the gentlemen yoo ont too high an mighty t' be a pig! Root root root! (GAULI *falls to his knees.*) Im the farmer's wife! How doo pigs goo when she threw scraps 'fore 'em in the dut? (*Calls.*) Gauli hev t' be a pig t' save his neck!

VILLAGERS (*off*). Pig ont save their neck! (*They imitate pig sounds.*) Pig it for the gentlemen Gauli! They want a pig, yoo be a pig like a good chap! Gentlemen know best!

MOTHER (*shouts pig sounds to the villagers*). Help him! (*Pretends to scatter scraps.* GAULI *roots and makes pig sounds.*) Root root root! Yoo got it boy! (*Calls.*) We'll do it if we pull t'gether! (*Off, the villagers join in.*) There sir! – ont ask better proof'n that! Rest of pigs heard him they'd think he's their brother had singin lessons!

VILLAGERS *off, imitate a pig farm.*

MOTHER (*aside to herself*). My Tygo's in there! He'll come out an play the fool! Then there'll be trouble! (*To* GAULI.) Root lad! Keep rootin till the gentlemen say they had enough!

MATSUO. He's not the emperor's son.

HENBA (*to* GAULI). Trot! Quick before I change my mind!

GAULI *runs off.*

VILLAGERS (*off*). My boy! Whass gooin on?

MOTHER (*aside to* TONAMI). Call my Tygo next missus.

TONAMI (*calls*). Fooshi!

MOTHER (*aside, to herself*). There! – she ont be advised when I tell her for the best!

FOOSHI *creeps from behind the screen.*

HENBA. Stop!

FOOSHI *runs back behind the screen,* HENBA *goes behind it and brings him out by the collar.* FOOSHI's *mouth opens and shuts but no sound comes out.*

MOTHER. Thass Fooshi! Old Mr Goffre's boy. All right Fooshi, Im here. Ont bother with him sir! Whole village know he's a pig.

MATSUO. He's not the emperor's son.

Silence. FOOSHI's *mouth opens and shuts.*

MOTHER. Honk Fooshi!

FOOSHI *mouths silently.*

HENBA. Cant he do a pig?

MOTHER. He honk with the best of 'em sir. Trouble is he's backward. Bag of nerves since his mother die. Cruel t' drive his sort too far sir: they ont know the way back. (*Calls to villagers.*) Fooshi cant git his pig out!

VILLAGERS (*off*). Want another pig? Well thass a rum un! Fooshi doo a pig or I'll larrup yer!

MOTHER (*to* HENBA). I swear t' god we're jist common muck from the bottom of the trash. Ont even best muck from the top. Ont fit t' contaminate your air! Let 'un goo.

HENBA (*suspicious*). See how she's set on saving this one . . .! A few rags and a foolish grin: fall for that?

MOTHER. Grunt Fooshi! Squeal! Honk! Root in the dut like the pigs! Yoo ont let me help yoo boy! (*Calls to* VILLAGERS.) Help him!

VILLAGERS (*off, imitating pig noises*). Fooshi be a pig when the gentlemen say! He doo a pig if yoo tell 'un t' shut up! Blast the boy why's he so stand-uppish? (VILLAGERS *imitate sheep*.) Ont want sheep! Want pig t'day!

MOTHER (*aside, to herself*). An I still hev t' handle my Tygo! He'll come out an say 'Im the prince!' Then all hell'll be let loose! (*Calls.*) Tygo yoo play me up when yoor turn come, there ont be enough of yoo left t' be a pig!

VILLAGER (*off*). Ont mind yoor lump of an ass missus – my Fooshi need help! Honk Fooshi! – yoo honk like a famish litter when yoo're asleep! (*The* VILLAGERS *make pig noises*.)

MOTHER (*beats* FOOSHI *with a cloth*). I'll pig yoo, git our lads kill! Pig! Pig! Pig!

FOOSHI *falls down in fright and gasps*.

MOTHER. There! Im gettin t' the pig in 'un now! (*Stamps feet.*) Thass the butcher – thass the butcher's knife flashin front the kitchen window – (FOOSHI *squeals in terror*.) – pig! – pig! – pig squeal now he smelt the butcher's apron! 'I'll hev the head off that pig! Singe that hide! Tie its guts for sausige!' (FOOSHI *squeals hysterically*.) There sir – thass prime pig! (*To* FOOSHI) 'Tip his blood in the black pudding bucket! Chuck his offal t' the dogs!' (*To* HENBA.) Now he's off yoo'll hev a job t' git him stop! Ont bin steady in the head since his mother die – an *she* ont normal!

HENBA. Chuck him out!

MOTHER *helps* FOOSHI *out – he squeals as he goes.*

VILLAGERS (*off*). Tie him down! Drop him in the pond –
thass help afore! Howd steady boy!

HENBA (*shouting after* FOOSHI). Tell your father to lock you
up in the sty! Not decent parading in front of the village!

MOTHER (*whispers to* TONAMI). Tygo!

TONAMI (*calls*). Chico!

MOTHER (*aside, to herself*). I despair of the woman!

CHICO *comes from behind the screen.*

HENBA. Stop!

CHICO *stops.*

MATSUO. He is not the emperor's son.

MOTHER. Chico – Chis' eldest.

HENBA. Family of pigs?

MOTHER (*thrown*). Hev yoo had enough pig sir? Shall he be
a dog? Gentry find dog a useful animal sir. Chico'd make
a good dog – allus larkin, full of spirits – hev us in heaps
of an evenin! Chico doo how a dog beg! (CHICO *imitates
a begging dog.*) There sir thass a perfect beggin dog! (Good
dog Chico!) Proud jist watchin 'un! Prince ont know dogs
beg. His dog eat off best plate an throw his scraps t'
footmen!

HENBA. Seen better dogs in a cat home.

MOTHER. Yoo'll see the dog when I thrash 'un! (CHICO
howls. To CHICO.) That racket's music t' my ears!

VILLAGERS (*off*). They got a pig that howl now? Wonders
never cease! Do they want every sort of animal?
(VILLAGERS *chorus farmyard imitations.*)

MOTHER (*calls*). Chico's doin dog!

VILLAGERS (*off*). Chico'll doo a crocodile if that helps the
boss! (*They imitate dogs and farmyard animals.*)

MOTHER (*aside, to herself*). Thass gooin too well! My boy'll

spoil it! Stand there barefaced an say 'Im the prince'!
(*Calls.*) Im gooin t' whip Chico's dog!

HENBA Teach the hound to kennel!

VILLAGERS (*off*). She's makin a proper job! Dog ont
entitled t' ask for mercy!

MOTHER (*mimes pointing to a wall*). That ont a crack in the
plaster – thass my whip – (*Mimes taking down the whip
from the wall.*) – come yoo down off my wall, whip!
(CHICO *whines*.) His whine hev set my whip a'twitch!

HENBA. Scare him!

MOTHER. Wicked beast know what it deserve! Slink in its
corner! (*She mimes whipping* CHICO.) Switch! Switch!
Mouth droolin on the floor – drag body 'long behind it
like a floorcloth moppin up its spittle!

HENBA. Whip him mother!

MOTHER (*miming*). I'll whip him father! I'll flay the hide off
my hound! There! Whip so hard the skin jump off an run
down the lane – left the carcas stood there –

HENBA. Howling!

MOTHER. – till I whip it so it run off after its skin – the two
of 'em make a race of it, see which can jump in the ground
first!

HENBA (*laughing*). Whip him till his bones play dice! Look
at his legs! Lame him! (*Calls to the* VILLAGERS.) She's
lamed our dog! Walked in on its hind legs – crawl out on
its belly!

VILLAGERS (*off*). Us'll git the whippin gooin out here sir!
Allus ready t' lend a hand! Whip us-selve! Put on a good
show! Good dog! Smash! Smash! We're a-whippin sir!
(*Dog howls.*) Im a good dog sir! Whip me! Im smartin!
Make me howl!

HENBA (*calls to the* VILLAGERS). Harder! Make the walls
shake! The ground rattle!

HENBA *goes out*.

HENBA (*off*). Lame that skinny one – thrash him! (*Howls*

with laughter.) They're all lame! Lame dogs floggin each other! Whip yourselves dogs! Bite! Round and round! The dogs are whippin like the masters!

Off, the VILLAGERS *imitate dogs, masters and whips. Suddenly there's a big shout: in the village the real dogs have started to howl.*

HENBA (*off*). The dogs in the village! Howling!

Off, the VILLAGERS *roar with laughter. Onstage,* GENZO, TONAMI, MATSUO *and the* NCO *are motionless.*

MOTHER (*tentatively touches* CHICO – *she's unsure how the others will react*). Chico. (*Gently strokes his head.*) Good boy – help me an I'll git you out . . . (*The stroking changes to patting.*) . . . good dog . . .

HENBA *comes in.*

HENBA (*laughs*). The dogs in the village joined in!

VILLAGERS (*off*). I holla-ed louder'n Chico – I ought t' git his biscuit! Boot 'un woman! Make an ignorant dog if yoo show mercy! Quickest way t' spoil a good animal! Gratitude ont in a dog's nature – no more'n sense!

MOTHER (*to* CHICO). What doo a good dog doo when the whippin stop? (CHICO *slinks to* MOTHER *to lick her hand.*) Thass proof sir: he know dog through an through. Can he goo?

HENBA. Look dog – a rat!

MOTHER (*points*). Rat boy! (*Aside, to herself.*) God he's had the sense he was born with schooled out of him! (*Screeches like a rat.*) Git the rat boy!

CHICO *chases the rat.*

HENBA. Pounce dog!

MOTHER *screeches.* HENBA *runs round pointing at an imaginary rat running beside him.*

HENBA. Big fat plump rat! (*Points to* TONAMI.) After it – up the lady's skirts!

TONAMI *freezes as* CHICO *chases the rat round her. The* MOTHER *stays on one spot, screeches and illustrates the rat's movements.*

MOTHER. Im leapin in the air out a' reach the dog's jaws!

CHICO. Snap! Eeaarrgh!

MOTHER (*high screech*). Thass it sir – caught! Dog swep up an took me out the air like a flyin graveyard full of teeth! O his fangs is sharp! Honed an oiled on spittle an sweat!

HENBA. Worry the rat dog!

CHICO *growls as he tears and worries the rat. Away from him, on another part of the stage, the* MOTHER *shakes as if she's being worried in the dog's mouth. She illustrates the rat's death and then the shaking of its limp body.*

MOTHER (*as the dead rat*). Done for sir! Dogs teeth rip the bone. Bits stick out like a pin-cushion struck with a hammer. Never git me t'gether again. (*Musical scale as she ascends to heaven. Etherial voice.*) I'll hev a tale t' tell the dead rats! Didnt I put up a rare show 'fore I die! Led that dog such a dance its fleas ont know which end the animal shit! Im dead but Im still pantin from the agitations of livin!

VILLAGERS (*off*). Hev he kill the rat? Rats is ugly brutes! Good guard dog keep the boss's store clean! Boss give dog a whack for every rat-droppin in the corn!

HENBA. Catch!

HENBA *throws a piece of real biscuit to* CHICO. *He catches it, eats it and begs for more.*

MOTHER. Mongrels work up a terrible appetite for morsels.

HENBA. You've had your wages! (*He notices* GENZO, TONAMI *and* MATSUO *staring icily at him. Calmly.*) Fossil dogshit staring like the whites of a blindman's eyes. No

you didnt pass through the bowels of a dog: they're too
human for you. – Late. (*To* CHICO.) Work hard. Scratch
your fleas out in the neighbour's yard. Look after the old:
you'll be old and mangey one day. Kennel!

CHICO *goes out.*

MOTHER. Now the calamity! Kep my boy last till the rest
git off safe. He delight in bein reckless. Play the fool with
the madman!

TONAMI (*calls*). Tygo!

TYGO *steps from behind the screen.*

MOTHER (*aside*). Now we'll hev it: 'Im the prince!'
HENBA. Stop!

TYGO *stops.*

HENBA. Who are you?

MOTHER *silently 'mouths' the words as* TYGO *speaks:*

TYGO. Im the prince!
HENBA. He's the prince. (*Pause.*) What do princes do?

TYGO *stares at* HENBA *a moment, then leans forward and
spits at him.*

HENBA. The comic interlude. Poor lad you're not the prince.
(*Turns away. Becomes quiet.*) You're two a penny. Cheer
the army. Trumpets and laughter. Then dead soldiers
poking out of the mud like tents stuck on horses' bones.
Wind in the dead trumpeter's teeth. The sound he made
when he was a novice. Broken cannons – like giants born
dead. At night the mist in the mountains: a sea with
upturned boats. I must go.
MOTHER. Ont taught him t' spit on gentry: his natural
wickedness come out. (*Bows deeply.*) Ont harm a lunatic
sir.
HENBA. Pig? Rat? Dog?

MOTHER (*lost*). He's anythin natural yoo choose sir. Rat – dog? Or let him be your table.

HENBA. Table?

MOTHER. Your table when you come in from fightin. Full of food. Ont say you're greedy! – celebration. Soldiers pick the best from all your farms an shops an spread your table. How else we show our gratitude? (*To* TYGO.) You saw the table in the magistrate's parlour when they took father in for stealin – an the priest's table when your sister die. What yoo come home an show me?

TYGO (*rubs his stomach and groans*). Ee-er-ah.

MOTHER. There sir: poor man doin a table. Rich man see table, mouth water: poor man, groan. Why? Table carry food on its head – which is tantalisin t' the mouth – but ont eat: so full table groan like empty stomach. There! An they say the mountain groan cause it carry the sky – if thass of interest. Be advised an let 'un goo. Easy pull a chap up by the roots or shut the sty gate on 'un till the butcher come: but might his god sit watchin on the roof? – or squat up in a tree? Who's t' say? Be advised – an let me take 'un out your road. (*No response. She calls.*) Tygo did a table! (*No response.*) Gone – hidin their young in the village. (*To* HENBA.) He'll do the fields when the wind's famished: shake like the mountain with the gut ache. Or the river in the drought: lie down like bones that grow without the benefit of flesh.

She realises HENBA *isnt listening and stops. He looks up, goes to* TYGO, *pulls his head down and boxes his ears.*

TYGO. Ouch that hurt!

HENBA. That'll teach you to scare your mother out of her wits! Now hop it!

MOTHER *frantically signs to* TYGO *to go. He stands and rubs his ears.*

TYGO. That truly hurt! Could've damaged my hearing! Ont

even spit t' hit!

MOTHER *pulls at* TYGO. *He goes.* HENBA *turns away.*
MOTHER *goes to him and holds out her open hand.*

MOTHER. Hope you liked our show sir . . .?

Her voice trails away politely. HENBA *looks through her and
points to the four desks by the screen.*

HENBA. Four. (*Points to* KOTARO'S *desk.*) A spare.
GENZO. The prince's.
HENBA. Finish it.

GENZO *goes to* MATSUO, *bows, takes the headbox and goes
out behind the screen. For a moment the* MOTHER *stands with
her open hand. Then she goes.*

Chiyo's Narration

CHIYO *comes on. Her scene happens in another place: the others
do not see her.*

CHIYO. When I left my son at the village school this morning
I lied. I ran along the road. I saw a vision. I thought the
tears in my eyes were a river in the sky. But I saw it was
this river on the ground.

Enemies heads are cut off. Common heads are thrown on
the victory pile but upper-class heads must be identified.
Matsuo betrayed his class. But he soon despised Henba
and his new allies. When they fight at his side – even
when their swords defend him – their sweat stinks worse
than the carnage of the wounded or the corruption of the
dead. And Henba doesnt trust him: when he looks at
Matsuo his eyes are like woodlice crawling along a crack
in a mirror. Today Matsuo must identify the prince's
head. Genzo wants to save him. Matsuo wants to help
Genzo. But Genzo can only get his hands on working-

class heads. He knows they'd never deceive Matsuo. Matsuo cant tell him he'd pretend to be deceived. Genzo would think its a trap. So Matsuo did the only thing he could: he sent him Kotaro disguised as a merchant's son – but Kotaro is his own son. He counts on Genzo using Kotaro's head. Its his duty to use it just as it was Matsuo's to send it. Their duty's clear – but they're human and what will happen is as uncertain as the path of pilgrims on the sea. Will Genzo kill Kotaro – or will he kill the prince to save himself? Which head will he show Matsuo? How will Matsuo react? With joy if the prince is dead – or grief that his son's alive? With joy if the prince is alive – or grief that his son's dead? With joy that his son's dead – and joy that the prince is alive? Or joy that the day is over – or grief that it ever began?

And me? When I go to the school you'll know more than I do. Will I be a bereaved mother – or a wife shamed by a husband who betrayed us all by weeping when he saw his son's head – or even shouted the truth before Genzo could kill him? Tonight will I weep with joy for a living prince – or shout in triumph over my dead son? You who know, pity those who must learn.

I walk under the willows. I tear at the branches. They hang like empty strings giants tore from their parcels and threw away – and ran off to play with the toys! Children never play: they pretend – and stare at the giants. Look! – willow branches! The air is full of prayerwheels! If a bomb exploded and smashed the prayerwheels – the flying pieces would spin faster! – faster! – as if they prayed for those the blast was maiming and killing! I tear at the willows! Let them pray for me when I go back to the school!

CHIYO *goes out.*

The Identification

HENBA (*brooding*). 'Im the prince'. Who tells the truth? Liars. But they dont know it is the truth. When they open their mouth the oracle speaks.

> GENZO *comes from behind the screen. His robe and hands are spattered with blood. He carries the headbox. He puts it on the ground in front of* MATSUO, *then sits beside* TONAMI *with his hands close to the sword under his robe. The* NCO *still stands guard with his raised spear.* MATSUO *places the ritual cloth on his thigh. Staring straight before him he takes the lid from the box, lifts out the head and balances it on his left hand. Still without looking at the head he takes the ritual cloth in his right hand, wipes the face and puts the cloth on the ground. Then he holds the head before him and lowers his eyes to look at it.*

MATSUO. The head of prince Kan Shu the emperor's son.

HENBA. Coin! (*Clicks fingers.*) These villages too high for war to reach – more ruined than towns put to the sword! Couldnt make a cripple's crutch from their huts. Thatch? – a corpse's eyelashes keep off more rain. He's dead but he'll go on bleeding other people's blood. His class are at home in the grave. Flourish in it. Chuck their earth over the living – we have to fight our way out like kids tearing open their mothers to be born. (MATSUO *gives him a coin.*) Too much. Brass. (*To* GENZO.) You can go. The school's shut. Try a church. (*The* NCO *lowers his spear.* HENBA *pockets the coin.*) When I tax people their grimy fingers cling to the coins – the dead teach them their grip. (*Takes another coin from* MATSUO *and glances at it as he drifts to the headbox.*) One head with a begging bowl for a mouth. (*Glances in the headbox. Shows the coin.*) Your father's head: take you a long time to suck that off. (*Drops coin into headbox.*) Dont say thanks. Im withdrawing his coinage. (*Turns to go.*) The village.

HENBA, MATSUO *and the* NCO *go out.*

GENZO. He was under the same roof as Kan Shu and walked away! – look at him marching to the gallows before they're built! – We must treat this body as –

TONAMI (*looking off*). The mother!

GENZO (*looking off*). Her? – Already?

TOÑAMI. O Genzo the gods are punishing us for killing her son and –

GENZO. Get rid of that!

GENZO *gives* TONAMI *the headbox and she goes out behind the screen. He wipes his hands, covers his robe in a wrap and sits as if deep in thought.* CHIYO *comes in.*

CHIYO. The schoolmaster?

GENZO (*looks up*). Yes.

CHIYO. I left my son. The lady –

GENZO. I hope it went well?

CHIYO. – ? –

GENZO. Your business in town.

CHIYO. I finished early. (*Gestures off.*) I saw the gentlemen. I waited.

GENZO. You wish to pay your son's fees. We charge board and lodging and any –

CHIYO (*packet*). These sweets – I hope you dont think its wrong? – presents – ?

GENZO. A few small gifts do no harm.

CHIYO. May I give them to him.

GENZO. We wont disturb him. I'll make sure –

CHIYO. Yes – not disturb him – he couldnt say goodbye –

GENZO. He'll soon settle in to his new life. I'll make –

CHIYO. Neednt know Im here – just look through the – (*She goes towards the screen.*) – is this where –

GENZO. Please leave. Parents are not allowed in the –. Let me help you. (CHIYO *is staring at the screen with her back to* GENZO.) Dont try to see him. Thank you for the sweets. I'll make sure he –

CHIYO (*calls*). Kotaro!

GENZO *takes out his sword and goes towards* CHIYO.

CHIYO (*calls*). Kotaro let me see you – let me see –

CHIYO *turns to see* GENZO. *He strikes. She dodges, screams and runs away.*

CHIYO. Help!

TONAMI *runs in from behind the screen.* GENZO *chases* CHIYO. *She picks up* KOTARO'S *desk, swings it at* GENZO, *then holds it in front of her as a shield.* GENZO *strikes. His sword hits the desk. One of* CHIYO'S *hands holding the desk is pinning* KOTARO'S *letter to the top. Instantly she knows the writing and lets go of the desk. It drops like a stone: she's left holding the paper in one hand. Instantly she automatically reads the first words.*

CHIYO (*reads*). 'Dearest mother you brought me here to die'!

GENZO *stops with his sword in his hand. He and* CHIYO *stare at each other. Then she reads on.*

CHIYO (*reads*). 'You and papa arranged it last night. Forgive me but your voices were so sad I listened at your door. It gave me great joy to learn that our prince still lived and even greater joy to learn that I would die for him. Perhaps you think I am too young to know what dying is? Your son has the courage to die since his parents have the courage to sacrifice him –'

GENZO. Who is this wonderful boy?

TONAMI. He wanted to finish the letter before Henba came!

CHIYO (*reads*). 'If only I were able to comfort papa when he holds my head. Alas this letter must come into papa's hands too late to lessen his pain at that moment.'

GENZO. Matsuo his father! Today we stood on the floor of a new shrine and didnt know it!

CHIYO (*reads*). 'Forgive your son for not bidding you farewell. I was afraid I would cry and leave you with unhappy memories. I bow to our dear earth before you and papa. When you die and come to the dark city of which we read, a small white figure will hurry from the shadow of the walls and run along the road with open arms – your son Kotaro.'

GENZO. Who are you?

TONAMI. Matsuo's wife.

GENZO. I report that your son's death was spotless.

CHIYO. Tell me! Forgive me – I need comfort now!

GENZO (*reporting formally*). I went to kill him from behind. There was no reason to let him know he was dying: it was not his concern. Commoners die as unknowingly as they live. Life and death arent trials for them. But he heard me and turned. He was waiting.

CHIYO. Thank you, thank you! Tell me! This is what I want to hear! Every detail!

GENZO. He stared at me – a look of respect. For one second I thought – crazily – 'He's studying my face to see what sort of schoolmaster I am – that's why he doesn't see the sword in my hand'. Astonished I looked to see if it was still there! Had I dropped it? No it was in my hand! I saw his face reflected in the blade – suddenly the reflection stretched as if it yelled in pain – distorted! I looked back at him: his face showed iron calm –

CHIYO. Thank you thank you! Tell me!

GENZO. The blade was swinging to his neck: that's why the image was distorted. His neck was reaching to the blade as if a hand was giving me his head!

CHIYO. And then! Tell me! Tell me! This is the moment!

GENZO. The image on the blade flew at the neck – cut into it – as if his spirit ate his living flesh –

CHIYO. Yes! Yes! Its come! His eyes look down inside the darkness in his neck – the head's lifting – a shaft of light –

GENZO. The image flew from the blade –

CHIYO. To paradise!

GENZO. – wiped off it by his blood!

CHIYO. No shout – groan – scream!

GENZO. He stands. Stock still.

CHIYO. O if I was there to kiss this hand as it killed him!

GENZO. His body rigid. Pumps the blood up through the neck –

GENZO *opens his wrap to show his blood-stained robe.*

CHIYO (*clutching the robe*). Kotaro's blood!

GENZO. He falls to the floor! His blood falls down on him –

CHIYO (*clutching the robe*). I smell him! In his blood! His skin! His breath! My boy! Kotaro! Kotaro!

GENZO. – like dead rain searching for a living sea . . .

CHIYO. Thank you thank you! You are so kind! So kind to this poor mother! I bless the feet that took you to my son!

GENZO. Now I'll give you his body. (*Starts to go.*)

CHIYO. No – dont take his blood away – let me smell his hair – his clothes – his skin –

TONAMI. We'll let you have his body.

GENZO *and* TONAMI *go behind the screen.* CHIYO *stares at the letter but doesnt read it.* MATSUO *comes in.* CHIYO *still stares at the letter.*

MATSUO (*points*). I sat there – the skin was dead – the scalp moved in my hand – like an animal burrowing – I was gentle, gentle – I must have pulled –

CHIYO. He wrote.

MATSUO. – his mouth fell open – slowly – as if he tried to speak –

CHIYO. Hush. Dont.

MATSUO. – the eyes were empty – but the mouth – puckered –

CHIYO (*half laughing, half angry*). Dont cry. They'll hear. Dont.

MATSUO (*crying*). – like a baby's – and spittle –

CHIYO (*cradles* MATSUO'*s head*). No no.

MATSUO (*crying*). – ran down his chin – onto my hand –

CHIYO. You must be happy!

Two masks: CHIYO *laughing and* MATSUO *crying.*

MATSUO. – a red rim on my hand – as if a bucket had stood there – and spittle – bubbles –! Cruel!: all that's left of my human son! – as if a cleaning woman put her bucket there and slopped the water down the side!

CHIYO (*laughing*). He wrote to us! He knew he'd come to die!

MATSUO (*crying*). Knew? How?

CHIYO (*laughing*). He wrote 'be proud'!

MATSUO (*crying*). Wrote? Our clever boy?

CHIYO (*laughing*). Such a letter!

MATSUO (*crying*). Read. Read.

CHIYO (*laughing*). I know it by heart! A mother doesn't have to read that letter twice! Look! The writing! Not one blot – one mistake! Every word spelt right! Send that to the examiners! My son would pass their test!

MATSUO (*crying*). Read.

CHIYO *holds the letter at arm's length and recites without looking at it.* MATSUO *cries and stares unseeingly. From time to time his hand gropes towards the letter.*

CHIYO (*recites*). 'Dearest mother you brought me here to die. You and papa arranged it last night. Forgive me but your voices were so sad I listened at your door –'

MATSUO (*crying*). He said that?

CHIYO (*laughing*). And more! More! Be happy! (*Recites.*) 'It gave me great joy to learn that our prince still lived –'

MATSUO (*crying*). All in his letter!

CHIYO (*recites*). – 'and even greater joy to learn that I would die for him.'

MATSUO (*crying*). Joy! – to die for him! He said that!

CHIYO. Listen! Listen! (*Recites.*) 'Perhaps you think I am

too young to know what dying is' –

MATSUO (*crying*). No no! My son – he knew!

CHIYO (*recites*). 'Your son has the courage to die since his parents have the courage to sacrifice him'.

MATSUO (*crying*). Praises his parents! In his last letter! To spare them! He was older than his parents! Wiser than all the past!

CHIYO (*recites*). 'If only I were able to comfort papa when he holds my head.'

MATSUO (*crying*). Such a son!

CHIYO (*recites*). 'Alas this letter must come into papa's hands too late to lessen his pain at that moment.'

MATSUO. No! No! No more! Its making me live again! I thought I could be dead! I threw my skin over his head like a living shroud! His fingers are inside me! Scrabbling at me! A baby! Beating its rattle on the ground! Playing with bits of earth! Stones! My son is making me! Look – my father's face in the street before I'm born! My father gave birth to my son! I was missed! Missed out!

CHIYO. Listen! His letter! (*Recites.*) 'Forgive your son for not bidding you farewell' –

MATSUO. There's a beast called nothing! It ate me! No no! Who are you? Chiyo! My wife! I know you! Help me! Chiyo!

MATSUO *cries.*

CHIYO (*recites*). . . . 'I was afraid I would cry and leave you with unhappy memories –.'

Slowly the masks change. As CHIYO *recites she begins to weep and* MATSUO *to laugh.*

MATSUO. No no! (*Wipes his face.*) Cry? – he says cry to please you! Give you satisfaction! He knew how to speak to women not just men! No one must cry! The prince – what does he say about the prince? Give me the letter! (*He takes the letter from* CHIYO *and skims through it.*) Hu huh –. (*Laughs as he reads*.) 'Gave me great joy to learn that our prince still lived –'. Always prince – never self! Chiyo dont cry! (*Laughs and reads*.) 'I bow to our dear earth before you and papa –'! I forbid you to cry! You're shaming our son! Prince country parents sacrifice!! Always for others! Give! Give! Give! (*Reads*.) 'When you die and come to that dark city –'! Stop that! Bellowing like a she-cow by its dead calf! Joy! Joy! This letter is a National Monument! A sacred heritage! Look its creased already! (*Smooths letter. Reads*.) 'Even greater joy to learn that I would die for him'! (*Skims*.) Huh-huh! – 'A small white figure will hurry from the shadow –'. The bit that says he couldnt say farewell – he wrote that under your influence! I shouldnt have trusted him to you! You flaunted your despair in front of him like a whore touting for trade at her husband's funeral! Shut up! Is there no shame? He was young – one little flaw cant ruin this letter! It shows he was human! Child's flesh! Not stone! His monuments will be stone! The prince will hold his ashes!

CHIYO *weeps and stammers words from the letter to herself.*
MATSUO *turns away from her.*

MATSUO. Two heads. All that's left of the world. A foot apart. His and mine. Young and old. He tried to speak. A sound. No words. Whisper – use your last breath! Only a sound! – dumb circus animals pulling their chains when the storm's coming! In every hole: eyes nose ears neck – all the feet in a city – creeping – drunken cripples. His tears falling in his blood – I heard them! His tongue curling like a snail on a mountain of salt. (*Imitation*.) 'Aaeeghghii!' What did he try to say? (*To* CHIYO.) Stop it! – you're drowning our son's last words in my head! Let me hear them! (*He stifles* CHIYO *with the ritual cloth*.) Damn you! Child hater! Murderess! You she-cattle market! (*Covers his ears*.) Forgive me Kotaro! Daddy will

keep the sound in his head! Till he understands! Not let
it die! What did you want to say? Tell me! Kotaro help
me!

MATSUO *crawls to a corner and covers his ears.*

Its in my head! Eeaarrgh! Yeeargh! (*Pain and frustration
together in one sound*:) *Eeiiaarrghgh*! No! No! Still!
Control! Break it up! Remember syllables! Ee! Aa! Ee!
Oo! Ahh!

CHIYO's *crying is now harsh and dry. Her words sound as if
barked by a tired dog.*

CHIYO. The dirt in the gutters will get on my skirt. The
brambles tear the stitches. Sparrows fight in the
doorway. Flies go round my head – so close I can see the
sun shine on the dust on their legs. But he'll never call me
or pull my hand. Only his letter. When he wrote it – his
arms – the mountains were rolled up on them like sleeves.

MATSUO. Iieeaarrgh . . .

GENZO *and* TONAMI *bring* KOTARO's *body from behind the
screen.*

GENZO. Matsuo!

GENZO *and* TONAMI *set* KOTARO's *body on the ground.*
CHIYO *and* TONAMI *kneel before it.*

GENZO. Father Matsuo it was my fortune to strike off your
son's head. Now it is my honour to bring you his body. I
report that his death was spotless.

MATSUO. Yes. Thank you.

GENZO. The gods put our old heroes in the sky. Now the sky
over Japan is full of holy stars. Our new heroes are fires
in the ground.

MATSUO. When I held his head he spoke.

GENZO. Spoke?

MATSUO. Eeaarrgh . . .

TONAMI (*to* MATSUO). I thought you made the sound.

GENZO. Errii . . .

MATSUO. If he could speak! The wind blows dead soldiers on their shields as if its rocking them in their cradles. There's no wind in this room – I cant even pretend he's speaking . . .

GENZO. I heard the sound. I thought it was the panic knocking on the inside of my skull – it was so clear. Eee-iii!

MATSUO (*bows to* KOTARO). Kotaro tell me! You are a wonder child!

MOTHER (*off*). Schoolmaster!

MATSUO. Eeaarrgh . . . (*Interprets:*) Emperor . . .? *Emperor*! Its not a sentence! A word! (*Distorted.*) Heeh-hher-herr! Proclaim the *emperor*! That's what he said!

GENZO. What?

MATSUO. The emperor's Kotaro's age! Kotaro was ready! Its wrong to hide him here! He'll die here! Proclaim him emperor and fight!

GENZO. Without an army!

MATSUO. With an oracle from the dead!

GENZO. Waste our last chance on –! No army? Led by a boy?

MATSUO. Fight or Kotaro's death is wasted!

GENZO. No! (*Tries to calm* MATSUO.) Our class isnt destroyed. But we need more than dead oracles. Matsuo there are years in front of us when we must be patient. Not act like toothless fanatics!

MATSUO. Now I know why I was a traitor! I understand everything at last! The gods sent me to Henba to learn from him! When he's beaten he fights! A great power comes out of nowhere and he's even stronger! And now he's won he *still* fights! He's raising a new army. Not from the military caste – from rabble!

GENZO. Good! Easier to cut down!

MATSUO. Give him time and he'll turn them into a modern

army! He doesn't need an elite. Just fodder! – human
mud to clog up the battlefields – cling to our wheels!

GENZO. He wont be ready to fight for years. The
administration's a stone round his neck. He needs civil
servants – tax collectors –

MATSUO. Fight him before he gets them! Say Kan Shu is
the emperor come back from the dead! Raise an army of
rumours! Recruit rabble that's too low for Henba! The
gods want chaos! That's how we'll beat Henba! An army
of skeletons armed with bones! The modern world! When
a city's destroyed the rats are let out in the ruins! Genzo
I long to live under a new emperor! Wash off Henba's
slime! The sun will lift me up from the bottom of the sea!
If we do our duty everything else will take its place.

The Proclamation

The MOTHER *comes in.*

MOTHER. Soldiers hev took our lads! Rid off on horse an
the lads gallop after on foot t' be soldiers!

GENZO (*to calm her*). Commoners cant be soldiers –

MOTHER. 'S all changed! Say our lads ont fight for bosses!
Foreigners come t' take our land – so they hev t' fight –
git a share of the loot! Ont true!

GENZO. Let these people mourn in peace.

MOTHER. World comes to its end t'day! Ont no respect t'
stay on your knees an let it pass! (*Goes to the other women.*)
If you're the mothers of kids . . .? (*She holds out her hand
in the gesture she used to* HENBA. *No response.*) Ont goo
empty handed. Cows roarin – old people cryin – dads
cursin! But no lads hollerin in the fields: whole world
seem empty! Why're you so hard? Where'll it end if the
common people fight your wars? Already one of the
chickens hev start t' mew!

CHIYO. Shut up you filthy hag! My son's talking to the gods

while they decide if he'll spend eternity in paradise – and you come and distract him! He's dead because we have to share the world with you animals! You smother us with your mountain of filth!

MOTHER (*wipes hands on the sides of her skirt*). Ont had time for a clean up.

TONAMI (*to* CHIYO). She cant understand. (*To* GENZO.) Get rid of her! She pollutes the dead! His corpse will go to heaven reeking of her breath!

CHIYO. How can she be so cruel!

KAN SHU (*off, behind the screen*). Be quiet! I am Kan Shu son of emperor Ry Shu. The earth shudders and the sky turns away from our enemy's cruelties and the restlessness of the poor. Now there is dissension among our followers. Today I assume the mandate of heaven and proclaim myself emperor.

GENZO, TONAMI *and* MATSUO *crouch before the screen. The* MOTHER *is left alone by the body. She hesitates, half bobs and then straightens.*

MOTHER (*to the screen, as she makes her open-hand gesture*). Mister . . .

KAN SHU (*off*). Genzo and Matsuo, defenders of the throne: drive the barbarian from the land!

MOTHER. Sir – the soldiers hev stole your schoolmates –

KAN SHU (*off*). Matsuo your son's death is amends for your treason. As a token of our grace we will send you Henba's head for identification.

MOTHER (*to herself*). No – waste of time t' ask. (*Looks at* KOTARO.) They kill you, my little ol' chap? Ont git no help here.

KAN SHU (*off*). Cremate your son in the playground. You may bring me his ashes.

MATSUO, GENZO, CHIYO, TONAMI. } Emperor!

MOTHER *watches the others take out* KOTARO's *body.*

MATSUO. My son's cremated under the new emperor! His letter – we mustnt trouble people with the bits to his mother – take them out. They were put in by Henba's spies. 'Err! Corr! Ah!' There are more sounds in my hand! Write them down. Interpret his messages in times of disaster!

They take KOTARO *out. The* MOTHER *is left alone on stage.*

KAN SHU (*off*). What d'you want?

MOTHER. Git rested. Soon be out your way.

KAN SHU (*off*). The lady left some sweets. You will see them on the floor wrapped in a paper. Place them before the screen.

MOTHER (*to herself*). Ont see the lads no more. Threw their toys in the river an crossed the bridge. Thought mine had more sense! 'Stead he comes up with new rubbish! Say the army'll teach 'un t' do tricks! More likely how t' git blow t' bits! Then who'll pity him an his mates? Other mothers'll cuss us who bore 'em. Who'll pity them? Who'll pity us?

The MOTHER *puts the sweets by the corner of the screen and goes.*

PART TWO: THE CITY

[A] Mrs Lewis's Kitchen

A pile of loot on the floor. MRS LEWIS *and her friend* MRS TEBHAM *try on clothes.* MRS TEBHAM *is in a brown dress.* PHIL *watches and tinkers with a radio.*

TEBHAM (*brown dress*). Like this.

LEWIS. That's yours then. (*Hands her a bright formal dress.*) Get this on.

TEBHAM. I couldnt.

LEWIS. Try it.

TEBHAM (*getting out of the brown dress*). No – spend all the time worryin I was markin it.

LEWIS (*to* PHIL). You're not supposed t' look when ladies are changin.

TEBHAM. Too good t' wear round 'ere.

LEWIS. O dont make me cross. Try it before I change me mind.

PHIL. She's a free woman.

TEBHAM (*starts to put on bright dress*). Just t' keep 'er quiet.

LEWIS. I'll manage the buttons.

TEBHAM. I feel awkward.

LEWIS. Its your colour!

TEBHAM. Dont try t' force me when I've got it on, 'cause Im not takin it. (*Stands in dress.*) What d'you think? (*The others stare.*) Told you. Dont even fit.

LEWIS. Not if you stand like that! Look like a sack with a 'ole both ends. Stand straight woman!

TEBHAM (*straightens*). Its not suitable.

LEWIS. That colour gives you the eyes of a young girl!

  PHIL *whistles.*

LEWIS. Dont she look a cracker! Right – that's yours!

TEBHAM. I'd never wear it.

LEWIS. Give a party! Pull all the fellas in that!

TEBHAM. I am tempted . . . If I keep it you must let me pay.

LEWIS. 'Ark at 'er!

TEBHAM. 'E's entitled t' somethin: 'e 'ad the risk.

LEWIS. What risk! (*to* PHIL.) You're not takin 'er money!

PHIL. I dont want 'er money!

LEWIS. Grabby little sod. (*Sorts clothes.*) The quality of this! Shouldn't be allowed! (*To* PHIL.) Oi stop oglin or wait out on the landin.

TEBHAM (*brown dress*). Let me stick with this. Least it'd get worn.

LEWIS. You're 'avin both so dont argue. (*Drops the brown dress on* MRS TEBHAM's *pile and hands her a coat.*) Try that. (*Sweater.*) O I love this! 'E's a good lad! Other lads'd come 'ome loaded with stuff for their own back – 'e thinks of his mum! (*She puts her arm round* PHIL's *neck.*)

PHIL. Get off!

LEWIS. Time we treated ourselves. Dont call this thievin. (MRS TEBHAM *starts to remove the bright dress.*) Leave that.

TEBHAM. Wont go with the coat.

LEWIS. You can slip the coat over for size.

TEBHAM (*puts on coat. To* PHIL). You be careful. They make films then pick out the faces.

LEWIS (*suddenly sharp, to* PHIL). You didn't see no one filmin?

PHIL. No.

LEWIS. Dont bring your troubles in 'ere! – Show Mrs T your jacket. And 'e got 'is radio.

PHIL *puts on jacket.*

TEBHAM (*coat*). I could wear this shoppin. (*Takes off coat and puts it on her pile.*) That dress worries me. It'd cost t' 'ave it turned up.

LEWIS. I'll turn it up. (*To* PHIL.) Pass me pins.

PHIL *hands* MRS LEWIS *a tin of pins. She kneels in front of* MRS TEBHAM *to pin the hem.*

LEWIS (*pinning*). If we're goin round this smart we'll need proper shoes.

PHIL (*jacket*). Good?

TEBHAM. Nice. 'S'got a mark.

PHIL (*shrugs*). Drop of oil.

LEWIS (*pins in mouth*). I'll take it t' the cleaners. (*Hem.*) Too high – too low?

TEBHAM. Must need me 'ead testin.

PHIL. Take you disco'in in that!

TEBHAM. . . . See?: waste . . .

Doorbell.

Police.

LEWIS. Not 'ere! They couldnt pick 'im out the crowd!

PHIL (*going to door*). Not police.

LEWIS (*to* PHIL). Put this away. I'll see t' the door. Stay in there.

They bundle the loot together.

One of the flats pryin. Not safe t' draw your curtains, they take a fancy t' the pattern an nick 'em.

PHIL *takes the loot out.* MRS LEWIS *opens the front door.*

(*Off*). I dont believe it!

MRS LEWIS *follows* BRIAN *in. He wears army uniform.*

TEBHAM. Brian! (*She embraces him.*)

BRIAN. Bin 'ome. Werent in – knew where t' find you! What you got on! Im on leave!

TEBHAM. How long? Why didnt you warn me?

BRIAN. Bin posted.

LEWIS. 'Ere?

BRIAN. Permanent.

LEWIS. What for?

PHIL comes in. He has taken off the jacket.

PHIL. Bri!

They exchange greetings.

LEWIS. 'E's posted 'ere!

PHIL. 'Ere?

BRIAN. The riots.

LEWIS. What riots! No riots 'less you lot come an start 'em! Few kids let off steam and they send the bloody army? My Phil was up there, so that's 'ow 'armless it was!

BRIAN (*to* MRS TEBHAM – *the bright dress*). That come from there?

TEBHAM (*realises she's wearing the bright dress*). O. (*She starts to take it off.*)

LEWIS. Yeh – that's what the army's for: not 'elp us – save their shops! (*To* MRS TEBHAM.) Dont you dare take it off!

TEBHAM. Pins catchin.

LEWIS. Looks a blasted sight better on you than some lanky cow can afford their prices! Begrudges 'is own mother a pretty dress!

BRIAN (*shrugs*). I never asked t' be posted!

LEWIS. Law forced the crowd up against the window – it broke – they stampede – an the clothes are left all over the road. 'E supposed t' stand an watch 'em trampled in the glass? Wouldnt've been there long if your crowd'd bin around!

PHIL. Let 'im alone.

LEWIS (*folding the bright dress*). Suppose this means we dont get our new shoes. (*To* PHIL.) Fetch 'er things. (*To* MRS TEBHAM.) Leave your nice dress.

PHIL goes out.

LEWIS. You'd better 'ave some tea or somethin. Now you're

'ere. Its not lifted.

PHIL (*off*). Lay off!

LEWIS (*calls to* PHIL). Well! Im allowed t' pull 'is leg! 'Is
uniform dont scare me. I knew 'im when 'e couldnt keep
'is nappies dry.

PHIL *comes back with a pile of clothes.*

BRIAN (*starts to go. To* MRS TEBHAM). Okay? – I only got a
twelve hour pass.

TEBHAM. I thought you was stoppin!

BRIAN. Confined t' barracks 'cept on duty. Got the pass
cause Im local. (*They stare at him. He shrugs.*) Uniform –
provocation – walkin target . . .

PHIL. How many's the army sent?

BRIAN. Two regiments. Support – armour – all the gubbins.

PHIL. Bloody 'ell!

LEWIS. Makes us feel like the enemy!

BRIAN. It'll quieten down now we're 'ere.

TEBHAM. Better go.

BRIAN. Cheerio.

PHIL. See yer!

MRS TEBHAM *and* BRIAN *go.*

LEWIS. Left some of this at your girl's?

PHIL. Yeh.

LEWIS. Tell 'er not t' wear it in the street for a while.

They go.

[B] Padre's Office

PADRE *and* OFFICER.

PADRE. Sit you down. What's your problem?

OFFICER. For two month's I've been waiting for the rioters
to act. So far they've only wounded twenty-nine of my

men – though to be fair two of them had to be invalided out. Now at last a bit of luck!: a dead policeman.

PADRE. I read the lesson at the funeral.

OFFICER. I sold his killers the gun.

PADRE. Ah – a confession.

OFFICER. No I did it on orders.

PADRE. On orders!

OFFICER. The rioters will get guns. If they get them from us we'll know what they're armed with.

PADRE. But what am I to think at the next military funeral!

OFFICER. We must provoke them into using force before they're ready. Then fewer soldiers will die. The policeman's death is a help, but we need a dead soldier. Then we'd be allowed street searches, mass arrests, internment without trial, new weapons – the whole situation would improve. The men need a dead soldier too. Fighting people who speak your own language isnt easy. A dead soldier would do wonders for morale. The young men would go on the rampage. As it is, they sit and twiddle their thumbs – all for the lack of one dead soldier.

PADRE. God will call him in his good time.

OFFICER. God's good time is often a bad time for everyone else. The rioters are becoming organised. I've arranged to meet their representative to improve the gun-running. It'll be a hair-trigger confrontation. If one small thing goes wrong they'll panic and open fire – and there's the dead soldier. We agreed to wear a white tie to identify ourselves. Instead, it will be black! That's all it needs: they'll shoot!

PADRE. You'll make that sacrifice! My son we scorn modern youth! Yet you're making the supreme sacrifice as if the past had never left us! I struggled to keep the faith! Im not insulting the army, but barrack life isn't the place to –

OFFICER. Im doing this on my own initiative.

PADRE. My son we'll miss you – the men as well. And think! – only I shall know your secret! My funeral oration will be magnificent! No no I must forgo that pleasure – be calm, simple – 'another soldier has done his duty in the field'. One day I shall speak out! Till then – silence. You have your trial, I have mine. But I mustnt depress you: let's make arrangements for your funeral. The hymns in your honour! The flowers! – from the hothouses of the mighty to humble allotment greenhouses! Choose the hymns carefully! Many sound fine on an organ that are lost on a brass band. So often I've felt how let down the deceased would be if they heard them. Alas! the next of kin are left to bear that burden alone. I beg you not to spoil their occasion. Of course the choice is yours, but *Behold the Awful Dawning Breaks* has a fine counterme-lody on the tuba if the bandsman is up to it.

OFFICER. It will be televised.

PADRE. What a pity there is no widow! But you've left it too late to do anything about that. Dying warriors have been married from hospital beds, but we can hardly expect a young English bride to walk up the aisle to be greeted by a coffin – even in these days of novelty. Should she wear white or black? Should one play *The Dead March from Saul* or *Here Come the Bride*? One couldnt please both families. The organist would resign in a tantrum and they're impossible to replace. No no I cannot consider it. Besides dissensions at the wedding ceremony would not augur well for the future of a marriage already so heavily burdened in other respects. Of course your honeymoon would have been spent in paradise (and how many can say as much?) but you'd have been on your own. Well at least you can provide loving parents and the army will provide old comrades, a band, a salvo over the open grave –

OFFICER. I shall command the gun party.

PADRE. On a tape machine? I know of nothing against it but I shall need the bishop's ruling. We must avoid an exhumation. The methodists would fuss. The ecumenical movement affects us all in ways we have not forseen. Mankind is frail! Next of kin seem to regard exhumation as a mark of distinction. It brings out their one-upmanship. Let it take hold and they're digging up bodies all over the place. One could not venture out of one's door at night for fear of falling into a hole. The dead are risen and we're confined to our kitchens! Not that I want to deny your last wish – if such it be. A tape machine! Your last command might issue from the grave itself! Thousands of souls saved by –! But forgive me! – you've turned your back on the frivolities of this world –

OFFICER. Im not going to die.

PADRE. Not die? But you gave your word – to a padre!

OFFICER. I cant die. It would be dereliction of duty. The soldier's death will set the city ablaze. I cant desert my men when they need me most. I see civil war.

PADRE. But this is wonderful! Forgive me – when you spoke of sacrifice, I thought 'we have a right to expect sacrifice from an officer'! But now you tell me a common private, a man of the masses, the lowest of the low, vermin, scum, a squalid blemish on society's face – snatched from the gutter by the army, dressed in khaki, taught to say 'country' and 'duty' like a babe saying 'ma' and 'pa' – steps forth from the ranks and cries 'Take me! I claim my right to be this sacrifice!' Your example inspired this outcast. How else could the idea have got into his thick head?

OFFICER. A private's death does far more good than an officer's. Their mother's make better TV. An officer's lady cant be seen behind her veil.

PADRE. True! – it might be a sheet on a parrot cage. I've seen privates' mothers stagger up to the open grave as if its just gone closing time. Wives tearing their hair – you'd think they'd had to leave bingo when they only needed one number for a winning line. The whole nation benefits! But the deceased's mother mustnt know our secret! She could've sold it to the papers! She'd tear her hair out if she knew the money she was losing! We must deny her the consolation. She too must make her sacrifice. And the army will give her a medal to fondle. Those distinguished initials that look so moving after a private's name, as if a costermonger were selling caviar from a whelk stall. (*Announcing.*) Private – (*Stops.*) Who is he?

OFFICER. The rioters may know me from earlier dealings. It has to be someone who'll pass for me. Fortunately there's a Private Tebham.

PADRE. Tebham? (*Shrugs.*) He must be a christian to make this sacrifice.

OFFICER. He doesnt know.

PADRE. Not know he – ? (*Vaguely mimes shooting a starting pistol into the air.*)

OFFICER. No.

PADRE. But you've ruined it again!

OFFICER. Our soldiers are well trained but we cant expect too much. A man'll go into any danger as long as there's a sporting chance the bullets will go into his buddies and not him. Soldiers are gamblers. When a gambler's desperate he puts his shirt on an outsider: the difference is the soldier puts his skin.

PADRE. You promised me a sacrifice!

OFFICER. I promised you a body.

PADRE. Its not the same.

OFFICER. Millions are sacrificed in war and they dont know. God doesn't mind. I spare Tebham the great burden of *knowing*. I carry his cross for him.

PADRE. Im confused. Who am I to pray for at the funeral?

OFFICER. All of us.

PADRE. How can I? Tebham might be watching! I'd feel as if I was in an argument and using 'amen' as a debating point. You need a better leg to stand on by the open grave. Couldnt you drop him a hint?

OFFICER. He doesnt know why he was born in one street and I in another. Why I went to Harrow and he went to Puddle Row. What the government's up to. Or the stock exchange. In fact no one told him what he's been doing all his life. If you told him now he'd die of shock before he could get to the people who're going to kill him. *I* dont know what *I'm* doing. But I cant let that stop me. If I did there'd be chaos. Frankly I dont even know if its right to kill him. Its the best I can think of. But I'm not god. I might be wrong. Then the thing would drag on till many more are dead – and he'd be one of them. Its cruel to ask too much of people. Let them jump when I tell them and let me worry where they land.

PADRE. Why've you told me this?

OFFICER. I have a spiritual crisis padre: I need someone to know how clever I am. But I dont believe in god, so there's no one watching. You know the story of the emperor's new clothes. Well now the emperor's clothed and the mob's naked. They think they own the world but its still ours. If they found out they'd kill us. That's why we're stiff and cold: we pretend to be dead.

PADRE. Try the MO.

OFFICER. No padre. When you pretend to be dead, you die. I am the walking dead.

PADRE. Ah yes the MO couldnt cope.

OFFICER. Im a candle that shines because it burns at both ends.

PADRE. In the age of electricity?

OFFICER. I clean my teeth but I still think they're yellow. My buttons are polished. I get my tunics from Saville Row – but I put them on and feel like a tramp. The skin's flaking on my Sam Brown. I drag the world round on my heels like a ball of mud.

PADRE. Change your batman. Can I speak to – (*Forgets name.*) He's going to be sacrificed but doesnt know!

OFFICER. Tebham. I'll send him to you.

PADRE (*wheedles*). Couldnt he be crippled? Im good with penitents in wheelchairs. I'd sit with him for hours. Nothing would be too much trouble – provided he oiled the wheels.

OFFICER. No. Wheelchair heroes are a menace.

PADRE. Alas yes! If royalty arent bobbing up all the time they brood and end up writing pamphlets. Then the military police have to arrange an accident with the brakes.

The OFFICER *goes.*

[C] Same – Later

KAN SHU *comes in in Japanese Imperial regalia. He bows to the audience.*

KAN SHU. Emperor Kan Shu. The sweets were inferior.

BRIAN *comes on. No one in the scene is aware of* KAN SHU *– he is invisible.* BRIAN *slumps on a chair downstage, staring ahead with his rifle on the ground beside him.* KAN SHU *goes to* BRIAN, *picks up his rifle, walks to the side and releases the safety catch. The* PADRE *comes from his office.* KAN SHU *aims at* BRIAN. BRIAN *springs to attention.*

PADRE. Tebham?

BRIAN. Sir.

PADRE. Your company commander's spoken to you.

BRIAN. Sir.

PADRE. You'll undertake the mission?

BRIAN. Sir.

KAN SHU *shoots* BRIAN.

PADRE. Stand at ease.

BRIAN *stands at ease.* KAN SHU *goes to* BRIAN *and puts the rifle beside him on the floor.*

PADRE. You realise your danger? You stand face to face with an enemy who speaks your language and walks your streets but inhabits another world. He might be from Japan. Dont trust him.

BRIAN. Sir.

KAN SHU *goes out.*

PADRE (*turning*). My office is quieter. (BRIAN *starts to follow him.*) Rifle, Tebham – its the infantryman's best friend.

BRIAN *goes back for his rifle and follows the* PADRE *into his office.*

PADRE. Sit you down.

BRIAN *sits.*

PADRE. Tebham when did you last think of the fiery pit?

BRIAN. Dont know sir.

PADRE. Before you undertake this mission there are many things you should think of. D'you pray?

BRIAN. Sorry sir.

PADRE. Unwise Tebham. None of us knows when we're in need of prayer.

BRIAN. Dont worry about me sir: I can take care of myself.

PADRE. Dont boast Tebham. You're dealing with lunatics. They might have you shot.

BRIAN. They've got more sense sir. They want guns. Shoot squaddies anytime.

PADRE. Tebham – god lends each of us a soul to take care of and we owe it to him not to be too trusting. You dont make my task easy! Its all lager and ladies of the street! And when it comes to your funeral I know I've failed. Your pain is past – I still have to pray for your soul when I know the task is hopeless! Can you imagine the torment of that?: no. In one afternoon I endure all the suffering you're allowed to spread out over eternity! Tebham please pay attention.

BRIAN. Sir.

PADRE. Every night my prayers went unheard. Yet no cry of despair broke from my lips like a lonely sergeant-major shouting at an empty parade ground. Till last night! – when my prayers were answered!

BRIAN. Is everything all right sir? My mother – isnt –?

PADRE. Your mother?

BRIAN. Is she all right?

PADRE. Of course she's all right. As far as I know. I expect she's at Bingo or asleep. Isnt that how the mothers of this city pass their time? She didnt spend last night on her knees! Well she may have missed the jackpot! Last night I heard god speak! O not to me! Such are the ways of god! – to humble the mighty of rank by letting them hear him talk to a common uncouth private: you Tebham! Share god's bounty with me! I am a padre! Let me hear again the words god spoke to you.

BRIAN. What did he say sir?

PADRE. Didnt you hear?

BRIAN. No sir.

PADRE. Not one word?

BRIAN. Perhaps the radio was too loud.

PADRE (aside). I suppose its possible he forgot? (Smacks his brow with his palm.) Stupid! Stupid! You have no theological grounding so you heard after your own fashion! God sent a sign? The curtain fluttered in the window?

BRIAN. Dont have curtains in barracks.

PADRE. Well – a dream?

BRIAN. Had a few beers in the NAAFI. Dont dream when Im a bit . . .

PADRE. Then what am I to think? Has pride misled me again? (Clasps hands prayerfully.) O lord you ask much – sift my weakness through and through – and now – is it possible? – am I thy vessel? – to speak like the prophets of old? Yes! Yes! He speaks in my mouth! Arise! Gird up thy loins and go!

BRIAN. Shall I leave sir?

PADRE. Yes! You understand? Yes Tebham! Run fleetfoot to your Golgotha! – the bones will crack underfoot like pistol shots and make you feel at home. Leave! Go forth! Meet thy enemy! – and be shot!

BRIAN (*half rising*). Yes sir rightie-o will that be all sir?

PADRE. Yes! – that will do! – at any rate for the moment. Arise! Go forth! Be shot! (*Looks at* BRIAN.) You do understand what the lord wants Tebham? He sends you forth to be shot!

BRIAN. O dont worry about me sir: I can take care of myself.

PADRE. Dont keep saying I can take care of myself! God doesnt want you to take care of yourself! He wants you to be shot! How can I put it to you? The wheels turn – the great engine shudders – and you are caught up. Is that clearer?

BRIAN. Sorry sir – if I can do anythin t' oblige – only too willin t' –

PADRE. Tebham there is a plot to have you shot. Is *that* plain enough?

BRIAN. You're tryin t' tell me somethin sir.

PADRE. Dear god must I show you your dead body before you know your days are numbered?

BRIAN. You want me t' flog raffle tickets for Army Orphans?

PADRE. God in heaven! – beer and videos have addled his brain! To think the defence of this poor realm is entrusted to his hands! (*Pause.*) Of course when I say plot I dont mean plot. That's egging the pudding as your mother would say. (I see you're fond of your mother – at least we may credit you with filial piety however limited your grasp of military intelligence.) There is no plot. God doesnt want you to be shot. How shall I put it? *I* want you to be shot. No again I phrase it clumsily! I want you to *choose* to be shot! Got it! – I knew I would if I persevered.

BRIAN. Shot sir?

Slight pause.

PADRE. . . . (*Looks up.*) Forgive me Tebham: I was following my train of thought. Indulging an idle fancy. You spoke?

BRIAN. You want me to be shot sir?

PADRE. You sound surprised! Surely its clear why god sent me to you? He saw your weak grasp of the transcendental and sent me as his mouthpiece. Arise – go to your meeting – antagonize the enemy – (I believe a black tie is to be worn?) – and be shot! Great heavens Tebham our fathers died for us! – shall we refuse the torch? I give you salvation of the soul! Dress you in the raiment of sacrifice! – the white khaki of the lord! Go in the dignity of man! Say yes to the lord! Arise! Go forth! Be shot! With a bullet! – Is that clear Tebham? (*Points.*) In the head. (*Chest.*) Or here. (*Stomach.*) Or here. I leave the details of your martyrdom to you and your assailants.

BRIAN. Permission to leave sir.

PADRE. No!

BRIAN. You're not well.

PADRE. Yes yes its so easy: anything beyond the narrow limits of your little minds – and 'you're not well'! D'you think a padre doesnt know when god speaks? I could have you court-martialled for refusing god's command! O I've heard it all so often! A minor peccadillo with a rattle – the first insouciance of blossoming youth – and nanny said 'you're noo the well'! (She had a Scottish accent.) At school classmates I'd called chums turned on me and said 'you're not well'! Even in theological college when I found them puffing their poisonous gaspers in the gardener's shed and denounced them to the dean: 'you're not well'! (*Tries again.*) Is it that the idea is new to you? This chance may never come again. It hurts me to see you throw it away. Your funeral will be far more

impressive than a person in your station has a right to
expect. Can you seriously say your life is a more
attractive alternative? Year after weary year – no job,
dole, debts, a leaking roof, screaming kids, ageing and
falling apart in a vandalised city, in dread of nuclear
armageddon (fry up) – I shudder at what lies before you!
– when all the time you might be sleeping at peace in your
grave and I might be leading pilgrims to pray at its side.
Tebham Tebham how have we failed you? Surely no sane
man could hesitate when the choice is so clear? – Your
mother would get a pension. I hope that show of filial
devotion was not a flash in the pan!

BRIAN. Permission to go sir.

PADRE. Yes yes go! No! – sit! Could I have said something
– out of place? (*Realisation: claps head with hands.*) O fool!
Fool! Yes humble me with that pitiless gaze! I've
misjudged you! I said *take*! Take the medal – take the
pension – take the glory – wallow in your funeral! Take!
Take! Take! And your word is *give*! I see it all! (Thank
you lord for showing me the way!) Yes Tebham prostrate
yourself in the dust: *there* you are at home! You'd rather
be blown to human confetti than burden your comrades
with the labour of burying you! Give for others! For the
regiment – the country – for nothing!

BRIAN. You're mad.

PADRE. Ah. Mad. We've come to that. (*Reflects, then:*) No.
Mad is a good word – indeed a favourite of mine. But I
have no right to claim it. I am too lazy. I see your gaze
is the Gorgon's stare. Betrayed, again I stand alone.
(*Pause.*) Tebham in – I wont keep you much longer – my
zeal for your welfare my approach – lacked finesse. The
mot juste I think. Forgive me. How hard it is to don the
cloth in uniform! The sniggers. Jibes. O the officers are
no better. D'you smoke?

BRIAN. No.

PADRE (*takes out cigarettes and smokes*). I only do it to put the men at ease. Sure? – they're Sobranie cocktails. Tebham – I find it humiliating to ask – but this is a private chin-wag – I'd be grateful if you didnt speak of this to anyone? (*Exhales.*) Of course if you feel its your duty – (*Shrugs.*) When d'you go on your mission?

BRIAN. T'morrow.

PADRE. Be silent till the day after tomorrow. Take a tip from you spiritual adviser. You need time to reflect on your future.

BRIAN. Yessir.

PADRE. O if you knew the crosses I bear. I – when I joined the regiment I volunteered – you know how keen one is when the ink's wet on one's commission – and perhaps there was a touch of pride in it? – a wish to ingratiate? – (are you sure you wont have a cigarette?) – I volunteered to look after the mess wine money. The auditors couldnt add it up. Dont even recall the sum. Of course I've lived it down. Almost paid off the last few thous – (*Stops.*) A weary life of scrimp and save. Couldnt even afford a hair shirt – just a few cigarettes. I dont want that reopened. Not that they'd take your word against an officer's.

BRIAN. Could you get me off route marches for six months sir?

PADRE. If I had your assurance you'd be gainfully employed. Perhaps you're learning French?

BRIAN. Sir.

PADRE. Useful as we're in NATO. (*Stands.*) Sorry to kick you out. (A Gorgon is a figure in Greek mythology.) You wont take it amiss if I pray for you.

BRIAN (*going*). Sir.

PADRE. Rifle, Tebham.

BRIAN *comes back, picks up his rifle and goes.* PADRE *sits at desk. He beats his cap against the side of his shin and buries his head in his arm.*

PADRE. Fool. Fool. Fool. You must control it! This absurd

obsession – crazy excess – this faith that drives you into –. It'll land you in trouble one day my lad. (*A great sob shakes him.*)

[D] Street

BRIAN *comes on in civvies. He takes a black tie from his pocket and looks round.*

BRIAN (*under his breath*). Jees.
PADRE (*off*). A word.
BRIAN. 'Op it sir.

    PADRE *comes on.*

PADRE. Apropos our *tête-à-tête* –
BRIAN. You've got to go sir.
PADRE. – which was private –
BRIAN. Please sir.
PADRE. So if the military police are snooping round –
BRIAN. Sir you'll drop me in the shit!
PADRE. – they're run by the KGB. Dont say shit Tebham. We never know when we're going to meet our maker. What if that were your last word? God wouldnt know whether it was your comment on this world or the next – neither would promise much for your future! (*Produces a paper.*) A paper! Of course I trust your word but you cant be too careful with the military police. Sign. (*Reads.*) 'I freely affirm that at no time has any officer of the corps of padres offered me a share in the mess wine money –'
BRIAN. Please sir!
PADRE. – 'or halfprice bibles donated for the eastern bloc –'
BRIAN. Piss off!
PADRE. I shall not stay to hear the cloth insulted. (*Goes. Stops.*) Your initials? It may be your last chance to do the good deed that will see you all right for the rest of eternity.

(*No response.*) Im not a prophet but I wouldnt be surprised if you came to a bad end.

PADRE *goes out.*

BRIAN. Hate ties. If I knew there was a tie in it I'd've said no.

BRIAN *puts on the tie.* PHIL *comes on behind him wearing a white tie and the looted jacket – his hand in one of the pockets.*

PHIL (*password*). Devonshire strawberries are very cheap for the month of –

BRIAN *turns to him.* PHIL *automatically pulls the gun from his pocket and aims: he shoots wide. They stare at each other.*

PHIL. You! Chriss!

PHIL *points the pistol at the black tie.* BRIAN *cowers and covers his head with his arms.*

BRIAN. Eeeaarrgh!
PHIL. Black tie! Black tie! Black tie!
BRIAN. They told me to wear a –
PHIL (*spinning round to search frantically*). Quick!
BRIAN. What?
PHIL. They 'eard the shot!

PHIL *tugs* BRIAN – *they run off together. The* PADRE *comes on wearing a white surplice and reading from the prayer book.*

PADRE (*reads*). 'Man that is born of woman hath but a short time to live and is full of misery. He cometh –' (*Stops.*) Someone's snaffled the body! (*Looks round.*) No blood? But I heard the –. O god its a miracle! At last! He's gone up to heaven! (*He is about to throw himself onto his knees – he notices a mark on the ground.*) What's this? Blood? No! No! (*Scrapes out the patch with his shoe.*) Not his blood! There was a miracle! That's been there for weeks! Blood all over the city! The sanitary department's a disgrace!

(*Realises.*) Ah its dogshit! – thank you Lord! – I saw him go straight up to heaven – there was a blob of chewing gum on his boot! My miracle! I'll get promoted! Be in charge of the bishop's wine money!

The PADRE *goes out.*

[E] Canal Path

PHIL *and* BRIAN.

PHIL (*controlled*). Saw the black tie. Gun out. Squeeze – look up – face: you. Couldnt stop the trigger – jerked wide.

BRIAN. Why d'you join that mob?

PHIL. I was in a store. Riot outside. Ground floor empty. Tailor's dummy on the stairs. Evenin jacket. Tried it on! Another dummy in the mirror: by the rails. Got a leather jacket. Went over. Bent down. Not a dummy: bloke tryin it on – shot in the stomach. I was in an evenin jacket strippin a corpse an there's a war goin on in the street. You cant live like that. *I'm* against lootin – not the lot who own the stuff! You loot it an duck through the streets dodgin the bullets – or slave your gut out every day till yer can afford t' buy it an take it 'ome in the bus. What's worse? – lootin from them or workin for them? Working for them! – so they can loot us! That's the crime – an it screws up all the rest! You're not 'ere t' stop us lootin – you're 'ere because *we* want *our* lives.

BRIAN. Yeh – well. *I'll* 'ave a few things t' say when I get back t' –

PHIL. You cant go back.

BRIAN. What?

PHIL. I dont know what they're up to but you're supposed t' be dead. Worse now you know! They'll *ave* t' get you!

BRIAN. The bastards! Yeh! – sent me straight in! Not a chance! I wouldn't go back if I could!

PHIL (*canal*). Fish live in that muck. Could've wore the evenin jacket fishin.

Pause. PHIL *takes a gun from his pocket.*

BRIAN (*turning away*). Dont Phil –

PHIL (*jerks gun to stop* BRIAN *turning*). 'Ave to – when you think it over.

BRIAN. No! Said I wont go back! Join you! Im trained! I can fight!

PHIL. 'He's okay – bloke next door – went t' school t'gether'. What's 'e been doin since? 'Joined the army – so okay they send 'im on special missions'.

BRIAN. Yeh – all right. So you dont know me. I go on the run.

PHIL. You know *me*! What if they pick you up? Dont 'even 'ave t' twist your balls anymore – give you a drug, plug a wire in your 'ead.

BRIAN. No!

PHIL. Or you're fed up bein on the run – want a meal or a hand-out – so you roll up t' the guard'ouse. Or you fancy yourself a hero with a medal –

BRIAN. No – its not like that! I joined the army t' get shot of this dump! Work – bit of dough, bit of life – before Im too clapped out t' use it!

PHIL. – or we blow your buddies up an you lose your rag (you're a good natured soul) – or you're stoned out of your mind and you want a fix – so you turn yourself in. Or you just miss the CO's smile. I dont know. Up to you. You know what's in your head. But we're not safe with you on the streets. Its not my neck. There's the others. We're organised now. I risk all that because we came from the same block? Never. – You got us into this mess. You think of a better way out.

BRIAN. You wont kill me. You'd've done it – not sat there! That's talk t' put it off.

PHIL. I dont do it for kicks.

BRIAN. I know when its real. Tell from the eyes. You dont even know 'ow t' use it! You missed once already!

PHIL. Im not trained t' make it easy. I dont go round in a uniform paid t' shoot mates. Dont gloat. When I look at you – I'd enjoy doin it! You're worse than that lot. They're looking after themselves – its their money, their jobs, their loot, their world – they own it! – its sense t' them! What're you lookin after? – your pig-ignorance – yes-sir-no-sir – the privilege of dressin up in their uniform an bootin your own people like a thug! Look at you! You're not even a tailor's dummy! You *should* be shot! Like hosin shit off the street! Suppose there was no black tie? By now you'd be sellin me – my girl – people you dont even know! *You're not fit to live!* (*Collapses: he keeps gun aimed but lowers his head.*) Piss off.

BRIAN. Dont Phil – for chriss sake dont – its all right – *dont look like that* – you're not shoppin your mates. I've learned somethin. Jesus I must 'ave – 'avent I? I give you my word I wont –

PHIL. I dont want to know. I didnt mean all – that rubbish. (*Silence.*) I've got to go on the run.

BRIAN. Why?

PHIL. We cant be in the same city. Not safe.

BRIAN. I told you: I wont split on you even if they –

PHIL. Yeh you told me. An I told you what I thought of it. (*Slight pause.*) I go, then I dont 'ave t' worry. Blab or 'old your lip: 's no difference. Funny! – we grew up round 'ere – now as long as one of us is alive you stood a whole bloody army between us!

BRIAN. Up to you. What else can I do?

PHIL. There is somethin.

BRIAN. What?

PHIL. Give me this afternoon. We put you in a hood an drove you round in a van – then you got out – they must've trained you t' get out of tight corners – think of somethin. Dont go back till t'night. You can keep your word one afternoon: Im not asking you t' keep it your whole life.

BRIAN. What'll you do?

PHIL. Go home.

BRIAN. If you go on the run I'll look after your old lady as if she was me own.

PHIL. Okay? – till its dark. I can watch telly. Chat. Look out the window. Afterwards she'll know I came to say goodbye – didnt just run off. You know how she is.

BRIAN. You said if I went back they'd shoot me.

PHIL. Sell yourself. They mixed you up in somethin – go in deeper. That's your way out. Go back. You tell them you know they're killers: they know you'll graft for their money. Creates trust both sides. Roll in the shit. Im not just thinking of your own welfare. Its best if *you* do it, not one of their class. From time t' time you'll look in the mirror and puke – then you might pass some duff gen or send one of their trucks over a landmine. That's the best you can do for us now: roll in their shit.

BRIAN. Okay: shoot me.

PHIL. Leave it. Its not a game.

BRIAN. Shoot me!

PHIL. What d'you –! I made my decision! Get one of your mates t' shoot you! They're not so squeamish! Its true: if I was like them I wouldnt be sittin 'ere! Right now I 'ate you too much t' even touch your face, let alone lift my 'and t' shoot you . . .! Go away. Leave me alone. Piss off you bastard! You landed me in this! . . . You took me t' pieces. Now d'you want t' play with the bits? *Shove off*! (*Calms down.*) All right. Its okay. Im okay. You're okay. Just get yourself through this mess.

BRIAN. Shoot me. What else can we do? Why did you say all that! Sell myself? – t' that mob! – you dont know what sort of animals they keep! Shoot me! Your mates'll be safe! You'll be 'ere when the real fightin starts! Its your postin! – You put your life on the line: I can put mine! I said I'd join you. You wouldnt 'ave that. Joke of the year!

Sneered! All right: I can do this! Shoot me Phil! Its your job!

PHIL. No – no – no – we mustnt, dont let – they're twistin us round each other's necks like ropes! I'll go. The struggles goin on everywhere, I can join it wherever I am. You want t' do somethin, you'll find somethin. Let's stop now – Im going.

BRIAN. Shoot me! Please! Please!

PHIL. Why?

BRIAN. Shoot me!

PHIL. Why?

BRIAN. For five minutes! For tea with your mother! For a look out the window! Even I'm worth that! Now shoot me!

PHIL (*offering gun*). Shoot yourself: there's the gun. (*Puts gun on floor.*)

BRIAN. I cant. I've seen it. I know what happens. You do it. 'Elp me. Why must we drag it out? Why didn't you shoot me before? The gun was ready. It would've been easy then! I'd be dead! It would've done you good! – trained you for the fight! Kill me! You promised! Look I'll 'old the gun against my 'ead for you! You pull the trigger!

PHIL. Please – it dont matter – we can give ourselves time – learn t' think. (*Walks away.*) Wont it be like that – sometime – when we dont 'ave t' talk t' each other like this? (*Stops.*) We'll run for it t'gether – t' different cities –

BRIAN. No – its gone – I missed the chance – before I joined the khaki. I cant go back. We 'ave t' 'elp each other in a new way now. I cant leave this path alive.

PHIL. I said all that – I was scared – I didnt –

BRIAN. Dont lie! You see, its gone: they've taken it away! You're insulting yourself t' 'elp me! You said it so clearly! The truth for once! Dont lose your 'ead, dont spoil it! It was good t' listen to! – I cant risk stayin alive. Go back? – that mad'ouse?: they sent me out t' be shot! On the run?

– you stopped that too: I'd roll up t' the guard'ouse – pat on the back – CO's smile – take their cash – pissed out of me 'ead – open me mouth – spew up anythin they want – the sky's pink – the sun's black – an if you dont shoot me I'll name the lot – my mother – yours – my mates – anyone – not in five minutes – before they can start the clock! I'll see you dead! – an go down so deep and come to you under all the rest – they'll bury you under the lowest of the low – and shit on your grave – because you wasnt fit to live! – or fit to fight! – for anyone! – because you're sorry for your mate – you shared the streets with! . . . Now shoot!

PHIL. No.

BRIAN *dives for the gun, struggles with* PHIL *for it, gets it, walks away and turns to face* PHIL. *He holds the gun in front of his chest with the barrel pointing up at his own face.*

BRIAN. Look at me! This face! Look! One quiver? Where? Point? Cant! Not one! And Im afraid! – Now see what I can do when Im pushed! This is who I am! And dont forget it! Im their enemy!

He crouches over the gun and shoots himself in the stomach. Groans quietly, falls onto his back and rocks from side to side with his knees up. PHIL *goes towards him.*

PHIL. The bloody – I cant –. (*For a moment he tries to stop* BRIAN *rocking but cant.*) Look at – look – the size of the 'ole in 'is – you stupid sod!

PHIL *turns to go, stops, takes off his jacket and covers* BRIAN *with it. He goes out.*

BRIAN *stops rocking with his body angled to one side. Dead.*

[F] Police Station

MRS LEWIS *and* MRS TEBHAM *in street clothes. They talk quietly.*

LEWIS. Course its 'im! Why'd else they bring me 'ere? Never stays out all night and not say.

TEBHAM. What about 'is girl?

LEWIS. Goin round 'er's when the police came.

TEBHAM. Could be somethin entirely –

LEWIS. Then where was 'e all night – lyin bleedin in some gutter?

TEBHAM. Im not listening t' that rubbish.

LEWIS. Thank god I stopped 'im bringin that stuff in the 'ouse! Riskin my neck on that trash!

TEBHAM. You chucked it out?

LEWIS. Yes – found some burned 'ouse.

TEBHAM. They'll search the 'ole flats if they're suspicious.

LEWIS. You're all right?

TEBHAM (*nods*). In the park.

LEWIS. Could've caught 'im floggin it in the street.

TEBHAM. No – 'e said he never sold it for –

LEWIS. Cant believe anythin they tell you that age! – You could slip out an phone.

TEBHAM. Who?

LEWIS. Brian.

TEBHAM. Why?

LEWIS. 'E'll know where the fightin was – could've seen Phil.

TEBHAM. Fightin everywhere. 'Ow could 'e pick 'im out?

LEWIS. Try. (*Money.*) There's the money. Find a box in the street – not downstairs in the –

TEBHAM. It'd only put ideas in their 'eads if –

LEWIS. Go through the welfare. Say its compassionate.

TEBHAM. We 'ave t' wait.

LEWIS. At least try!

TEBHAM. Barracks wouldnt put me through.

LEWIS. You think 'e's dead.

TEBHAM. I told you I'm not listen t' that rubbish. We'll go round 'is girl's. She can say 'e spent the night there. If they find any –

A POLICEMAN *comes in with a white plastic bag.*

POLICEMAN. Sorry. Packed out there. Double time but we cant keep up. (*He takes the jacket from the white plastic bag and shows it to* MRS LEWIS.) Know this?

LEWIS. Im not sure.

POLICEMAN. You know if you've seen it. Distinctive article.

LEWIS (*looks at* MRS TEBHAM). All their stuff looks alike. Always buying. Too much money.

TEBHAM. Where d'you get it?

POLICEMAN. What's it matter if its not her's?

TEBHAM. Could jog 'er memory.

LEWIS. My lad's got a wardrobe full of jackets. 'E 'ad one similar.

POLICEMAN. 'S got your tab inside – cleaners.

TEBHAM. Why didnt you say? Worryin 'er if you know! (*To* MRS LEWIS.) It must be Phil's – if they got the cleaner's tab.

LEWIS. What's 'appened?

POLICEMAN. When did you last see 'im?

LEWIS. Yesterday lunchtime – I expect – I dont know. Where is 'e? What's 'e done?

POLICEMAN (*unfolds jacket to show blood stain*). A body was found last night by the canal.

LEWIS. 'E's dead.

POLICEMAN. Shot.

LEWIS. I knew it.

TEBHAM. Talk to 'er later. I'll take 'er –

POLICEMAN. She has to identify the body.

LEWIS. I said last night: 'Why did you let 'im out? If I 'ad 'im 'ere I'd 'old on to 'im. Both 'ands. All the time. Let people laugh! We could live like that'. 'Ear meself say it.

Tie a string to 'im like I did when 'e was a kid. Mothers with kids in wheelchairs – *they* keep two 'ands on 'em – they live like that. Why wasnt mine in a wheelchair? That's not a mother bein selfish: 'e'd still be alive! – Cant 'e 'ave 'ad an accident? Be lyin in some hospital?

TEBHAM. Let me bring 'er back when she's –

POLICEMAN. Form says it has to be done now – so it can be filled in. Best for her too.

LEWIS. The police shot 'im! What was 'e doin? – larkin about – too full of life – so they shot 'im! It'll all come out! I'll 'ave a proper enquiry!

POLICEMAN (*to* MRS TEBHAM). Keep an eye on her. (*Turns to go.*) We'll see if she can recognise her son.

The POLICEMAN *goes.*

TEBHAM. Dont antagonise them.

LEWIS. Why not? 'E's dead! Im not lyin now! I want the truth!

TEBHAM. You dont know 'e's dead.

LEWIS. 'E said! They found 'im on the –

TEBHAM. That could be a trick. They caught 'im liftin from shops – put 'im in cell – got you down 'ere so's they can search your place – they could string you along for weeks –

LEWIS. Not dead? That's the sort of thing they do . . .! Trip me up! That's why 'e stared at me! – not because I'm a mother with a dead son, they seen plenty of *them*! 'E's playin cat an' mouse! 'Is eyes – I can tell 'e knows Phil's alive –

TEBHAM. We cant be sure –

LEWIS. No no you're right: 'e's alive! Thank god I got rid of that stuff! They find anythin in yours, you didnt get it from 'im. Fair's fair. You took your chance. Always was 'is fault: too generous. You can say you seen 'im in is jacket, only nothin about the – (*Stops.*) But why's there blood? (*Goes closer to the jacket but stops someway from it.*)

It looks like blood. It must be blood. 'Ave they dropped 'is jacket in someone else's blood then showed it to 'is mother? They couldnt be so cruel!

TEBHAM. They're cruel or they couldnt do the job.

LEWIS. Then he isnt dead?

TEBHAM. I dont know.

LEWIS. You said 'e isnt!

TEBHAM. I dont know! I dont know everything! I said 'e might not be!

LEWIS. Stop it! Stop it! I wont listen to you! (*She goes nearer to the jacket and crouches to stare at it.*) Its blood. Its nearly wet. I can smell the blood from 'ere? Why did you say 'e's alive – an now 'e 'as t' be dead! Who're you t' drag 'im in an out of 'is coffin? Tell me why there's blood on 'is jacket? God rot you woman! Why did you say 'e was alive? 'Ave I got t' be told 'e's dead twice!

TEBHAM. 'E lent 'is jacket to a friend?

LEWIS. Lent it? Lent it? 'Ark at 'er! No! I wont listen! She's a monster! – Lent it? Why should 'e lend it? Its 'is favourite jacket! What d'you know? What are you up to? You've got somethin 'idden! You're always 'angin round 'im! O dont think I'm jealous! I dont care what goes on – crawl into whose bed you like! – as long as they let 'im live!

TEBHAM. I dont know! 'E might be dead!

LEWIS. There! – she's at it again! Why're you doin this? They pay you? How many mothers you sold? You want us all dead? No no I shouldnt say such things. I dont know what t' do! . . . Lent. Lent. Shall I believe it? – or would I be a stupid woman? Why? Its the sort of thing 'e would do! Lend to anyone – always lendin – *give* it away the fool! – just cause it *is* 'is favourite jacket! – an it ends up on the back of someone who's not even grateful! Yes yes of course I believe it! That's not deceivin myself! Its starin me in the face an I didnt see it! A fine mother I turn out t' be! You'd think I *want* 'im dead! 'E lends 'is jacket – doesnt say – an then there's all this fuss! When did 'e last put it on? When did you see it last?

TEBHAM. I dont know.

LEWIS. 'Asnt wore it for weeks! 'E give it away! I think 'e said! I know 'e said somethin! – Why cant I think?

TEBHAM. Wait an be quiet. You only 'urt yourself jumpin t' conclusions. Dont do their job for them. Wait an be ready t' fight for 'im – even if it comes t' the worst. That's the only way we can 'elp ourselves. Let them play around with their little surprises: when they've gone they've got nothin. Then it'll be our turn. (*Shivers.*) But I 'ate their places. You think the paint was alive before they spread it on these walls. (*Pause.*) The jacket was stolen.

LEWIS. . . . O yes. Yes . . . (*Takes* MRS TEBHAM's *hands.*) that's the best one of all. Thank you, thank you. Stolen. By a complete stranger. Nothin t' do with us. My boy's just the victim. 'S not 'is blood – not even 'is mates'. You're so good t' me! Im sorry I said those things – silly silly, didnt mean it – forgive me. I'll tell 'im 'ow good you are. I let go of 'im, I wont let go of you. If you knew 'ow it 'urts: but you wipe the blood off the knife even when its in the wound.

TEBHAM. Not long now. Perhaps the lad'll belong t' some other woman – goin on with 'er work and doesnt know what she's got in front of 'er. I 'ope she forgives us when she suffers. What else can we do?: I 'ope when 'er times comes the pain's so sharp she cries out! – so she 'as t' see why we were too weak to bear it an 'ad t' push it on to someone else.

LEWIS. Let's go. We can walk in the streets. Keep goin for days an still find places we've never been. We can be 'appy. Even the sun's out!

TEBHAM. You'd turn back at the corner. We 'ave t' know. If its good news, you'd've wasted all that time runnin away when you could've been sittin at 'ome with 'im.

LEWIS. Dont.

TEBHAM. And anyway they wouldnt let you out.

LEWIS. Suppose they mixed two jackets up? Someone's shot
– the police get it right for once – its a murderer– molests
little kids – strangles old people – anythin – the sort of
beast the police *would* run into – why should I feel sorry
for *is* mother? – she brought a monster in the world to
terrify us! – good riddance! That's 'ow the blood got into
it. Then Phil's brought in – drunk or brawlin – or 'e did
the murders an molested the kids – an Im the wicked
mother – I dont care as long as 'e's alive! Dont judge 'im!
– you're no better! Well. That's 'ow they got the two
jackets. Then they take them off an search the seams an
pockets – 'ow they do – an when they chuck 'em back
Phil's lands on the corpse. That's 'ow the blood got on it.
An accident! Phil didnt notice they give 'im the corpse's
jacket cause 'e's drunk or upset. There's bin a mix up!
Look what 'appens in maternity wards! *They* mix the
babies up! What's the difference between a baby an a
corpse? None! – I dont see it! The corpse cant say that's
my jacket – the kid cant say thats my mother! 'S always
'appenin! Maternity wards! Prisons! Morgues!
Mad'ouses! Everywhere! There's no difference! They're
all their places! They mix 'em up!

TEBHAM (*tired*). Somethin like that.

LEWIS. What's the matter? Dont you believe me? You said
'e was alive – came out of the blue – I 'ad t' believe it! It
'urt me as much as when they said 'e was dead! Now I
tell you the truth – *prove* it – you see that sort of thing on
the news – an its too much bother! 'E's my only kid Mrs
Tebham . . .

TEBHAM. I know.

LEWIS. No. Yours is alive. Rides round in a tank. Mates t'
watch over 'im. Mine 'as t' run through the streets on 'is
own. You dont know. I stand 'ere – that little bit of floor
between us – an you might be in China. Even if 'e's dead
'e feels my pain. They can bury 'im – pile the earth on

top t' keep me from 'im – put the whole world between us if they like – and my pain would still get through and 'e'd feel it. Now I wish I knew for sure 'e's dead so I could give up 'ope an put 'im out 'is misery.

The POLICEMAN *wheels in a stretcher. On it the body lies under a white sheet. He stops the stretcher and puts on the handbrake: a slight squeak.*

POLICEMAN. We'll do this without fuss. (*To* MRS TEBHAM.) She wont react. Noisy one's crack up later. Get her home fast.

LEWIS. Im not lookin. (*To* POLICEMAN.) You got yourself in a mess: get yourself out of it. I 'avent done anythin! You cant keep me 'ere! . . . I cant look.

TEBHAM. I'll look for 'er.

POLICEMAN. The form says no: next-of-kin – in this case the mother. Please wait there. Its a serious offence to obstruct an identification.

TEBHAM (*to* MRS LEWIS). Im sorry, I cant 'elp you anymore.

LEWIS. Its all right: I 'ave t' do it.

POLICEMAN. Get it over so I can take him back to the quiet. No reason to parade him just because he's dead. In this job the dead are the only ones you respect: they dont try to cheat. They restore your faith in human nature. Stand there.

MRS LEWIS *stands at the head of the stretcher.*

POLICEMAN. I've taken hold of the sheet – I'll now lift it.

The POLICEMAN *lifts the sheet.* MRS LEWIS *sees the head but it stays hidden from* MRS TEBHAM.

LEWIS. It – it (*She looks at* MRS TEBHAM *and then points at the head.*) – it – its (*She bursts out laughing.*) – its not 'im! – not 'im! – not Phil! – not 'im! – not 'im!

TEBHAM. O – no? What did I say? Its wonderful! Thank

god! The wrong man! Mixed 'em up – or the jacket –
what's it matter? The relief! Im so glad!

LEWIS (*laughing*). Not – not – not like –

Still laughing MRS LEWIS *and* MRS TEBHAM *hug each
other. The* POLICEMAN *covers the head with the sheet.*

LEWIS. ⎫ Thank you! What you said! Couldnt believe it!
      ⎬ 'Elped so much!
TEBHAM. ⎭ Not 'im! Its marvellous! We'll 'ave a party! I
      wish I'd kept that dress!

MRS LEWIS *laughs and turns to face the body. She talks half
to it and half to the* POLICEMAN, *trying to control herself.*

LEWIS. Im sorry for the – I didnt mean to – no disrespect to
– (*She goes to the sheet and touches the covered foot.*) – sorry
– if you knew my son you'd understand my – your mother
would tell you 'ow I – so 'appy you're not mine! (*She
laughs and picks up a corner of the sheet to dab her eyes.*) The
relief – the relief – any mother would forgive the way –
the relief to know you're – (*She bursts into convulsive
laughter and stuffs the sheet into her mouth to stifle it.*) – sorry
– all this noise for – *it's someone else's!* (*Howls with
laughter.*) Eeeaarrghgh! Thank god thank god! (*Clutches
her stomach.*) The pain! 'Avent laughed so much since –!
My son's alive! 'E's 'ere – someplace – come back! Quick!
Pull meself t'gether! Go 'ome! 'E's waitin – (*Renewed
bursts of laughter.*) – tell me off: 'Where's me tea? Im
starvin!' – Pull meself t' –

TEBHAM. No laugh laugh I'd rather 'ear you laugh than
cry. Let the 'ole buildin know. New sound for some of
'em. Let 'em 'ear it in the drains. Give the cells a treat.

POLICEMAN. Glad Im not a bettin man. One comes in, not
a tear: next, clean out – whiter than the corpse – wouldnt
know who's identifying who if it wasnt for the tag. *This
one's* the cake-walk at the fun fair! (*Putting the jacket into
the white plastic bag. Nods at* MRS LEWIS.) There's our

good deed for today. (*To* MRS TEBHAM.) Take her home
but she mustnt leave her notified address. Neighbours
can do the shopping.

TEBHAM. That's as bad as lockin 'er up! Its not 'er son so
why's she –

POLICEMAN. Let the desk know. You need an exit pass.

LEWIS. Give the little bleeder a piece of my mind when I see
'im. Pig! Pissed! – that's 'ow 'e got 'is jacket pinch! Little
perisher upsettin me! Wish 'e was dead when I finish with
'im! (*To* MRS TEBHAM.) 'E say we can go?

TEBHAM. Yes.

The POLICEMAN *releases the stretcher brake: slight squeak.*

LEWIS. Dont worry me bein shut up there. Enough roamin
chasin after 'im. 'E can stop in where I can keep an eye
on 'im. 'Ave a few undertakin's before 'e sets foot outside
that door again . . . (*She looks at* MRS TEBHAM.) Mrs
Tebham – (*Looks round.*) – somethin's not right –

TEBHAM. What?

LEWIS (*gestures towards the stretcher*). I – its not – somethin
in my 'ead –

The POLICEMAN *starts to wheel out the stretcher.*

POLICEMAN. Thanks for the co-operation.

LEWIS. – I – so relieved – it went – came out of me! – and
– (*To* POLICEMAN.) No. (*To* MRS TEBHAM.) Tell 'im.

TEBHAM. What is it?

LEWIS (*sudden vehemence*). Tell 'im! Tell 'im! Stop 'im! If
that's – (*Confused again.*) – its – my 'ead's full of –

MRS TEBHAM *glances at the* POLICEMAN *and he stops the
stretcher.*

POLICEMAN (*quietly to* MRS TEBHAM). I've got other cases
out there.

LEWIS. – faces – or –! Its not my son – but then – why do I
know 'im? Seen 'im somewhere? Or was I – wrong an got

it –? Terrible! Tryin t' see 'im in my 'ead! 'Elp me! Its wrong! I knew 'im! White – thing – plastic! Its my son! – what 'e looks like when 'e's dead!

TEBHAM. No no there never was such a woman for scarin herself! Come 'ome in the peace an quiet. Come back t'morrow. No more fuss t'day. Let 'im take the poor lad away.

The POLICEMAN *releases the stretcher handbrake: slight squeak.*

POLICEMAN. Remember: exit pass.

LEWIS. Its my son!

TEBHAM. Its not!

LEWIS. Then why do I – know 'im? I didnt look properly! I was too – me nails dug 'oles in me 'ands – I couldnt see! Let me look! I must know!

TEBHAM. Poor woman, I'll never get 'er 'ome like that. (*To* POLICEMAN.) She's said its not 'er son. Let me look t' set 'er mind t' rest.

POLICEMAN. Nothing on the form against that.

The POLICEMAN *stops the stretcher and puts on the handbreak: slight squeak.*

POLICEMAN (*sigh*). Drop of oil.

MRS TEBHAM *goes to the top of the stretcher as the* POLICEMAN *is pulling back the sheet. She reaches it and stares down at the head. Her face is blank. Silence.*

LEWIS. Why's she starin? She frightens me! Its my son!

MRS LEWIS *goes to the stretcher. She faces* MRS TEBHAM *with her back to the audience. Slowly she doubles over in silent laughter and – still completely silent and doubled – totters away. She stops, bent double.*

LEWIS. Didnt recognise 'im! I was so relieved – I – (*She whoops with laughter.*) – I didnt recognise 'im! (*She laughs and hobbles to* MRS TEBHAM.) Sorry, sorry – I thought 'e was – told 'er 'e was –

She claws at MRS TEBHAM, *trying to turn her towards her to comfort her but laughter makes her too weak.* MRS TEBHAM *stands as before and stares blankly at the face.*

POLICEMAN. You recognise the deceased?

LEWIS (*pointing to* MRS TEBHAM). Its – its – (*She clutches at the sheet and buries her face in it.*) – its – (*She shrieks with laughter.*) – I told 'er – she stood there an I told 'er – I said it was a –!

She roars with laughter and as she hobbles away from the stretcher she holds the sheet against her face and drags it with her – the body is uncovered. MRS TEBHAM *stares down at the face.*

LEWIS (*clutching the sheet to her*). I looked at 'er an said – it wasnt mine – I said it was – (*She clutches her stomach and laughs.*) The pain! I said – I said – I said –. (*She sits on the ground roaring with laughter and drumming her heels.*) The pain! The pain! The pain! The pain!

She stuffs her hands into her mouth to stop the laughter. She covers herself with the sheet till she's completely shrouded. She rocks and her gentle laughter comes from under the sheet. MRS TEBHAM *glances across at her once, then looks back at the dead face: otherwise she doesnt move. Her blank expression doesnt change.*

LEWIS (*gently as she rocks under the sheet*). Nineteen years – sat at my table – days – days – washed 'is cuts – christmas toys – didnt know – no idea – swear it on this sheet – didnt see – said a stranger – and its– . . .

POLICEMAN (*to* MRS TEBHAM). Im keeping you in pending enquiries.

The POLICEMAN *releases the handbrake: slight squeak. He*

wheels out the stretcher. MRS TEBHAM *goes with him without looking back.* MRS LEWIS *takes off the sheet and sits with it crumbled in her lap and round her on the floor. She sighs once. She presses the side of her thumb against her teeth: one small jerk as if she's biting a thread. Then she calms herself by folding the sheet. She goes out with it.*

[G] Mrs Lewis's Kitchen

MRS LEWIS *and* MRS TEBHAM *both sit in chairs facing the audience.* MRS LEWIS *is upstage of* MRS TEBHAM *and* PHIL *stands beside her with a saucer and cup of tea. Near* MRS TEBHAM *there is a framed photo of* BRIAN.

TEBHAM. If I moved in she wont be on 'er own. You wouldnt be so tied down.

PHIL. 'Alf asleep. Struggled all 'er life. In the end you sleep on your feet.

TEBHAM. Only one rent.

PHIL. She liked company.

TEBHAM. That's settled then. Next door'll 'elp you shift my stuff along the landin. Then I neednt go in.

PHIL. You cant spend the rest of your life bein scared of the past.

TEBHAM. Brian's dead. If that didnt 'urt it wouldnt be worth goin on, would it? Going out?

PHIL. No.

TEBHAM. Go: we're all right.

PHIL (*blows on tea*). Gettin cooler.

TEBHAM. Dont treat 'er like a child.

LEWIS. Washed 'is face out of a medical bottle.

Doorbell.

TEBHAM. If its me, I went t' bed.

PHIL *gives the tea to* MRS LEWIS *and goes out. Slight pause.*

The OFFICER *comes in. Halfway through the* OFFICER'S *next speech* PHIL *slowly comes in and stands in the doorway to listen.*

OFFICER (*unsure who is* MRS TEBHAM, *to* LEWIS). Mrs Tebham . . . (*Turns to* TEBHAM.) I knew you'd be cross if the young man sent me away. No chance for a word at the funeral. Had to nurse the top brass. The padre was very moving. (*Slight pause.*) Brian was the best type of young soldier. Clean. Loyal. Carried his share of the burdens and enjoyed his share of the laughs. (*Looks around.*) We'll miss him. (*To* MRS TEBHAM.) I was a bit apprehensive about coming – me and Brian being alike. (*Picks up photo.*) Same hair – same eyes – same height though you cant tell from the head. (*Smiles and goes on looking at the photo.*) One christmas we swapped hats! – that sort of party! Tebham went round the barracks and was mistaken for me! (*Imitates* BRIAN.) 'They was throwin up salutes like a stop-watch goin backwards sir.' We're proud of our regimental christmases. Can I have this for my scrapbook?

TEBHAM (*snatches the photo from the* OFFICER). Who are you? What you come 'ere for? (*Without looking at the photo she wipes it on her sleeve.*)

OFFICER. I came to spend a moment with you today.

TEBHAM. You're nothing like him!

OFFICER. Different backgrounds. The mother's bound to see that.

TEBHAM. Come 'ere pretend . . .!

OFFICER. I wont intrude. (*Preparing to go.*) The regimental almoners fund is available should any need arise.

LEWIS. Your tea!

OFFICER. Thank you I wont –

LEWIS. Must 'ave tea – its a funeral!

MRS LEWIS *stands, pours her tea into the saucer and hands it to the* OFFICER.

TEBHAM. 'Umour 'er.

OFFICER. Mouth *is* dry.

Before he can drink MRS LEWIS *fills the saucer to the brim and then lowers it in her hand. They stare at each other in silence.* MRS LEWIS *grins. Carefully the* OFFICER *raises the saucer to his lips. He drinks silently without spilling a drop.*

LEWIS. Clever little sod. (*She cackles shrilly and pokes him in the ribs.*) Cocky little bastard.

The OFFICER *finishes drinking and hands the empty saucer back to* MRS LEWIS.

OFFICER (*cold anger*). Brian died on duty. That's still something to be proud of. His death wont be wasted. Read the newspapers in the morning. You'll have a surprise.

PHIL. You give 'im a good send off sir.

OFFICER. That was our duty.

PHIL (*slowly coming into the room*). I went t' school with 'im sir.

OFFICER. Accept my condolences.

PHIL. Thank you sir that's much appreciated.

OFFICER. Tonight this city will be sealed off. The whole garrison deployed.

PHIL *carefully changes from slippers to street shoes.*

PHIL. 'E always said 'ow well organised you was sir.

OFFICER. Wish we had him with us tonight. Reinforcements dropped in from helicopters. That's a 'first use' against civilians.

PHIL. Landin on a city at night sir? – (*Sucks in breath through his teeth apprehensively.*) dont want no more Brians.

OFFICER (*reassuringly*). Its all in hand. Cordon the ring roads. Stop all civilian transport. As safe as anaesthetising a corpse. The code name's Fallen Warrior. My idea. The men cheered when they heard it. The heat's coming through the barracks walls. The city parks will be temporary holding pens – some of those we put in them wont hear the dawn chorus. I couldnt restrain Brian's chums if I wanted to. Tonight's the night. I hope you feel better about things Mrs Tebham. (*To* MRS LEWIS.) Your tea was excellent.

The OFFICER *goes.*

LEWIS. The dead are entitled to their tea. (*She starts to go back to her chair, then stops to explain vaguely.*) I always say – if they're dead – since I got it wrong . . . (*To* MRS TEBHAM.) You died too – but *you* came back. Now I'd let you lead me anywhere.

MRS LEWIS *sits in her chair.*

TEBHAM. You're goin out?

PHIL. Remembered somethin.

TEBHAM. Its dangerous if all 'e said 'is –

PHIL. I'll be all right.

TEBHAM. Be long?

PHIL. Try not. Dont wait up.

TEBHAM. Tell me –

PHIL (*calmly*). 'Ave t' 'urry.

TEBHAM. I may not see you again.

PHIL. Im only goin out t' –

TEBHAM. So was Brian. Who shot 'im?

PHIL. 'E was a soldier. Okay – is it better if 'e shoots someone t' take 'is place? Someone on the street t'night? You ask some 'ard questions. (*Goes to* MRS LEWIS.) Bit of luck Mrs T's movin in. (*No response.*)

TEBHAM. 'Ow did 'e get your jacket?

PHIL. She'll pull through. Only while you're 'ere we wont lie to each other. We dont 'ave to. (*Gesture to* MRS LEWIS.) Asleep. – 'E needed the jacket so I lent it. – 'Ave t' 'urry.

PHIL *goes out.* MRS TEBHAM *and* MRS LEWIS *sit facing the audience.*

In the Company of Men

Businessmen:
OLDFIELD *early sixties*
LEONARD OLDFIELD
HAMMOND *fifties*
DODDS *late forties*
WILBRAHAM *forties*

Servant:
BARTLEY *twenties*

In the Company of Men was first produced in Britain by the Royal Shakespeare Company at the Barbican, London, in the Pit Theatre, on 16 October 1996 with the following cast:

OLDFIELD	Karl Johnson
LEONARD OLDFIELD	John Light
HAMMOND	David Ryall
DODDS	Alan David
WILBRAHAM	Richard Cordery
BARTLEY	George Anton

Directed by Edward Bond
Designed by Eryl Ellis
Lighting by Andy Phillips

Unit One:	The Lounge of Oldfield's Town House
Unit Two:	The same as Unit One
Unit Three:	The same as Unit One
Unit Four:	The Hall Lobby of Oldfield's Country House
Unit Five:	The Ground Floor of a Derelict House
Unit Six:	'The Two Armchairs' – the same as Unit One
Unit Seven:	Oldfield's Office
Unit Eight:	The same as Unit Seven
Unit Nine:	The Cellar of a Derelict House

The present time in London and Kent.

Unit One

Oldfield's House.

A room with two armchairs.

LEONARD *and* DODDS *standing.*

LEONARD. You neednt wait. I'll pass on your congratulations.

DODDS. He wont be long.

LEONARD. The television's caught him.

DODDS (*shakes his head*). He was on the earlier news. (*Slight pause.*) I spoke to him on the phone. He told me to be here at nine in the morning. He's going to give me his new plans for the company. (*Slight pause.*) Did he say what he'd've done if we'd been taken over?

LEONARD. He was sure he'd win.

DODDS. Is it all right if I change the subject? Wilbraham came to see me. Its been a seesaw sort of day. Your father was still fighting to keep his company – the last thing I wanted to do was deal with Willy and his disasters.

LEONARD. Could he kill himself?

DODDS. Willy hasnt got the initiative. Leaves all the big moves to others.

LEONARD. Why do people gamble like that?

DODDS. Because they cant solve their problems. It gives them problems they dont have to solve – the decision's up to fate. His company's run up debts of four millions. With his reputation he cant get another loan. The debtors are meeting tomorrow. They'll bankrupt him.

LEONARD (*half attention*). Im sorry he's in a mess.

DODDS. Its his father's fault. *He* learned to run a company by founding one. He thought he could just die and hand it to Willy on a plate.

LEONARD (*shrug*). He'll be free when its gone.

DODDS. With nothing to restrain him he'll go to the bottom.

LEONARD. *You* lend him money. He's your friend.

DODDS. You didnt think I was going to ask you to *lend* him money? That *would* be throwing it down the drain.

LEONARD. You were working up to something.

DODDS. I was going to –

LEONARD. Tomorrow.

DODDS. The creditors meet in the morning. Let me tell you the situation. His order book's patchy but the trade outlook is good. He's got a modern factory – well equipped – there's over-manning but some of the top dressing's gone – rats leaving the sinking ship. If you go in – cut the workforce – collect what's owing – went after new orders – you could get the company back on its feet. The potential's there but because of the debts it'll be closed down.

LEONARD. How much?

DODDS. Half a million to hold off the debtors for a year. But its not money that's important – the company needs an input of energy and talent. Willy would pull himself together if you were –

LEONARD (*shakes head*). Too many complications.

DODDS. Complications yes – but they can be *seen*: it isnt a gamble. Your father's like a lot of intelligent men – sometimes he's very stupid.

LEONARD. Stupid?

DODDS. You know you're being wasted. At your age time's decisive. If you dont develop your potential over the next year – even the next few months – you'll pay for it for the rest of your life. Willy's creditors are moving in because before long there wont be anything left to sell up. You wont get another chance anywhere near as good. Its as if someone had set up the ideal test to let you find out

what you can do – and at your age that means finding
out who you are.

LEONARD. My father wouldnt allow it.

DODDS. Good heavens we mustnt tell him!

LEONARD. No?

DODDS. I've worked for him for thirty years and I've never
wanted to leave. But I learned his faults long ago. He'd
be breathing down your neck telling you all the right
things to do. The company'd be a success – Willy would
be saved – I'd've helped a friend – and you'd get nothing.
It'd be a triumph and feel like the biggest ditch-job of all
time.

LEONARD. You think I should go behind my father's back?

DODDS. He spits out the bait and chews the hook – he had
to learn to do that. Well you learn more from your
mistakes than someone else's success. Even if you fail it'd
be money well spent. You can use your own money – or
I'll raise a loan without your father knowing. If you
succeed you'll be giving him more than money.

LEONARD. A lesson in cheating?

DODDS. Your father's trouble is he admires you too much.
He wants you take over from him – its a passion: that
makes him afraid of you. If you fail you'll get over it,
you're young. But he's old so its *his* future at stake. You
have to live out his ambitions. If you fail it means he dies
a failure. He couldnt bear that after a lifetime of success.
He's never going to let you take a risk. Sometime in the
next year you'll have to go behind his back.

LEONARD. Give me a report on the company.

DODDS. I need something for the creditors tomorrow. Can
I say you're seriously interested?

LEONARD. How many do you have to persuade?

DODDS. Five main suppliers.

LEONARD. This is my father's lucky day. You've left *my*
chance till almost midnight.

DODDS. Willy was too ashamed to tell me about the

creditors before. He had a few drinks and turned up. You wont believe it but –

BARTLEY *comes in. He wears dark trousers, dark tie, white shirt and a servant's light-khaki house-jacket. He carries a glass of whisky on a tray.*

BARTLEY. Your father's in the hoose Mr Leonard.

LEONARD *takes the whisky from the tray.*

BARTLEY. Did you want anythin?
LEONARD. No.
BARTLEY. Mr Dodds?
DODDS. No thanks Bartley.

BARTLEY *goes out with the tray.*

DODDS. I was going to say Willy was like you once. His father was always going to give him his head, let him stand on his feet. By the time he died Willy was hooked on risk: gambling with fate instead of controlling it.
LEONARD (*curt amusement*). Have you noticed Bartley's wristwatch? The dial's a human face. My father tolerates his whims.
DODDS. *You* must decide.
LEONARD. That's like sentencing someone to death to encourage them to escape.
DODDS. If you were your father I'd be giving you the same advice.

OLDFIELD *comes in. He wears a city overcoat.*

DODDS. Congratulations sir.
OLDFIELD. Thank you. We did well today. Its turning into a stampede. When the stock exchange closed over sixty per cent of our shareholders had accepted my offer. Hammond will hold on to his ten per cent but we'll end up well into the eighties. Safe from take-over for all time.
DODDS. Have you heard from Hammond?

OLDFIELD. He'll send a line. Wont want to appear miffed.

LEONARD. I dont understand why he tried to take us. He could've got a better return on his capital somewhere else.

OLDFIELD. Was there anything in particular you wanted Dodds?

DODDS. Just to say thanks for seeing Hammond off so brilliantly. Its been a tense time. Our loyalty to you would've cost some of us our jobs.

OLDFIELD. Thank you. Hammond's patient – never moves without a purpose. And clever – doesnt even let his buttonholes know what buttons are for. (*Drink.*) Mine? (*He takes his whisky from* LEONARD *but doesnt drink it.*) O the shareholders didnt support me out of loyalty – never look for that! I put on a world-weary pose – gave the impression I was losing interest – that started rumours in the press – and it didnt cost me a lunch! They said I might withdraw my offer – and the shareholders panicked! – What dont you understand Leonard? D'you need a clairvoyant to tell you a bag of crisps is a bag of crisps? The prospects in the arms trade are good – its difficult to get in on our level – and Hammond was shopping: it was so clear I was even able to warn the accountants to prepare our defence in advance.

DODDS. Are you taking a rest?

OLDFIELD. No I feel as if I've got another leg – Im learning to walk again! We've beaten Hammond but we must be vigilant. An *internal* weakness: the wrong design compromise, a misreading of international relations – a *strategic* error of that magnitude could destroy us five years from now. When you make the guns you must be more alert than the soldiers who fire them. *They* need allies not enemies: *we* need enemies. We cant trust our allies, they're our commercial rivals – we cant trust our workers, they're like scavengers on the battlefield, they'd strip the dead – we cant trust our government, they use our rivals to beat us down – and then there's the

Hammonds and their fifth columns. We've got only one good reliable friend: our enemies. We build our life on trust in them, they're always at our side. That makes us lonely: but the ground under our feet is very solid.

DODDS. I must be off if Im to be fresh in the morning. Congratulations again sir.

OLDFIELD. Goodnight.

DODDS *goes*.

OLDFIELD. He hung on to congratulate me . . .!

LEONARD. I thought you'd gone on to celebrate.

OLDFIELD. No. You should've gone. You earned it.

LEONARD. I hardly saw you.

OLDFIELD. Yes it was a busy time. I can turn to Dodds and the accountants – but no one else. You're inexperienced but the fresh eye often sees what we miss.

LEONARD. Thank you.

OLDFIELD. O dear. Im tired and put it badly – (*Sighs.*) and you interpret me ironically.

LEONARD. No.

OLDFIELD. One day you'll know why I wish I'd had time to talk to you. When you're in my position most people tell you what they think will flatter you or flatter them. You have no reason not to tell me the truth. You have a valuable gift Leonard: you make people talk. But you dont always listen when they do.

LEONARD. If you end up with eighty per cent of the shares you as good as own the company. Will I get it when you die?

OLDFIELD. You get everything.

LEONARD. I want to go on the board.

OLDFIELD (*smells drink*). O no . . .!

LEONARD. There's no reason to wait.

OLDFIELD. Its too late to discuss this now. We wouldnt have time to finish.

LEONARD. It doesnt take long to say yes or no.

OLDFIELD. Dont be difficult. There are options – various ways of doing things. It needs to be – (*Stops.*) No I refuse to start. Its important, it deserves all my attention. Tomorrow afternoon after I've spoken to Dodds – and the accountants – Im seeing them after lunch. Then we'll shut ourselves away and –

LEONARD. Tomorrow you'll be busy.

OLDFIELD. Yes yes tomorrow's full. I wont mislead you. We'll set aside a definite time in the next few days and put it in the diary.

LEONARD. What's wrong with your drink?

OLDFIELD. My drink? – O my drink's unimportant. (*Puts the glass on the floor.*) Nothing wrong with it. Over the years I've built up a good board – they're all fighters – many of them are ex-service. Most of them have their sights on my chair. Now I own the company they wont get it. We must understand their disappointment. If I push you in over the top they'll resent it – rightly. Give you a hard time.

LEONARD. I'll learn to survive.

OLDFIELD. Survive? Why approach a great opportunity in such a grudging spirit? They want to be your friends.

LEONARD. Then there's no problem.

OLDFIELD. One cant even get a decent drink in this house.

LEONARD. Let me fix it for –

OLDFIELD. No no it doesnt matter. I can get by without my –

LEONARD. Its no trouble.

OLDFIELD (*weary*). Please Leonard – this fuss about a drink! Im not alcoholic. After the energy I spent today I'll sleep without a soporific. Did you *see* me on television?

LEONARD. You were very good.

OLDFIELD. I wondered since you didnt say. Was I good . . .? What were we talking about before you got agitated over my drink?

LEONARD. My place on the board.

OLDFIELD. In my opinion you're not ready for the board. If I put you on now they'll always associate you with weakness – I know men! – treat you as a spoiled pup on the grab. And as ninety per cent of the job is acting as transmitter between them – you can never be better than they're able or willing to make you. If they see you as weak, you become weak: *that's* the only basis on which they can deal with you. I've seen it so often. Men make their worst fears come true and call it fate but really its their own bad habits. If I was a foolish father I'd force you onto the board – teach you the hard way. That doesnt work. If you're thrown in at the deep end you break your neck on the ones who were thrown in before you. If I put you on the board you'd be an instant success! I have to think what you'll be when the honeymoon's over. You must learn patience. Its the hardest part for an able young man – it means taking a risk on yourself before you've proved its worth taking. Fortunately I have faith in you: I can wait.

LEONARD. If the board obstruct me I'll get rid of them.

OLDFIELD. What a reckless thing to say! I chose a board who could stand up to the leader – be their own men – and already you're sacking them for those very qualities! What sort of justice punishes people for being right? When I listen to you I feel I have to *protect* them from you! – that you'll never learn how to earn their respect!

BARTLEY *comes in.*

BARTLEY. Everything okay sir?

OLDFIELD. Yes thank you.

LEONARD. His drink isnt as –

OLDFIELD. O for heaven's sake! Why did I ever mention the drink!

BARTLEY. Is somethin nae right wi' the drink sir?

OLDFIELD. Its perfect. Exactly what I was looking forward to.

BARTLEY. That's all right then sir – I would'nae want t' think there was anythin wrong wi' it. Eh – ah understand congratulations are in order the night sir?

OLDFIELD. That's kind of you Bartley. I appreciate it. Yes its been a good day. I shant need you now. Go to bed.

BARTLEY. Is it the office in the mornin sir? Ah laid oot a suit.

OLDFIELD. Thank you.

BARTLEY (*stares at drink*). It'd be nae bother t' fix the drink sir. Was it the soda again? I cannae get the hang o' it.

OLDFIELD. No its fine. I shall drink it in a moment.

BARTLEY *goes out.*

OLDFIELD. How thoughtless of you to upset him in that way! You know he spills things. He'll be jittery all tomorrow. You might have spared me that. Harrassing servants is a sign of weakness of character. And I do not allow you to slight my board! You speak as if you were scrapping for a fight. Anyone can be tough with others: be tough with yourself. If you were ready for the board you'd be begging me to keep you off so you could enjoy your freedom a little longer. Other fathers would have to force their son on – but Im denied that pleasure.

LEONARD. I didnt say I wanted to get rid of them. I said I would if they tried to get rid of me.

OLDFIELD. Please dont tell me what I heard – I know the spirit of what you said. They offer you their friendship and you condemn them! This terrible impatience blinds you to every – (*Stops.*) Dont you see that if the job wasnt kept for you they'd be cutting each other's throats to get it? Some of the remarks reported to me – and I trust Dodds absolutely – make me despair of the havoc ambition causes even among comrades. You can come to them as the peacemaker.

LEONARD. Then there's no problem.

OLDFIELD. None – unless you make it. (*Picks up the drink*

and is about to drink it but smells it first.) . . . I wouldnt
have believed it. (*Puts drink on floor again.*) I understand
your frustration, but you must understand the responsibility I – I feel more than if you were my actual son. When
I adopted you, in my eyes that was a contract. I honour
my contracts. Natural fathers have rifts with their sons
– we should be spared that. It should be our advantage.

LEONARD. Father I wont be put off. If Im to do your job I
must have determination. But when I show it you say it
makes me unfit for the job!

OLDFIELD. Precisely! Why is that a mystery? Learn to get
what you want without grabbing – and without this
shocking abuse of innocent people. Putting you on the
board – I looked forward so much to that. I meant
'pleasure' when I said it just now. But you've turned it
into an ordeal. I feel like a blindman groping across a
minefield. I cant do anything right for you. Get rid of
your ambition – every scrap of pride – and start to think
of the responsibilities you owe to others. Then I can be
happy with you. I never had any ambition – it would have
got in the way of my mission. The leader's life is service.
There are no rewards – and it gets harder. If you dont
know that in your bones then perhaps you should look
round for a more comfortable future.

LEONARD. Is that what you want?

OLDFIELD. Dont be a child.

LEONARD. Then what do you want?

OLDFIELD. I told you! I'd hoped you'd begun to see! Or is
this some new twist in your game? He served me neat
whisky. Does he think I buy soda to clean the drains? Its
impossible to make the most innocent remark without
offending you Leonard. You fly off the handle and
everyone feels guilty. You wont believe it, but I sit here
asking myself if *I've* done wrong! Now you see why I
asked to be spared this conversation . . . O god he's
going to sulk! Its a father's duty to show his child his

weaknesses so that he doesnt have to parade them in front of others. In your situation they could destroy you. Would you rather I lied? I've no intention of lowering the intellectual standards by which I live so that you can go on believing you're faultless – and that your talents will make running any company childs play! Im tired – this conversation must stop.

LEONARD. I cant win with you father.

OLDFIELD. Very smart. (*Silence.*) You certainly manoeuver yourself into a comfortable position: if you fail you blame me. That'll be next. I offer you everything and Im blamed because you cant take it: all I ask is a little patience. I dont want gratitude but – (*Stops.*) I shall never understand why you had to do this today! I thought for once I'd be allowed to come home to peace. (*Pause.*) Why should anyone expect gratitude? We work – and give others their livelihood and expect to have the skin flayed from the backs of our hands.

LEONARD. I dropped the subject five minutes ago.

OLDFIELD. I will not sit here and be tormented! The subject's dropped when I say – not when you want! You start a row and say drop it when you see how crude – and pushing your behaviour's been! You're intolerable! (*Slight pause.*) Dont try these tactics on the board. They wont handle you with kid gloves. (*Low, gruff.*) There are limits to what I'll accept. I tell you Leonard, if I didnt already have doubts this conversation would have given me them. Its a warning. I put you on the board – the first disagreement and you're squabbling with me in public! What's your scheme for handling the ministry when they welsh on a procurement? – order the unions out on a mass sulk?

LEONARD. Im sorry. Im sorry. Im wrong. It wasnt fair to ask you today when you're in a –

OLDFIELD. O? When Im in a what? (*No answer.*) Today's no different from yesterday or tomorrow. I can deal with

Hammond and that crowd without losing the ability to attend to my responsibilities. I could sit here till I'd settled the future of a hundred sons – if it was in their interest I did so. What you're doing is in no one's interest! Hammond wanted my property: you seem to want my peace of mind!

LEONARD (*slight pause*). Hammond wasnt such a push-over.

OLDFIELD. What did you say?

LEONARD. I said you sweated when the bankers took time over raising your second loan.

OLDFIELD. I see. You start off touting for your future and now you're holding an inquest on my past! Is there more? (*Silence.*) You may regret what you've said tonight. Your last remark – I hope it was your last – was not merely contemptible. I have to say this Leonard: you can be cruel. Its the worst vice.

LEONARD. Yes well the truth can be cruel.

OLDFIELD. Go on!

LEONARD. I told you: *I'd* stopped. But you – so I – (*Stops.*) O god. Please. Please. Its finished.

OLDFIELD. Six weeks fighting for your future and you treat me to this! Dodds and Bartley gave me their congratulations. You said 'Gimme-mine!'

LEONARD. Im not letting you blame me for this.

OLDFIELD *stands.*

OLDFIELD. Blame? You've a right to be heard with respect. We shouldnt end the day like this. When two people start talking about blame they're both in the wrong – that's my experience. Im always busy – on the move – it must seem as if I didnt care. Its really only when Im tired, isnt it? Im tired now. Hammond scared me. I wish you'd never have to deal with people like him. He thinks with his mouth open – *eats* everything. I try not to be impatient. When you're old, that's ugly. I shant change.

Its good we had this conversation, it forces me to say something essential to you. I dont have the rights of a proper father. You dont owe anyone that. If I cant be lived with – you mustnt deceive yourself: you should go. My money isnt worth it. You'd become corrupt. That would be the worst thing that could happen.

LEONARD. I shouldnt have asked. I knew the answer.

OLDFIELD. You should have gone out to celebrate what I'd won for you. Its not too late. If I was your age I'd have something to celebrate. (*Shrugs.*) I've burdened myself with my responsibilities for the rest of my life – I could've burdened Hammond with them. We'll make an appointment in the diary and sort this out. Goodnight.

LEONARD. Goodnight.

OLDFIELD *goes.* LEONARD *stands in silence.* BARTLEY *comes in quietly.*

BARTLEY. Could ah have a word Mr Leonard?

LEONARD. – ? –

BARTLEY. What the hell's goin' on? Ah cannae figure the half o' it. Mr Oldfield was in a shockin sweat the last weeks. The explanations in the press only make the whole thing more of a riddle.

LEONARD. Hammond tried to take over my father's company –

BARTLEY. Ay Hammond Hammond Hammond yous cannae get away from the name!

LEONARD. He tried to buy the shares. If the shareholders had sold him more than half he'd've controlled the company.

BARTLEY. Is that legal? A man can just buy up people's livelihoods like that?

LEONARD. My father offered them more money. Then Hammond offered more and so on. Today they sold my father over half –

BARTLEY. That means there'll be nae more Hammond the morrow?

LEONARD. Yes. The banks lent my father enough money to buy almost all the shares. We're now a private company.

BARTLEY. That must be an awful relief t' your father. It is t' *me*! I learned t' survive the hard way Mr Leonard – I have t' read between the lines before they're printed. If Mr Oldfield had lost he'd've nae worked for Hammond – and it'd've been doon the lavvy for me.

LEONARD. Im sure he'd –

BARTLEY. No no – ah rub along with Mr Oldfield. But ah'm dam sure he'd nae want me roond him all day when he's retired. An there's nae many gentlemen want a man with ma background – an most of *them* left the service with their own batman. We're nae nannies: the employer cannae increase his need! Ah'm nae talkin too much Mr Leonard?

LEONARD. My father doesnt need you tonight.

BARTLEY. Then there's the court martial. Mr Oldfield saw the unfairness o' that. But the prejudice is shockin! People think a court martial's roond one o' the last judgement. Telled them they gi' a wrong verdict an its blasphemy! – you're quarrelin' wi' god all mighty!

LEONARD. You'd get a reference.

BARTLEY. O nae doobt – a reference. Mr Oldfield'd gi' me that. He's one o' the best – as you ken yourself. In a manner o' speakin wor both his weans – he took wor both in. Have you never thought o' that? Oh ah'm nae sayin ah'm qualified t' stand side by side wi' yous – ah wouldnt go that far. You're sure ah'm nae talkin too much Mr Leonard? Yous said a wee crack wor in order. An then there's yon glass. Set like a trap for the dilatory servant. If ah took it in would ah m'bee disturb him? If he'd've wanted it he'd've took it or drank it afore he left. But if ah took it awae would he m'bee come lookin for it? An if ah leaves it it looks as if ah'm treatin the place as a midden. Would yous tell us wor ah'm expected t' do Mr

Leonard? (*No response.*) I would'nae want yous thinkin ah'm nae willin t' deal wi' the glass cause ah'm off duty. On or off never stop nae body givin me orders in this hoose!

LEONARD (*low, flat*). For chrissake.

LEONARD (*sudden malice*). Sorry t' land yous wi' the decision. Shall ah hang on or come back later . . .? (*Recovers.*) Och there's nae call for me t' adopt that tone. Yous must think ah'm a snotty-nosed little tear-arse. Im over-conscientious. (*Low.*) Scared t' shit ah'll lose my job, so ah do everythin perfect. (*Normal tone.*) I wor on my last roonds t' lock up afore ah switch on the alarm. Then ah saw your father's glass an had a slow panic. Best leave it where it is. Its doin nae harm.

BARTLEY *goes out.* LEONARD *sits in an armchair. He dozes – not in the comfortable position of a sleeper but as stiffly and awkwardly as a soldier shot and left in the street.*

Unit Two

The same.

Dawn. The electric light is on and the curtains are drawn. LEONARD *still sleeps in the armchair. His face is blank and his body is even more rigid and awkward, as if it had dried and contracted.*

DODDS *comes in. He has changed into a different business suit. He looks at* LEONARD *and draws the curtains.* LEONARD *wakes.*

DODDS. Morning. (*He switches off the lights.*) You slept here?

LEONARD (*wristwatch*). Is my father up?

DODDS (*shakes his head*). Im very early. You're all right?

LEONARD. Dropped off.

DODDS. Wilbraham's in my car.

LEONARD. You dont want me to see him now?

DODDS. Calm him down. If the creditors see him in this state they'll pull the plug.

LEONARD. I cant.

DODDS. Five minutes. I'll bring him up.

DODDS *goes out.* LEONARD *curses under his breath. He straightens his clothes.* BARTLEY *comes in.*

BARTLEY. Mornin sir. I did'nae recollect you said anythin aboot an early breakfast . . .?

LEONARD. Coffee for three.

BARTLEY. D'you want anythin cooked? (LEONARD *shakes his head.*) Mr Leonard – last night –. When Mr Oldfield's tense he takes it oot on me – he pays so its his privilege. When it was settle ah had a little bevvy celebration – ah was that happy for yous. I would'nae want any little-bit indiscretion t' get on ma records or any o' that. You can rely on me Mr Leonard. So its no cooked breakfast then?

DODDS *comes in with* WILBRAHAM.

DODDS (*introductions*). Leonard – Eric Wilbraham.

WILBRAHAM. Howdyoudo? Mr Oldfield its most decent of you to receive me at this hour.

BARTLEY. I'll serve coffee in ten minutes gentlemen. (*He turns to go.*)

WILBRAHAM. I say d'you think your man might kit me up with a shirt? Colin kindly bedded me down for the night but I've no fresh linen. In the daylight my shirt's a bit grubby.

BARTLEY. Nae bother sir.

BARTLEY *goes out.*

WILBRAHAM. Awfully good of you.

LEONARD. Im sorry about your problems.

WILBRAHAM. I've been a fool. But the main thing is I know it. I've told Colin everything – opened the books – and I gave him permission to disclose everything to you. Im glad its come to this. I feel as if this morning I'll be driven to my funeral and afterwards I'll walk away and leave an empty casket.

LEONARD. I cant commit myself. Colin's preparing a report on your company. I look forward to reading it.

WILBRAHAM. Life is always worthwhile. The great offence is to deny that. Gamblers are used to coming home in the early morning when its daylight but the rest of the world's asleep. Drawn curtains, locked-up shops, a milk-bottle in front of a great office tower – the caretaker comes out and stoops to pick it up like some old crone – at least a thousand years old. You feel young – and your losses and drinking dont matter. The mornings are always beautiful, before the day soils itself and becomes shabby.

DODDS. Be positive eh Willy?

WILBRAHAM. That's how one must live. If you stand before a firing squad believe – absolutely – the army's about to mutiny or war will be declared and they'll be ordered to save ammunition. I inherited a company in profit – good prospects – good people – they hardly needed me – I had time on my hands – so I went on gambling. You wouldnt believe how much you lose! Not lose: it *vanishes* – as if you went to sit down in a chair and suddenly the room's gone – you're sitting in an empty field. You live in a world of illusions. But you dont want to hear this! – you dont gamble. I promise you you wont lose one penny of your investment. I *have* learned. Whatever I do now – right or wrong – is my responsibility. The past cant help me or harm me anymore. Perhaps this is what I've been striving for? I recall reading a magazine article ages ago which said that gamblers – O in some fearfully complicated way I didnt grasp! – wish to lose. That's the only way I can make my losses look like gains!

BARTLEY *comes in with a folded white shirt.*

BARTLEY. This'll fit the neck fine sir.

WILBRAHAM. How kind. To lend me a shirt.

> WILBRAHAM *takes off his jacket, tie and shirt.* BARTLEY
> *puts the jacket on an armchair, unfolds the clean shirt, holds
> it up by the outer tips of the shoulders and waits.*

WILBRAHAM. So – you'll back me.

LEONARD (*to* DODDS). Will Mr Wilbraham's creditors
leave the bankruptcy petition on the table for a week?

DODDS (*reassuring*). I'll phone round before the meeting.

WILBRAHAM. They'll jump at the offer. If they shut me
down they'll be lucky to get 10p in the pound. Your
father's name will carry the day. (*To* BARTLEY.) Thank
you. Of course Colin explained that your father knows
nothing about this. All the same. If things go wrong again
– he'd be bound to bail us out. What better security could
they want?

LEONARD. Im not interested in merely lending money.

WILBRAHAM. No. Colin spoke of that. Its to be as you wish.
I'll put you on the board.

LEONARD. I want –

WILBRAHAM. I welcome your contribution. Fresh eye of
youth – that's not a cliché, it means money.

LEONARD. I want to be managing director.

WILBRAHAM. O. (*To* BARTLEY.) It *does* fit.

BARTLEY. Yessir.

WILBRAHAM (*to* LEONARD). Colin hadnt spoken of that.

LEONARD. *If* his report removes my considerable doubt.

WILBRAHAM. My people – there's been a misunderstanding
– they wouldnt accept a new MD. The position isnt
offered. I've hidden nothing – it would be pointless to try
to do so. Our situation is desperate. But I've learned my
lesson – forgive me if I repeat myself but I must assume
I wasnt clear – and now Colin has arranged this last

chance for me. I cant throw it away – it would be worse than a gamble.

LEONARD. Im not interested in less.

WILBRAHAM. I must think. (*Cuff-links.*) I've spoken to my colleagues of – our rescue plan – they gave me their support – heart warming – I no longer had a right to it. If I go back to them with – say I've put them in the hands of –. (*Controls himself.*) Let me just say I couldnt carry my board.

LEONARD. Carry's the word! Chuck them out! They helped you to get in this mess –

WILBRAHAM. No no you mustnt say that! If I'd heeded their advice –

LEONARD. – and now I've got to get you out of it! If they want their jobs they'd better earn my confidence sharp!

DODDS. All this –

WILBRAHAM. You cant treat them like that! Some of them were my father's friends – they've served the company for years. I couldnt face them, knowing what I've heard. The offer of a seat remains, of course – but I cant put them in a position where I wasnt able to protect them. (*Pause.*) I've fooled myself. I thought for once I hadnt! Colin – its your fault – you brought me here under a misapprehension –

DODDS. What nonsense! We havent time to thrash out these details now. Leonard wont be silly and jeopardise his position before he's read my report.

WILBRAHAM. Suppose you were MD. The company wont be easy to save. We know the competition – the wrinkles – you'll need our help. I wouldnt have the heart to offer it if I'd been humiliated.

LEONARD. Chairman-MD. Full personal control. Or no money. No one deserves charity – in my experience they drink it or gamble it.

BARTLEY *goes out with* WILBRAHAM's *jacket.*

WILBRAHAM. You want to take my company from me.

LEONARD. Stay on the board – if you think you can contribute.

WILBRAHAM. For how long – and under what sufferance?

LEONARD (*conciliatory*). Suppose I put money in and the company fails? If you're not chairman you've got an excuse, you say it failed because I –

WILBRAHAM. A highly paid messenger! – not even highly paid!

LEONARD. Anyway the board'll be glad to be shot of you – if they're not too geriatric to notice you've gone!

WILBRAHAM. Im in trouble. I may lose my livelihood. But Im not a pauper. Dont push me. Im not speaking from pride. This is my last chance. I know Im ready for it. Im chastened and sober. Otherwise I wouldnt have come here – it would've been wrong. Colin will bear me out if your own judgement cant tell you. You can still make good money out of me. – You silly man! I know what Im doing, *you're* the one who's in confusion. You'd burden yourself with the daily running of my piddling company when you've got the Oldfield giant to absorb you? Anyone would think you were in a trap you show such confusion!

BARTLEY *comes in with* WILBRAHAM's *jacket, giving it the final flick with a clothes brush.*

BARTLEY. I'll put your dirty shirt in a carrier Mr Wilbraham.

WILBRAHAM. Thank you.

BARTLEY *helps* WILBRAHAM *into his jacket and then goes out with the brush and the dirty shirt.*

WILBRAHAM (*to* LEONARD – *the shirt*). Thank you. I'll have it returned.

DODDS. This is absurd! Leonard must state his interest to the meeting. That doesnt commit anyone. It gives you a week of discussions without costing a penny.

LEONARD. I want his agreement on paper before the meeting.

WILBRAHAM. No. I'd sooner dig up my father and pawn his graveclothes. I've been a bloody fool. But when I got up from the gambling table and left appalling losses behind me – my affairs in ruins – I could look the others in the face. It was my money I'd lost. Im sorry I cant put it any better. There are some things – they get talked about so often because they're so important – and then anything we say about them is a cliché. That's the only way we can tell the truth. Listen: if we cant hear the clichés as if they were the truth told to us for the first time – then I think we'd all be dead. Last night I was like a condemned man in a cell. But I looked forward to the morning. I'd found a purpose. The drink, stupid night time sweats, the illiterate gossip in the press (their style is far worse than the imbecilities they're describing – not even honest clichés: frigid banalities) all that was in the past. The last ten years ripped from the calender. And now Im asked to put my inheritance and my expectations in the hands of a boy who – grabs so brashly that he crushes everything he touches! I wont do it. I'd be gambling in a week. I'd rather face my creditors Dodds, they want my money (*Turns to* LEONARD.) – I dont know what you want – it lies beyond my experience, and that's been shady and desperate enough. I see it in your face – your features are like your prison number.

DODDS. Willy Leonard's right: no one can trust you after all the –

WILBRAHAM. You cant know! You havent been in my situation! (*To* LEONARD.) You dont teach dogs to walk on their hindlegs by cutting off their front ones! – they die of your cruelty.

LEONARD. Perhaps this report will show your company's prospects are good. Brilliant! But they're out of your reach. You cant get them without me!

DODDS. Willy dont be unreasonable. Let Leonard –

WILBRAHAM. Shut up! (*Pause.*) Shut up! (*To* LEONARD.) Send this employee from the room! 'Thrash out the details'? If I were suicidal – Im not – you'd both have murder on your hands! (*To* LEONARD.) So cocky! So sure! You dont know what you're doing or even who you're talking to. I could stab you in the back through a three foot wall. I should give in to you and destroy you. It'd almost be worth it to see the surprise on your face! And you wouldnt even have the fun of gambling (*Bitterly.*) or the comfort of walking home in the morning – just the despair.

DODDS (*wristwatch*). We're getting nowhere.

LEONARD. Run him to his creditors. He can tell them he's a reformed rake – signed the pledge – a born again christian – discovered monetarism! It'd almost be worth going to see! A revivalist meeting!

WILBRAHAM. Im so bored with you. I feel like a scientist watching mice when he's forgotten what experiment he's doing. When you ask so much you can only take it from yourself.

LEONARD. I dont want you to give me anything but your enmity! Not the chair – I can *take* that! But when its mine be my enemy! Trick me. Cheat me. Swindle me. Promise me. Please. Enmity! Enmity! Enmity and hate! I'll thrive on the worst you can do! The more stones you throw at me the more I can bury you with! Dont tell me you cant hate? I couldnt stand the let down! If I took all you've got and you didnt hate me – I'd be robbed! All I ask of you is *honesty*: hate me and say it! I'll help you – give you every reason to hate me. Im a gambling machine designed so you cant win: you never have a chance – that's what the machine's *for*! But you must go on gambling. That's our situation. Now do something.

WILBRAHAM (*cries*). I dont know why Im crying. 'S not appropriate. 'S what fathers do: whip their child and cry.

– Why are we so sordid?

LEONARD (*flat*). You'll spoil the shirt.

WILBRAHAM. We're bastards but we dont deserve to live like this. No – (*Sniff.*) not a spoiled shirt. I put on a show. (*Sniff.*) Bloody fool – crying over you doesnt help you. If I could make your mistakes and let you stand by and watch, I would. When it was over you'd pay me far more for what you'd seen than what you'll pay me now. The degradation wouldnt hurt me, Im hardened to it. Yesterday I was at the bottom. Last night was a consolation. Now its the bottom again. What next? What d'you want from me? (*Hand on* LEONARD'S *shoulder.*) I hope you have all the luck – the big successes. (*Sniff.*) Come to me if things go wrong, I'll help. Looking down at a gambling table's like looking down at a map of the world: its surrounded by a ring of ghosts. (*To* DODDS.) Scribble his bit of paper.

BARTLEY *comes in with a carrier bag.*

BARTLEY. Your shirt's in the carrier Mr Wilbraham.

LEONARD. I wont be at the meeting.

WILBRAHAM (*to* BARTLEY). Thank you for your help.

BARTLEY. Let me put it in the car for you sir.

LEONARD (*to* DODDS). They'll accept your verbal assurance.

BARTLEY (*to* WILBRAHAM). Coffee's in the mornin room sir. 'Long the passage – ah left the door open. Its sunnier in there.

WILBRAHAM *goes out.*

LEONARD. He's drunk. There arent any overnight conversions – you cant escape from yourself.

DODDS. He's not drunk.

LEONARD. Only because the facts have caught up with him. All *that* was pride and guilt. When the pressure's off he'll be back to his bottles and wheels. Glad to be rid of his responsibilities – probably realise it before he gets to the coffee.

LEONARD *and* DODDS *go out.* BARTLEY *picks up the glass left the night before. It is full. He drinks it and goes out with the empty glass.*

Unit Three

The same.

A few weeks later.

LEONARD *and* DODDS. LEONARD *has a file of papers.*

LEONARD (*evenly*). It could never have worked. Start ruthless or pay later. The meeting was vital – a full board – the accountants. Plans for expanding after recovery. He sat in a haze of whisky fumes pushing a piece of paper up and down with one finger. Terrified to pick it up – it'd shake.

DODDS. He warned you.

LEONARD. Im not taking stick for him. (*Mutters.*) He'll booze when he's a skeleton – use his bones for straws.

DODDS. What?

LEONARD. Gambling's *his* problem, his booze is the. *company's.*

DODDS. Indeed.

LEONARD. If he had any guts he'd make a clean break – start something new – open a gambling hell. Follows me round like dogshit on my shoe.

DODDS. Nasty.

LEONARD. The whole company know he's a failure. Surely he suffers under that? Well the board's agreed: he's out. I can turn the company round in a year – we've even had some luck: the orders are better than you forecast – but not if I carry passengers. Anyway for the first time in my life Im happy. Why should I let him spoil it? Get him in. (DODDS *starts to go*.) He hasnt been drinking? Cant stand him like that.

DODDS. No.

LEONARD. Take him out to Annabel's if they still have him. The company's farewell gesture. Let him off-load his bile on you.

DODDS *goes out*. LEONARD *goes to an armchair, sits, opens the file and immediately begins to study the papers in it. The door opens and a large man in a brown suit comes in.* LEONARD *reads for a few more seconds – not long enough to be impolite – shuts the file and stares at it for a few more seconds before looking up.*

LEONARD. Mr Hammond – ? (*Stops.*) My father's not – was he expecting you? (*Silence.*) He's in the country. (*Slight suggestion of intrigue.*) You knew.

HAMMOND. Morning. We'll get this straight out in the open.

LEONARD. Wait . . .! (*Rapid think.*) All right – I'll talk to you and we – (*Stops.*) Im in the middle of – I'll put it off and –

HAMMOND. No need. You're not keeping Willy waiting – I sent him packing.

LEONARD. Who let you in? You've come to hurt me.

HAMMOND (*puzzled*). Hurt? I dont know about such things.

LEONARD (*moves towards door*). I want a witness to this conversation.

HAMMOND. That's the last thing you want. I dont believe you've even guessed? As managing director of Wilbra-ham Engineering you owe me four million three hundred odd pounds. Overdue. I want immediate payment.

LEONARD. I've got a debtors' waiver for one year.

HAMMOND. No.

LEONARD. Yes. You werent on the list.

HAMMOND. Not when you checked. Dodds gave you five names. Between then and the date of the waiver I bought the debts. The waiver says 'debts outstanding' – nothing more. For the sake of form you do owe the five a few thousand each. Your bit of paper doesnt cover my four millions.

LEONARD. Why was the paper worded like that?

HAMMOND. I told Dodds to word it like that.

LEONARD. And not serve you notice of the creditor meeting.

HAMMOND. That would've been Willy's slip. Seen worse. Busy time – company upheaval. Mistakes happen in the best run companies – and he's known to drink.

LEONARD. Any lawyer would rip through that in his sleep.

HAMMOND. Let sleeping lawyers lie, they do less harm. I knew Willy's dad – the evil bugger. Sorry for the lad. When his firm got in a bad way I bought the debts. Give my old friend's son a breathing space. Then I find he's been took-over, kicked out the chair – now kicked out the company (I read his dismissal notice on the desk on my way in) – by a young pop-up artist who doesnt give a monkey's who he hurts! We're not safe. That young tear-away's pants need taking down for the sake of decent public life.

LEONARD. What did you pay Dodds? Or did he do it out of the malice of a pure heart? This is to hurt my father.

HAMMOND. Hurt? I dont have time or inclination to go round doing hurt. Listen: I dont have to present my bill, now or ever. I reckon you might get this company back in profit. You started right – kicked Willy out – but any sane man'd rid himself of that louse. Suppose you fail? Trade slump – labour trouble – reorganisation snarl-ups – a whole host of things! – not to mention your own mistakes: you trusted Dodds. I wouldnt have. I dont trust *myself* – and I dont know half what Im up to! Dont *you* trust me neither. We'll put it on a business basis. I'll bail you out and see you through any rough patches – you'll

get all the resources of my organisation behind you –
money – insider gen –

LEONARD (*candid*). I have to ask you to explain Mr
Hammond. Are you threatening me or offering me
something?

HAMMOND. I own twelve percent of Oldfield's equity. When
time takes its toll and you inherit, you top me up to fifty-
one per cent: controlling interest. Your father's getting
on and lately he's been under a strain. Dodds has put it
all down nicely on a bit of paper. I checked it, its safe to
sign – no catch: it says what it says.

LEONARD. I'll pay you off. Borrow from my father.

HAMMOND. Dont haggle if you cant offer something with
a bit of relish. Would I go to all this bother if you could
wriggle off the hook so easy?

LEONARD. The other creditors had faith in me! I'll give you
a good return on capital! All I ask is – (*He stops.*)

HAMMOND (*after a short pause*). I wish there was another
way. (*Slight pause.*) You cant even try borrowing behind
my back – Hong Kong or somewhere – they'd want your
balls and they'd be mine by then: the first sign of messing
and I'll stick my bill where your father sees it. And if that
didnt scare the Willies out of you you'd've gone to him at
the start – when Dodds came to you with his evil little
plan. I'd've gone to him. So would Dodds. So would
Tom, Dick and Harry. You're the only person in the
world who couldnt. And its got worse! The first move you
made on your own you put his whole company at risk!
Dear o dear. If he saw the cock-up you're in – just try
lifting a corner so he can peep – he'll cut you off. He'd
never forget. O he'll fill your pockets – but his company'd
vanish out of sight like Mont Blanc going down the plug
hole. So would all the other loot I dont know about –
(*Taps his chest.*) the treasure store up within. The whole
world really. That's what you're scared of losing – not
the company or the money. The little no-man's land

between father and son. That's where it all turns. That's
what handed you over to me. Dodds was right. Strange.
I can see it in your face. It'd be a different world if we
went round with our boots on our heads – as we would if
we had the sense. We walk on our feet but drag our face
through the dirt. Its painful to see you lad. There's one
certain thing left in your young life: you wont get your
hands on a spanner from your father's works unless it
comes through me. They say he's a right bully. I'll make
amends. Controlling share – not the lot. Leave you your
proper incentive. And if you're hoping I'll die before your
father, that wont help – apart from the incidental
pleasure it'd give you. My shares go to my assigns.
(*Calls.*) Dodds! – you dont mind me being free? Im taking
the risk out of your future. Me behind you, you cant fail.
When your company's a success, come out in the open –
partly: bounce about in front of your father – rattle his
bones.

DODDS *comes in*. LEONARD *ignores him*.

HAMMOND. We've been building paper castles.
LEONARD (*half-musing, half aloud*). No no that's not the
problem. My father's slow because he doesnt want his
company wrecked. Its every father's problem: hand on
because they die. If its an athlete – runner – jumper – he
gives up early and trains the young. Then he's happy.
Business men are in their prime when they're old. That's
why there's distress. Not hate and treachery – that's for
friends. In families – there's distress *because* they're loyal.
He'll take his share of blame. Its wrong to judge him.
HAMMOND (*to* DODDS). You comment.
DODDS. Your father came to me as company secretary and
raised his doubts about you officially. When you help to
arm the nation you have obligations.
HAMMOND. Be inventive! Expand! All sorts is possible!
When you sign my paper I'll sell you my shares in

Oldfields – for a price. Then you give them to your dad as a present. Say you talked me into it. How's that! He's not to know I'd just be putting money in my own piggy bank! The things you've got to learn! Take Respectability Dodds – a perfect specimen of the devious and corrupt. Or Willy – the Inexplicable. No one needs to stand alone in this world: we can share each other's enemies. Just remember whose back your knife's in. If I push you too hard you run to dad and get disinherited: then you disinherit *me* at a stroke! Not every lad's in a position to disinherit a man old enough to be his father. I'll have to be a good boy! When I bind you to me, Im the rope: if I bind too hard, I break. Our friendship's based on betrayal. Not many friendships have such a solid base my son – that's usually reserved for love affairs.

LEONARD. Go to hell. You havent thought of everything.

HAMMOND. I have, I have! I bet you Wilbraham Engineering I have! Cheer up! It looks like collapse and its the rocket taking off. Dont judge by the common man's standards. If a strangler got his hands round my neck I'd crush his wrists with my chin. I would. I wouldnt let him tear hisself away. Hold him eyeball to eyeball and let him plead while his fingers dribbled down my shirt. I succeed because I enjoy my enemies: but I dont let them enjoy me – Im not an ecumenisist!

LEONARD. I cheat my father every day till he dies?

HAMMOND. Well you made a nice start when you went behind his back to Willy and it'll come easier with practice.

LEONARD. If I get a chance to hurt you I shant hesitate.

HAMMOND. I wouldnt want you to. You'll be my trainee by then. Its only the humbug I cant stomach. (*Pats* LEONARD's *back.*) We'll do.

LEONARD. I wont sign.

HAMMOND. I'll give you a couple of days for the sake of

your dignity. I enjoyed meeting you – helping a young lad by putting opportunity in his way. But you're not the only iron in the fire. (*To* DODDS.) I'll expect the paper by Monday. (*Starts to go.*) You were a sitting duck and as you were sitting on the roof of an armaments factory it seemed wrong not to take a shot.

HAMMOND *goes out.*

DODDS. We'll go to your father's shoot. It'll look suspicious if we both dropped out.

LEONARD. What's the first thing I'll do when I get the company?

DODDS. By then we'll know so much about each other we'll both have to keep to heel. Hammond's a bad friend but a worse enemy. If you want anything to use on your father, I can let you into the –

LEONARD *has walked out.* DODDS's *voice doesnt rise or trail away but stops abruptly in mid-sentence. He goes out.*

Unit Four

OLDFIELD's *Country House*

The Hall Lobby.

Apart from BARTLEY *everyone in the scene wears shooting clothes.*

BARTLEY *comes in carrying the Oldfield AS42 Rifle and a case of magazines and rounds. He wears a dark suit with a fawn windcheater over the suit jacket, and calf-length wellingtons. He sets the AS42 down on its dipod and puts the case next to it. He starts to shell rounds from their packets.* WILBRAHAM *comes in.*

BARTLEY. Like spring oot there the mornin sir.

WILBRAHAM. Good morning. Is this where we assemble?

BARTLEY. The hoose party ay. Day guests oot on the drive. Yous can join them if yous wish sir.

WILBRAHAM. I'll hang on. Somewhat nippy. (*Looks at the AS42.*) . . . Good lor . . .!

BARTLEY. Ay sir – new Oldfield AS42. Nae a prototype – first factory run. Mr Oldfield's takin it oot the day. He allus takes a new –

WILBRAHAM. You couldnt find me a drink?

BARTLEY. Ay sir. Can ah offer you ma flask? (*Takes out his pocket flask.*) Mr Oldfield does'nae like liquor drunk before the shoot. (*Fills flask cap.*) Has t' act canny in his line o' trade. Accident here – the peaceniks'd put it doon t' the hand o' god. When you're desperate you bring god in t' anythin. I carry a wee drop for the gentlemen's emergencies. (*Hands cap to* WILBRAHAM.) There you go sir.

WILBRAHAM. Obliged to you.

BARTLEY. Not at all.

WILBRAHAM (*drinks*). I had intended not to drink before lunch. This nip in the air . . .

BARTLEY. Och it'd be suicide t' go oot in that damp wi' oot a liquid breakfast. Could yous manage another sir? I'd advise it t' dilute the first.

WILBRAHAM *holds out the cap.*

BARTLEY (*pouring*). Mr Oldfield does'nae let me join the beaters. But ah flit aboot. Ah keep *this* top up.

WILBRAHAM *drinks. He holds the empty cap in his hand.* BARTLEY *poises the lip of the flask over it and looks questioningly at* WILBRAHAM.

WILBRAHAM. No no please. (*Hands cap back to* BARTLEY.) I mustnt.

BARTLEY *takes the cap and screws it back on the flask.*

BARTLEY. It'll come t' nae harm if wor leave it t' mature a while longer.

WILBRAHAM. I was up at six.

BARTLEY. Is that right sir?

WILBRAHAM. I intended to take a brisk walk. Then I thought: ridiculous – let the poor bloody birds spend their last morning in peace.

BARTLEY. O ay sir?

WILBRAHAM. I sat in the armchair and looked at the trees.

BARTLEY. Much more sensible sir. You'll get plenty brisk walks the day.

WILBRAHAM. Yes.

BARTLEY (*pocketing flask*). I dont know if you'd agree with me sir but there's a fine view o' the trees oot your room. Panoramic.

WILBRAHAM. Bird song always makes the world seem empty. I played in a wood when I was a boy. My aunt owned one in the country.

BARTLEY. Tell me the lad wor's nae at haim in a wood.

WILBRAHAM (*quietly*). How bloody stupid it all is . . . I wish I didnt have to go out. Im not at all in a fit state to kill things. I could say I was indisposed – stay in? (*Shakes head dismissively.*) I'd drink. (*Looks at AS42.*) How barbarous . . .

BARTLEY (*offering a small tin box*). Would you take a peppermint sir?

WILBRAHAM. No thank you.

BARTLEY. T' keep the kelt oot.

LEONARD *comes in. He stops in the doorway, looking at the AS42, sees* WILBRAHAM *and turns to go.*

WILBRAHAM. Dont go.

LEONARD (*going*). Im looking for my father.

WILBRAHAM. I must have a word.

LEONARD *stops*.

WILBRAHAM. Im most grateful.

BARTLEY. I'll tell Mr Oldfield you're lookin for him Mr Leonard.

BARTLEY *goes out*.

WILBRAHAM. I've been trying to speak to you since I got here.

LEONARD. You have nothing to –

WILBRAHAM. Im absolute scum. You cant possibly forgive the harm I've done you. I destroyed myself and now Im used to harm others. Odd isnt it? I've nothing against you. Dodds came to me with his filthy proposal. He poses as my friend. Men like him are vermin. I wouldnt be his friend if he were my one salvation on the day of judgement. What could I do? Im not in control of my performance. Before I met you I prayed (of course I dont believe in god, my gambling losses cured me of that: he's just a nervous tic left over from school chapel) 'O god let him be a crook, a bastard – and let my innocence shine out'. Then I'd be exonerated in the eyes of the mythical bystander in books on ethics: he'd see *Im* the victim. I was only doing to you what you'd spend your life doing to others – my one fault was to punish you before you'd had time to commit the crime: but surely in the eyes of heaven that's almost a virtue? And there you were: innocent. Its cruel to be that innocent! I was so ashamed. I had one hope: he'll see Im scum. Surely he wont trust me? O god he's so innocent he does! I reek of deceit – fraud – dishonesty – filth! Even he must see it! Find me out! Get on my scent! Run me down! Expose me! Help me you fool! I chatted on about early morning walks and milk bottles – I was as bogus as I dared – extravagant under the circumstances – remember Dodds was watching. You were too greedy to notice what you were eating.

Yum yum you lapped the poison up and asked for seconds! Make me chairman! You were like a victim pointing out the places to stick the knife in. I was to blame – I led you on. That was my crime: I let you make me your victim. I couldnt believe the confusion you were in. This man is more evil than I am, I thought: yet he's innocent. Dont you think the world's in great danger when such things can happen? When corruption's so deep it comes from innocence, everything's contaminated by innocence! We can never get away from it! And I connive. Always I let it happen. Yet I long to do good! Im such scum! Such scum! Such scum! How can you stay and listen to me Mr Oldfield?

LEONARD. Why're you here?

WILBRAHAM. Hammond sticking me under your nose. What can you expect from a man who always wears brown? He'd wear a brown dinner jacket if he could get a decent tailor to make it for him. Im the stench of failure – if you dont sign his paper you're supposed to end up like me. Last night I was reformed – again. I put a bottle of Laffite under the bed. I even got up at six to torment myself by sitting with it. Its still unopened. Then I came down and scrounged a guzzle from that gillie. I had to chat him up. How the homespun philosophy comes to one's lips! I invented an aunt who owned a wood. Always stay down-wind of a servant – they turn nasty. He offered me peppermint: how low I've fallen! Scum! I told you I didnt deceive you from malice? There was no pleasure in it. You seemed a long way off. It was like god shooting at cardboard cut-out men for target practice. Thank you for hearing my confession while Im fairly sober. This evening I'll get drunk and buttonhole you. You'll have to listen to the most fearful sentimental garbage. I do apologise. D'you know why a drunk buttonholes the sober? He tries to force his own self-love onto them by making them tell him he's wonderful – it might even sound true coming from someone sober. But they tell him he's a drunken swine – and bring him face to face with his own self-hate. Then the anger swells up. – My confession didnt interest you?

LEONARD. No.

WILBRAHAM. A mistake. Adding to another's torment doesnt lighten our own. (*Shrugs.*) Why should you accept the apology of a scum?

LEONARD. Sell up what's left and go.

WILBRAHAM. Too late. I gamble any money I get hands on. If I was wounded I'd sell my bandages to bet on the 2.30 though I'd bleed to death before they came under starters orders. I told you you were my last chance. You did right to squash me – a civic duty – but its a pity you had to damage yourself so badly to do it. Im scum beyond redemption. Not even a ruin: a waste lot where the builders dumped their things to rot. Even now when I apologise Im a puppet doing Hammond's dirty work: I exhibit my admonitory vileness. Would it help you to call me scum?

LEONARD. No.

WILBRAHAM. You may should you wish. To relieve your feelings. I shant take offence. (*No response.*) We're civilized men who've found this small way to help each other. Relieve yourself on me. Please. Say scum. Scum. Its a useful word – not easily confused except with skunk. Almost an anagram of muck – and mucus. (*Silence.*) You make people talk but you cant listen. Two sides of a coin but they cant see each other, the head's so close to the tail its got its eyes up its own bum. Is that the secret? Perhaps that's to be your downfall. (*Pause.*) Scum. I flatter myself I have the *mot juste*. As distinctive as the old school tie – which you dont claim unless you're entitled to. *Cads* do: but *I'm* genuine scum. I dont demand repartee: just the odd insult. You wont oblige? No matter. I do brilliant imitations. The only thing I learned at school. Cut lawns

– oak panels – mullioned windows – tradition like bloodstains in the cloisters – libraries bulging with the wisdom of dilapidated books – and I learned the arts of a low comedian. (*He imitates* DODDS. LEONARD *walks away*.) 'I have prepared this piece of paper. I've lined up the dots with a ruler and counted them. They're all there. You can sign'. (*Imitates* DODDS *in Gilbert and Sullivan*.)

'I am Dodds the dots – dots – dots
I am Dodds of the dotted line'

(*Imitates* HAMMOND.) 'Trust me lad and I'll peel the skin off your back and flog it to you for wallpaper. Hate me, and we'll sit side by side on the same cadaver and nibble the same bone.' (*Brief shrill laugh. Imitates* LEONARD. LEONARD *moves away but he follows him*.) 'Mr Wilbraham this is young Master Oldfield. Im king of the castle! I want to be chairman! Only triple-scum would bring that up Wilbraham! Scum! State of the art scum! S for shit – c for crap – u for uckers – m for mess: scum!' Now for my *pièce de résistance* – my imitation of myself! (*Parodies himself*.) 'Rightie-o young Oldfield! Jolly fine insulting weather! What's that you say? Bum? – no need to be personal. Rum? – I dont mind if I do. Slum? – my aunt used to own one! Dumb? Hum! – 'tis a mite pongy, could I scrounge the loan of a pair of socks? O *scum*! – Scum! Scum – scum – scum!' (*Weeps*.) And who's the weeping – who's that imitate? The world, the whole bloody bloody world! (*Slight pause, stops weeping*.) I shouldnt have drunk. Fancy that! O god was that me? I was looking forward to a nice normal weekend away from the London alley-louts, harmlessly shooting birds out of the sky. And now I've been a reformed drunk at night and a lapsed drunk in the morning and we still havent shot the birds. There's no limit to my vileness. Its a conspiracy against the world – certainly against myself. I listen to my imitations to find out what they say about me behind my back. They say Im scum. Utter scum. Yesterday I ruined your life, now Im ruining your weekend. What scum!

OLDFIELD *and* BARTLEY *come in.*

OLDFIELD (*to* BARTLEY, *pointing to the AS42*). Put an empty magazine on the gun.

BARTLEY *kneels by the AS42 and loads magazines. He puts one on the gun.*

OLDFIELD. I hope you're comfortable Mr Wilbraham? If you need anything my servant will look after you.

WILBRAHAM. Delightful house. Reminds me of my aunt's.

OLDFIELD. I wonder if you'd mind finding my assistant Dodds?

WILBRAHAM. Where should I look?

OLDFIELD. He's around. I'd be most grateful.

WILBRAHAM *waits a moment and then goes out.*

OLDFIELD. For god's sake what made you invite him? The man's absolute scum. If he's not careful one day someone will tell him.

LEONARD. I felt sorry for him.

OLDFIELD. You're so naive. I dont like you mixing with his sort. Reeks of failure.

LEONARD. He's in trouble.

OLDFIELD. Im not surprised. Any other weekend I wouldnt mind if you invited Bedlam and Pentonville for their annual cricket match. You know Im putting on my little show with the AS42. Over the years its become a ritual with a new gun. A celebration for friends. Its certainly the most innocent use it'll ever be put to. Now I feel like a clown performing to a stranger. Why you –

LEONARD. Shut up! Its stupid to waste – (*Stops.*)! Does it matter? Be a clown! (*Tries to be calm.*) I shouldnt have brought him. *He's* the clown . . . (*Angry.*) But its my house too! I might have something to celebrate!

OLDFIELD. What? (*No immediate answer.*) Well what? (*Pause.*) Was I going on . . .? *You* know the man's irritating. I made a resolution not to quarrel. I had a special reason for wanting a good weekend. I wasnt going to tell you till the evening. I'll put you on the board.

LEONARD. You changed your mind.

OLDFIELD. Not straight away – I'll approach the directors over the next few months. They wont oppose. You'll come on as trainee-director. I hope that's what you want?

LEONARD. Yes.

OLDFIELD. So you *have* something to celebrate. Frankly this isnt how I wanted to do it. You're impetuous – of course you cant see it, but its what you are and you have to come to terms with the consequences. With a gun you test and discard and the tears go on the drawing board. With people, they learn by wounding themselves – or others: though *that* tells them about guns not wounds. (*To* BARTLEY.) Find Dodds. With any luck that fool's got lost in the fields. (*To* LEONARD.) You're responsible if he strays in front of the guns.

LEONARD. Why didnt you tell me before?

OLDFIELD (*to* BARTLEY). Leave that – I want Dodds.

BARTLEY *goes out.*

OLDFIELD. You've begun to pull. If I hold you in you'll get – fractious . . .

LEONARD. If you'd said this – you passed me in the house every day with this in your head – why didnt you – ? – as if we were cars passing on the street! –

OLDFIELD. Would it've made a difference?

LEONARD. No – when you know what you're doing nothing does. (*Sudden change.*) You can still chuck me off, old lad!

OLDFIELD. The board hires and fires.

LEONARD. Hostile board – I fail – out! Rid of me!

OLDFIELD. Are you being bloody minded – or is it lack of

confidence? I've done what you wanted! (*Conciliatory.*) I took you by surprise. Well at least we can look back – our lives havent been without their strangeness – and see how we survived. Your first parents left you on a doorstep. I've opened doors. What would you say to them today?

LEONARD. I'd ask them to forgive me.

OLDFIELD. You mean you'd –

LEONARD. No – I mean *that*.

OLDFIELD. Would you try to find them? Give them money?

LEONARD. Mother burned the rubbish I was found in. Might've been a clue. D'you ever wonder about my father?

OLDFIELD. No – I've always had a very clear picture of him in my head. The reality you see in – O, doll's houses and gravestones.

LEONARD. Yes, but we're talking about strangers.

OLDFIELD. Children are born with nothing. I gave you things because I have them – its how I made you mine. Women are different. Your mother had to strip you to make you hers. Dont begrudge her her bonfire. She had a withered womb. I'll tell you something I – but she's been dead long enough now . . . She ate nothing for days (I found out later) and then swallowed a colic – a violent mixture of bitters. I came home. I thought at first it was the burglar alarm, not working properly. Her whimpering was drawn out like a scream. Real pain and fear. She pretended to give birth to you and you almost killed her. She tore the sheet with her teeth – along the top – holes and rents. She'd smeared you with something to resemble blood. I dont know what it was. You were beside her on the bed sleeping naked.

LEONARD. Cosier than a doorstep.

OLDFIELD (*controlled*). God you can be icy-blooded. You'll listen with respect when I talk about your mother. After she got well you werent a gift I'd bought her. There was

something between you. You'd given her fear and pain:
you were hers. And you gave me a new woman. I didnt
know she had such tenderness in her – that it was in
anyone. She became all I wanted, and I lost her. She was
a stranger – like your father in a way: a doll. Its precious
– you're happy its yours – but it cant be changed – you
take it as it is. (*Explains.*) Though your father was a
fiction. Not real. – You're right, dont pry into the past.
The detectives cant earn their fees. Put your arm round
me.

LEONARD. Bartley – he may come in –

OLDFIELD. Does a child found on a doorstep worry about
such things? – You should be at home with all doors. Sons
put their arm round their father. Do it today. You're my son.

*They stand side by side, their bodies barely touch, and put an
arm round each other's shoulder – they are like two dummies
each with a human arm.*

OLDFIELD. There. Our pact. (*Hand-pat on* LEONARD's
shoulder.) Strong. Not my flesh – but good. I was strong
once. Now its your turn. Our talk of birth makes me think
of death. No rituals can take *its* place.

LEONARD. Rituals?

OLDFIELD. Naked on your mother's bed. Your ritual birth.
Its hard to care for others as they deserve.

LEONARD. We have – we know what we should do.

OLDFIELD. And my gun! You must use that! Have to! Yes
– have a go! Bang it! Bang bang bang! (*They part.*) The
press office have hired a photographer!

DODDS, WILBRAHAM *and* BARTLEY *come in.* BARTLEY
has OLDFIELD's *coat over his arm and carries gloves,
mittens and a scarf. He goes to the AS42 and finishes loading
the magazines.*

DODDS. I've sent off the beaters trucks. Havers said to give
him twenty minutes.

WILBRAHAM. You must be proud of your new gun Mr Oldfield. I hear you're putting on a show? Just the normal shooting? – or do you juggle with it?

OLDFIELD (*to* DODDS). Mortingham turned up?

DODDS. No.

OLDFIELD. Ha ha all his land and the old scoundrel's jealous! He's had his chauffeur in and out his garage ten times this morning! He'll come – never miss a shoot! Watch the envious old bugger when he sees my gun! The ermined old faggot rang up the Game Conservancy to see if it was legal! The pettyness! He doesnt know I know!

DODDS. You should put a shot in him.

OLDFIELD. I'll wear my coat Bartley.

BARTLEY *goes to* OLDFIELD *and helps him to dress.*

LEONARD. Are you a good shot Wilbraham?

WILBRAHAM. The world's worst.

OLDFIELD. We cant all be good at everything.

LEONARD *picks up the AS42 and starts to demonstrate it.*

LEONARD. The new generation of personal weapons: sniper and assault rifle combined. Weight four kilogrammes. Barrell thirty-three inch. Calibre standard NATO 7.6. Muzzle velocity 2900fs – 860ms. Gas operated.

BARTLEY (*to* OLDFIELD). I brought a choice o' lined gloves or gun mittens.

LEONARD (*aiming at various targets*). Out performs the rival SSG69 Manfred Schöner with RWS match rounds. Ten shot groups of under forty centimetres diam at eight hundred metres. Thirteen centimeters dispersion at four hundred metres. The salesmen boast that guarantees a killing.

BARTLEY (*to* OLDFIELD). Shall ah put the gloves in your pocket?

DODDS (*to* WILBRAHAM). If you want to get into history Willy get shot by that. You'd be first.

OLDFIELD. So far its only put down pigs. (*To* BARTLEY.) Dont fuss.

BARTLEY. I was wrappin the gloves in the scarf so they'd nae go lost.

OLDFIELD (*to* DODDS). Make sure they ring the office for messages before they bring down our lunch.

WILBRAHAM. Whenever Im on a shoot I dread being peppered by someone who's an even worse shot than me – if there is such a thing. I wouldnt mind being put down with *that*. Die in the forefront of technology. Not like dying – more like enlisting for the future. When I see –

LEONARD (*aiming*). Image intensification using the wavelength of visible light and an infra red facility for seeing in night and mist. Image controlled by voltage on the plate. Two cheap torch batteries.

BARTLEY (*almost to himself as he watches* OLDFIELD). Mittens must be pulled on tighter than gloves.

OLDFIELD (*to* BARTLEY *as he starts to push the mittens down on* OLDFIELD'*s fingers*). The head gamekeeper can be photographed with it. No one else. I dont want the crowd clowning. They may be the elite but they're like a coachload of borstal escapees when they've got guns. Send one of me out with a press release. I dont want to pick it. They complain I choose the unflattering ones.

LEONARD (*aiming through the sights*). The feathers on the blackbird's back. The line along the tips. A grey hair in the sea. So clear. You dip your finger in the pool in the trees a thousand metres away and wonder why it isnt wet.

BARTLEY. Pardon sir.

BARTLEY *goes to* LEONARD *and unclips the magazine from the AS42. On the way he drops a mitten.*

OLDFIELD. What – ?

BARTLEY (*to* OLDFIELD). Its nothin sir. (*To* LEONARD.) Beg pardon sir.

OLDFIELD (*pointing to the magazine in* BARTLEY'*s hand*). Give me that.

BARTLEY (*throws the magazine into the case. Under his breath*). Nothin nothin nothin.

OLDFIELD (*going towards the case*). I will –

BARTLEY (*jerking passed* OLDFIELD *to get to the case before him*). Will yous leave the bloody – ! Its nothin sir. The guns are ready. Ah believe ah heard the beaters – (*Stops. Slight pause. He stands between the case and* OLDFIELD.) Ah dropped your mitten. Tch tch.

OLDFIELD *goes to the case, takes out a magazine and examines it. He wears one mitten.* BARTLEY *watches him.*

OLDFIELD. Loaded. One round.

BARTLEY. Och well I was in the middle o' loadin when – (*Stops.*) That's nae the magazine wor on the gun.

OLDFIELD (*magazine*). Dodds kindly confirm this round.

BARTLEY. That was nae on the gun.

OLDFIELD (*to* DODDS). It was on the gun. (*Goes to the AS42 and rapidly checks.*) With the safety catch released.

BARTLEY (*explaining firmly*). Now sir. Three magazines – and the one in Mr Dodds' hand I'd started – wor loaded. The empty magazine's in the case.

WILBRAHAM. Good lor' have we all been in danger?

OLDFIELD. Mr Wilbraham please confirm that you witnessed the gun loaded with that magazine.

WILBRAHAM. O guns guns I know nothing of guns. Depend utterly on my loader.

BARTLEY (*quietly explaining to the others*). If he'd'nae snatched – an mix em up – such a terrible awkward thing t' – like an old wuman wi a weapon in his –

OLDFIELD (*to* BARTLEY). Get your things together. Dodds see a waggon runs him to the station. (*To* BARTLEY.) You're dismissed with a month's salary. (*To* DODDS.) Warn the security guard in London to accompany him the whole time he needs to remove his things. (*To* BARTLEY.) Go. (*To* DODDS.) Go.

BARTLEY. Ah dinnae understand – Mr Leonard – ?

LEONARD *stands holding the AS42.*

OLDFIELD. Your irresponsibility might have caused a tragedy. And burdened my son with guilt. You're partly to blame Leonard. The magazine's provided with a transparent view strip. However I suppose one round is easily missed. (*Starts to turn away but turns back.*) And you were aiming. I wanted to stop you but I'd've been told I was treating you like a child. (*To* BARTLEY.) He's still there! Cant he move? Has he shot *himself?*

WILBRAHAM (*quietly singing Gilbert and Sullivan*). 'O Im the dots dots dots and Im underlined'.

BARTLEY. Sir –

OLDFIELD. If the magazine wasnt loaded why did you snatch it from the gun?

BARTLEY (*immediately*). I thought ah heard Havers hoot oot the yard t' say the beaters wor in place.

OLDFIELD. I might have reconsidered but after that blatant affrontery I wont. All employees are issued with the Company Laws. Careless handling of weapons-stroke-rounds: instant dismissal.

BARTLEY. Och that does'nae apply t' domestics an such type o' –

OLDFIELD. It applies.

BARTLEY. Anyway I wor nae mistook! Ah swear t' god ah –

OLDFIELD. You're in no fit state to swear to anything. You rarely are. Its my fault for – (*Stops.*) Mr Wilbraham did you have something to say?

WILBRAHAM *stops singing.*

OLDFIELD. Its my fault for asking you to load.

BARTLEY. Well in that case ah think its –

OLDFIELD. I refuse to stand and argue with an ex-employee! You're on my property! And drunk! (*He reaches out and takes the flask from* BARTLEY'*s jacket.*)

Like the magazine this flask has a viewing strip – so the owner's not caught with it empty – as it now three-quarters is!

BARTLEY (*appeal*). Mr Wilbraham – ?

WILBRAHAM. I wouldnt know the lethal end of a pea-shooter.

BARTLEY. This is unfair unfair unfair. Will none o' yous speak for me? (*Blunt, angry resignation.*) Ach t' hell wi' the lot o' yous!

OLDFIELD (*flask*). Take it. I shant be short of evidence. The cupboards will be full of empties.

BARTLEY (*under breath*). Yous bastard. (*Apology.*) Ah'm sorry sir. If ah accidental clip on the wrong magazine that's cause ah wor sent oot in the middle o' loadin. Ah'd've check. Ah'm like a hen: check check check. I check when Mr Leonard had it up in the air. Ah'd never've let ma governor oot the door wi' nae check. Take your mitten sir. Its just that – (*Stops and turns to* WILBRAHAM.) Mr Wilbraham its nae right t' treat any man like this. (WILBRAHAM *starts to hum 'Dot' tunes.* BARTLEY *tries to edge* OLDFIELD *aside.*) Man yous know fine why ah carry the flask. Hoo many times've yous seen me in the bushes gi' the gentlemen a wee nip when their fingers's numb? Ah *need* my job. Please take your mitten. Its kelt oot there. (*Indicates* WILBRAHAM.) Ask yon what he took for breakfast an wor he got it. It wor liquid but it wor nae oot the udder.

OLDFIELD. I've been waiting for a chance to dismiss you and by god you've given me one. Any doctor will confirm you're an alcoholic. I should explain Mr Wilbraham, he was courtmartialed from her majesty's navy. I gave him a chance – I hoped he'd been taught his lesson.

BARTLEY *turns on his heels and goes out quickly.*

OLDFIELD (*to* WILBRAHAM). Sorry about this. Must be firm, y'know. Christen a gun with accidental death –

imagine the effect on the minds of men going out to kill! We all know the military are superstitious. If the procurement came down to a fine choice *that* could tip the scales against us. Now promise me you wont let this spoil your weekend Wilbraham. Fortunate you were here! I may need a statement – though I dont think he'll cause trouble. Went off smartish! – fraid to lose his sack-money. You recall how he insulted me? – not so much words but tone. He swore twice and was over-familiar.

WILBRAHAM *hums.*

OLDFIELD (*to* DODDS). See him off! Is the whole world coming to a halt? (*Takes the AS42 from* LEONARD.) And bring back my mitten – he tried to make off with it. (*To* LEONARD.) Bring the rounds. – My dear Eric I cant believe this about you being a bad shot.

WILBRAHAM. You soon will.

OLDFIELD. We'll get you a good loader. Wrong chap ruins the sport. If Mortingham didnt bring his own I'd give him one with aftershave – ha! (*Going.*) Dodds!

OLDFIELD *and* WILBRAHAM *go out.*

DODDS. I'll bring Hammond's assignment to your room before dinner.

DODDS *goes out.* LEONARD *follows with the case of magazines.*

Unit Five

Derelict House

The only piece of furniture is a traditional wooden kitchen-chair, with a curved back and a support across it, a cane or drilled-plywood seat, and a strengthening hoop between the legs. There is an empty bottle beside the chair and a small bottle in a corner.

LEONARD *sits on the chair.* BARTLEY *has a blanket. Both wear shabby trousers, shirts and raincoats and muddy shoes.*

BARTLEY. Lyin prat . . . yous got money . . . your ol' fella would'nae cut yous off . . . get your hands on a fortune . . . stop wor us: yous pay . . . malignant bastard . . . What d'yous want? What d'yous want? . . . Have a few bevvies one night, see black in my head: kick yous t' pieces! . . . If ah had money ah could get oot this coffin . . . you could help us . . .

LEONARD. If you had money you'd –

BARTLEY. Booze it! Ay but that would'nae last. Scroungin every penny t' drink *drives* a man t' drink, yous dinnae have the strength left t' kick it . . . You think yous can live wi'oot money! Few months doon this hell, you'll murder for money! Why must ah suffer till then? . . . What d'yous want? What d'yous want? If ah knew that . . . God ah could murder a drink . . . Ah'll settle yous sonny: next time you're drunk you'll come to in a empty hoose! – cope on your own!

LEONARD. No one goes while they can still screw you.

BARTLEY. Is that right? I'll maybe teach you different laddie! . . . My god there must be somethin else! Sat here persecutin each other! . . . Ah wonder if its nae me wor's cruel? . . . If ah knew what yous want! . . . If you left yous have t' come t' your senses. Nothin t' stop yous, not even a door on the hinges . . .

LEONARD. You'd be running after me before I was round the corner.

BARTLEY. Dinnae be too bloody sure! Ah'd be better off shot o' yous even if you are rollin! Im still nae but the skivvy! Wouldnt slash your wrist if ah was'nae here t' swab up!

BARTLEY *stands, goes to* LEONARD *and grabs for his wrists*
– LEONARD *pulls away.*

BARTLEY. Ah'll bloody look man! (*Unwinds rags from*
LEONARD'*s wrists.*) No gangrene in my place! Stink o'
that on top o' your spewed up guts! Worse'n sewers!
(*Examines* LEONARD'*s wrists.*) Pathetic! Look at it –
scratches! Cant even open his veins! I hate yous bloody
amateur suicides – messin wor other people have t' live.
(*Goes to the corner and picks up the small bottle.*) Next time
tell the skivvy. 'Cut my wrists Bartley there's a good
man'. Ah'll do a proper job! Leave yous t' swill oot the
gutter. Leonard man shall ah tell yous somethin? (*No
answer.*) Is this how wor t' live, stuck starin at scabs? –
If ah telled yous would yous listen? D'you know why the
navy chuck us oot?

LEONARD (*flat*). You lied to my father.

BARTLEY. Ay – but it wor a good lie: it stop him checkin up
the real reason. Why should ah tell such nonsense if its
nae true? I came t' the interview wi' a cock an' bull story
work oot: Victimized by wor officers – the *lie* came t' me
while I wor talkin. Ah start off tellin him bout the sub –
anthin nuclear, people are fascinated. (*Iodine.*) It does-
'nae hurt on whole skin. Hardens it magic. You'd need
a stone mason t' get in those veins noo. Ah thought it
policy t' stress the danger. I said in every chamber o' the
sub that has t' do wi' weapons there's a truncheon hangin
up. If someone goes beserk – or acts peculiar – yous beat
the laddie's brains oot – that's if he has'nae beat yours
oot first. Official yous give him a wee tap an a tablet
when he comes round. But when the master-at-arms (O
they worship titles!) instructs yous in the use o' truncheons, its 'Beat the bugger's brains oot – nae loonies in
my sub!' Your ol' fella's sat there listenin. There was
dead silence. Uncanny. He give the impression he's asked
a question an he's waitin for the answer – but he has'nae

asked. Then the lie came t' me. I swear it wor in his head
first – an ah told him the lie he wanted me t' told him.
His mouth wor set – like a stone – but a bitty open – like
the gob on a wee angry ol' woman – an then ah said it.
It wor like lip-readin a corpse. Ah said on christmas
mornin ah went roond t' every truncheon an put a
condom on it. Shall ah tie these rags back on? The
wounds – if they deserve the name – dinnae need it but it
stops the iodine gettin rub off. Its expensive stuff. The
girlie in the chemist thought ah wanted t' drink it dilute
wi' water. Nuclear sub – under the atlantic – christmas
mornin – wi' novelty decorations. Ah says the captain
took it personal: ah wor callin him a prick. When wor
got home t' Faslane – court martial. Is that what we got
wor hands for: for t' cut wor wrists? Ay well, none o'
that's true – 'cept the court martial – the discharge – the
nae pension – an the poverty. Ah almost told him I put
a condom on the weapon-officer's trigger – the one he uses
t' fire the rockets. But that's kep lock away in a safe:
behind its own wee flies. So ah stops meself an thinks:
yous'll have t' settle for the truncheons ol' fella. Where'd
ah get thirty condoms on an all male sub that's been
under the sea for eight weeks? He did'nae think t' check
the mucky beast.

BARTLEY *goes to his blanket.*

Ah could teach yous a lot. Ay. Ah've blowed up the world
hundreds o' times. Five years in the service: eight months
shore, four months dived. Every few days, London order
– fire. Captain knows its practice. Wor dont. Everytime
could'a been real. They cannae tells us in case wor says
no. The deterrent works on the ignorance o' the rank an
file. Afterwards wor knows it was'nae real cause wor still
alive. If wor'd fired, wor rockets 'd've telled the enemy
where we wor: he'd've turned us int' human krill for
whales – if wor rockets had'nae killed him first. If they had
wor officers would've killed us.

HAMMOND *comes in.* LEONARD *and* BARTLEY *dont see him*

Once we'd blew up the world we'd be spare bodies wor nae world left t' blow up. The lads might feel bad – turn on the officers – or just fancy bein in charge for wor few days left. In the last war jerry used prisoners t' gas the yids. Every so often they gassed the prisoners. Had to – they can'nae trust lads wor did work like that. The crew of a nuclear sub's like the prisoners: same work, same pay. Yous owe us for the iodine: ah made a note. People reckon when the war comes t' forces'll kill the civvies – an then be the ones t' survive. Sheer ignorance. The captain has his orders – an if he did'nae have em its still: bang bang bang. He could'nae risk keepin wor alive. (*Sniffs fingers.*) That lassie was on t' somethin: the smell o' my iodine-fingers gi's us a thirst. The captain's a prat – but he'd run the sub wi' his officers for the wee while left till the grub ran oot an their time's up. Or maybe the poor ol' sod'd just put a bullet in his own head? The crew would've shat oot o' every orifice when the rockets left the tubes – the blood when he shot us – the air conditionin could'nae cope wi' the stink o' carnage.

LEONARD *is staring at* HAMMOND – BARTLEY *sees his stare and turns to see* HAMMOND.

BARTLEY. Chriss a brown ghost . . .!

HAMMOND. I came on my own. We can talk. No one'll interfere.

BARTLEY. Who's that?

HAMMOND. It doesnt seem right in this hovel: but congratulations. You're the first to get the better of me in a long time. I always allow for an element of chance. Oldfield might've had another son – gone bust – war been abolished. Far fetched but you cant tell fact from fiction when it happens to you. But I didnt allow for this.

BARTLEY (*penny drops*). Dodds!

HAMMOND *gives* BARTLEY *a bottle of whisky.*

Ah. One? Wor's the crate?

HAMMOND. One for the moment.

BARTLEY. One? I want more than bloody one! I told Dodds a crate! What bloody moment?

HAMMOND. Later.

BARTLEY. There is nae bloody later! My pals'll blow the world up before bloody later!

HAMMOND. I thought I was home when I had your undertaking to give me control of Oldfields when your father died – assuming he wasnt immortal. Instead you've deliberately run yourself off the rails and got yourself disinherited. That's what I call determination. You're a fanatic.

BARTLEY (*drinks*). O yes – the right stuff – fair dues. Will it be a crate o' this?

BARTLEY *drinks.* LEONARD *sits with his wrists tucked in his armpits.*

HAMMOND (*after a moment's silence*). Shall I go?

BARTLEY. Stay there! (*Goes to* LEONARD *and hisses at him.*) By god ah took trouble t' fix this – yous spoil it an ah'll give yous hell. That man's money – you respect him! (*To* HAMMOND.) He's listenin mister. (*He stands in the doorway.*) Nae one passes me till ah'm paid. What sort o' cheapskint d'yous think ah am? I dinnae betray a pal for a bottle – ah want my crate!

LEONARD. Why d'you want Oldfields?

HAMMOND. Would it change your mind to know?

BARTLEY. One bottle! – an ah drink it! Ah've known the time ah'd've chuck it in his face! God ah've fallen!

HAMMOND. Im in clothing – transport – construction – but mostly in food: the biggest chain of supermarkets in Europe. Half the world's starving but they cant afford my stores. That ought to upset you.

BARTLEY (*drinking*). They call em coffin ships. Lads have coffin dreams. Medically recognised condition! Wake up screamin – all o' em! 'Let me oot!' In the middle o' the ocean!

HAMMOND. Im supposed to be too European. The trade says it takes two generations to change what people eat. The food in the bellies of kids running round the streets is the same as the food in the bellies of their parents lying in the grave. But things are changing even in food. We could adapt. Its the governments that wont let us in: not desperate enough.

BARTLEY (*drinking*). Been roond the world more times than the sun! Chriss! – niggerland – chinkland – yankyland – saw nothin – not even the sea – (*Swig.*) – only the inside o' wor subs – pipes an tubes – an laddies crawling on em like maggots in their own guts.

HAMMOND. The governments say they cant afford to eat *and* arm. Guns or butter. So they tell the people to starve. You cant afford to eat but you must be able to kill: that's history. Sacrifice.

BARTLEY (*waves bottle*). Shut it! Shut it! You're one good reason t' press the button!

HAMMOND. These days the West cant afford to make arms for itself unless it exports them. But they're expensive for the third world. They tried making their own – not much cop and no R and D. So all the time they're getting into debt. Soon so many'll die it wont look like sacrifice anymore: just bad government. Then they'll be desperate – and I'll make my offer. Let my stores in – and I'll sell you arms.

BARTLEY. One bottle an ah cannae drink that in peace!

BARTLEY *goes out.*

HAMMOND. If I sell both I can sell cheap. But the margins'll be low. So I cant afford to buy in arms to resell. I must make my own. That's why I want Oldfields. I'll start in a small way: guns – mines – PGMs – then educate the consumer – branch out. The next century will be a great gaping mouth – wide as a continent – with rows of missiles for teeth. Out of that mouth there'll come a great roar for food – as loud as the fire-storm from a burning city, a great wind so loud it'll make the screaming of bombs sound like the whistles of errand boys going home on their bikes. People must eat. First its need – then greed – then fear – and then you're back to need. That's why people will always want weapons. I'll feed them and arm them – and if they pay I'll transport them – house them – build their shelters – amuse them – dress them: and I'll make their civvies as bright as they like, they'll still be battledress – because they'll all be in the front line. Harsh? The old myth of peace is harsh. Peace caused more misery than all the wickedness of war. Peace was the time when people trembled – went without – and sweated to arm themselves for war – that's more history. Now I'll make life easier for them. I'll provide swords and ploughshares, tanks and tractors, and do it cheap. Once it was guns and butter. Now it has to be both. They can never be parted again. That's the Great Pieta I see for the twenty-first century: guns *and* butter. No government can refuse it: the starving wouldnt let them – and more important, nor will the rich. Old men make plans, young men see visions. I shant live to see it – but you can. Im offering you the sales franchise on a century. All you have to do is go back to your father.

LEONARD. I havent got a father.

HAMMOND. I know your sort. If anyone lets you in you tangle up in their bowels. That's why Oldfield had enough. A man wants his guts to be his own. Im offering you more than I've offered anyone else. What do you want? I've come to this ruin like a door-to-door salesman trying to flog you the twenty-first century. I dont know why. (*Slight pause.*) One of my sons makes clay pots. One's a specialist in grass. The rest do business. There are five thousand species of grass – more. Someone couldnt make up their mind. (*Shrug.*) I talk to so many fools, perhaps its the novelty of talking to someone who's only mad . . .?

LEONARD *still sits with his hands in his armpits.*

LEONARD. Tear up the paper I signed.

HAMMOND. No its my only hold.

BARTLEY (*off*). The bloody – bloody – bloody – bloody – (*A crash.*)

HAMMOND. What the – . . .?

LEONARD. Cellar. A fit. Lasts five minutes. His brain sucks in alcohol like a live sponge.

HAMMOND. You think you're still young enough to play games. If you stay here you'll crack up for real. Pneumonia or drink. What d'you want from me? Tell me.

BARTLEY (*off. Crash, roar*). That – that's doon wi' yous laddies – come on! – naebody messes me! – ah'll smash the – ah!

HAMMOND. Shouldnt we . . .? (*No answer.*) There's no middle road between us. You can break rules and change facts, but hunches are like the laws of fate: they cant be changed. You've got the gift of hunches or you're in the herd: I've got it, so've you. You wont end here.

BARTLEY (*off*). The stairs – he threw the stairs at me – the railings tore the – a hole! – a hole! – is that hair? – or people? – its seethin in the – no no no! – I didnae do wrong! – the people in the hole! – let them oot t' die! –

LEONARD. Machines: my father's workshop. Little metal arms with rows of snapping teeth making prehistoric reptiles. We become human and make tin dinosaurs. Why are people scared of death? A bit of pain and then – peace. A statue picking up a sheet to use it as a cover for itself. It never has to take it off. Its never tired of standing there. Never even feels the weight of the sheet. The linen turns to stone. And no sculptor can prise him out of it. Death is the last thing to be afraid of. Its our living monument.

BARTLEY (*off*). Agh! Agh! O! Help me! Leonard! The bricks are turnin roond – the light beween the bricks – the walls turned in t' teeth! (*Crash.*) Gi' me back my bones!

HAMMOND. There's no romance in squalor. Dirt and drunkenness are dirt and drunkenness. Dodds says your father wants you. He's got no one to hand on to. He blames his stubbornness. You dont have to ask – just walk in.

LEONARD. I could've done so much. I was strong. Fit. I was like a child who always had its arms open. What had I done to deserve so much hatred? I knew there were enemies. But why were you waiting to break my back? What had I done to you? What machine made you in what swamp? I didnt even check. What you offer – you break everything as you hand it over. People massacring each other – faces screaming at TV cameras – soldiers' hands blotting out the cameras – why should I be interested in their suffering? – turn the sound off. Give them power and watch them torment their tormenters. Airmen bombing little children. Would they stamp on their faces? The answer doesnt interest me. Women making bombs. If you gave them a bonus they'd make them in their womb. D'you think that can go on? They learn nothing – not even the numbers tattooed on their arms. Who says Im doing this – this is on my hands? They say they're not doing it while they do it. Words mean nothing to them: they communicate with signs with blood on their fingers. And then they celebrate. Parties and parades. Corpses wanking in the grave to kill the time or fill their loneliness.

HAMMOND. You shouldnt say those things.

LEONARD. Go away.

HAMMOND. You wont get one penny from this! All this spite will be wasted! . . . Im rich, I can afford defeat: but when I want I get! I'll get Oldfield's when he's dead. The rubbish'll move in – not class! That's when I get! – I can hound you sonny! That lunatic! – five minutes – under lock and key and soaked in carbolic.

LEONARD. You'd be doing him a favour.

HAMMOND. Why did I come here? What d'you want from me? Tell me? (*Plea.*) Dont sit there, your arms curled up . . . you look like some crippled foetus. Let me fetch you clean clothes? I cant leave you here. What d'you want? If only I knew. I stand here like a servant begging for scraps of attention. I dont know why. Come with me. If you're ill, lean on me on the stairs. I've hurt you . . . maybe harmed you . . . Now I'll take you away from offices and paper, where no one will hurt you, quiet, and make you well, and my life will be cured by your wounds and make amends as if I could wash the greyness out of hair like common dirt, which no one can . . . of course its not to be. But I can do a simple act of kindness, that's allowed. I'll take you where you can think, and there – in that place – you'll tell me what you want. I'll get it for you. Anything. Im rich. I can afford one folly. If things worked out I'd make you boss of Oldfield's. And there's *my* companies – if things worked out, if there was an interest. But dont ask me to destroy my paper. I must have my paper. It was a hunch. Dont block it. Its the one thing I couldnt humour. Its not allowed. No doubt I shouldnt tell you – its a bad mistake. You'll find a way to use it against me, wont you? Dont. Dont. Dont lad. Please dont. Let it stop here. Im older, I know where these things lead. One day we'll all be dead. Is it worth struggling in the meantime? I wonder more and more. I need my paper – to get me through the time. (*Slight pause.*) I dont think you can listen. A pity. Now I'll tell you something different: People are hard, so the rule is: be harder on yourself. Say no to me – I'll drive off and I wont say no to myself fifty or a hundred times: one no will be enough with me. (*Slight pause.*) Five thousand sorts of grass. – So you'll send me through that door alone? You wont exist. The door wont exist. You wont even be dead – you never were. A stain in an abortion clinic. The last time? – no. If I had your blood on my hands I wouldnt even see it as I washed it off.

HAMMOND *waits a moment, then turns and goes out.* LEONARD *fiddles with the rags on his wrists.* BARTLEY *comes in with the empty bottle. He is blind drunk.*

BARTLEY. I have come up wi' my empty bottlesh: it floatsh. (*He raises the bottle in front of him and holds it there.*) Not all drunk. Much slop. 'S'plenty damp dust if yous thirshty. 'S rests gone – 's way of all watersh 'n runny thingsh thash flow. Ah have exhaust. 'S no more bottlesh? – O god ah'll gesh sober an real – ish – the predic – immensh! (*Holds out the bottle to the side.*) You crushify me wi' one hand an let me hang! No bottlesh! No money! No nailsh! No nailsh – in all t' world – t' decent hang a man!

BARTLEY *crashes unconscious to the floor.* LEONARD *fastens the last knot with his teeth and free hand.*

LEONARD (*to* BARTLEY). I swapped the mags. I tried to kill my father. I'd've killed him as sure as two sides of a coin. Its easy. Extra sugar in your tea. A slight sense of self-indulgence. Shouldnt something defend us from ourselves? There was nothing interested enough to stop me. No hand out of the cloud. Then you spoke – that silly stupid voice. (*Imitates* BARTLEY *and* OLDFIELD.) 'A moment sir – I think your laddie has a loaded weapon pointed at your head'. 'You're sacked!' 'Ah'm innocent!

Unfair! Unfair!' 'Out of my house! You'd steal the fingers from a man's mittens!' – frothed and waved his arms and you'd tried to save his life! (*Laughs shortly and stops.*) You were down for sacking anyway. And he'll die sometime. (*Sings and makes Black-and-White Minstrel gestures.*)

> O de camp town races five miles long
> O de camp town races sing this song
> Ready to run all night
> Ready to run all –

He continues making the gestures and silently mouthing the words – and then he adds little puffer-fish choo-choo breaths in the song's rhythm. Stops. Silence. BARTLEY's *eyes are shut – stiff as a signpost, one arm rises and points at* LEONARD.

BARTLEY. Why yous starin at us for?

LEONARD. Your eyes are shut.

BARTLEY. Sub-men see in the dark. (*With his eyes closed he feels for the bottle, finds it, holds it to his ear and shakes it.*) Jees. Would yous look-see if its empty? For ah cannae open my eyes – nae even the one.

LEONARD. Yes.

BARTLEY. All that drunk? He didnae bring my crate? – god bless the man that spared me that. Was ah oot long?

LEONARD. Five minutes.

BARTLEY. O god that's bad when its short. My head's in another world. I'd have t' droon in the stuff t' get any lastin benefit.

LEONARD. The boards boom when you walk on them. Dust crunches like icing sugar.

BARTLEY. I wor happy once. At sea. M'be that wor wrong? – just satisfied wi' the servility? Ah'll never be happy noo. Its all pretend pretend an gettin old. A rat drownin in a puddle cause its roond like the door o' its hoose – he thinks he's inherited a palace. I dinnae tell yous why I was discharge. I'd like t' telled yous if you'd listen: ah dont know why. There's no education in it: only officer stupidity. I was eatin in wor mess. A ratin cut his arm – quite nasty – an come through rollin up his sleeve t' keep it oot the cut. He stop t' get his breath – leant against the table an steadied his-self wi' the flat of his hand on top. The blood ran doon his arm. Its no on t' show sympathy on a nuclear sub: its no but an underwater raft for murder. I went on eatin. Some fella crack a joke. The cut man went on t' the sick bay. Where his hand had rest on the table there's some spots. Some wingey drops o' blood. I had a little-bitty bread ready in ma hand. I dipped it in the blood – t' mop it up – an ate it. No special thought. The blood was red – the bread was that stark white – they seemed t' go t'gether. I should explain we wor encouraged t' be clean. Are yous sure yous listening? They're fanatical for cleanliness in all that water: dirt's a capital offence – an bein sick – an wor gear oot o' place – they have machines t' purify the air. So my hand cleaned up the mess. It did it on automatic pilot – an drop it doon me gob. Wor cook was squintin oot the galley. He telled the captain. He telled the MO. I did his tests. Blobs on paper. Would yous credit it? Blobs. Ah felt ashamed – like a kid had mess its briks! Ah cannae see what ah did wrong. Can yous? That fuss 'bout a wee-bit-bread-roll dip in blood? It was bread so ah ate it. In wor hoose you learned yous dinnae waste man! You'd think ah'd dip my hand in the laddie's pocket – or lift his wallet oot his locker. He did'nae complain ah'd pinch his goods – if his blood's so precious why's he flitter it on the walls? – he's nae jasus chriss ah'm tellin yous. Ah give the cook squint: jab the bugger's eye wi't the handle o' wor breadknife. Fightin on a sub on active service: *oot*! Yous wrong cause yous innocent. Will yous hold my hand noo Lennie-man while ah open my eyes. (LEONARD *holds his wrist.*) Ah'll be all right. (*Kneels.*) Steady it is. (*Opens his eyes and crouches down with his face to the ground.*) Jees-jees-jees.

The light blinds yous but wor need it. Ay – ah can see. (*Straightens up.*) Ah'm goin t' be all right man. Jees. Jees. (*Looks at the empty bottle.*) Terrible. Nothin. An ant could'nae lick it oot.

LEONARD. You spilt some.

BARTLEY. Was ah away below? (*No answer.*) O god one day ah'll tear up the foundations o' the hoose an the roof'll jump doon on wor heads. (*Pause. Tries to remember.*) Was that yous singing when ah come roond?

LEONARD. Yes.

BARTLEY. Lenny go away. Dont be offended noo. Let go o' me. The two o' us are nae good t'gether. Its a hunch. If yous left, ma ol' ruin'd be as snug as a fortress-hoose. By the time yous get your money ah'll be dead. What is it yous want? (*Pause. Cries.*) I dinnae want t' die in a mac. That's the worst death of all. Ah could'nae show me face in another world. M'be ah cannae die – is that ma problem? If ah could die ah'd've been dead long since. They shovel the dirt on me – I'ld lick it off like a street-dog lickin its jaw. (*Silence.*) Singin – he kep that quiet. Your singin, my mouth organ – should get a pitch. Make a bomb. 'The Man Who Blew Up the World a Hundred Times an the Poor Millionnaire'. Could catch on. (*Stands and covers himself in his blanket.*) I need a pal t' push me under a bus an bugger his scruples – then ah'd see if I cannae die. If I cannae, we'll put it in wor act. Yous reek o' piss an iodine. Gi's that bottle – we'll get it filled. By chriss ah could drink the booze oot a dead man if ah could find a tit. (*Points to the other bottle.*) An that. One each fella.

BARTLEY *pulls the blanket tighter round him.* LEONARD *picks up the other bottle. They go out.*

Unit Six

'The Two Armchairs'

A room in OLDFIELD's *House (as in Unit One).*

One of the two armchairs is covered in a white dust sheet.
OLDFIELD *dozes in the other. He wears a pale dressing-gown.*

LEONARD *is standing in the doorway. He wears the mac and
the other clothes he wore in the ruined house, but he has brushed
them and smartened himself up. From time to time he pulls his
sleeves down over his hands and then pins them against his palms
with his second and third fingers.*

LEONARD. Father.

OLDFIELD (*sees* LEONARD.) What d'you want?

LEONARD. I woke you.

OLDFIELD. Money.

LEONARD. The house is quiet.

OLDFIELD. I'll authorise my accountant.

LEONARD. I have to talk to you.

OLDFIELD. Leave me alone.

LEONARD. Five minutes.

OLDFIELD. No. (*Silence.*) I cant. Im tired. Its not your fault
– its age: the fight with Hammond took more out of me
than I knew. It was hard to get on with my work when
you left. Now I've settled down. Please leave me alone.

LEONARD. Im sorry if I hurt you.

OLDFIELD. Young people must turn against their elders,
everyone knows that. I didnt know that understanding,
patience, regret have nothing to do with it. They fight
each other to the finish so they can get away from each
other. Its a curse on us.

LEONARD. I have to tell you why I left.

OLDFIELD. You dont even know. I thought we could end

our constant quarrelling. Then suddenly you're gone. No luggage – your jacket hanging on a chair – you dont use your bank account: were you supposed to be dead? – a hostage? – amnesiac? I read the daily listings from the morgues and learned how terrible the city I've spent my life in is. Three months later Dodds finds you in a hovel sharing the grudges of an ex-employee. Are you drunk? You've come to rob me?

LEONARD. Father when I've told you I'll go away for good.

OLDFIELD. Im not your father. Dont pretend. A poor man might have made you his son. From the street to this house – the distance is too far. When you went I loved you as a son. Now I feel nothing. I stare at you and there's nothing. You no longer give me pleasure – and you cant hurt me.

LEONARD. That's how fathers talk.

OLDFIELD. Go away.

LEONARD. Criticise their sons and kick them out.

OLDFIELD. *You left*!

LEONARD (*shrugs*). I made a mistake.

OLDFIELD. I dont condone the right to make mistakes – that's modern cant. Your natural parents made mistakes. If that's what you want, go and find your mother: dont waste time looking for your father – even your mother couldnt help you there.

LEONARD. That's jealousy.

OLDFIELD. Jealous of people who abandon an infant?

LEONARD. The day after they left me they probably went dancing. That's what you envy.

OLDFIELD. You're mad.

LEONARD. Shall I get you a drink?

OLDFIELD. Is that your way of scrounging one?

LEONARD. I've been to the street where I was left. I dont think she knew the house. She came a long way – crossed the river by bus – walked miles – then turned into a gateway where there were lights. I must've had her tears on my face every day I was with her. Her arms would've felt light – unnatural – after she'd carried me for days. The street's pulled down. New blocks. My doorstep's rubble under a motorway. I walked on the pavement – that's still there. If the doorstep had been there I'd've touched the stone that touched the back of her fingers when she put me down. I hope it didnt graze them. Every few years your whole body changes. There isnt one part of me she's touched. Every bit of her child's gone. Dead skin flaked off. If she saw me now she'd see a ghost put in its place. The stone would be the same if it hadnt been pulverised for rubble.

LEONARD *sits down in the armchair covered by the dust sheet.*

OLDFIELD. You strung me along for years – an inherited trait – but you finally showed your true self. Dont try it on anymore! All you needed was a little patience – a little cunning – to wait till I died. You've come to tell me the truth? Lie. The only way *you* can help anybody is to lie. Why didnt you leave me the comfort of my foolishness? I was happy. You only had to tell a few more lies . . . Suppose you came back here? Yes it would be companionship for me – you're the nearest I had to a son. But it would be another lie dragged into the open. Sons inherit: but would *you* leave your life's work to a drunken wastrel – a tramp? No one can trust you anymore. If I made you my heir you'd have *this* quarrel with your own son – he'd object to you just as I have, for the same reasons. You'd learn the quarrel from the other side and find how bitter my role is! (*Flat.*) No no you're not coming here. I accept my legal obligations – Im not vindictive – I'll pay. But that's all. My wife's dead. I dont have friends. I dont even need a servant. We couldnt look each other in the face. The constant self reproach: 'Have I been unfair – should I change my mind?' All the old horrors. Im not up to it. Let me live in despair. Each time I tried to help you I damaged you. I dont understand. Im afraid of you. When you came in I thought you were from a dream.

LEONARD. I went away to be ill. The only movement I made for days was shivering. My eyes and tongue seized up – stopped like print on a page. Even my bowels. I heard breath going on inside me like a little animal leading its own life. I saw the light on a broken window – brighter in the cracks. And rags – the weave comes through when they're worn. Everything was beautiful. I wanted to put the rags and dirt on and let them make me beautiful. I felt sad – a sorrow – for the air. Why doesnt it struggle in our mouths – choke us as if we're dragging it down a filthy corridor to an execution shed? Our lungs are charnel houses, mausoleums. If they were cities we'd pull them down. The air takes all the filth away. It stinks of us. Yet lets us breathe. I thought when I could move I'd cut my wrists: I held the knife against them – but I went to see the doorstep. My parents arent survivors – dead, not lucky people. You're my father. I didnt deserve your kindness when you took me in. I wasnt anyone – I lay in my shit and cried. You werent kind to *me* – I was a *thing* in the way: something's in the way of a bullet – I was in the way of kindness. But I survived and grew up and made it mine. I dont mean I have a legal right. *This* is a law that can only be made by crime. I grabbed. I shut you inside my body. The body shuts up tight – like iron in cement. My mother left a ghost. I found you. You're in every hair I've got – every bit of flesh. And what I didnt shut in I shut out. Everything outside's in the same prison. You cant escape from outside. We're in the same prison – we're just on different sides of the wall. It made me ill, and then it made me well. I've come to confess.

OLDFIELD. You're in trouble! I knew it! Something shady!

LEONARD. You know I took over Wilbraham Engineering?

OLDFIELD. The accountants found out. An impetuous waste of money! Dodds tried to speak to Wilbraham – the bounder wouldnt!

LEONARD. I was tricked. There was a debtor with a death-grip – perhaps you should have a drink?

OLDFIELD. Go on!

LEONARD. It was Hammond.

OLDFIELD. Hammond? My Hammond? (*Rapid thought.*) Is he – he sent you! He's manipulating you! Still after my company!

LEONARD. He tried to force me to give him control when you died.

OLDFIELD. Yes?

LEONARD. I couldnt turn to you –

OLDFIELD. What?

LEONARD. You couldnt help me –

OLDFIELD. Of course! Of course! I'd've bought him off! Anything! My company's at stake – still! What's the situation? What's –

LEONARD. Listen! Listen! Listen!

OLDFIELD. I dont understand.

LEONARD (*short laugh*). No – you dont. You said it again just now, you're always saying it: no one could ever trust me. So if I'd told you what a mess I'd made of –

OLDFIELD. Yes?

LEONARD. – you'd've disinherited me: its what you *have* done!

OLDFIELD. Of course – so? So? For god's sake Leonard! – we've got more important things to deal with than your future. My company! Yes yes of course your future's important but we can settle that any time. *Has Hammond got a hold on me?*

LEONARD (*wearily*). Would you believe me if I told you?

OLDFIELD. O god he's impossible! Impossible! Totally impossible! Self! Self! Self! The everlasting whining! *What's my position?* (*Silence.*) It doesnt matter. I apologise for betraying an interest. (*Slight pause.*) Fancy – some nights I sleep in this chair to spare myself the journey to bed. I take my meals at a dining club. One gets used. So you found the house quiet? My lawyers will tell me in the morning. They may have to trouble you with a question or two – I apologise.

LEONARD. I didnt sign his paper.

OLDFIELD. Are you sure? You might've signed when you were drunk. (*Silence.*) I'll never understand. You wait three months! God knows what Hammond's been up to!

LEONARD. There's no more.

OLDFIELD. How could you know? Hammond twists boys like you round his finger. You put me in this terrible situation and then have the temerity to *reassure* me! – as if your opinion could ever be worth anything! That's gall even from you!

LEONARD. You see.

OLDFIELD. No. Whatever we see isnt the same – thank god! You'll stay here tonight. In the morning we'll try to limit the damage. Dodds will arrange a meeting – lawyers – accountants – we'll call in private detectives – a Grand Council! Not that I look forward to it. I cant even enjoy the fight – with you involved there can only be alarms and fiascos!

LEONARD. I have more to tell you.

OLDFIELD. O god now it'll be interesting. He's sold my organs for research. Hammond gets my eyes transplanted so I can watch him counting my money when Im dead.

LEONARD. If I'd signed you'd've died without knowing. An easy lie! When I was trapped one thing became clear – it surprised me. I'd betrayed you – you'd driven me to it – but it was difficult to hurt you. For the first time I felt what it is to be a son.

OLDFIELD. Well – that's handsome of you – and Im sorry if you had –. But three months! You put everything in

jeopardy – then take three months sick leave! Couldnt
you have managed with a week – or come to me first like
a proper son? Hurt me? You destroy me! Even now you
come out of office hours!

LEONARD. And I betrayed you on the day you beat
Hammond. Imagine! – you were going on about new
beginnings and I was buying nails for your coffin! Now
you can use them in mine.

OLDFIELD. O dont despair – Im sure we can find you a
suitable profession. You show all the talents necessary to
a member of a minor soap opera. (*Calculating to himself.*)
Its unlikely but Hammond may have stepped outside the
law.

LEONARD. And what's worse, you loved me as a son.

OLDFIELD. Not more self pity! You disgrace yourself – put
my company at risk – go on a celebration (for all I know)
lasting *three months* – then talk of love! You certainly
demand patience. Love is responsibility to others, above
all those you dont know. Its not meant to give us
satisfaction. Or pleasure. What it gives us in compensa-
tion for the suffering it causes, I dont know – something
we need to make us put up with the folly! Whatever it is
its like the old names of gods: it cant be spoken. If we
could get away from our bodies so that our minds were
pure – unbiased – aloof – then we could deal with the
squalor. The body creates problems and stops us solving
them. – Let others judge: I carry out my responsibilities.
I know what it costs. And all those who've ever been
anyone's victim, will know if they should be grateful . . .
We're as alone as statues and pictures in a gallery. We
stare at each other and see nothing. But isnt that the
shrine? – the memorial to *some* sort of civilization?
Perhaps its the distance that keeps us together. – Not one
word of apology. Im even blamed for your blunders. You
make me sad. A man accepts responsibility for his
actions. Go to your room – try to imagine how others see

you. If you cant it might've been better to leave you on the doorstep. I begin to think it was cruel to pick you up.

LEONARD. Dodds works for Hammond.

OLDFIELD. O?

LEONARD. Dodds drew up the paper to hand me over to him when you're dead.

OLDFIELD *gets up from his chair, goes to* LEONARD *and stares into his face.*

OLDFIELD. Have you gone mad? Is this revenge? I cant smell drink. Im at a loss to know how to handle you.

LEONARD. Dodds is on Hammond's payroll.

OLDFIELD (*tense bemusement*). You've come to set the house on fire. You offered to get me a drink so you could poison it. My god is there nothing he wouldnt stoop to? They cant wait for the fathers to die – they make them visit their graves! Touch the spade! Watch the earth being thrown! You come here and in that quiet tone say monstrous things – lower your voice as if you're going to pray and utter profanities! You have no secrets to flaunt at me! I will not be patronised! Dodds is my friend! I tell him everything! He knows all my secrets. Never never never will I believe what you've just said about Dodds! Dodds is Dodds! Not a drunken – rip! I insist you tell me it isnt true! (*Slight pause.*) O Im being stupid. You're treating me to my own medicine. Because I said you had the talents of a soap opera (*Claps hands twice.*) – you're playing this terrible joke. I deserve it! Hammond – Dodds – everything you said since you came . . .? (*No answer.*) You're telling me I must believe it? No Leonard dont – this is not good for my head. I shouldnt go through this. You're turning me into a circus animal! – dragging my past behind me like a monstrous tail! I'd be aghast to try to live with what –. (*Stops.*) The liftman takes bribes – the secretaries work for the Mafia – but not Dodds!

LEONARD. I must be firm with you father: you've been as

gullible as a schoolboy. Its important you own up to it.
Dodds must be trapped. Im sorry I told you quietly. All
this is sad for me. It was hard to come and confess – and
harder because I knew it'd turn into an accusation: you
rejected your son and crawled to your enemy.

OLDFIELD. You'll say this to his face! I'll get to the bottom
of –. (*Calls.*) Dodds! Dodds!

LEONARD *jumps from his chair, goes to* OLDFIELD *and
literally puts his hand over his mouth.*

LEONARD. No no dont!

OLDFIELD. Ah! ouf! He's stifling – ! Help! My throat!

LEONARD. Father please. No. You're putting your head in
the snake's mouth. I've got more to tell! (*Releases*
OLDFIELD.) Dont betray me. Not now. Please. O god I
didnt know he was here. Im shaking. Let me help you.
O god father I see you on the doorstep and me bending
down to pick you up. See how frail you are. Your face in
my hand. Let me be your son for one day and everything
will solve itself.

DODDS *comes in.*

DODDS. Leonard.

LEONARD (*arm round* OLDFIELD). The prodigal returns.

OLDFIELD. Yes. Leonard's . . . as you see.

DODDS. How nice. It's been a bad time.

OLDFIELD. So I thought . . . drinks? . . . Dodds – would
you mind? Some whisky?

DODDS *goes out.*

OLDFIELD. His tie's straight. There's no blood on his face.
Dodds, Dodds . . . (*To* LEONARD.) But you're not
deceiving me.

LEONARD. Why should I?

OLDFIELD. To make me doubt? Dont dont – no matter how
much it matters to you. You'll regret it. Running a

company's like walking a tightrope in burning shoes. You cant do it if you doubt. Blind foolish faith – let me keep that. Let me have my illusions. I dont know what you're up to. There's some scheme. What is it? I feel you must want something. I look so foolish – all this bewilderment over a colleague. The company's my life. My legs are trembling. I've no right to put on this suit. How stupid.

LEONARD (*explaining*). Dodds is to be told you know about Hammond. I'll tell him I kept his *own* part secret so we can both rook you – he has more experience.

OLDFIELD. Yes yes if that's . . . I'll be in control tomorrow. I could believe you cheated me – you're always changeable. Sometimes I paraded you – to show you off – you didnt know – but you found a way to spoil it – always – it seemed like spite. But Dodds was always Dodds, the faithful servant. Now I have to watch him like a common spy.

DODDS *comes in with three glasses of whisky.*

DODDS. We'll all have a restful night at last. – Your father was very worried.

OLDFIELD. Yes – Dodds . . . these are worrying times. (*To* DODDS.) Your health – old friend.

DODDS. To Leonard.

LEONARD. To father.

They drink. DODDS *starts to go.*

OLDFIELD. Stay, stay . . .

DODDS. You two must talk.

OLDFIELD. Yes Dodds – you're right, as always . . . Goodnight – till the morning Dodds . . .

DODDS *goes.* LEONARD *listens at the door.*

OLDFIELD (*whisper*). O god he's bugged the room.

LEONARD (*whisper*). No need, you tell him everything.

OLDFIELD. What have I done? God knows the damage

he's – ! And not one sign! Yet there were mysterious – I
thought I'd slipped – coincidences. Thats why Hammond
almost beat me! . . . Since you left he stays late. Snooping in case I got his scent.

LEONARD. Im here now. It'll all be gone into.

OLDFIELD. But we're acting as if he cheated me for years.
We know one slip! And you're as much to blame – I
warned you you were gullible! Im thoughtless – I push
him too hard. Do I pay enough? You dont think he's
being blackmailed? Dodds could never do anything to
give a – but if he's betrayed me he's capable of anything!
Such infamy under my own roof!

LEONARD. O before you go to bed: put me on the board.

OLDFIELD (*groan*). Not now.

LEONARD. You cant trust Dodds and you need someone to –

OLDFIELD. All right – yes! God knows you've earned it –
by moral right and force of arms!

LEONARD. Cheer up! Paper isnt sacred. The hand that
writes it can tear it up! But I think you'll make a new sort
of decision from now on . . . you'll be bound by your
word.

OLDFIELD. Yes yes when you're on you'll stay. I shant live
to see the changes. I need my bed. This is more than
tiredness. We must leave the rest till the lawyers open
their offices.

LEONARD. Goodnight.

OLDFIELD *goes out.* LEONARD *sits in an armchair.*
DODDS *comes in.*

DODDS. Why?

LEONARD. The smell of iodine. He knows about Hammond
– I had to explain my 'break down'.

DODDS. You didnt say he has the rights?

LEONARD. Fool . . .!

DODDS. You scared Hammond. He said you were destroying yourself to spite him. I said no one's so stupid.

LEONARD. He was right: I found I could destroy myself to *get*. Im on the board, tomorrow I'll fix his will: I'll get Oldfield's when flesh and bone pass to time's grave . . . And Hammond can use his paper in the loo. I'll have to give him something to stop him going to my father: twenty per cent – his proper incentive. Do the paper work at the same time as the will. That leaves Dodds-is-Dodds.

DODDS. You and Hammond can go to your father: so can I. Anyone call tell the truth if they'll put up with the inconvenience.

LEONARD. Why did you hand me over to Hammond?

DODDS. Greed. (*Shrugs.*) If you want another reason: fear of poverty? They say when a dog's whipped it bites everything except the whipper. No, it bites everything except the whip. If it sees the whip chucked in a corner – the tip doesnt even flicker – it howls. The power of the tool: me. You're the dog who's learned a few elementary tricks. Two things you mustnt trust: god and the servants. They know too much about you. So, the tool has the power of god – if that's not immodest? While Im drawing up Hammond's paper I'll draw up another one in my favour. We'll talk about it tomorrow – in office hours. Your father doesnt pay overtime.

LEONARD *goes out.* DODDS *picks up the empty glasses and goes out after him.*

Unit Seven

Oldfield's Office

At the back a tall Georgian window with small panes. In front of the window a desk with a desk chair and a desk lamp. In front of the desk, left and facing into the room, an office armchair.

DODDS *sits at the desk with* OLDFIELD'S *will in front of him.*
OLDFIELD *comes in.*

DODDS. Going through your will. A duplicate of the one you
tore up. (*Stands.*) To be signed by you and two witnesses
in your presence and the presence of each other. The
lights?

OLDFIELD. Desk lamp please.

DODDS *switches on the desk lamp.* OLDFIELD *sits in the
armchair.*

DODDS. I'll be in my office.
OLDFIELD. Working late?
DODDS. Checking the Zaire report.
OLDFIELD. Zaire.

DODDS *goes out, leaving the will on the desk. A few seconds
later* LEONARD *comes in. He wears a business suit, dark tie
and shoes and a white shirt with conspicuous white cuffs.*

OLDFIELD. He was sitting on my chair.
LEONARD (*picks up the will from the desk*). I've checked it.
OLDFIELD. Have it photocopied. There'll be interpolations
– invisible ink that comes through when he sprinkles my
ashes on it. Turns black into white, honour into how
much!

LEONARD (*half musing*). I wish you werent so absurd.
OLDFIELD (*not hearing* LEONARD). . . . sitting at my desk,
fingering my will. He'd charge you a hiring fee on the
knife he sticks in your back. I must not be bitter . . . In
my chair like a spider spinning a hangman's rope!

LEONARD. He's a little man.
OLDFIELD. They have big ambitions. They make the ruins
we live in – and we spend our lives struggling not to be
rats. Give it here! (*He takes the will from* LEONARD.) I'll
sign it.

OLDFIELD *sits at his desk, silhouetted against the window. As the sky and the room darken only* OLDFIELD's *hands, the will and the pen are seen in the pool of light from the desk lamp – and, caught in the reflection,* LEONARD's *face and white cuffs.*

LEONARD (*unscrews the top of the pen*). Your pen father. (*He walks away.*) I've something else to confess.

OLDFIELD (*murmur*). Im reading.

LEONARD. I must tell you now you have the will. You'll sign, but you must do it when you know.

OLDFIELD (*reading*). . . . whatsoever goods and chattels I may die . . .

LEONARD. I'll tell the truth. Dont leave – or speak – or make a sign. Perhaps you'll want to *keep* it secret? Its your truth as well as mine. The two halves of a code come together – and there's the meaning. Truth's a 'one off' – like losing your virginity or getting conceived. You only tell it once. Afterwards you're changed – you cant get away. When you tell it it may ruin you – and you have to live off your attempt to tell it.

OLDFIELD. Sh. Later.

LEONARD. Suppose a child before the age of speech – in a kitchen or a shed with a woman who's afraid to look at it – if it spoke – with all the inflections of a lifetime's experience – you'd listen. Even if it only said good morning you'd listen as intensely as the dead would listen to the living if they could.

OLDFIELD (*reading*). No Leonard please . . . Im doing my duty to you. Sole beneficiary.

LEONARD. I cant stop. If a cliff as big as the world was leaning over to fall it'd be as silent as if nothing was happening – but nothing could stop it. When it hits the ground everything will change.

OLDFIELD *turns a page.* LEONARD *is sitting in the armchair with his back to him.*

LEONARD. I tried to kill you. I would've done it. You can hear it in my voice. You're listening to a recording of your killing. (*Sudden collapse.*) No! – its not! I should have to . . .! (*Stops.*) Still! Still! Dont move! . . . I changed the magazine. A strange gun – an accident was plausible. That was my first advantage. It was as if the gods were smiling at me. They were far more cunning than I could ever be. I meant to shoot you in the fields while the photographer snapped me – that was the second advantage, no one poses for photos while they're committing murder. Dont move! Still! Its our only chance! – I would've aimed well. A clean death. – I can tell you: its going to be all right. Words are like things. That helps. They share the responsibility. Just prod with them – they're little bits of iron or stone. I considered wounding you so you'd live for a few minutes – in case you had something you wanted to say. Then I saw that was an insult. Who'd condescend to speak to the living when they're being handed over to the dead? So I'd make it a clean shot like a diagram on a shooting chart. I promise you you wouldnt even wince. Then I had another bit of luck. The third advantage. I could kill you indoors. I couldnt miss! The whole sky was grinning at me. The loaded gun was in my hands. I aimed at different things. Then I focused on you through the sight. The optic dragged your face so close – you were bending down to kiss me. The technical virtuosity, the gun's workmanship – astounding. I could count the stubble on your chin. Measure the thicknesses. Your pores were old bomb craters. But no smell. A world of glass between us. Only Wilbraham's stink – his breath – armpits – crutch: a corpse sprinkled with eau de cologne – the scent brought out the stench of his dried sweat, that no movement would ever bring to life again – the wells were dry. I counted. I was a war-machine registering hundredths of a second. You were so close to death and didnt know. I

lived your last seconds for you. Filled them with life.
Stretched them. They were as long as all the time you'd
lived before. I gave you a long life. But the clock's looking
for the last second. It'll find it. Children putting away
their toys – turning their heads to look for the last piece
– the little fist comes down. All children are giants. You
werent in the morgue but the morgue's in you. A handful
of gravel thrown at the wind: it gathers it to a stone. In
a moment you'll be dead. You'll fall – go down. Your
hands will wave above you as if they're trying to pluck
the bullet from your brain. And now you think: Bartley
spoke – an idiot reprieved you. No, it was a bird. In a
bare tree. Leaves would have blanketed the sound – a
fraction of a decibel – but I was living in millionths of a
second. The bird sang in the tree. So innocent and clear.
The time to die had come and you were saying –
something irrelevant, when its all irrelevant. Your voice
grating like stones on the bottom of a *maelstrom* – that's
the word. You couldnt say no. The word would fall into
the gap between the millstones. The grating roar. An ogre
had cut its throat. There was blood. A lot. And then I
saw your words – I told you words were things. A red
carpet stretched between your mouth and the gun. The
words were moving on it. Ghosts. The air movement
behind a jet. Or the wires that guide a T.O.W. to its
target – something like that. A great suction comes from
your head to draw my bullet to it. The trigger's curved.
My finger. Millions of fingers – crawling from the mud.
The filth. The nails were eyes: they cried to wash away
the mud. Anything should be pitied if it lies in its
own tears. The rags of skin. The claws. The rot. Decay.
And so I thought, as Im a kindly man, clean and well-
educated, sent to sit among the wise, like my sort – the
bird must sing. If you shoot it flies. Rattles up through
the trees – a whole army looks up – the food drops from
its forks – their footprints in the mud – the crying bones.

There was only the bird's sound. The metal sheets in a shipyard. Iron wings. Music – but exact, precise, a total grammar – that said nothing. So I let it sing. (*Pause.*) Then I couldnt kill you. It would've been a tactical mistake. Two incidents with a gun? – and I had a motive. If the idiot had spoken on his own: bang! I'd've said his lurch to grab the gun had startled me. It was the bird – that's all between you and death. Think of it when you hear one sing. Im glad you know. It wasnt difficult to tell it. I'll never try to kill you again: I've set us free. One last thing. This time I must say it all. I said I didnt kill you father. That's a lie. I did. You're dead. So am I. I wont hide it from you. You walk about and breathe but I killed you even more than if we'd been buried together and I killed you in our coffin. I made you the living scene of a crime. The embryo of everybody's death. We keep it secret by parading it in the streets. Everywhere you go – every cup you put on a saucer – every crumb you brush from your trousers – tells everyone I killed you. I couldnt have killed you – got through your last seconds – on my own. You had to help me: Im a parasite on your death. I got inside your dead skin to kill you. That's where Im sitting now – and your bones are in me as if they'd been wrapped up in the wrong parcel. And as that's so, what do we do? How shall we go on? The dead must think of the future. Take stock. I have to give you a good reason why I killed you. One you can respect – that makes sense of your life. Then we can go on living. I killed you to prove Im fit to take your place. I'll live for you. Your successor had to be aggressive and patient – the disciplined patience that's a sort of knowledge. A man who kills to *get* proves his aggression. A man who waits to let a bird sing – proves he knows. Who else can you trust your company to? – only your killer. I've earned the right to your place. Well?

No answer.

All other fathers would envy you. I prove myself by killing you and let you live to share my inheritance. Im a worthy son – you must prove you're worthy to be my father. That's the catch: I set you free, chucked you out of prison. Of course you hesitate. Its sudden. But you must choose.

No answer.

If you get it wrong it shows you have a weakness that's infected all you've done – so you've only got second-hand goods to leave me. What son wants that? I told you truth was dangerous.

No answer.

(*To himself.*) I've untied the riddle. I killed – now Im giving life. Im father and son. (*To* OLDFIELD.) We cant pretend I havent spoken. (*To himself.*) If you choose properly you're the father I wanted: we'll live together as brothers. (*To* OLDFIELD.) I shocked you. You'll get over it. They used to wound god in the side to make him live. (*No answer.*) Im being inconsiderate. I've tired you. These last few months I've made you old. Let me hold your pen. Dont be a child father. Someone may come. This is the one time in our whole lives we must be alone together.

LEONARD *stands, goes to the desk and picks up the will.*

You signed. Im grateful. (*He puts the will on the desk.*) Father.

LEONARD *shines the desk lamp in* OLDFIELD's *face.*

Why dont you – ? (*Touches* OLDFIELD.) He doesnt –.

LEONARD *goes to the centre of the room and stands behind the chair. He turns to face* OLDFIELD *and clasps his hands together.*

He's dead.

LEONARD *goes back to the desk and lurches across the top to peer into* OLDFIELD's *face.*

Dead! Dead! The cunning bastard! The wicked – cunning – ! I told him all that – and he – ! The shit! (*Starts to go, talking to himself.*) No he wont get away with that. Im not so easy to beat! Right! You play dirty? There are machines – life support! (*Goes to the desk and kicks it.*) You wont get away with it you bastard!

LEONARD *goes out. Pause.* OLDFIELD *slumps from the chair and goes out of sight behind the desk.* LEONARD *and* DODDS *come in.*

He's gone!

DODDS *switches on the lights.*

DODDS. Is this a joke?

LEONARD. O god he's turned into a ghost and walked! No no! – not dead! Tricked me! He's hiding! I'll teach that shit to play his jokes on – ! O god he's gone to the police! (*Picks up the phone on the desk.*) It's dead.

DODDS. Miss Shrewsbury's gone home. (*Sudden thought.*) The will.

LEONARD *finds* OLDFIELD *behind the desk.*

LEONARD. Ah!

DODDS. What?

LEONARD. There! Fell! (*Starts to pick up* OLDFIELD.) Help me!

DODDS (*examining the will*). You bloody fool!

LEONARD. What?

DODDS. Incompetent bloody fool! Look! Half a signature! – he wrote half his name and stopped!

LEONARD. Is that – bad? O my god – what's he up to? What's he doing to me?

DODDS. Quick – the chair – it may be a stroke – not dead. He must sign the will!

LEONARD *and* DODDS *set* OLDFIELD *in the desk chair.*

LEONARD. Yes yes not dead – air came –
DODDS. His mouth – I saw it – gasped –

OLDFIELD *sits in the chair.* LEONARD *flattens the will on the desk in front of him.*

DODDS. Mr Oldfield its Dodds here. Dont die before you sign the will. Leave us with happy memories. (*To himself.*) The lawyers' fees on a half signed will! O god *Hammond*! (*Aloud.*) Mr Oldfield – please.
LEONARD. Father!
DODDS. Pen pen pen! He cant sign without a pen!
LEONARD. He had a – ! Where's the bloody – ! He must've knocked it when he –. (*Calls.*) Miss Shrewsbury my father needs a –
DODDS. Miss Shrewsbury's gone home!
LEONARD (*going*). There's an office full of – !
DODDS. The same pen! The same pen! D'you want to finish it in red biro?
LEONARD (*searching*). Pen . . . pen . . .
DODDS. There!
LEONARD. – ? – Ah!

LEONARD *gets the pen.* DODDS *takes it from him and holds it upright in front of* OLDFIELD. LEONARD *flattens the will on the desk.*

DODDS. Mr Oldfield Dodds begs you. A last gesture of farewell. (*He puts the pen in* OLDFIELD's *hand – it falls out. Dodds turns away with the will.*)
LEONARD. But breath came from –
DODDS. Wind – when you kneed him in the belly. The dead are always belching and farting. That doesnt make it the day of resurrection.

LEONARD. He's hot!

DODDS (*studying the will*). Gone to hell – making a take-over bid!

LEONARD *watches* DODDS *as he walks away with the will. Behind them* OLDFIELD *falls out of sight again.*

DODDS. At least he didnt tamper with the text. Fool! – fetching me – he was probably still alive. You could have made him sign – told him no doctor till he did – (*Shrugs.*) under the circumstances. To think the company's in your hands! (*Stops.*) Why should he go to the police?

LEONARD. He's dead – what does it matter?

DODDS. Of course the police matter if he's dead.

LEONARD. O my god he's gone again! (LEONARD *and* DODDS *look behind the desk.*) He's trying to get up! The kiss of life!

LEONARD *heaves* OLDFIELD *onto the desk top.* DODDS *pulls* LEONARD *back.*

DODDS. No! You've done enough harm! He might've heard what we said! What did we say? Its impossible to think with a dead – or dying – man in the room! He always kept the big decisions to himself – now he leaves us in the lurch! We mustnt go to pieces! Mr Oldfield is it better if we let you live or finish you off? What an absurd question! (*Looks closer.*) Well he's come to a firm decision on that: he's dead.

LEONARD (*sits and cries*). O god what can I do? What'll become of me! I'll never get away from him! No one can help me! It's unfair!

DODDS. Im sorry I shouted, I didnt mean to make you cry. I lost my grip. I'll finish his signature. He taught me to do his hand for minor documents. A simple bit of forgery is far less complicated than the kiss of life. We've had the kiss of death, and if you ask me we got the best of the bargain. (*Pushes* OLDFIELD *aside.*) Clear a space. (*Signs the will.*) There. A baby's hand patting its mother's cheek couldnt be more sure.

LEONARD (*crying*). What can I do?

DODDS. Spare me the hypocrisy. We'll say he signed his will this morning. He'd better be found out of reach of pens and desks. He collapsed in the corridor and we carried him to the VIP reception room. Leonard.

LEONARD *helps* DODDS *to pick up* OLDFIELD's *body. He is still crying.*

DODDS. I believe your tears are genuine! Death plays funny tricks – no one's safe. The suddenness after a run of shocks. I could cry with relief. (*A flurry of tears.*) People say I have no feelings – but when I think of all that could've gone wrong! (*A flurry of tears.*) But you came back in time – Hammond stuck to his guns – and I was on hand to forge his signature! That's a lot to be grateful for! And if the truth's told he's better off dead than having to live with Hammond – and you – and me! (*A gush of tears.*)

DODDS *and* LEONARD *cry as they carry* OLDFIELD *out.*

Unit Eight

The same

Next day.

LEONARD *sits in the armchair with his eyes shut.* BARTLEY *comes in. He wears his mac and the other clothes from the ruined house. He walks to* LEONARD *and stops.* LEONARD *opens his eyes.*

BARTLEY. Ah come through the wall. You're wore oot. Countin the loot? Ah saw the old sod's death on telly. (*Explains.*) Servant's key. – Have ah been the bloody fool!

BARTLEY *sits at an askew angle on the top of* OLDFIELD's *desk.*

BARTLEY. I could'nae figure oot why yous come t' my hovel. The scratches on them wrists'd fool nae'body. What's the laddie want? Is he m'be sorry for us? – pourin oot the ol' sunny-treacle for his pal? You're nae'body's pal. You're a bastard. When ah got the sack ah'd supped a drop, ay – but that never put a man wi' my stomach in a state o' homicidal confusion. It was nae'body's confusion – it was your cold cunnin calculation. You switch the mags – yous tried t' kill yous dad. Then yous stuck t' me t' see if the penny drop – if it had you'd've murdered me! When yous saw ah wor too innocent t' guess – you was away. Well ah've guessed noo! Ay. Ah'm too smart for yous laddie. Nae'body's fool me – ah'm tellin yous. If yous want t' catch me yous dont get up early – yous dont go t' bed! And noo yous'll pay. Ah'm nae drunk – ah walked oot that pub an left a full jar – less one gargle – stood on the table. Nerves o' steel man! Do ah go t' the police? I cannae prove wor ah knows – but others can: they've got the money t' prove the world's flat. Plenty o' that sort like t' see the back o' yous. Two times ah wor kick oot – once by toffs an once by offal: an yous'll pay – for your old man – the navy – the whole bloody world – ay for every crick o' my cradle: they even rocked that wi' a boot.

LEONARD. I envy you. You want so little.

BARTLEY. Little? Ah want the bloody lot – murderer!

LEONARD. You stupid bastard! I could've killed him! – knew who I was! Knew what I'd done! Now you come and shoot your mouth off! Too late! You should've come a month ago – yesterday – and told him! He'd've made you rich – so would I! Your stupid voice . . . had more in it than all the wisdom of philosophy. It stared you in the face but you did nothing. (*Shrugs.*) Isnt that worse than murder . . .? How can the world be so cruel? Because you're its servant and help it do its stupid tricks. No you're so stupid you're the master.

BARTLEY. Ah-ha, ah-ha! – the police are on t' yous kid! Ah'm your man. Ah swear an oath ah loaded the gun accidental. Ah'll swear anythin. But yous pay first. Ah'm nae the skivvy noo – ah'm in wi' a chance o' partnership. A hundred thousand in the bank.

LEONARD. There's no police.

BARTLEY. Then what? – By god I'll murder yous an then there'll be police! This bloody hoose – yous bloody people! Ah'd get some peace in prison! Ah have t' twist an turn an try an be degraded for every penny o' my share! Wait on murderers wor practice cuttin throats on their own wrists! (*Calmer.*) No matter – ah still know, an yous'll still pay.

LEONARD. The middle drawer.

BARTLEY. My money? My big moment? (*He goes to the front of the desk and opens the drawer.*)

LEONARD. The will.

BARTLEY *takes out the will.*

LEONARD. I got everything. It needs one more bent witness. Dodds is hunting the clubs for Willy. (*He reaches a hand for the will.* BARTLEY *gives it to him.*) My whole life would be different if I'd sat in another chair. I heard the page when he turned it: as if a piece of paper could sigh at what was written on it. But he said nothing. Why? If you could tell me that . . . Perhaps he didnt hear a word I said. Concentrated on the will and died by coincidence. Or did he stop to listen and then die? But why no sound? Perhaps he wasnt shocked – stopped because he didnt take me seriously, but I went on pouring my poison in his ear, and he slipped away in confusion, as if he *found* that he was dead? Or was the shock so deep he *couldnt* speak – a fist screwing him up inside and throwing him down through his own anus? Or was it malice? Or something I dont know? There's no life after death. No voice to tell us anything. The worms swallow us up and go off on their journey as if we were their luggage. Or we're burned and our smoke drifts off in the air, which is full of waves. Sound waves, shock waves, radio waves, light waves, time waves, quantum waves. When we're dead the waves pass through our dust and ashes drifting in the air. The dead carry the news of the living. The chatter from radios, threats from satellites, children's crying, the banging of hooves in the slaughter house – they all travel through waves. That's science. The laws of physics: a joke really. They even carry the past. Once something happens its recorded – voices, events, spectacles – its all recorded and goes out to the edge of the universe and then begins the journey back. The dead are always speaking the laws of physics. Our last words grind backwards and forwards over our first cries. Jokes and shouts from the holocaust, the orders to shoot and the pleas for mercy – all passing through each other in silence. The axe keeps falling. Mothers keep pleading, fathers cursing. The waves that guide missiles are full of human voices. Our ignorant little acts are dragged round and round the universe – they never lose their ignorance – and deepest space goes on shuddering at things we did millions of years ago. The waves recorded what my father heard and why he died. But they can never tell me. The dead spend eternity telling the truth and no one can listen. The dead dont even know they're talking. No wonder living in such brutality we die. Bartley I told the truth – and no one listened. I've come to the place where we stumble over the dead and their skeletons sit up and spit at us and dribble down their chins. The dust uses us for a little while and then the wind blows us out of it and howls. And that's all there is.

BARTLEY. Is that gabble supposed t' put me off? Im one ahead laddie. Ah know ma bit o' truth an (*Imitates bouncing coins in his palm.*) it chinks! Sacks an sacks an sacks o' it!

LEONARD. My father and Hammond. I couldnt beat two of them. If he'd left one sign – one thumbprint – to show he'd heard – I'd've had to spend my life pondering that. No. Old men with long beards waiting like children for their questions to be answered. I wont live like that. I think our trouble is we're never born. If he came to the door now and tried to tell me, I wouldnt listen. There's nothing to say.

BARTLEY. Whist!

LEONARD. What?

BARTLEY. Door. (LEONARD *shakes his head.*) The door man! My servant's ears! Dodds has a key. Ah'd better see.

BARTLEY *goes out.* LEONARD *puts the will into his inside pocket.* BARTLEY *comes in with* WILBRAHAM.

WILBRAHAM. Forgive me. Dodds left messages – Hammond wants to see me here.

BARTLEY (*to* LEONARD). Did ah do right?

WILBRAHAM. So sad. Deepest sympathy. You know Im scum so you wont be offended if I change the subject? I've gambled heavily. I made my bank send out a notice they wouldnt honour my gambling debts. The clubs said (*Imitation.*): 'Gamble old sport. You've lost so much old cock you must win!' They've turned me over to the mobsters. My pocket's ripped. I put talcum on my eye.

BARTLEY. The bloody vulture beggin before your da's buried! Let me thrash him Lennie!

WILBRAHAM. Yes yes despise me. Thank god decent people

still know scum when they see it – even if we do have to depend on servants to keep up our standards. The streets are full of buses. I cant throw myself under one. The passengers would stare at my body. Being dead wouldnt make it easier to bear their pity. I dont mind anger – Im *used* to angry servants – but I wouldnt even pray to god for pity – only his anger, which I deserve in the full majesty of its diapasm. My immediate debts are ninety-five thousand. Thirty would call the bullies off.

LEONARD. No.

WILBRAHAM. Why should you? But you're so rich its like being immortal! The first time we met I asked you to help me – you wouldnt. Look what happened to you! Im asking you to help me now. Fifteen thousand?

LEONARD. No.

WILBRAHAM. Then its over. I cant hide. I'll turn up at some club. Its my destiny to be thrashed to encourage the others – so the owners can get the pennies out of the pockets of those who still have any. Ten thousand? – a pittance to you, and me in my days of glory.

LEONARD. No.

WILBRAHAM *kneels.* LEONARD *ignores him.*

BARTLEY (*amazed*). He drop doon like a turd!

WILBRAHAM. Would you pay for abasement? I've knelt before. I had a regular appointment with an eccentric in the city. The panelled office – churches peeling by the river – a ritual from the middle ages. It was his price. To be fair he knew he'd never see his money. People bewilder me. What do you want? This posture is ridiculous. The thugs are waiting in the street. I cant kneel to them – they kick you when you're down. (*Crouches forward and hides his face in the ground.*) Pity me. Pity me. I've come to that at last. Have pity on me.

LEONARD (*to* BARTLEY, *going*). We must hurry.

BARTLEY. You'll nae leave this shit here?

LEONARD. We'll get your money on the way. (*To* WILBRA-
HAM.) Tell Dodds I'll be at Bartley's dosshouse. You're
ugly –

WILBRAHAM. Yes yes odious!

LEONARD. – because you're innocent. That's why you're
punished.

WILBRAHAM (*face on ground*). Dodds – Bartley's doss – *any*
service I can render –

LEONARD *goes out.*

BARTLEY. You touch any o' this I'll break your fingers.
Your thuggie-pals'll look like holy sisters! Yous wont
have knees – yous'll crawl on your belly. All this is mine!

WILBRAHAM. Thank you thank you. Implicit trust. I'll wait
quietly for the clubs to open. I'll enjoy the peace.

BARTLEY *goes out.* WILBRAHAM *gets up and looks at the
armchair.*

Unit Nine

The Cellar of the Ruined House

Empty. A bracket on the proscenium arch.

LEONARD *comes in carrying a rope. He looks round, goes to the
proscenium arch, sees the bracket and turns back to the centre of
the room. He ties a noose in the rope.*

BARTLEY *comes in carrying the kitchen chair.*

BARTLEY (*chair*). What's it for? (*Stops and sees rope.*) What's
that?

LEONARD (*points to the spot under the bracket*). There.

BARTLEY (*sees bracket*). Ah'm nae gettin in t' this. O no.

LEONARD. There.

BARTLEY. Yous nae right in the head.

LEONARD. Money.

BARTLEY *places the chair under the bracket.* LEONARD *gives him the rope.* BARTLEY *hesitates.*

LEONARD. Money.

BARTLEY *climbs onto the chair and fastens the rope to the bracket.*

BARTLEY (*as he works*). Ah'm nae doin this. (*He finishes fastening the rope and steps down from the chair.*) Is that for yous – or one o' your pals?

LEONARD. Test it.

BARTLEY. That'll hold.

LEONARD. Test.

BARTLEY. I bloody tested it! I bloody tested it!

Slight pause. BARTLEY *gives the rope two savage jerks.*

BARTLEY. Now yous play on yous own. Gi' me my money. Ah'm off.

LEONARD. Kick the chair.

BARTLEY. Yous nae serious?

LEONARD. Money.

BARTLEY. O nae. I've done some stupid things. But ah kep a little innocence left t' live on. Yous nae draggin me doon t' your cess. Give me my money an ah'll away.

LEONARD. When Im dead.

BARTLEY. Dead! (*Grabs chair.*) I'll beat your bloody brains oot! Then I'll take me money!

LEONARD. Dont rob – earn.

BARTLEY. I'll rob – an keep my self-respect!

LEONARD. Watch.

BARTLEY. Watch?

LEONARD (*shows watch*). Watch.

BARTLEY. Yous cruel bastard! Rich scum! Yous wont get away wi' it! There's some justice left!

LEONARD. The man who blew up the world.

BARTLEY. O ah'm nae so easy beat! When yous up there ah'll cut the rope – get a knife an – bite it wi' my teeth! I'll take my money – an leave yous on the ground! You'll kick yourself back t' life! That'll settle your hash!

LEONARD. Knock a chair over for fifty thousand pounds.

BARTLEY. My god what monster are yous! (*Starts to leave.*) Stick your fifty thousand pound! Get your pals in – they'll offer yous a discount! (*Stops.*) Fifty thousand pounds. How do ah know yous didnae drop it in the gutter when us left wor bank. Your idea o' a sick joke – me workin for nothin!

LEONARD. Pocket.

BARTLEY. What d'yous want? An audience? Ah can roond up the wino's – junkies – kinks – every sort o' crap an prat! Pack the room! Gi' us the money – ah have t' pay em. Ah guarantee some'll be wide enough awake t' know what they're watchin – honest man!

LEONARD. Tell you when to kick.

BARTLEY. Yous'll kick when yous hang – kick the bloody chair for practice! No no Lenny please. No son dont. Its nae necessary – none o' this. Yous stand there lookin soaked and its nae rainin. I dinnae mean ma brutality. You're no a bad lad Lennie son. Come away – wor'll still find us some laughs. Ah'll show yous how t' live – not help yous t' die. O my god – the door! (*He goes to the doorway and listens.*) Dodds. People wi' him.

LEONARD *stands on the chair and puts the noose round his neck.*

BARTLEY (*sees* LEONARD *and points at him*). O god look at that! He means it! A harmless little blackmail an ah end in this shit! God if ah come away sane I'll never take another penny from another man! Lenny show a bit o' pity! What yous puttin me through'll drive me t' drink myself t' death! Im standin here in hell! How can you do this t' yoor pal? Kill yourself fine – but why must ah suffer? They're off up the stairs – the missin treads 'll hold 'em up. I dinnae know what you hopin oot o' this – but I reckon yous in for a colossal disappointment. – Fifty thousand quid! Ah'd be free for life! Yous got your money through stark wickedness – put it right by doin good! Lift me oot the gutter! You'll never spend a better penny. The best flowers for the hearse lad, an ah'll live a credit t' you. Ah'll swear ah'll never touch a drop! The holy saints'll pray t' me! Lenny think o' the shit-hoose world you're leavin me in! Im nae better'n an orphan! For the sake o' the good times pal!

DODDS (*off*). Mr Oldfield.

LEONARD. Soon.

BARTLEY. O god they'll break ma bloody neck for helpin yous! We might as well swap places! Shall ah go an telled em yous ran off? Then yous can take wor time. Dont let em rush yous in t' it. No – they'd find yous body and ah'd be for the high jump – innocent or not! Jump Lenny – there's nothin else for it! Jump for god's sake! Let me get my money an go!

DODDS (*off*). Oldfield I know you're up there.

BARTLEY (*hovering in the doorway*). Jump jump jump! Are yous a bloody coward! Its a disgrace standin there so ah have t' plead. Jump!

DODDS (*off*). Dont do anythin rash. I've fixed the will.

BARTLEY (*hovering in the doorway*). They're comin back t' the hall. They'll come down here. Jump! (*Wringing his hands.*) Have yous no shame! Do it Lenny! Yous promised! Ah *need* that money! Jump!

LEONARD (*flat*). Soon.

BARTLEY. Jump! You little cock-teaser! You're an insult t' wor manhood!

LEONARD. Fifty-thousand pounds.

BARTLEY. Jump jump jump! Ah'm pissin meself wi' suspense!

HAMMOND (*off*). Oldfield.

BARTLEY. Hammond . . .!

LEONARD. Now.

> BARTLEY *creeps towards* LEONARD.

BARTLEY. Ay so ah will. There's nothin reckless in it . . .
its on request an a clean rope, not second-hand.

WILBRAHAM (*off*) One might try the garden – the gardener
seems lax!

BARTLEY. Hark at em bellow – an here's a man aboot t'
hang hisself assisted by his pal an they do nothin – nae
notion o' the urgency they're in. Ah'll top yous an be off.
I know a hole wor goes up t' the street. Shant even meet
em on the stairs t' stand aside an let em through. This is
where I allus wanted the boss – an ah almost miss ma
chance for wor little voice o' conscience they would'nae
hear anymore than you will when you're dead.

HAMMOND (*off*). Oldfield – you down there?

BARTLEY. Yous arms! Wor should've tied yous arms – shit
– you'll reach up an grab! The struggle'll be shockin!
They'll cut yous doon alive!

LEONARD (*puts his hands in his jacket pockets*). Gone.

BARTLEY. Bloody keep em gone! (*Suddenly stops to listen.*)
Ah dont believe it! (*Goes to the doorway.*) They're havin
a conference. The ineffectual bastards! Captains o'
industry! No wonder wor in us mess! Shall ah go up an
get em organised? They'll be oot on top o' the roof pigeon-
spottin! Hup – they're comin! (*Goes back to* LEONARD.)
Goodbye pal!

LEONARD. Wait!

BARTLEY. Wait! Wait! Bloody wait? – when ah've screwed
meself up t' –

LEONARD (*hands the will to* BARTLEY). Teeth.

BARTLEY. Teeth? – Does he want me t' take his false teeth
out?

LEONARD. Bite. Blood. Gag.

BARTLEY. Gag? Blood? *Teeth!*

BARTLEY *puts the will into* LEONARD's *mouth. A noise outside.* BARTLEY *runs off and vanishes into his hole.* LEONARD *stands on the chair with the will in his mouth, his hands in his pockets and his neck in the noose.* WILBRAHAM *comes in very bored.*

WILBRAHAM (*calls back immediately*). 'S empty.

WILBRAHAM *slowly waddles round the room, looking for a place to sit. He mutters to himself.*

Up and down broken stairs. One could break one's neck. So pleasant in that armchair. Anonymous. Cosy. Peace. Nice. (*Starts to go, but loiters.*) Better make it look as if I searched – had the floorboards up. (*Taps foot.*) Blue magazines. Hot rod cars. Shit. Filth. Greedy old man. Moronic youth. Lascivious insects. And so Rome fell.

WILBRAHAM *starts to leave.* LEONARD *coughs through his teeth clenched on the will.* 'Huh-humph'. WILBRAHAM *turns, sees* LEONARD, *walks a few steps towards him and stops.*

Good lor.

WILBRAHAM *looks away, hesitates for a moment, adjusts his tie-knot and goes out. Immediately* BARTLEY *runs out of his hole.*

BARTLEY. That's it! Ah'm nae leavin tuppence for that toe-rag! Its my life's wages! See yous pal!

BARTLEY *kicks the chair from under* LEONARD. LEONARD *hangs.* BARTLEY *searches in* LEONARD's *pockets.* LEONARD *reaches up and grabs the rope with both hands to take the weight of his body from his neck.*

My money! My money! Will yous keep still – wrigglin like a bloody tart as hadnt had it up for a year! (*Finds the wad of banknotes.*) Dear god ah hardly dared t' hope the world could be so good t' me! Halleluja! Fifty thousand quid! It is! It is! (*Starts to count the notes.*) One two three four – O god let it be there! – yous would'nae cheat me at a time like this pal? – four five six – nae! – six seven five – och I should o' listen more at school! – what the shit ah'll have t' take his word! (*Starts to run out. Stops.*) 'The watch!' 'Yous can afford a hundred watches!' 'It was the laddie's last request!' 'You superstitious prat!'

BARTLEY *runs back to* LEONARD, *rights the chair, stands on it, and starts to undo* LEONARD's *wristwatch.* LEONARD *is clasping the rope with both hands.*

Will yous – you said yous – get your bloody hands off – yous stubborn git – you'll spoil the mechanism!

BARTLEY *gets the wristwatch, jumps down from the chair and starts to run out again.* LEONARD *gets one foot onto the chair to support his weight.*

O god son ah hope that's nae too painful!

BARTLEY *stops, turns and across the distance mimes shaking* LEONARD's *hand in farewell.*

Yous turned oot trumps pal! Ah'm sincerely grateful for all yous help!

BARTLEY *goes out through his hole. For a moment* LEONARD *teeters with one foot on the chair. He takes huge breaths and then kicks the chair away.* HAMMOND *and* DODDS *come in.*

HAMMOND. Hanged. I told you: reckless. I'd've run a book on something like this!

DODDS. The dirty little wrecker! Years of scheming thrown away! The sheer bloody-mindedness! Burned the will or put it through the shredder!

HAMMOND *and* DODDS *come down to* LEONARD.

HAMMOND. What made you leave a valuable document with him? You knew the lad suffered impulses. God knows he gave us warning.

LEONARD (*jerks*). Yrgh!

HAMMOND. If it had been deposited in my safe in the proper way we'd be laughing. A man of your experience making elementary mistakes. Its downright diabolical.

WILBRAHAM *comes in and hovers round* HAMMOND *and* DODDS.

DODDS. I think you're totally unjust. How could I know he'd destroy the will? He was the beneficiary. There's usually some twisted logic in what he did – but this?

LEONARD (*jerks*) Yrgh!

HAMMOND. An avoidable blunder. I hate bodge.

WILBRAHAM. Er –

DODDS. If you foresaw calamity would strike, it would've been a help if you warned me.

HAMMOND. You're paid to know not be warned.

WILBRAHAM. Er –

DODDS. Its been a difficult day. The cigarette smoke in those clubs has given me a headache. And now I see Im to have my feelings trampled on. However, I do of course apologise.

HAMMOND. Excuses are always late and apologies never meant. I dont accept either.

WILBRAHAM. Excuse me I do apologise but – (*Points to* LEONARD.) he's alive.

HAMMOND *and* DODDS *look at* LEONARD.

HAMMOND. What's that in his mouth?

DODDS (*takes the will from* LEONARD's *mouth*). The will.

LEONARD. Hrg – hrg – hrg –

HAMMOND. I suppose he wiped his bum on it? That lad's

sense of humour contributed to his downfall.

WILBRAHAM. If we had a knife? (*Going to* LEONARD.) We could take the weight from his legs so –

DODDS *violently pushes* WILBRAHAM *away*.

DODDS. Fool! We've got the will and he lived to inherit! Let him hang!

LEONARD *is still*.

HAMMOND. The pair of you give over. Anyroad its too late – he's a gonner. Best call the police. We passed a phone box on the corner – if its not been rifled by some spark taking a crash course in private enterprise. And get an ambulance – it'll look good. (*Pen.*) Wilbraham if you'd be so kind. And for god's sake dont shake lad. They might not know you're alcoholic and think its fear. No point in stirring suspicions.

WILBRAHAM (*signs*). Anything anytime anywhere. Could I mention the sum the chap with the Mohican haircut hissed in my ear as he twisted it?

HAMMOND (*examining the will*). As efficient a piece of perjury as we can expect in the present slapdash company. (*Pockets pen.*) Look sharp – or must I draw a map?

DODDS *and* WILBRAHAM *go out*. HAMMOND *picks up the chair*.

HAMMOND. 'Scuse me lad. You wont object if I borrow a loan of your chair? Its yours by rights. Always yours. If that doesnt make you sole proprietor nothing will.

HAMMOND *sits on the chair beside* LEONARD. *His head is bent over the will. He mutters to himself as he reads.*

Getting short-winded – which you'll understand is an affliction. Dont mind telling you I can do without too many of these days – will or no will. (*Reads.*) Have they spelt my name right? These modern hussies use their imagination when it comes to names. If you're Smith they put down Jones. Brazen.

LEONARD's *left hand comes from his pocket, with smooth silent jerks. There is a pistol in the hand. Slowly and smoothly the arm jerks sideways and upwards, as stiff as a blindman's stick searching for a wall.*

You did me proud lad, according to your lights. Not all I wanted but plenty to build on.

LEONARD's *arm falls silently and swiftly to his side.*

(*still muttering as he reads*). As to the rest, Im sorry. I warned you. I distinctly remember. 'Say no to me an you're a dead-un'. (*Looks ahead of him and contemplates space, caressing his jaw with one hand.*) Wouldnt heed – couldnt heed. Strange lad. You moved me to the bowels. Didnt know I could still be touched. Wont happen again. (*Goes back to reading the will.*) It was a nice dream and they're bad for you. There's a lot to be said for grass. Five thousand sorts and no questions.

The arm has silently risen again, in smaller jerks. The rest of LEONARD's *body is still. The pistol searches till it finds* HAMMOND *and then stops – aimed.*

(*Suddenly sucks in air through his teeth*). Ysssss: grass! Might the fuzzy-wuzzies start to eat it and shut my shops? Put a stop to that: root it up! No no – worrying for nothing. (*Ruminates over the will for a moment.*) . . . The world changes. No bridge between the ages. The shores move further apart.

A shot. HAMMOND *jumps up, sending the chair flying. He darts to the centre of the room, frantically looking round to see who shot. The pistol fires into the ground.* HAMMOND *retreats to the back wall and stares at* LEONARD *in shock. The pistol falls to the ground.* DODDS *comes in.*

DODDS. – ?

HAMMOND. He shot me!

DODDS. Are you – ?

HAMMOND. A dead man tried to kill me!

DODDS (*looks at* LEONARD *and then at* HAMMOND). Well he missed. Death hasnt improved his aim.

HAMMOND. Then he shot the earth!

DODDS. Now now, the onset of rigor mortis – a spasm jerked the gun. (*Slight sneering amusement.*) Im surprised you didnt forsee it.

HAMMOND. We'll wait outside.

HAMMOND *and* DODDS *start to go.* HAMMOND *goes back to* LEONARD *and kicks the pistol away from under his feet – it slithers along the ground.* HAMMOND *and* DODDS *go out.*

LEONARD *hangs dead.*

Methuen World Classics *and* Methuen Contemporary Dramatists

Methuen Modern Plays

include work by

Jean Anouilh	John McGrath
John Arden	David Mamet
Margaretta D'Arcy	Patrick Marber
Peter Barnes	Arthur Miller
Sebastian Barry	Mtwa, Ngema & Simon
Brendan Behan	Tom Murphy
Edward Bond	Phyllis Nagy
Bertolt Brecht	Peter Nichols
Howard Brenton	Joseph O'Connor
Simon Burke	Joe Orton
Jim Cartwright	Louise Page
Caryl Churchill	Joe Penhall
Noël Coward	Luigi Pirandello
Sarah Daniels	Stephen Poliakoff
Nick Dear	Franca Rame
Shelagh Delaney	Philip Ridley
David Edgar	Reginald Rose
Dario Fo	David Rudkin
Michael Frayn	Willy Russell
John Godber	Jean-Paul Sartre
Paul Godfrey	Sam Shepard
John Guare	Wole Soyinka
Peter Handke	C. P. Taylor
Jonathan Harvey	Theatre de Complicite
Iain Heggie	Theatre Workshop
Declan Hughes	Sue Townsend
Terry Johnson	Judy Upton
Barrie Keeffe	Timberlake Wertenbaker
Stephen Lowe	Victoria Wood
Doug Lucie	

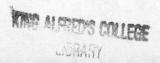

Methuen Student Editions

John Arden	*Serjeant Musgrave's Dance*
Alan Ayckbourn	*Confusions*
Aphra Behn	*The Rover*
Edward Bond	*Lear*
Bertolt Brecht	*The Caucasian Chalk Circle*
	Life of Galileo
	Mother Courage and her Children
Anton Chekhov	*The Cherry Orchard*
Caryl Churchill	*Top Girls*
Shelagh Delaney	*A Taste of Honey*
John Galsworthy	*Strife*
Robert Holman	*Across Oka*
Henrik Ibsen	*A Doll's House*
Charlotte Keatley	*My Mother Said I Never Should*
John Marston	*The Malcontent*
Willy Russell	*Blood Brothers*
August Strindberg	*The Father*
J. M. Synge	*The Playboy of the Western World*
Oscar Wilde	*The Importance of Being Earnest*
Tennessee Williams	*A Streetcar Named Desire*
Timberlake Wertenbaker	*Our Country's Good*

For a Complete Catalogue of Methuen Drama titles
write to:

Methuen Drama
Michelin House
81 Fulham Road
London SW3 6RB